POLITICS AND POLICY IN BRITAIN

LEONARD FREEDMAN
University of California at Los Angeles

 Publishers USA

Politics and Policy in Britain

Copyright © 1996 by Longman Publishers USA.
All rights reserved.
No part of this publication may be reproduced,
stored in a retrieval system, or transmitted
in any form or by any means, electronic, mechanical,
photocopying, recording, or otherwise,
without the prior permission of the publisher.

Longman, 10 Bank Street, White Plains, N.Y. 10606

Associated companies:
Longman Group Ltd., London
Longman Cheshire Pty., Melbourne
Longman Paul Pty., Auckland
Copp Clark Longman Ltd., Toronto

Executive editor: Pamela Gordon
Production editor: Linda W. Witzling
Cover design: Kevin Kall
Text art: Fine Line Inc.
Production supervisor: Winston Sukhnanand
Compositor: University Graphics

Library of Congress Cataloging-in-Publication Data

Freedman, Leonard.
    Politics and policy in Britain / Leonard Freedman.
        p.   cm.
    Includes bibliographical references and index.
    ISBN 0-8013-1366-X
      1. Great Britain—Politics and government—1945–
2. United States—Politics and government—1945–1989.
3. Great Britain—Economic policy—1945– 4. Great
Britain—Social policy—1979– 5. Comparative
government. I. Title
JN318.F86 1996
320.941—dc20   95-12853
                                          CIP

1 2 3 4 5 6 7 8 9 10-MA-9998979695

Once more, to Vivian

Contents

Illustrations xv
Tables xvii
Preface xix

Chapter 1 / INTRODUCTION: WHY STUDY THE BRITISH SYSTEM? 1

The Decline from Greatness 2

The Rise and Fall of the British Empire 2
The Erosion of the Economic Base 3
The Fraying of Civility 4
Questioning the Governmental System 4

Defending the Study of British Government 5

The Original Parliamentary System 5
A More or Less Common Language 6
The Heritage of Institutions and Ideas 7
Similarity of Policy Issues 7
The Quality of the Political Dialogue 8
The "Special Relationship" 8
Decline: Not Only Britain? 9
Conclusion 10
Some Questions to Think About 10
Suggestions for Further Reading 11

Part One: CONTEXTS 13

Chapter 2 / THE CULTURAL SETTING 15

Class 17
- *Middle and Working Classes* 18
- *The Upper Class* 20
- *The Decline of Class* 22
- *The Persistence of Class* 24
- *Assessments of the British Class System* 25

Individualism and Authority 27
Religion 28
Ethnicity 30
- Conclusion 31
- Some Questions to Think About 32
- Notes 32
- Suggestions for Further Reading 33

Chapter 3 / THE DEBATE OVER THE CONSTITUTION 34

The Evolution of the Constitution 35
Contrasts between the British and U.S. Constitutions 36
- *A Mostly Unwritten Constitution* 36
- *The Interconnection of Executive and Legislative Branches* 37
- *The Lack of Judicial Power to Overturn Legislation* 38
- *The Absence of Federalism* 38
- *The Separation of Head of Government from Head of State* 39

Limits on the Power of Government 40
- *The Rule of Law* 40
- *Democratic Accountability* 40
- *The European Union* 41

The Case for the Constitution 42
Pressures for Constitutional Reform 44
- *The Growing Supremacy of the Executive Branch* 45
- *Secrecy* 45
- *A "Predominant-Party System"?* 45
- *Reform Proposals* 47
- Conclusion 47

Some Questions to Think About   48
Notes   48
Suggestions for Further Reading   48

Part Two: THE PARTY SYSTEM   49

Chapter 4 / GROUPS AND VOTERS: ORGANIZED AND MASS INFLUENCES ON THE PARTIES   51

Interest Groups   52
Business   53
Trade Unions   55
The Corporatist Connection   59

Voters   60
Interest and Knowledge   61
Involvement   62
Voters and the Parties   62
Conclusion   65
Some Questions to Think About   65
Notes   66
Suggestions for Further Reading   66

Chapter 5 / INSIDE THE PARTIES   67

Party Differences   68
Party Similarities   69
Conflicts in the Conservative Party   71
Locations of Power in the Conservative Party   72
Leadership Contests   74
Conflicts in the Labour Party   79
Locations of Power in the Labour Party   80
The Rise of the Left   82
Leadership Contests   83
The Decline of the Left   84
The Liberal Democrats   88
Conclusion   89
Some Questions to Think About   90
Notes   90
Suggestions for Further Reading   90

Chapter 6 / ELECTIONS IN THE TELEVISION ERA   92

Differences between British and U.S. Elections   92

Brevity   92
No Paid TV or Radio Commercials   93
Less Campaign Spending   94
No Debates   96
A Larger Role for the Press   96

The Americanization of British Elections   98

Television and the Projection of Personality   98
Trivializing the Issues   100
The Polls   101

In Defense of British Elections   102

Manifestos Matter   102
Communication Skills Are Relevant   102
Leadership Preferences Are Not Necessarily Decisive   103
Television News Is Important and Balanced   103
Campaigns Rarely Decide   103

What Determines Election Results?   104

Longterm Factors   104
Shorter-Term Factors   106
Prospects for Future Elections   109
Conclusion   111
Some Questions to Think About   111
Notes   112
Suggestions for Further Reading   112

Part Three: THE INSTITUTIONS OF GOVERNMENT   113

Chapter 7 / THE MONARCHY: WILL IT SURVIVE?   115

The Erosion of Royal Popularity   116

The Role of the Tabloids   117
Royalty and the Establishment   118
Damage to the Monarch's Constitutional Standing   119

The Constitutional Roles of the Monarch   119

Ceremonial Duties   119
Dealing with Constitutional Conventions   120
Consultation   122

Proposals for Change   123

Restoring the Mystique   123
Abolition   124
Simplification   125
Conclusion   126
Some Questions to Think About   126
Notes   127
Suggestions for Further Study   127

Chapter 8 / PRIME MINISTERS AND THEIR CABINETS   128

Prime Ministerial Powers and Limits   129

Relations with the Cabinet   129
Control of Parliament   131
Election Timing   132
Influencing Public Opinion   133
Making Foreign Policy   133
Patronage   134

The 1945 Labour Government   135
The Thatcher Government, 1979–90   138
Other Prime Minister-Cabinet Relationships   140

Conclusion   148
Some Questions to Think About   149
Notes   149
Suggestions for Further Reading   149

Chapter 9 / CIVIL SERVANTS AND THEIR MINISTERS   151

The Competence Question   152

Educational and Class Background   152
The Lack of Technical Expertise   153

Accountability   154

The Ethos of Subordination and Impartiality   154
Civil Service Assets   155
Is There a Civil Service Bias?   158
The Politicians' Assets   159
Conclusion   162
Some Questions to Think About   162
Notes   163
Suggestions for Further Reading   163

Chapter 10 / PARLIAMENT: DOES IT MATTER? 164

The House of Commons 165
Representation 165
Resources 167
Interest Group Influence 168
Making (and Breaking) Political Reputations 169
Relations with the Executive Branch 170
Roles for Backbenchers 174

The House of Lords 182
A Weak Chamber 182
Remaining Functions 183
The Party Line-up 183

Proposals for Parliamentary Reform 184
The Commons 184
The Lords 185
Conclusion 185
Some Questions to Think About 186
Notes 186
Suggestions for Further Reading 187

Chapter 11 / THE COURTS AND CRIMINAL JUSTICE 188

The Structure of the Courts 189
The Judiciary 189
The Legal Profession 191
The Police 191
The Critics of the Criminal Justice System 192
Class and the Judges 193
Problems with the Police 193
The IRA Cases 195

Some Qualifications to the Critics' Case 196
Judges versus the Government 196
Expeditiousness 197
Reforms in Progress 198
The European Court of Justice 199
Conclusion 199
Some Questions to Think About 199
Notes 200
Suggestions for Further Reading 200

Chapter 12 / LOCAL GOVERNMENT AND THE NATIONALITY QUESTION   201

The Pull of Centralization   202
The Absence of Federalism   202
The Loss of Functions   202
Finances   203
Partisan Elections   204

Labour and Centralization   204
Early Trends   204
Recent Shifts toward Decentralization   205

The Conservatives and Centralization   205
Strong Leadership   205
Money   206
Politics   206
The Poll Tax   207
The Conservatives after Thatcher   209

The Nationality Question   210
Scotland   210
Wales   212
Northern Ireland   213
Conclusion   220
Some Questions to Think About   220
Notes   221
Suggestions for Further Reading   221

Part Four: ISSUES IN PUBLIC POLICY   223

Chapter 13 / THE TROUBLED ECONOMY   225

The Economic Consensus, 1945–79   226
Emerging Problems   228

Conservative Economic Policies since 1979   232
The Thatcher Administration's Policies   232
The Major Administration's Policies   234
The Results of the Thatcher-Major Policies   234

Opposition Responses   240
Conclusion   241

Some Questions to Think About   242
Notes   243
Suggestions for Further Reading   243

Chapter 14 / THE WELFARE STATE AND ITS CRITICS   244

Social Security   244

The Party Consensus, 1945-79   245
Thatcherism   246
The Labour Critique   248

The National Health Service   249

Inauguration and Minor Modifications, 1945-79   250
The Limited Impact of Thatcherism   250

Housing   253

Fluctuations in Policy, 1945-79   253
Thatcherism in Housing   254
Conclusion   258
Some Questions to Think About   259
Notes   260
Suggestions for Further Reading   260

Chapter 15 / EDUCATION: ACCESS AND QUALITY   261

Secondary Education   261

The State Schools   262
The "Public" Schools   266

Higher Education   269

Expansion   269
Changes in Student Composition   269
Thatcher versus the Universities   271
Higher Education under Major   272
Conclusion   273
Some Questions to Think About   273
Notes   274
Suggestions for Further Reading   274

Chapter 16 / RACE AND GENDER: HOW MUCH DISCRIMINATION?   275

Race   275

Immigration   275
Race Relations   278

Gender   282

Early Discrimination   283
Changes since the 1960s   283
The Remaining Gaps   286
Margaret Thatcher and the Role of Women   288
Conclusion   289
Some Questions to Think About   290
Notes   290
Suggestions for Further Reading   290

Chapter 17 / CIVIL LIBERTIES UNDER THREAT   291

The Threats to Liberty   292

The Paramount Executive   292
Secrecy   292
The Law of Libel   294
Crime and Terrorism   294
The Decline of Traditional Morality   295
Government Policies in the 1990s   295

The Role of the Courts   296

Official Secrets   297
Journalists   298
Protesters   299
Property Rights   300

Protections for Civil Liberties   301

Interest Groups   301
The Media   301
The Courts   302

The Bill of Rights Controversy   303

Conclusion   304
Some Questions to Think About   305
Notes   305
Suggestions for Further Reading   306

Chapter 18 / FOREIGN POLICY: FROM EMPIRE TO EUROPEAN UNION   307

Adjustments to Decline   308

Empire to Commonwealth   308
Association with Other Nations   309

Incomplete Adjustments to Decline   310
Wars to Preserve Residual Imperial Interests   311
The Independent Nuclear Deterrent   313
The Reluctant Europeans   316

Bipartisanship in Foreign Policy   322
Conclusion   323
Some Questions to Think About   324
Notes   324
Suggestions for Further Reading   325

Chapter 19 / SUMMING UP: TRANSATLANTIC LESSONS   326

Institutions   326
What the British Can Learn from the U.S. System   326
What Americans Can Learn from the British System   328

Policies   330
The Economy   330
The Welfare State   331
Education   331
Race and Gender   331
Civil Liberties   332
Foreign Policy   332
Conclusion   332
Some Questions to Think About   332

Appendix: General Election Results, 1945-92   333
Index   335

Illustrations

Figure 2.1: The United Kingdom *16*
Figure 2.2: A still-topical 1920s cartoon on the honors system *26*
Figure 3.1: The British Constitution: Executive-legislative relationships *39*
Figure 5.1: Organization of Conservative Party *73*
Photo: Margaret Thatcher disposes of Edward Heath *76*
Figure 5.2: Organization of Labour Party *81*
Photo: Tony Blair *86*
Figure 6.1: Conservative and Labour newspaper ads, 1992 *95*
Figure 6.2: Manifesto covers: Neil Kinnock in 1987, John Major in 1992 *100*
Cartoon: A cartoonist's caustic view of the royal family *116*
Photo: Clement Attlee flanked by senior cabinet members Ernest Bevin and Herbert Morrison *137*
Photo: Margaret Thatcher at the peak of her power, 1988 *138*
Photo: Lord (Sir Alec Douglas-) Home: the last aristocratic prime minister *141*
Photo: Anthony Eden: successful foreign secretary, failed prime minister *142*
Photo: Edward Heath: better at controlling an orchestra than the unions *143*
Photo: Winston Churchill: not quite as great in peace as in war *144*
Cartoon: Harold Macmillan: "Supermac" *145*

Photo: Harold Wilson: more dominant, but less successful, than Attlee   *146*

Photo: James Callaghan: surviving without a majority   *148*

Figure 10.1: How a bill becomes law   *165*

Photo: The House of Commons in session: Neil Kinnock challenging the Thatcher government   *172*

Photo: Betty Boothroyd, elected in 1992 as the 155th Speaker of the House (and first Madam Speaker)   *176*

Figure 11.1: Structure of the courts (England and Wales)   *190*

Figure 12.1: Map of Ireland   *215*

Photo: Campaign for Nuclear Disarmament poster   *300*

Cartoon: Kennedy, Macmillan, and the Polaris negotiations   *314*

Tables

2.1: Cross-cultural comparison of selected religious concepts   *29*
3.1: 1983 Election results   *46*
4.1: Party alternations in power   *63*
4.2: Voting in 1992 election   *64*
6.1: 1992 Voting by housing tenure   *105*
6.2: 1992 Voting by age   *105*
6.3: Issues and voting in 1992 election   *107*
10.1: Social class in the House of Commons, 1992   *166*
13.1: Unemployment, inflation, and the Misery Index for selected years   *236*
13.2: Public sector borrowing requirement for selected years   *237*
13.3: World Competitiveness League, 1993   *239*
14.1: Age structure of the population   *247*
14.2: Public and private housing starts   *255*
15.1: Scores on standardized math tests, 1990   *263*
16.1: Nonwhite British residents, 1994   *279*
18.1: British attitudes toward the EU, 1994   *321*

Preface

This new text on British government and politics is built around a number of features I have found especially useful in my 30 years of teaching undergraduate students at UCLA. The first is to demonstrate the relationship between political processes and institutions on the one hand and policy outcomes on the other. Obviously students must be well-grounded in the structure of the system. But politics to most people who are not going to be political actors or political scientists is primarily a matter of how the major issues of public policy affect their lives. Thus, we first set the cultural and constitutional contexts then examine the party system and the institutions of government. The six chapters that follow review key public policy issues as arenas in which parties and governmental institutions come into play.

Second, the book provides a strong United Kingdom-United States comparative perspective—a natural product of my own background as a transplanted Britisher. This is clear from the opening chapter which asks (and explains) why Americans should bother to study the British system. Each chapter on the party system and governmental institutions highlights comparisons and contrasts between the two systems. The policy issues selected are all parallel to issues confronting Americans today. And the final chapter asks what the Americans and British might learn from the strengths and weaknesses of the other's system. Moreover, at the end of each chapter "Some Questions to Think About" are posed, many of which are comparative in nature. (I should note that economic comparisons between the two countries are complicated by the fact that the dollar-pound exchange rate has fluctuated considerably over the years. At the time of writing this the rate was hovering between $1.50 and $1.60 to the pound.)

Next, I pay rather more attention than is common in introductory texts to individual political leaders, particularly prime ministers. There is always the danger, of course, of overstating the importance of individual participants in the process. Yet we are in an era of the growing personalizing of politics; and it is clear that some institutional and policy matters in Britain have been very much influenced by the characteristics of particular leaders. Margaret Thatcher is a case in point; Thatcher and Thatcherism are seen as a watershed phenomenon in British politics and as an effort to reverse the earlier watershed—the Attlee government of 1945-51.

Finally, I have aimed at an accessible style designed to stimulate discussion by presenting the controversies surrounding each topic. At least two sides on the various controversies are presented throughout. However, the reader will quickly discover that while I am still very much an Anglophile and an admirer of many aspects of the British system, I am sharply critical of some attitudes, practices, and institutions that in my view have inhibited Britain's ability to address its problems since the end of its empire, and will need to be changed if it is to be able to confront the challenges of the twenty-first century.

I want to thank Neil Jesse, a UCLA political science graduate student, for invaluable research assistance, and of course, all the scholars in the field of British politics whose works I have cited in this text.

Thanks are also due to the perceptive critiques and helpful suggestions provided by faculty members who reviewed the manuscript of this book, notably

Adrian Clark, James Madison University
Clay Clemens, College of William & Mary
Mark N. Franklin, University of Houston
Lewis G. John, Washington and Lee University
Richard R. Johnson, Northwestern Oklahoma State University
Carol Mershon, University of Virginia
Henry Steck, State University of New York, College at Cortland
David S. Wilson, University of Toledo
Graham Wilson, University of Wisconsin, Madison
Thomas P. Wolf, Indiana University Southeast

Finally I am greatly indebted to the publishing team at Longman Publishers USA: Pam Gordon, Linda Witzling, and the others who participated in the production of this book.

1

INTRODUCTION
WHY STUDY THE BRITISH SYSTEM?

A half century ago, the answer to this question would have been self-evident.

Britain as it emerged from World War II was a power to be reckoned with. Here was a small island—slightly less in area than Oregon—that had brought within its sway a vast empire, an empire that was still intact at war's end with the restoration of territories overrun by the Germans and Japanese. And as a victorious power, it occupied one of the five permanent seats on the Security Council, the inner group of the United Nations.

The war had taken a severe toll on the economy, and for a time Britain was heavily dependent on loans and grants from the United States. But it was Britain that had led the way into the industrial revolution and performed remarkable feats of production during the war, and although the damage inflicted by the Blitz was indeed painful, the British economy by no means suffered the level of economic devastation experienced by the Russians, the Germans, or the Japanese.

Americans had greatly admired the way the British had comported themselves during the war; the people of postwar Britain continued to display a stoic willingness to accept shortages and austerity for the common good. The British appeared to have a well-ordered society in which people behaved courteously and considerately toward one another, and in which a civilized balance was maintained between the claims of the individual and of the community.

Finally, there was the British system of government and politics. In contrast to the defeated dictatorships of Germany and Italy, and the still-potent autocracy of the Soviet Union, Britain stood as a beacon of democracy. At the same time, Britain was a model of stability and effectiveness, in sharp contrast to prewar France with its repeated collapse of governments. In the United States there were many political scientists and others who even preferred the British parliamentary system to their own constitutional structure.

Yet in all of these four respects—great power politics, economic strength, the quality of the civic culture, and the reputation of the governmental system—the days of British glory have passed. The high status accorded Britain in the immediate postwar period was short-lived. Since then, one word has appeared over and over in commentaries on the condition of Britain: *decline*.

THE DECLINE FROM GREATNESS

The Rise and Fall of the British Empire

By the end of the nineteenth century, orators could boast of a globe-spanning empire on which "the sun never set." Until the late 1940s British schoolchildren were still learning their geography from a map that showed Britain as the center of the world, and the countries of the empire—including India, Burma, Malaya, close to half of Africa, and much of the Middle East, as well as Canada, Australia, and New Zealand—standing out from the rest in bold pink. The French, Dutch, Belgians, Germans, and Italians were as eager as the British to establish control over territories in Africa or Asia. But none could compare with the British for imperial scope and importance.

However, this situation could not last indefinitely. Self-government and democracy had long since come to the predominately white dominions—Canada, Australia, and New Zealand—and by the 1940s the pressure in India and several other countries for independence was becoming overwhelming.

For by this time, empires were out of fashion. Colonial overlords claimed that they were acting from a sense of duty to less advanced civilizations, that they were carrying "the white man's burden." But even in the imperial countries this view was increasingly attacked as sanctimonious and racist, as a cover for exploitation and repression. Moreover, the scale of military force needed to contain rising levels of resistance among so many populations was well beyond Britain's resources.

Winston Churchill, Britain's magnificent leader in war, hoped to defy the inevitable. Preserving the empire was one of his principal war aims. He had not, he declared, become "His Majesty's First Minister to preside over the liquidation of the British Empire." But immediately after the war in Europe ended, he lost his position as "His Majesty's First Minister," and the incoming Labour government launched the process that was to lead quickly to the independence of India, Burma, and Ceylon. Although, as we shall see in chapter 18, there was reluctance to let the rest of the empire go the way of India, the trend toward independence was inexorable, and it was accepted by Conservative as well as Labour governments.

Today the British empire is no more. In its place is a "Commonwealth" of 66 nations. The queen is the nominal head—in effect, the chair—of the Commonwealth. All but 16 of its members have declared themselves republics; of those 16, Hong Kong will become part of China in 1997; and there is a strong movement in Australia to end the formal allegiance to the British crown.

There are still bonds of mutual sympathy, and some limited economic advantages, that justify the annual meetings of Commonwealth leaders. But Britain's dominant role in world affairs was a reflection of its imperial stature, and only a fading shadow of empire remains.

The Erosion of the Economic Base

The building of empire was closely related to the growth of the British economy, both as a source of cheap raw materials and of markets. But this is not the principal explanation for the fact that Britain, in the late eighteenth and early nineteenth centuries, became the first of the world's industrial nations. To a large extent this was the product of Britain's own resources—abundant supplies of coal and iron and the technological genius of its inventors. The great migration from the countryside and farm to the town and factory carried with it appalling working and living conditions. But these improved as the economy grew and protective legislation was passed, and as the twentieth century dawned, Britain was clearly the wealthiest and most productive of any nation other than the United States.

Beginning in the early twentieth century, however, Britain's lead over other industrial nations began to narrow; the competitive advantage Britain enjoyed in the aftermath of World War II quickly disappeared. By the 1970s Britain had become by some estimates the least wealthy and least productive of the world's industrial nations. Its rate of growth and its output per capita had fallen well behind those of its erstwhile broken adversaries, Germany and Japan, and a particularly severe blow to British self-esteem came when their gross domestic product was overtaken by the Italians—whom they had traditionally stereotyped as hopelessly unmethodical and inefficient.

In the 1980s, the administration of Margaret Thatcher introduced policies aimed at jolting the economy back to health, and, following a deep recession, there was a spurt of growth and signs of revitalization. After another severe downturn in the early 1990s, the British economy again showed signs of recovery, while economies throughout western Europe languished. But skeptics doubted that Britain would be capable of the many years of sustained growth that would be necessary to overcome the long slide in performance.

A number of factors have contributed to this weak economic record, as we shall see in chapter 13. But whatever the combination of causes, the result is what has been called, ignominiously, "the British disease"—an affliction characterized by poor productivity, loss of competitiveness in world markets, and a pattern of living beyond the nation's means.

It is important to emphasize that we are speaking here of decline *relative to other nations*. There has certainly been no decline in absolute terms. Most of the British people enjoy much greater material prosperity than previous generations, and Britain is still included in the category of the world's rich, advanced industrial (or emerging postindustrial) nations. Just the same, relative to other countries, Britain has fallen behind economically. And in world politics, relative standing is what counts.

Empires, says Paul Kennedy in his *Rise and Fall of the Great Powers,* cannot long survive the deterioration of the home economic base. And with the interrelated decline of empire and economy, Britain's status has fallen from that of a great power to a nation somewhere below the top of the second rank.

The Fraying of Civility

We shall see in the next chapter that Britain, much more than America, is a class-conscious country. Yet disparities between the classes did not in the postwar period overwhelm the general civility between individuals and groups. Consequently, this was a society with fairly low rates of crime, where the local "Bobby" covered his beat on foot or bicycle with no weapon other than a truncheon, and where people could walk through city streets at night without fear.

Today the media is full of accounts of the breakdown of civility. Crime, including violent crime, has increased sharply. Drugs are epidemic among the young, especially in the inner cities. There are racial tensions, serious enough in the 1980s to erupt into riots. British soccer fans have disrupted games with savage attacks on players, referees, and each other, and terrorized European cities when their teams played abroad. The British police themselves have been caught up in charges of brutality, forced confessions, and fixed evidence; instances of corruption have reached even into Scotland Yard's senior ranks.

Here again, the evidence for decline depends on our point of reference. Compared with Dickens's mid-nineteenth-century world of degraded criminality, ferocious treatment of the poor, and debtors' prisons, today's Britain seems a benevolent, well-mannered country indeed. Or if we compare Britain with America today, we note that there were fewer than 1,000 murders in Britain in 1991, whereas in the United States (with four times Britain's population) there were some 17,000.

Nonetheless, within the living memory of the British people, there are all too many signs of a frayed social order; as we shall see, this has important consequences for political attitudes and behavior in Britain.

Questioning the Governmental System

The admiration that Americans and others lavished on British governmental and political institutions during the 1940s and 1950s was based on a perception of effective decision making combined with democratic accountability. The system, it was said, enabled the government to get things done, yet set limits to government power through a vigorous tradition of free speech and strong political parties that presented clear alternatives to the people. In this view, the British system offered advantages that were conspicuously lacking in the U.S. constitutional structure.

By the 1970s, however, some of the gloss had worn off the reputation of British government, which encountered increasing skepticism abroad and demands for reform at home. These challenges stemmed in part from questions—which we will discuss throughout this book—about the adequacy of restraints on the centralized power of government's executive branch. But the skepticism also resulted considerably from the country's unsatisfactory economic performance and a general sense of decline. After all, the advantage claimed for the British system over other forms of democracy was precisely that it was efficacious, well-equipped to make decisions. But it was increasingly evident that the decisions emerging from this system had not succeeded in preventing the nation's relative decline. As a result, the system itself came into question.

By 1993, Gallup Polls revealed a deep disaffection with British governmental institutions. Only 30 percent of those polled believed that the country was well governed. There was growing dissatisfaction with Parliament, the monarchy, the church, the legal system. Most dismaying of all: Polls indicated that half the British people—and 70 percent of British teenagers—said they would like to emigrate.

DEFENDING THE STUDY OF BRITISH GOVERNMENT

For students of politics, there is no better way to gain perspective on one's own system of government than to study the institutions of other countries. But, given the extent to which British power and reputation have fallen, can a strong case still be made for the study of British government and politics?

There are, in fact, a number of reasons why—for Americans especially—studying British institutions can be highly instructive. In general, the study of Britain provides a special advantage in that it offers us a system that is significantly different from our own, yet through certain similarities sets those differences in a familiar and thus readily understandable context.

The Original Parliamentary System

Even the most casual U.S. observer of the British scene will recognize some familiar features in its political process—a constant barrage of criticism of the government in the legislature and the press, periodic free elections, a predominately two-party system, and so on. Yet it is no less obvious to Americans that the structure of British government is very different from their own.

And although the U.S. constitutional system has influenced the making of constitutions elsewhere, particularly in Latin America, the parliamentary system is much more prevalent among world democracies. It was Britain that first shaped this system, and it is the British parliament that is referred to as the "Mother of Parliaments."

Not surprisingly, countries settled by Britishers—Canada, Australia, New Zealand—adopted versions of the British model. Even others, like India, that had fought for independence from British domination, continued to use that model. So, too, did most countries in western Europe. And it is especially noteworthy that when the U.S. occupation forces imposed a new constitution on the defeated Japanese, they decided on a parliamentary model rather than one based on American institutions.

A system that is so widely used is clearly worth studying. To be sure, each parliamentary system has its own distinctive features and thus differs somewhat from the British structure; nevertheless, Britain itself has the most mature and extensive experience with this form of government and thus provides a valuable starting point for understanding parliamentary democracy.

We have noted that over the past 50 years, there has been dissatisfaction with the British system and increasing demands for reform. Throughout this book we shall be forthright in exposing the system's deficiencies. Yet along with the shortcomings we will discover some major strengths, and although there is no possibility that the United States will convert to the parliamentary model, in our final chapter we shall suggest some potentially useful ideas for Americans in the British practice of government and politics.

A More or Less Common Language

It is not only the "Queen's English" that is spoken in Britain. American tourists are sometimes baffled by the local dialects with which Britain, despite its small size, is so profusely endowed. (The regional dialects in a few British movies are so impenetrable that they are shown with subtitles in America.) Then there are idiomatic differences. Britishers today *whinge* rather than whine, and wear pants *under* their trousers; to be *knocked up* in Britain is merely to be exhausted. There are also minor differences in spelling: in this book we shall use the U.S. spelling when we discuss the *labor* movement but the British spelling for the *Labour* party.

Despite these differences, the similarity of language provides ready access to the vast riches of British literature from Chaucer and Shakespeare to Dickens and T. S. Eliot, as well as contemporary television programs such as those featured on "Masterpiece Theater" by the U.S. Public Broadcasting Service.

Much of the popular culture, too, is interchangeable. The British have flocked to American movies since the earliest days of the industry; in 1990 the U.S. share of movie box office receipts in Britain was almost 90 percent. Although British productions still play the major role in their television schedules, *Cheers, Golden Girls, L.A. Law,* and *Roseanne* have been among the most highly rated shows in recent years. Earlier generations in Britain listened to the songs of Irving Berlin and Cole Porter; later, when rock was imported to Britain, the Beatles and other groups made rock a valuable British export. Although no two nations can have an identical style of humor, many of the leading American comedians have been popular in Britain, and devoted followings exist in the United States for the "Monty Python" repertory and the broader, lewder antics of the late Benny Hill.

British politics as an area of study is accessible to Americans without the distortions that come from imperfect mastery of a foreign language. Also, resources abound: most college libraries offer British newspapers, periodicals, and journals; and

C-SPAN each Sunday carries Prime Minister's Question Time from the previous Tuesday and Thursday.

The Heritage of Institutions and Ideas

The fact that the Mayflower came to the Americas from England—as did many of the immigrant ships that followed—has had a profound impact on our institutional practices and our cultural attitudes.

Subsequent waves of immigration have reduced Americans of English descent to one among many minorities, and today a focus on the British, or even the broader European, heritage is regarded by some as "politically incorrect." To be sure, it is entirely appropriate to recognize that the sources of U.S. culture go far beyond Britain and Europe and include Africa, Latin America, Asia, and the Middle East; however, at the same time, it is useful to remain aware of Britain's influence in American culture and institutions. Our legal system may differ in many ways from the British, but the principles of the common law are derived from British practice. And the framers of our constitution, though determined to produce a system very different from the British, were themselves steeped in British cultural attitudes, literature, and works of philosophy; these, as we shall see, were reflected in various ways in the constitution and its first ten amendments.

Similarity of Policy Issues

The basic policy issues facing British politicians are remarkably similar to those confronting their U.S. counterparts.

In both countries, the standing of governments depends heavily on the state of the economy. In both, there is the struggle to increase the rate of growth while keeping inflation under control and to improve industrial competitiveness in the global economy.

In Britain as in the United States, the aging of the population and new medical technologies place enormous upward pressures on the cost of healthcare. In both societies, people demand action in response to falling standards in the schools, rising rates of crime, television violence, immigration, welfare, and racism. In the 1992 presidential compaign, the Republicans injected the issue of family values and criticized television's *Murphy Brown* for championing the single, unmarried mother. In 1993, the British Conservative party complained of the decline of traditional family values and criticized the increase in single, unmarried mothers.

These are among the topics to be addressed in Part IV of this book. As we transpose these painfully familiar issues from British to U.S. context, we find that the two systems sometimes respond in very different ways. Thus Americans struggle toward a comprehensive health program; the British National Health Service is 50 years old. The British race problem is much more recent than that in the United States, and the largest minority in Britain originated not in Africa but in the Indian subcontinent. And even where the substance of the issues is almost identical in the two countries the issues tend to be handled differently because of the dissimilar nature of the governmental systems.

The Quality of the Political Dialogue

Many observers find the cut and thrust of political debate in Britain generally more interesting than that in America. This may reflect the greater attention to the spoken and written word in the education of most British leaders. It is also related to the style of debate in the House of Commons, where the parties confront each other more directly than in the U.S. Congress, and where the ability to think and speak on one's feet are key to political advancement.

Finally, the spectrum of political ideas ranges wider in Britain than in the United States, where the left is an insignificant force, and socialism has no serious place in the political arena. In Britain, the left has lost much of its former impetus and socialism is on the defensive, but a number of leading politicians still embrace the socialist label, which makes possible the injection into politics of more provocative economic and social criticism than is commonly experienced in the United States.

The "Special Relationship"

If Americans are asked whether there is any one other country with whom they have a particularly close bond, the answers will vary widely. Some will mention Britain; others may suggest Israel, Canada, Mexico, Ireland. If you asked the same question in Britain, the overwhelming response would be that their country does indeed have a "special relationship" with one other country: the United States.

Although the relationship began inauspiciously, and there was British support for the losing side in the U.S. Civil War, the twentieth century has seen the emergence of a strong alliance between the two countries. Two world wars found them on the same side. In the second, there was a close personal bond between Franklin Roosevelt and Winston Churchill. The two nations were then allied in the Cold War; and the apotheosis of the relationship came with the concurrent administrations of Reagan and Thatcher—two leaders who had utterly different styles yet were mutually admiring friends and policy soulmates. Following Thatcher's departure, the relationship between the two countries was again reinforced when British forces were the most actively engaged of all U.S. allies in the Gulf War.

The alliance has not been without discord. No two nations have identical interests in the world. Roosevelt and Churchill had sharp disagreements on wartime strategy and Roosevelt did not share Churchill's passion for preserving the British empire. Even Thatcher and Reagan took contrary positions on some issues, as we shall see in Chapter 18. A coolness between Bill Clinton and John Major resulted from the efforts of British Conservative party emissaries who acted as advisers to George Bush's 1992 presidential campaign. In the 1990s Britain will be directing its policies more and more toward Europe; and the United States was bound to see Germany as a more important player than Britain in the European economy.

Nevertheless, British leaders continue to assert their dedication to a special connection with the United States. And the United States will no doubt continue to find the relationship a useful one. Both countries have large financial investments in the other. Their tradition of partnership in foreign policy has produced a pattern of close and easy cooperation between their diplomatic, military, and intelligence staffs.

Although British power has fallen considerably, its experience and diplomatic skills enable it to play an international role larger than its objective resources and stature seem to justify. Even if Germany and Japan gain permanent seats on the U.N. Security Council, it is unlikely that Britain will be demoted, and Britain can usually be counted on to side with the United States on the Security Council and in most other international arenas.

So the special foreign policy relationship between Britain and the United States will survive into the next century, even if it changes and perhaps weakens in the course of time.

Decline: Not Only Britain?

The decline from great power status, Paul Kennedy tells us, has been experienced by several countries throughout history; as he brings his account up to date, he speculates that the United States might have to be added to the list.

Beyond question, the United States was the dominant world power at the end of the second world war. Militarily, it possessed overwhelming weaponry including a monopoly on the atom bomb. In economic terms, the United States produced half of the world's total output in the late 1940s, and through the Marshall Plan it helped repair the devastation of war in Europe.

Before long, however, the United States was confronted by intense competition on the world scene. The Soviet Union led Americans into space in the 1950s, then caught up with them in the nuclear arms race in the 1970s. In Vietnam, the United States suffered humiliating defeat—the first in U. S. history. Pride in the economic and technological record was shaken when Japan took away a large part of the U. S. domestic automobile market and almost all of the market for television and other electronic consumer products.

In 1980, Ronald Reagan came to the presidency with the promise to end the decline in his country's standing and to have the United States "stand tall in the saddle again." By 1984, he claimed, "It was morning again in America." Subsequently the collapse of the Soviet Union and victory in the Gulf War seemed to confirm Reagan's assessment. Indeed, in the 1990s the United States was once again the world's preeminent military power.

Yet the restoration of economic leadership was another matter. The arms race may have bankrupted the Soviet Union, but, combined with tax cuts, it had left the United States hamstrung by enormous budget deficits. The bills for the Gulf War were met mostly by the Gulf oil states and Japan. There would be no more Marshall Plans from U. S. largesse, and the United States was hard-pressed to find the necessary funds for infrastructure repair and the welfare state.

So "morning again in America" seemed to be a false dawn. Just as in Britain, polls indicated a sharp falling away of confidence in leaders and institutions (though the British urge to emigrate was matched only by small numbers of Americans, and far greater numbers were desperate to migrate to the United States). Nor was there much consolation for Americans in the fact that the leaders of most other democratic countries, including Japan and Germany, were experiencing a similar loss of public support in face of intensifying economic and social problems.

Perhaps all this will pass. By the mid-1990s there were indications of improved U. S. competitiveness in a number of fields, and a reasonable recovery from recession could help restore public confidence in U. S. institutions. However, it is unlikely that the United States will return to anything resembling its unquestioned world economic leadership in the late 1940s.

Consequently, although the United States will continue to be a much more potent international force than Britain, there may be useful lessons for Americans in observing how the British have responded to the situation of relative decline. The lessons to be learned are not merely negative. We shall see that some aspects of British policy have been self-defeating, blinded by a nostalgic reluctance to face new realities. But we shall also encounter evidence of adaptability to changing circumstances. And the extent of Britain's ability to adapt to contemporary needs without destroying its rich institutional inheritance will be a central theme throughout this book.

CONCLUSION

Despite Britain's decline as a world power and the erosion of its reputation for effective self-government and civility, Americans can learn a great deal by studying the British system. In particular, they can find instructive insights by examining British political parties and governmental structures, and by examining how the British have confronted major policy issues. We will address these points further after reviewing the cultural and constitutional contexts of British politics.

SOME QUESTIONS TO THINK ABOUT

Where would you place Britain today among the world's powers?

What do you see as the main reasons for Britain's decline?

What is meant by the aphorism that Britain and the United States have "a common language separating two cultures"?

How important is the British heritage of institutions and ideas in the United States today?

Do you see the United States as having a "special relationship" with Britain?

Are there any warnings for the United States in the decline of Britain?

SUGGESTIONS FOR FURTHER READING

Among the many general histories of Britain, the introductory reader will find useful the Pelican-Penguin series, *The Pelican History of England,* including David Thomson, *England in the Twentieth Century* (Pelican, 1965); Glyn Williams and John Ramsden, *Ruling Britannia* (Longman, 1990); Asa Briggs, *A Social History of England* (Penguin, 1985). E. J. Hobsbawn provides a neo-Marxist analysis in *Industry and Empire* (Pelican, 1969) and Paul Johnson's *A History of the English People* (Perennial Library, 1985) presents a contrasting conservative interpretation. For the post–1945 era, which is the main focus of this text, see Kenneth Morgan, *The People's Peace* (Oxford University Press, 1990).

The voluminous literature on British decline includes Andrew Gamble, *Britain in Decline* (Beacon Press, 1981), Correlli Barnett, *The Pride and the Fall* (Free Press, 1988), and, in comparative context, Joel Krieger's *Reagan, Thatcher and the Politics of Decline* (Oxford University Press, 1986), and Paul Kennedy, *The Rise and Fall of the Great Powers* (Random House, 1987).

Anthony Trollope's "Palliser" novels, particularly *Phineas Finn, Phineas Redux,* and *The Prime Minister,* published between 1869 and 1876, provide brilliant accounts of British politics before the decline, and despite all the changes since then, much of Trollope's description of parties, politicians, and Parliament seems remarkably contemporary.

For more recent reference purposes, *Britain: An Official Handbook* and *Social Trends* are published annually by Her Majesty's Stationery Office (HMSO), and the *Guardian* newspaper publishes an annual *Political Almanac.*

British journals dealing with political institutions and issues include *British Journal of Political Science* and *Political Studies,* as well as the less technical *Parliamentary Affairs, Political Quarterly, Public Administration,* and *International Affairs.*

The most useful weekly magazines of opinion are *The Economist,* whose section on Britain provides informative analyses from a free-market perspective, the left-of-center *New Statesman and Society,* and the conservative *Spectator.* In addition, *Private Eye* provides a scathingly satirical (and often allegedly libelous) commentary on British politics and politicians.

Most college libraries carry the daily *Times* of London, and may also include the *Guardian* and the *Independent.* The *Manchester Guardian Weekly* (the *Guardian* used to be published in Manchester) provides selections from the daily *Guardian,* and is published jointly with weekly versions of the *Washington Post* and *Le Monde.* Libraries are also likely to include two Sunday papers, the *Sunday Times* and the *Observer.* Newsstands in some American cities also sell some of the London daily tabloid newspapers.

PART ONE
CONTEXTS

In which we review first the cultural setting of British politics, with particular reference to social class, individualism and authority, religion, and ethnicity; and second, the constitutional framework, setting up the debate about the need for constitutional reform that will be explored throughout this book.

2

THE CULTURAL SETTING

Is there such a thing as *the* British culture?

We have used the words *Britain* and *British* so far, although the correct designation of the country we are studying (shown in Figure 2.1) is the United Kingdom of Great Britain and Northern Ireland (Great Britain comprising England, Wales, and Scotland), and there are major disparities between the four quasi-nations. England has by far the largest population, with 48.6 million people in comparison to Scotland's 5 million, Wales's 2.8 million, and Northern Ireland's 1.6 million.

The joining together of these territories did not come easily. The Welsh fought English domination for centuries until they were finally subdued in 1536; Scotland's relationship with England was even more turbulent until the Act of Union in 1707; and Northern Ireland consists of six counties that refused to join the rest of Ireland in 1920 after the resolution of that country's long and bitter struggle for independence.

Given these disparities of scale and history, it is not surprising to find significant variations in cultural patterns. Although English is the principal language throughout the United Kingdom, Welsh is spoken in parts of Wales (and on one of its TV channels); Gaelic is spoken in Scotland and Northern Ireland. Scotland has its own church, separate from the Church of England, and its own school system (generally regarded as superior to the English). Each of them has its own music, poetry, and folk arts. Accordingly, many of the inhabitants of these smaller countries prefer to describe themselves as Scottish or Welsh or Northern Irish rather than British.

Even within England, cultural patterns vary widely from region to region. A great

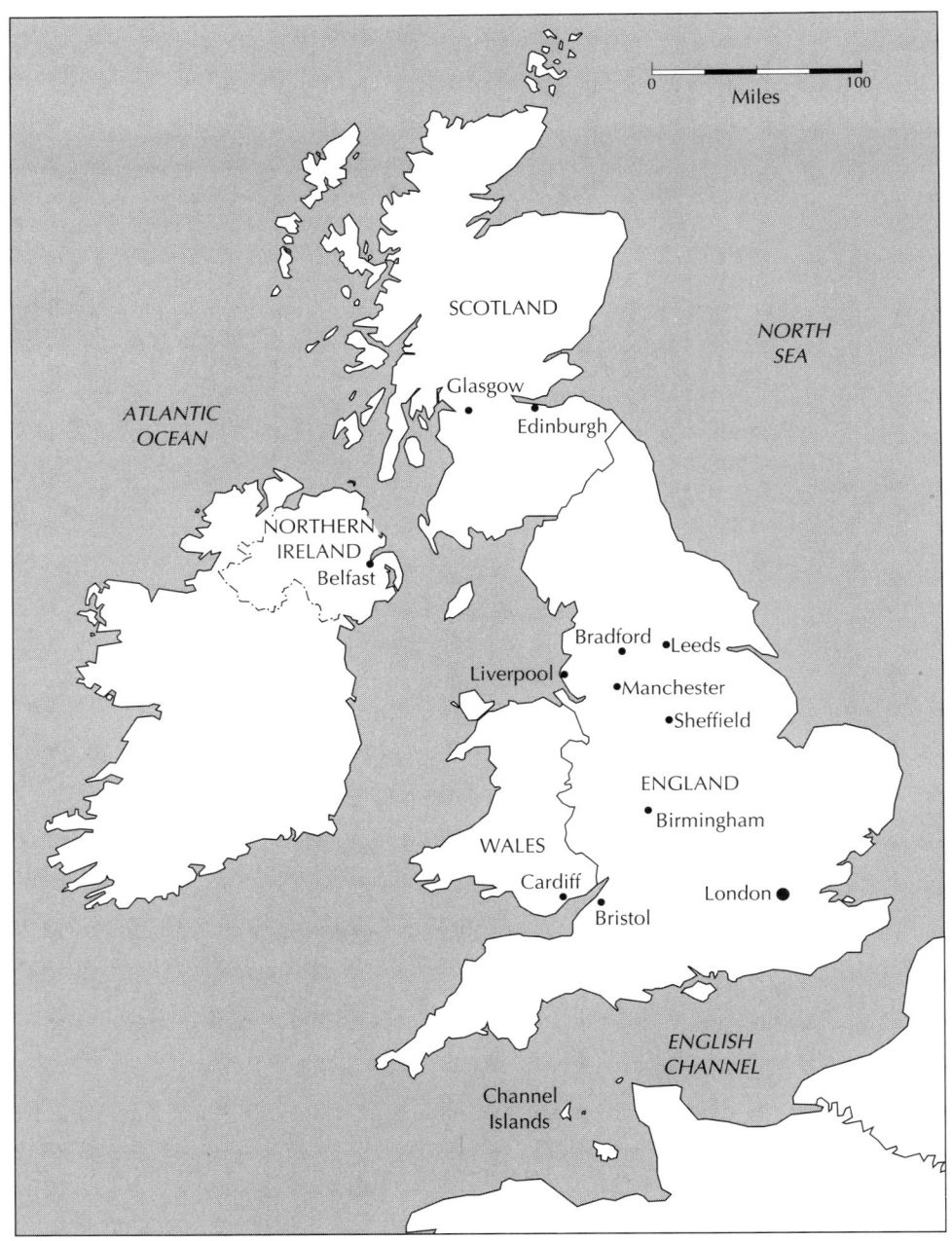

FIGURE 2.1 The United Kingdom

divide exists between the poorer north and the more prosperous south, and the profusion of dialects within and between each region reflects a considerable diversity in ways of thinking and behaving.

Yet this diversity is set within some important commonalities. The United Kingdom's population, after all, is crammed together in a very small space. It is subjected to the homogenizing influence of national television and national newspapers. The governmental system is highly centralized, and the worlds of politics, the media, finance, and the arts are focused in London.

The rolling countryside of Britain's "green and pleasant land" is still there to delight the eye. But Britain is urbanized to an even greater extent than the United States. And, as in the United States, urbanization and suburbanization, modernization, and the impact of technological change bring with them dramatic cultural changes. It is a well-known list: consumerism; the shift from manufacturing to service industries; the trend (still far from complete) toward equality of the sexes; rising rates of divorce and weakening of the traditional family; sexual permissiveness; and the catalog of problems associated with the alienation of life in the inner cities.

So amidst diversity, common patterns of culture emerge with increasing strength throughout the United Kingdom. And, as we noted in the opening chapter, these patterns are remarkably similar in many ways to those in America. Yet we also noted some significant differences between the two countries, and a useful way of gaining an understanding of the British cultural setting is to examine the extent to which it differs from the attitudes, values, and behaviors most commonly found in the United States. We focus here on four areas that have particular significance for British politics and policy: social class, individualism, religion, and ethnicity. Of these we shall consider class most extensively, for it will be a recurrent theme throughout this book.

CLASS

To a much greater extent than the United States, Britain is a class-conscious society. Class distinctions, as we shall see, have been eroding among the British since the 1950s. Even so, the idea of class still permeates British social relationships. It is an obsessive theme in British novels, plays, movies, and television programs, reflecting the reality of a hierarchical social structure.

Definitions of class vary widely, for the concept is ambiguous and perpetually evolving. When Britain was a mainly agricultural country a small number of classifications, modified from their feudal origins, served reasonably well, distinguishing large from small landowners and both of these from the mass of farm workers and servants. But the Industrial Revolution created the need for a sizeable number of employees at a level between owners and factory workers, as well as a need for many others in retail, distribution, and finance. In other words, a large and growing middle class was emerging.

Middle and Working Classes

Today most political surveys are based on the distinction between the middle class (or classes) and the working class (or classes), and various schemes have been developed to divide the British people into class categories. The most widely used in both commercial and political surveys is a market research classification, which divides the population into six groups—three middle-class and three working-class, each defined by *occupation:*

Middle Class
- **A.** Top executives and senior professionals (doctors, barristers, architects, etc.)
- **B.** Middle managers and lower professionals (e.g., sales managers, realtors, social workers, teachers, nurses)
- **C1.** White collar staff (e.g., clerks, shop assistants)

Working Class
- **C2.** Skilled manual (e.g., machine tool operators, butchers, hairdressers)
- **D.** Semiskilled and unskilled manual (laborers, bus conductors, hospital orderlies, etc.)
- **E.** The very poor (welfare recipients, longterm unemployed, elderly living on small pensions)

We shall use this marketing scheme for our purposes throughout this book. However, it is important to note that, like all classifications, it can be criticized as ambiguous and misleading. Among social scientists the most trenchant criticism has come from Anthony Heath, Roger Jowell, and John Curtice.[1] Where in this market research system, they ask, are small self-employed businesspeople? And neither *C1* nor *C2* seems to fit two categories of great importance in modern economic systems: the immediate supervisors of manual workers and the rapidly growing numbers of technical staff. So Heath and his colleagues propose a five-layer classification: the *salariat* (all senior and middle-level managers and professionals); routine nonmanual workers; *petty bourgeoisie* (small business proprietors, independent tradespeople, and farmers); foremen and technicians; the working class.

In turn these categories, too, have been criticized. Why, for example, should the entire working class be lumped together in one classification? And the debate grows more confused as both scholars and government agencies design their own classification schemes, some proposing an even larger number of categories. Still, all of them are based on the notion of social class, all of them make the distinction between middle and working classes, and all of them use occupation as the principal defining characteristic of a person's class.

Yet the category *occupation* itself encompasses a complex array of factors including cultural inheritance and experience, family background, personal and societal values, as well as social and economic standing. These factors work together to produce certain advantages, and these advantages are for the most part enjoyed by the middle classes.

Thus the middle classes are seen to have more and better *life chances*. They generally have higher incomes than the working classes, and because they have more, and frequently better, education, they are equipped with more of the skills that command higher incomes.

Middle and working classes tend to have somewhat different *lifestyles*. Middle-class people are more likely to live in the suburbs with more housing space and facilities than working-class people, who are heavily concentrated in the cities and are the main occupants of public housing. Foreign travel and golf are also associated more with middle- than with working-class people. Even newspaper readership is an index of class. British daily and Sunday papers are divided between the "quality," "broadsheet," or "class" publications on the one hand, and the mass circulation tabloids on the other. The quality papers (the *Times,* the *Guardian,* the *Independent,* the *Daily Telegraph,* and their Sunday equivalents) are read mostly by people who fit market research categories *A* and *B* as defined above. Among the tabloids, the *Daily Mail, Daily Express,* and their Sunday versions draw readership principally from the *B* and *C1* middle-class group, whereas the readership of the more sensationalist *Sun, Daily Mirror, Star,* and *News of the World* is largely working-class.

Some novelists and social analysts have expressed a preference for working-class lifestyles as more authentic and less prone to conformity and anxious upward-striving than life in the middle-class suburbs. Yet, as we shall see, the variety of factors that bring political, social, and economic advantages to the middle class are indeed increasingly attractive to the working class.

Class and Self-Definition. This distinction between middle and working classes is no mere theoretical construct imposed on the population by academics and advertisers. It strongly represents how the British people see themselves. Most of them place themselves in one of these classes and are not reluctant to identify themselves by class in response to surveys. Various surveys yield somewhat different results with respect to the numerical division between the classes, but all reveal that more people call themselves *working class* than *middle class.*

Results based on self-identification may be somewhat misleading. The market research industry has established its own criteria for distinguishing between middle and working classes, and surveys based on these criteria yield smaller working-class majorities. So a significant number of middle-class people appear to be calling themselves working class—perhaps defining the phrase to mean simply "working people." Nonetheless, the studies are unanimous in indicating that the *working class* designation is accepted by a clear (albeit declining) majority of the British people.

The Upper Class

The division of the population into middle and working classes ignores the very important fact that there is also a British upper class. The reason for this omission, as explained by a leading British pollster, is that

> such a class, however defined, would be too small to make a significant impact on statistical inquiries covering the whole nation. Even the holder of the most ancient and exalted dukedom in the United Kingdom and Great Britain and Northern Ireland must therefore accept middle-class status within the system.[2]

But if we are not to fall into the statistical fallacy that "if it can't be quantified it isn't important," we must take a close look at the British upper class; for although its influence is declining, this class, often referred to as the "Establishment," is still much more influential in the British social and political system than its numbers would indicate.

The concept of an upper class or Establishment is obviously compatible with radical left interpretations, and the Marxist scholar, Ralph Miliband, sees it as a *ruling class*, a "power elite" which, he contends, controls "the main institutions through which power, responsibility and influence are mainly exercised."[3] However, the idea of an Establishment is also employed by a broad spectrum of non-Marxist interpreters of the British system, and although their definitions vary, they all see the Establishment as an informal interconnecting elite involving both economic-political power and social status.

The centers of upper-class power are located in both the public and private sectors. Included in the public sector are the top leadership of the executive branch of government (prime minister, cabinet, and senior civil service), the judiciary, the military, and public corporations like the British Broadcasting Corporation (BBC). Positions of private power are held by presidents and boards of major industrial and financial corporations, and by the proprietors of national newspapers and television channels.

At the apex of the system of social status stands the monarch, whose political power, as we shall see in Chapter 7, is largely ceremonial, but whose social preeminence is beyond question. Below the monarchy we find the aristocracy—the approximately 35,000 dukes, earls, countesses, marquesses, and baronets listed in *Debrett's Peerage*. Others without titles may be included, especially if they receive a mention in the "Court Circular," published daily in the "quality" newspapers, which chronicles the activities of each member of the royal family (and everyone in their company) as they set a foundation stone or depart from an airport.

The power and status strands, though obviously not identical, share certain characteristics. First, the upper class owns a high proportion of the *personal wealth* of the country, because some 17 percent of the stocks, bonds, land, houses, art, jewelry, etc., are in the hands of 1 percent of the population. Among the richest are the queen and some of the old landed families of the aristocracy (the Duke of Westminster's fortune has been variously valued from $3 billion to $8 billion); and more recent huge fortunes have been made in industry, finance, commerce, and show business. Of course, most of those who occupy positions of governmental power are not wealthy on this scale, though the perks that go with high office in Britain are not unlike those associated with the lifestyle of the very rich.

Upper-class incomes provide for the purchase of a privileged form of *education* in exclusive private schools, which the British call *public schools* or *independent schools*. The top nine are all boarding schools for boys only; and among these Eton, Harrow, and Winchester are the most prestigious. All of them emphasize character building and leadership training along with the academic preparation needed for entry to a university—and particularly to the two most prestigious universities, Oxford and Cambridge, colloquially referred to as Oxbridge.

We shall have more to say in Chapter 15 about this educational sequence from public school to Oxbridge. For now the key point is that it provides a springboard to positions of power and influence. A high proportion of Conservative Party leaders in recent years went to a public school, and close to three-quarters graduated from Oxbridge. The proportions are considerably lower on the Labour Party side but over one-half of the last two Labour cabinets were Oxbridge graduates, and the current Labour Party leader, Tony Blair, is a public school product. The public school/Oxbridge connection also applies to a majority of judges, senior civil servants, and members of the boards of the BBC, the *Times,* and major banking and industrial concerns.

Members of the upper class also manifest certain *personal characteristics and mannerisms* that distinguish them from the rest of the population. There is a special speech pattern associated with a British upper-class upbringing. For those who do not absorb this accent from early childhood, the public schools will provide it. As one graduate of an exclusive girls' academy explains: "The first thing they did was get rid of the Lancashire accent I didn't know I had. Rather Pygmalion, really."[4]

A further common upper-class characteristic is a comportment, a way of carrying oneself that conveys a combination of self-assurance, restraint, and understatement. It was said of Sir Alec Douglas-Home that he appealed to rank-and-file Conservative Party members because of his "aloof self-confidence, his patrician voice and his air of disdain when meeting strangers."[5]

Given these characteristics we would expect members of the British upper class to be defensive of their privileged position and thus *conservative in their political attitudes*. In general this is true. The larger number subscribe to traditionalist doctrines including respect for monarchy, aristocracy, the church, the military, and the rights of property. But this does not mean there is a monolithic Establishment ideology. Many upper-class members temper their conservatism with an acceptance of the need for moderate reform. And some with impeccable upper-class credentials have repudiated their inherited loyalties and become prominent leaders of the Labour Party.

The Gentlemen Traitors.   Others have gone even further. Thus in the 1930s several sons of the Establishment, undergraduates at Cambridge and Oxford, joined the Communist Party. Among them were Guy Burgess and Donald Maclean, who became members of the diplomatic service after World War II, and defected to the Soviet Union in 1951 to escape arrest as Soviet spies. They were tipped off by another ex-Cambridge student and diplomat, Kim Philby, who also defected to Moscow in 1963. In 1979 came the disclosure that there was a fourth man in the spy ring: Sir Anthony Blunt, who had been an art tutor at Cambridge in the 1930s, was then a member of Britain's counterespionage agency, MI5, during the war, and subsequently became the queen's official adviser on the royal art collection. After his exposure, Blunt was stripped of his knighthood and his royal appointment, but was never prosecuted.

The ability of the four spies to establish themselves in important positions and escape discovery for so long is related to another characteristic of the British upper class—the tendency of its members to provide *mutual protectiveness and support*. Thus Blunt admitted in an interview with the editor of the London *Times* that MI5 recruited him despite their full knowledge of his communist affiliation because he was recommended through "the old boy network."[6] And all four were part of that network, for all four came from upper-class families, had attended public schools and were, in their speech and style, English gentlemen.

Subsequently it was rumored that a former head of MI5, Sir Roger Hollis, had been a fifth man in the network. The rumor was almost certainly false, but not for the reason given by another archetypal Establishment figure, former *Times* editor Sir William Rees-Mogg: "I very much doubt . . . that Hollis was a spy. I do not believe he was an ideological man at all, much more an old-fashioned, patriotic, upper middle-class Englishman."[7] In other words, despite the examples of Burgess, Maclean, Philby, and Blunt, it was still inconceivable that an English gentleman could be a traitor.

These cases provide an extreme illustration of the special advantages accruing to members of the British upper class, as a result of the contacts formed through family connections and by public school and university friendships, often reinforced by membership in elite London clubs. The networks thereby established have played a major role in helping members of the upper class advance in industry, finance, the professions, and politics.

The Decline of Class

Despite the evidence of class consciousness among the British people a number of social trends gathering force over the past 40 or 50 years have been weakening the impact of class on attitudes and behavior. This erosion has been taking place at both ends of the social scale—among the working class at one end and the upper class at the other.

The Shrinking of the Working Class.
Several of the factors that tie people to a working-class identification have been weakening, with a resulting trend toward "embourgeoisement"—a shift to middle-class conduct and tastes.

The key to this shift has been a substantial increase in family income, even allowing for inflation, for all but the very poor. The consequence has been a transformation of the living standards of working-class people. In 1950 few among the working class owned their homes, and even fewer owned a car or a telephone. Today a majority of working-class families own their home, in many cases a public housing unit they formerly rented. Ownership of a car is now a norm among the working class, and most also own a telephone, a color television, and a VCR.

There has also been a general increase among the working class in number of years of schooling, and it is not at all uncommon for working-class families to enjoy packaged holidays in Mediterranean resorts. Moreover, there is more social mobility than in the past, and considerably more people see themselves as moving up in the social scale than as moving down.

It is clear that numerically the working class has shrunk. And since the 1970s, the size and strength of the principal organizations representing working class interests—the trade unions—have also lessened. Thus there is general agreement among social scientists today that, however people identify themselves in terms of class, an increasing share of the British population has been adopting more middle-class behavior and attitudes.

The Decline of Upper-Class Influence. Until the latter part of the nineteenth century, the British upper class was clearly a ruling class. Since then its power and influence have been slipping.

First, with the decline of land values in the 1880s, and the coming of income tax and death duties early in the twentieth century, some of the old landed fortunes are no more, and a number of large country estates have been broken up or donated to the National Trust as stately homes to be visited by tourists (sometimes with the provision that the former owners may continue to live there).

Several members of the aristocracy have taken paid jobs outside the traditional range of company directorships. Some work in the media, in auction houses, in interior design, in senior sales positions. But Lord Simon Conyngham has been an assistant in a delicatessen; Earl Nelson worked as a police constable; and Lord Teviot drove a bus and married his conductor, then worked in a supermarket with his wife as cashier.

Then, as the mass of the people have gained the vote, educational opportunity, and increased affluence, they have been less inclined to award the upper class the deference that was the legacy of Britain's feudal past. After World War II, plays and novels were written by a group dubbed the "Angry Young Men," protesting their sense of suffocation in a system dominated by the old boy network. On television *That Was the Week That Was* lampooned all of Britain's sacred cows, *Monty Python's Flying Circus* depicted the upper classes as mental defectives, and *Spitting Image* made savage fun of everyone in public life, including the royal family.

In pop music the Beatles, a working-class group from Liverpool, showed no respect for their elders or authority figures; they were followed by punk rock, which derided everything considered proper and respectable. The punk attitude was well exemplified when Lord Hailsham complained of a horrible experience on the M1 motorway: he was mooned by a carload of youths. "I was flabbergasted," he said. "There was this huge pair of buttocks exposed before me. It stayed there all the way up to London. Obviously he didn't realize who I am."[8] Or conceivably he did.

A further indication of the decline of deference came with the growing onslaught on a favorite upper-class sport—foxhunting. A bill banning foxhunting and hare coursing passed one of its stages in the House of Commons in 1995, and although there were still several legislative hurdles ahead, an opinion survey indicated that close to 70 percent of the public supported the ban.

The clearest political expression of the decline of upper-class authority has come in the transformation of Conservative Party leadership. This is the party that in its origins had expressed the interests of the hereditary aristocracy and the smaller landed gentry. Yet Sir Alec Douglas-Home (Lord Home before and after he became prime minister) was the last of the bluebloods to head the party. The next three leaders—Edward Heath, Margaret Thatcher, and John Major—all came from lower-middle-class backgrounds, and none went to a "public school." Heath and Thatcher did graduate from Oxford, but Major did not go to a university at all.

As prime minister, Thatcher attacked several bastions of the Establishment. Then John Major announced his intention to make Britain a "classless society." This did not sit well with the Duke of Westminster, who—when the Conservative government announced its intention to enable people to buy the apartments they were leasing from private landlords—declared that his property rights were being infringed and resigned in disgust from the Conservative Party.

The Persistence of Class

To recognize the extent to which class distinctions have declined in Britain is not to suggest that they have disappeared. In comparison with the past, the British are less class-conscious than they were. In comparison with most other industrial countries today, especially the United States, the British are still remarkably aware of differences between the classes. John Major's goal of a "classless society" will clearly not be achieved in this century.

Of course, there is social stratification in all societies. In the United States we have extremes of wealth and income at least as great as those found in Britain. The concept of the Establishment is widely used here, too, both by radical sociologists and conservative writers, and so is the notion of a ruling upper class. Our newspapers chronicle the activities of the wealthy in the "society pages." And there are obvious parallels to the British experience in the expensive private schools that feed into Ivy League universities and in turn open the way to top law firms and financial institutions in New York and Washington.

Yet in U.S. voting surveys, the classifications used are by income, occupation, race, and gender, among others, but never by the kind of class-based categories used in Britain. Moreover, to the extent that they are prepared to assign themselves to a class, the large majority of Americans see themselves as middle class, not working class. As for the U.S. "Establishment," it is a weak imitation of the British model. The U.S. upper class is not clearly differentiated by accent and deportment from the rest of the population. The only recent American president born to the upper class, George Bush, emphasized his fondness for country music and bacon rinds.

In Britain, much more than in the United States, social class is still an important influence on voting behavior, even if not the controlling factor it once was. Although Heath, Jowell, and Curtice agree that the size of the working class has been falling, they insist that "Britain is still divided by class,"[9] and that a strong working class consciousness persists.

Moreover, the upper class still possesses a degree of influence and power far beyond its numbers. If some members of the aristocracy have lost their fortunes, others have used primogeniture (leaving all the property to the eldest son) and a variety of techniques for avoiding inheritance tax to keep their holdings intact and build them further. Great fortunes have also been amassed by new breeds of entrepreneurs, and within a generation or two the new money is absorbed into the upper class by virtue of public school education on the one hand and the honors system on the other.

The Honors System. Twice a year a list is issued of approximately 1,000 individuals who are to be honored by the queen (most of them on the recommendation of the prime minister, who nominates an additional list on his or her resignation). The honors list may include a few peerages, which entitle their recipients to sit in the House of Lords (though most are now for the life of the recipient only and cannot be inherited). Other honors create knighthoods, which place the title "Sir" before the individual's name, and "Lady" before his wife's name.

Then there are various "orders of chivalry," including the Order of the Garter, the Order of Merit, the Order of the Bath, the Order of St. Michael and St. George, and the multipurpose Order of the British Empire. There is a hierarchy of prestige among the orders, and some of the orders have rankings within them, with the lower grades most likely given to athletes or pop entertainers like the Beatles. (Lennon sent his back.)

The distribution of honors, although it extends to wide sections of the population, has been directed primarily to bestowing status on those who occupy positions of power and influence in both private and public sectors. Peerages and knighthoods go not only to former cabinet members, members of Parliament, and civil servants but also to newspaper proprietors and to industrialists and financiers who make large financial contributions to political parties. Thus, the 1920s cartoon in Figure 2.2 is still topical.

Some steps in the direction of democratization of the system were announced by Prime Minister John Major: senior civil servants were no longer to receive Knighthood "automatically" on retirement, and nominations for honors were invited from the general public. The result from 1994 was an increase in the number of "ordinary" people included on the list—but almost all at the lower levels. The honors system continues to pull together the two strands in the Establishment—power and status—and to reinforce the social stratification that characterizes the class system.

Assessments of the British Class System

To critics of the class system, its persistence is in large part attributable to the survival of the upper class, for the middle classes seek to emulate the upper class, and the "embourgeoisement" of the working classes then carries the process further down the social scale.

Yet the British Establishment is not without its admirers. Some have praised its

"I COULD NOT LOVE THEE, DEAR, SO MUCH,
LOVED I NOT HONOURS MORE."

FIGURE 2.2 A still-topical 1920s cartoon on the honors system

SOURCE: Reproduced by permission of *Punch*.

members for their adaptability to changing circumstances, and—in contrast with some of their European counterparts—their instinct for knowing when to give ground, how to make adjustments and still survive. This was attributed to a shrewd assessment of their longterm self-interest combined with a sense of *noblesse oblige*—the belief that the privileged classes have obligations toward those less fortunate than themselves.

Others have suggested that the combination of upper-class background and education has produced able and experienced leadership, which has been particularly valuable in establishing a high reputation in the world of international diplomacy. Then, too, the urbaneness, restraint, and good taste of the upper class are often credited for infusing British culture with its respect for moderation and civilized behavior. In this view, the decline of respect for the upper class has been the main cause of the disastrous loss of civility that we noted in Chapter 1.

But the critics are unpersuaded by these views. They doubt the Establishment's readiness to accommodate change, and argue that, like the present Duke of Westminster, they have fought rearguard actions against every inevitable reform.

Then there is the charge that in general, the upper class disdains real work, as distinguished from sitting on boards of directors, acting as gentlemen farmers, and supervising charities. As one Saville Row tailor put it: "I don't think you should wear [a watch] because it shows you have an interest in time. Real gentlemen don't."[10] This disdain is particularly directed at manufacturing work, and the permeation of this posture throughout British society has contributed grievously to the decline of Britain's economic competitiveness.

INDIVIDUALISM AND AUTHORITY

It is frequently suggested that Americans are more dedicated to individualism, more suspicious of authority than are the British. This is said to be the consequence of two principal factors: first, the U.S. frontier tradition, under which individuals moved on restlessly into vast open territories relying on their own initiative rather than government support. The small British Isles have offered no such frontier, and a densely populated country has required people to develop a strong sense of interdependence.

Second, when the Normans conquered Britain in 1066, they imposed the system of feudalism, and a central characteristic of feudalism is deference to authority. Feudalism has no place in U.S. history, and deference has no place in U.S. character.

Although these historical differences are significant, the consequences in contemporary behavior are sometimes overstated. Thus, the picture of the supremely individualistic American has been challenged by novelists like Sinclair Lewis, writing in *Babbitt* about small-town pressures to conform, and by sociologist David Riesman's analysis of the shift from inner-directed to other-directed behavior. Moreover, despite the protestations against government and taxes that Americans tend to indulge in, most of them resist strenuously any interference with Social Security and other benefits provided by the welfare state.

As for the British, the emphasis on "deference" should be questioned. They have not been nearly as deferential or respectful of authority as, for example, the Germans or the Japanese. And we have already noted that to a considerable extent, the deference of the past has eroded. With this erosion has developed a growing dissatisfaction with the institutions that represent authority. Thus an opinion survey published in 1990 asking to what extent people were satisfied with the performance of various institutions found only 39 percent approving of the civil service, 31 percent approving of Parliament, and 26 percent approving of government ministers.[11]

Moreover, deference and acceptance of authority in Britain have existed side by side with strong individualistic impulses. Among the intellectual influences behind the Declaration of Independence and the United States Constitution were British philosophers like John Locke, with his emphasis on individual rights. And in the 1980s the administration of Margaret Thatcher launched a fierce attack on previous government policies in the name of the same kind of economic individualism that was being pursued concurrently by Ronald Reagan.

Still, if British and American attitudes on individualism and authority appear to be converging, the convergence is far from complete. Margaret Thatcher's effort to convert her people to a thoroughgoing economic individualism never really overcame an obstinate attachment to communitarian values. When people were asked in a survey toward the end of her tenure whether they favored "a mainly capitalist society in which private interests and free enterprise are most important" or "a mainly socialist society in which public interests and a more controlled economy are most important," the socialist society was preferred by 47 percent to 39 percent—an inconceivable outcome in the United States. Again, 54 percent preferred a society that "emphasizes the social and collective provision of welfare," compared with the 40 percent that opted for one where "the individual is encouraged to look after himself."[12] We shall also be observing later that outside of economic policy, Thatcher stood for a strong reassertion of respect for authority and law and order.

Two examples illustrate the differences between the two cultures in the context of individualism versus communitarianism. The first relates to radio and television. Today in Britain there are commercial stations and channels that carry advertising. But this has been the case only since 1955. Before that a semiautonomous public corporation, the British Broadcasting Corporation (BBC), created in 1927, held a monopoly of broadcasting and allowed no advertising; the breaking of that monopoly faced strong resistance even by some Conservative Party leaders, who believed that advertising on the air would be demeaning and would bring down the high standards established by the BBC.

Despite having to face strong competition, the BBC is still very much alive, and it is funded not by advertising, nor by the kind of subscription appeals resorted to by U.S. public television and radio, but by a license fee set by the government and paid by every owner of a television set. An arrangement so socialistic would seem to contradict the ideas propagated by the conservative governments of Margaret Thatcher and John Major. Yet the Major government decided to renew the BBC's charter for another ten years after 1996, and to continue its support from the license fee (although the BBC was to supplement this by vigorous efforts to sell its programs and services worldwide).

A second example illustrating the differences between the two cultures concerns the role and control of guns. Of course, there have been occasional incidents in Britain involving crazed individuals shooting people at random; however, these are rare occurrences—there are no counterparts to the regularity of drive-by shootings in American cities and of gun battles between rival gangs or between armed criminals and armed police (other than those involving the Irish Republican Army). The sale of guns, other than for hunting, is carefully controlled. Most Britishers cannot comprehend why the Governor of Virginia's limiting the right of individuals to purchase guns in his state to one a month was regarded as an act of high political courage.

RELIGION

There is no separation of church and state in Britain. On the contrary the Anglican Church of England is the "established" or official church (as is the Presbyterian Church in Scotland). Bishops and archbishops provide the spiritual leadership of the Church of England, but the queen is its secular head, its supreme governor. One-half or more of the population say they belong to this established church. In all state schools, prayer and religious education are not simply allowed—they are required (although some schools have not implemented the requirement).

Thus Britain is officially a Christian country, and, ever since Henry VIII wrested control of the church from Rome, it has been a Protestant country. However, a wide range of religions, some not Protestant, some not Christian, exist alongside the official church. There are the Methodists, Baptists, and other "nonconformist" Protestant churches, with about seven percent of the populace. Close to 13 percent declare themselves to be Roman Catholics. There are about 110,000 active members of Jewish temples (out of a total Jewish population of some 400,000). Among the religions of the nonwhite immigrant groups, Mohammedanism is easily the largest, with close to 1 million church participants out of a total Muslim population of over 1.5 million. There are also significant numbers of Sikhs, Hindus, and Buddhists.

With many other faiths thronging the religious scene—Jehovah's Witnesses, Spiritualists, Scientologists, Theosophists, new age "travelers," and so on—it might appear that the British are a very religious people indeed. But in fact, judging by church attendance and demonstrated extent of belief in church teachings, the British are much less religious than Americans.

Over one-third of Americans claim they go to church at least once a week. The corresponding figure for Britons is 14 percent. In the section on religion in the statistical survey, *British Social Trends Since 1990*, the heading for the summary is: "Does It Matter?,"[13] because over the past 15 years actual registered church membership (as opposed to vague assertions of church affiliation) had declined from 8.5 million to less than 7 million, and 3,000 church buildings had been closed. Membership continues to decline in all the mainstream Christian churches.

It is true that 61 percent of British adults say they believe in God. But the corresponding figure in the United States is 89 percent. And only 24 percent in Britain are prepared to say they have no doubts about God's existence, as against 63 percent in America.[14] As suggested in Table 2.1, much the same is true of other religious beliefs.

TABLE 2.1 Cross-cultural comparison of selected religious concepts

Percent Surveyed Who Believe In	U.S.	U.K.
Life after death	78%	54%
Miracles	73%	45%
Heaven	86%	54%
Hell	71%	28%
The Devil	65%	28%

SOURCE: Adapted from tables in *American Enterprise*, November–December 1992.

Given this relative lack of religious intensity, it is not surprising that there is nothing in British politics comparable to the impact of the fundamentalist right wing in American politics. Still, religious affiliation does play a role, albeit a limited one, in British politics. Conservatives generally have seen the Church of England as one of the pillars of the established order and have argued that the decline of respect for religion and the Church is a prime cause of the breakdown of traditional values and the loss of civility. On the other hand, some Church of England bishops have criticized Thatcherite conservativism. As for the Labour party, it is said to have been inspired more by Methodism than by Marx, for the nonconformist chapels have been a major influence in the party's history, and the two most recent leaders of the Labour Party, John Smith and Tony Blair, have defined themselves as Christian Socialists.

As we shall see, religion has entered into the controversies affecting the royal family, as well as the threats to assassinate Salman Rushdie because of the offense perceived by members of the Muslim religion in his book *The Satanic Verses*. And on the issue of Sunday trading, the Church, in combination with the shopworkers' union, repeatedly defeated attempts in Parliament to allow major stores to open on Sundays. Only when several large stores flouted the law did the pressures of commerce overcome the claims of religion, and since the passage of the 1994 Sunday Trading Act, large stores may stay open for six hours on Sunday and small stores all day.

Because the Church of England is the official state religion, changes in its structure require approval by Parliament. Thus Parliament debated and endorsed the decision of the Church's national synod voted in 1993 to allow women to be ordained as priests; the issue attracted extensive media coverage as some members of the clergy, and even a Conservative government minister, defected from the Church of England in protest.

And if religious issues are secondary concerns most of the time in most of Britain, they are primary matters *all* of the time in Northern Ireland. As we shall see in Chapter 12, the agonizing conflict in that province has not been solely religious, but the Protestant-Catholic divide has provided much of the emotional force of the contending groups.

ETHNICITY

A year before she was elected prime minister, Conservative Party leader Margaret Thatcher told a television interviewer that British culture was in danger of being "swamped" by immigrants who brought with them "un-British" beliefs and behavior. She was referring to the nonwhite populations who had been arriving since the early 1950s from parts of the old colonial empire—the West Indies, Africa, and especially India, Pakistan, and Bangladesh. Polls indicated that a substantial majority of the voting public agreed with her. Yet the population of nonwhite immigrants constituted a much smaller proportion of the British population—approaching 6 percent—than the nonwhite minorities in the United States.

We shall discuss in Chapter 16 the party politics of the immigration issue and of the resulting problems of race relations. But it is important to establish at the outset that this issue contains one of the keys to understanding contemporary British culture. For Britain until the 1950s had not had anything like America's experience in absorbing successive waves of immigration—not, that is, since 1066.

Before that time Britain had been settled or overrun by a succession of groups from different parts of Europe. The New Stone Age was brought to Britain by peaceful agriculturalists. These gave way around 2000 B.C. to tribes of invading warriors, the "Beaker Folk," who inaugurated the Bronze Age. Later Celts arrived from France and western Germany, and they gave way in turn to the Romans, who extended their empire to much of Britain starting in 55 B.C. With the disintegration of the Roman empire, the last centurion left Britain in 407 A.D. In the fifth century we enter the era of the Anglo-Saxons, who originated in the Jutland peninsula and north Germany. The seventh century saw a series of mostly successful attacks by Vikings from Scandinavia. Then in 1066 William of Normandy defeated King Harold and became William the Conqueror, King of England.

Each of these waves of foreigners (except the Romans) came to settle in Britain, and each (including the Romans) left their mark on the British landscape and culture. The Beaker Folk built Stonehenge; the Romans built towns, roads, and great walls. The Celts and Romans brought different versions of Christianity. Much of British law and its early literature derives from the Saxons. The Normans introduced various French influences on customs and language and—more important—centralized royal power and feudalism. All these influences and the groups that brought them fused together in an early version of what Americans have called (though never fully achieved) a melting pot.

However, the process we have described was more or less completed almost a thousand years ago. Since then there have been other arrivals: small numbers of French Huguenots fleeing persecution in the seventeenth century, Jewish refugees from Russia and eastern Europe in the late nineteenth and early twentieth centuries, and a continuing influx from Ireland. But the scale was always easily manageable. So Britain was able to build a culture within a fairly homogeneous population. Moreover, the 22 miles that separated Britain from the closest point in France served to generate an attitude of insularity, of suspicion of foreigners. Europe was "abroad," and the defining joke was: "Heavy fog in the Channel. The Continent cut off."

So it is not surprising that, as we shall see, Britain was slow to join the European Community and then dragged its feet at every step toward fuller integration into Europe. And its long history of homogeneity has not prepared it to deal comfortably with a major increase in immigration, especially from countries with cultures very different from its own; charges of racial prejudice and discrimination have become an increasing part of the British political debate during the past half-century.

CONCLUSION

The four topics discussed in this chapter play important roles in the political arena and will be reviewed again at various points throughout this book. Class, as we have indicated, will be a consideration no matter what the subject, despite its decline in recent years. Economic individualism is the central element in Thatcherism, and becomes the focus of political debate from Mrs. Thatcher's accession to the prime ministership in 1979. Religion will be considered in relation to parties and elections and some of the public issues discussed in Part IV. And ethnicity and race will be given particular attention in Chapter 16.

As we examine each of these topics we will be reminded that, for the all the similarities between Britain and America noted in the opening chapter, and for all the economic and technological forces that propel them in the same direction, there remain significant differences between the two political cultures.

We turn next to an area in which these differences are particularly marked—their respective constitutional structures.

SOME QUESTIONS TO THINK ABOUT

Are there equivalents in the United States to the British class system? Does the United States have an upper class comparable to theirs?

Has the influence of the upper class been beneficial or harmful to Britain on the whole?

What advantages and disadvantages do you see in Britain's leaning more to community values than individualistic values? Would you support the creation of a broadcasting system analogous to the BBC in the United States? What do you think of the much stronger gun controls in Britain compared with the United States?

Why do you think Britishers tend to be less religious than Americans? Should the Church of England be disestablished?

What are the advantages and disadvantages of a relatively homogenous ethnic population?

NOTES

1. Anthony Heath, Roger Jowell, and John Curtice, *How Britain Votes* (Pergamon Press, 1985); Heath, Jowell, Curtis et al., *Understanding Political Change* (Pergamon Press, 1991).
2. Eric Jacobs and Robert Worcester, *We British* (Weidenfeld and Nicolson, 1990), p. 138.
3. Ralph Miliband, *Capitalist Democracy in America* (Oxford University Press, 1982).
4. Nancy Banks-Smith, *Guardian Weekly*, 1994 February 13, p. 24.
5. Anthony Howard and R. West, *The Making of the Prime Minister* (Jonathan Cape, 1965), p. 94.
6. The *Times* (London), 1979 November 21.
7. The *Independent*, 1986 December 2.
8. *Evening Standard*, cited in *New Statesman and Society*, 1989 February 23.
9. *How Britain Votes*, p. 39.
10. The *Daily Mail*, cited in The *New Statesman*, December 1993, p. 29.
11. Jacobs and Worcester, *We British*, p. 68.
12. Jacobs and Worcester, pp. 25–26.
13. A. H. Halsey, ed., *British Social Trends Since 1900*. (Macmillan, 1988), p. 522.
14. The *American Enterprise*, November-December 1992, pp. 93, 95.

SUGGESTIONS FOR FURTHER READING

On British culture generally: Arthur Marwick, *British Society Since 1945* (Penguin, 1982) and *Culture in Britain Since 1945* (Blackwell, 1991), and A. H. Halsey, *British Social Trends Since 1900* (Macmillan, 1988).

On class: John H. Goldthorpe, *Social Mobility and Class Structure in Modern Britain* (Clarendon Press, 1980), and Arthur Marwick, *Class: Image and Reality in Britain, France and the USA Since 1930* (Fontana/Collins, 1981).

On the subject of upper class, Ralph Miliband (see NOTES) provides a Marxist analysis; critical assessments are offered by David Cannadine, *The Decline and Fall of the British Aristocracy* (Yale University Press, 1990), and Jeremy Paxman, *Friends in High Places* (Penguin, 1991); and a contrasting, admiring view is presented in W. D. Rubenstein, *Capitalism, Culture and Decline in Britain: 1750-1990* (Routledge, 1993).

On religion, see Grace Davie, *Religion in Britain Since 1945* (Blackwell, 1994).

3

The Debate over the Constitution

❖ ❖ ❖ ❖ ❖ ❖ ❖ ❖ ❖ ❖ ❖ ❖ ❖ ❖ ❖ ❖ ❖ ❖

Underlying the laws and practices of any legitimate political system is a constitution—the basic framework that assigns power, sets limits to that power, and establishes the rules of the game.

The United Kingdom operates under such a constitutional structure, although unlike the United States it does not have a single document defining its fundamental law. Instead the constitution has evolved over the centuries, with power shifting from the monarch to the Parliament and then to the executive branch. For some in Britain the process of evolution has produced a generally satisfactory framework for government, wherein only minor adjustments are called for. Other voices are heard, however, protesting that there are profound defects in the present constitutional arrangements, and these critics are forcing a vigorous debate over the very foundations of the British system.

We begin this chapter with a brief account of the evolution of the constitution. Then we review the major differences between the British and U.S. constitutional systems. Next we present the case for the British constitution, followed by the arguments for reform.

THE EVOLUTION OF THE CONSTITUTION

For the past three centuries or so, the British constitution emerged gradually, unmarred by the kind of revolution that preceded constitution-writing in the United States and France. However, the earliest stages of constitutional development were anything but peaceful.

First, limits had to be set to the power of the monarch, other than those imposed by the periodic threat of being overthrown by a rival claimant to the "divine right" of kings. The *Magna Carta* was the initial step in this direction, when King John submitted in 1215 to the demands of his barons that his feudal duties be listed in writing.

Then as the feudal system faded it was Parliament's turn to challenge royal authority. In the seventeenth century this challenge erupted in a violent confrontation between Charles I and his parliament, which charged that the king was acting arbitrarily and planning to overturn Henry VIII's break with the Roman Catholic church. Civil war broke out in 1642, with massed armies clashing in ferocious battles. (Britain, too, has its Civil War buffs, who dress up in armor and period costumes and reenact the battles.) The royal forces lost, King Charles was beheaded, and a republic was declared under Oliver Cromwell.

This proved to be the last great paroxysm of violence in the development of British institutions. The republic lasted only eleven years and the monarchy was restored in 1660. There was one more impasse between king and Parliament. Again an army took the field against the incumbent monarch, James II, whom Parliament accused of scheming to bring back Catholicism. This time the insurgents were an invading force led by William of Orange, who had been invited by parliamentary leaders to take over the throne. But this time there was no civil war. James, with his army defecting, remembered what had happened to Charles I, and fled into exile without a struggle. Thenceforth the British spoke of the "Glorious Revolution" of 1688, so named because it was successful, popular, and bloodless.

With the installation on the throne of William and his English wife Mary, the clear ascendancy of Parliament began. Yet we can hardly date the inauguration of British democracy from that event. Parliament then represented mostly great landowners, rural squires, and wealthy merchants. The first halting move toward enfranchising the middle classes did not come until 1832. Step by step the franchise was extended: to working-class men in 1867 and 1884; then to women over 30 in 1918 and over 21 in 1928; and finally in 1969 to everyone over 18. The democratic principle was further entrenched in 1911 when the House of Lords, the hereditary upper chamber, lost much of the power that it had previously shared with the popularly elected House of Commons.

The process since 1688 has not been entirely free from turbulence. In the 1830s and 1840s, the Chartist movement was organized to demand the inclusion of the working and lower-middle classes in the system. Huge petition drives were organized and a Chartist faction erupted into riots in 1841. The petitions were rejected, the riots were put down, and the movement collapsed. Yet most of their demands had become part of British constitutional practice by 1918. Militant challenges, including bombings, arson, and hunger strikes, were also mounted by the Suffragette movement until at last women won the vote. Violent opposition to British rule was instrumental in the establishment of an independent republic of Ireland, and violence continued until recently in the six northern counties that are still part of the United Kingdom.

But none of these movements have forced a fundamental redirection of the British constitutional order. The constitution emerged a step at a time, responding piecemeal to pressures from one group or class and then from another, evolving by trial and error over the decades and centuries.

CONTRASTS BETWEEN THE BRITISH AND U.S. CONSTITUTIONS

A Mostly Unwritten Constitution

There was no occasion in British history when—as in Philadelphia in 1787—a group of leaders gathered to set down a comprehensive, codified declaration of procedures and principles. We must therefore turn to a variety of sources from which the British constitution can be derived.

Some of these sources are, in fact, written down. For example, *Magna Carta*, by setting some limits to power at the center, is cited as a fundamental constitutional source in all English-speaking democracies.

Then there are various *statutes* passed by Parliament, which go beyond current policy issues to change the way the system works as a whole. Examples are the laws extending the franchise or reducing the power of the House of Lords. These are matters that would involve formal amendments to the constitution—if there were such a single constitutional document.

Judicial decisions may also underscore or even establish constitutional principles. Courts, by finding that certain long-established customs or rules should be given legitimacy, have established a body of *common law*. Included in common law is the principle of *prerogative powers*—powers once exercised by the monarch but now by the government, which do not require parliamentary action. These government prerogative powers range from the awarding of honors and the granting of pardons to the declaration of war. On the other hand, the writ of *habeas corpus*, a fundamental limit on arbitrary authority, was established in common law before it was incorporated into acts of Parliament. And in the absence of the level of protection for the accused built into the U.S. Bill of Rights, judges have issued rules that provide some of those same protections.

Other writings that are often cited as constitutional sources are *authoritative books* by leading constitutional scholars including A. V. Dicey, Sir Ivor Jennings, and E. C. S. Wade.

There are also *documents that govern the behavior of the institutions of government*. Thus cabinet members are issued *Questions of Procedure for Ministers*.

This lays down not only procedures but also the principles that govern the relationships between the members, and because much of the power in the British system is vested in the cabinet, any document intended to guide their conduct of business takes on a quasi-constitutional force. Similarly, the speaker of the House of Commons uses a standard reference work by Erskine May[1] as her procedural bible.

There is yet another source of written contribution to the British constitution, and it is a recent addition, resulting from Britain's increasing involvement in Europe: The *European Union treaties*, which Britain has entered in to award the European Union authority to determine law in important areas of British life—important enough in some cases, as we shall see, to be of fundamental, constitutional significance.

But all of these documents together constitute only a portion of the total constitution. The rest is made up of custom, established political practice, *conventions*. For example, there are no official documents that declare that the queen *must* sign a bill passed by Parliament, or that a government *must* resign if it is defeated in the House of Commons on a vote of confidence, or that a prime minister *must* today be a member of the House of Commons, not the House of Lords. Yet these consequences *will* transpire as surely as if they were formalized in a written constitution.

So, in contrast not only to the United States but to every other industrialized country except Israel, the British constitution is not set forth in a single, comprehensive document, but is made up of a patchwork of writings and an array of political conventions.

The Interconnection of Executive and Legislative Branches

The relationship between the executive branch of government and the legislature is close enough to be considered almost symbiotic. The system works this way:

1. In 651 local districts or constituencies, the voters choose among candidates aspiring to be their representative in the House of Commons, or member of Parliament (M.P.). Candidates are selected by local political party organizations and run under the banner of their party. Only one round of voting is required, and the candidate receiving the largest number of votes is elected.
2. When the election results are known, the queen sends for the leader of the party that has won enough seats to form a majority in the House of Commons, and asks him or her to become prime minister and form a government. If no party has a clear majority, the queen sends for whichever party leader is able to attract enough support from other parties either to form a majority coalition or, at least, to avoid defeats on key votes in Parliament.
3. The prime minister names a government of about 100 members, and within the government an executive committee, the cabinet. All of the government members will normally be drawn from the majority party or coalition of parties, most from the House of Commons, a few from the House of Lords.
4. *The government members retain their seats in the legislature*, presenting and arguing for their legislative proposals from inside Parliament.

5. *The government remains the government as long as it keeps its majority in the House of Commons.* If the government is defeated on a vote of confidence in the Commons, it must resign and usually will dissolve, or terminate, Parliament and call a new election.
6. If the government is able to avoid a defeat on a crucial vote it may stay in office for no more than five years, at the end of which time new elections must be held. However, there is no fixed term of office, so the government may decide to call new elections at any time it decides within the five-year limit.
7. Strong party discipline is essential, for the survival of governments depends on their ability to retain the support and votes of the members of their party or coalition of parties in the House of Commons. Thus the British constitutional system is, to a large degree, *party government*.
8. Because the House of Lords is composed of hereditary and appointed peers, it lacks democratic legitimacy, and thus it has been stripped of most of its power. Since reforms in 1911 and 1949, it has had the ability only to delay bills passed by the House of Commons for nine months to a year (unless they are financial bills, which are ready for royal assent within a month of their approval by the Commons). It is now an established constitutional convention that prime ministers must be members of the House of Commons; therefore, peers who want to become prime minister must first renounce their peerage.

We illustrate these principles in Figure 3.1, which presents the essential elements in the relationship between the electorate, the two houses of Parliament, the government, and the cabinet, with government and cabinet drawn mostly from the House of Commons and retaining their power only as long as they retain the support of a majority in the Commons.

The Lack of Judicial Power to Overturn Legislation

The British courts do not have the authority, which has been vested in the United States Supreme Court since *Marbury v Madison*, to review acts of the legislature and determine whether they are consistent with the constitution—and to strike them down as null and void if they are not.

In Britain the courts face the constitutional doctrine of *Parliamentary sovereignty*—whatever Parliament passes into law is the supreme law of the land and may be repealed or amended only by Parliament itself.

The Absence of Federalism

Unlike the United States and many other democratic systems, in Britain no powers are constitutionally vested in units of government below the national level. Local governments, like the courts, are limited by a further manifestation of Parliamentary sovereignty—Parliament itself, as the ultimate source of authority, decides what func-

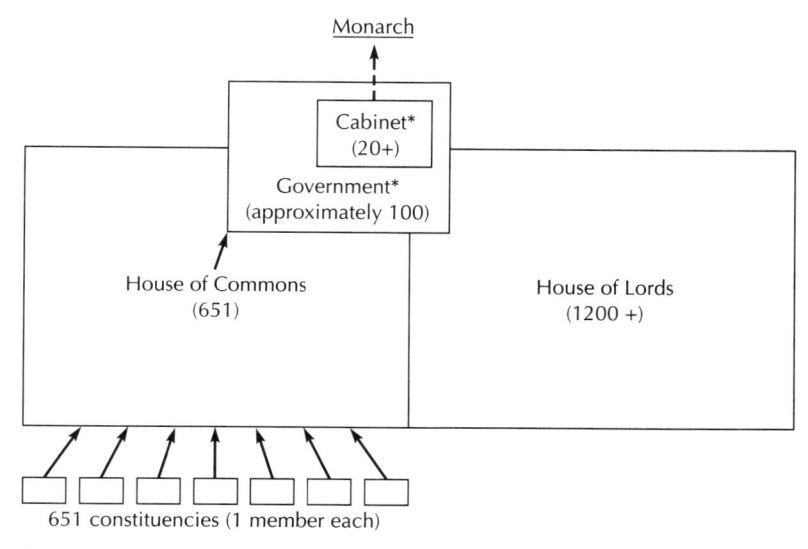

```
                              Monarch
                                 ↑
                          ┌─────────────┐
                          │  Cabinet*   │
                          │    (20+)    │
                          │             │
                          │ Government* │
                          │(approximately 100)│
┌─────────────────────────┤             ├──────────────────────┐
│             ↗           └─────────────┘                      │
│    House of Commons                        House of Lords    │
│         (651)                                 (1200 +)       │
│                                                              │
│  ↑  ↑  ↑  ↑  ↑  ↑  ↑                                         │
│  □  □  □  □  □  □  □                                         │
└──────────────────────────────────────────────────────────────┘
   651 constituencies (1 member each)
```

*Members of government/cabinet retain seats in Commons or Lords. Government must have support of majority in Commons.

FIGURE 3.1 The British Constitution: Executive-legislative relationships

tions may be performed by local or regional governments, and may expand or abolish the roles and the very existence of the local units by simple parliamentary statute.

The Separation of Head of Government from Head of State

Although the British do not separate the powers of the different branches of government (nor separate church from state), their constitution does separate the functions of the prime minister from those of the monarch.

That kind of distinction is not made by the U.S. constitution, which recognizes the president as both our governmental and political leader as well as ceremonial head, speaking for the continuity and public traditions of the nation as a whole.

In Britain, when Parliament broke the power of the monarch it made itself "sovereign" and vested the formerly royal prerogative in the elected government. Yet the symbolic role of representing the nation historically, as opposed to politically, remained with the monarchy. The monarch also carries out a number of constitutional functions, in some of which she retains small areas of independent discretion, and if the monarch lacks real power she may still be in a position to exert some degree of influence.

However, when Walter Bagehot in 1867[2] wrote his brilliant study, *The English Constitution*, he distinguished between what he called the "dignified" or ceremonial parts of government and the "efficient" or real power-wielding institutions. The monarchy, even then, was classified among the "dignified" elements and it has not augmented its power since then.

LIMITS ON THE POWER OF GOVERNMENT

In describing differences between the two constitutions, we have focused on elements that we in the United States consider to be essential to the checking and balancing of governmental power—and that are notably absent from the British system. The British scheme provides for Parliament to be sovereign over the courts and local governments, and for the executive, using tight party discipline, to be sovereign over Parliament. The separation between head of state and head of government does not act as a real limit on the power of government.

However, among the central principles of the British constitution there do exist various constraints on the power of government.

The Rule of Law

Judges cannot invalidate an act of Parliament. Nonetheless they can, and sometimes do, find that the government has acted beyond the powers granted it by the laws of Parliament. For example, in 1994, the Court of Appeal found that a government minister had "acted unlawfully and abused his prerogative or common law powers" in issuing some regulations without parliamentary approval. So an essential concept of democracy, that government is not above the law, is well established in the British constitution.

Moreover, principles derived from the common law and from judicial interpretations of Parliamentary statutes have built into the constitution those protections for individuals and groups essential to the rule of law—the rights of the accused in criminal cases, and the rights of free speech, assembly, and religion.

Democratic Accountability

The other component of the British constitution that establishes its claim to be a democratic system is that it makes government responsible to the people at large in a variety of ways.

First there are periodic elections. These can be suspended by act of Parliament, as was the case when Britain faced the prospect of imminent invasion by Nazi Germany in 1940; however, a binding convention dictates that this kind of intervention is only permissible in extraordinary wartime circumstances when extreme danger threatens the very survival of Britain itself. Otherwise the government must submit to the verdict of the electorate, and usually new verdicts occur with a frequency greater than the five-year intervals provided by law. (There were two elections in one year in 1974.)

The elections are no mere formality, as they are in authoritarian countries. They are vigorously contested by rival parties, who usually present somewhat clearer policy alternatives than those provided by competing parties in the United States.

Thus the party system in Britain is not only the principal means by which the government keeps itself in power; it is also an essential check on the power of government. Even after an election, the opposition parties take their place in Parliament and subject the government to a constant barrage of questions and criticism. Indeed, the leader of the largest opposition party has an official role in the British constitutional structure and is given the title "Leader of Her Majesty's Opposition." Nor is open criticism of government limited to the parties and their leaders. Dissenting voices are heard in the press, on television and radio, in organizations of all kinds, on Sunday mornings at that bastion of eccentric oratory, Hyde Park Corner. The right to assemble, to march, and to demonstrate is also established by court decisions and by constitutional convention.

The European Union

Another limitation on the power of government in Britain has been taking shape since Britain entered the Common Market in 1971. (The Common Market subsequently became the European Community, and then, in 1993, the European Union.) The agreements attached to the entry into the Common Market, and to the passage in 1987 of the Single European Act, provided for British acceptance of the authority of various European bodies in several areas of public policy. This could only mean that Parliament would be less "sovereign" than before—and as Parliament goes, so goes the executive in Britain.

Now, nations commonly concede, at least on a temporary basis, some degree of sovereignty—or the right to do what they want without outside interference—whenever they negotiate a treaty. But no treaty entered into by the United States, even the North American Free Trade Act, limits its freedom of action to anything like the extent imposed on the members of the European Union. This limitation provides a new source of opportunities for groups concerned about the power concentrated in the British executive branch, for litigants may appeal from the highest British courts to the European Court of Justice, as well as to the European Court of Human Rights. There are, however, those who complain that under the European Union the decision-making process becomes even more remote from the ordinary British individual, for power is gravitating toward bureaucratic bodies in Brussels and Strasbourg rather than being concentrated exclusively in London.

Participation in the European Union can thus be viewed as both a limitation and an enhancement of centralized power in general. But it certainly reduces the power of government in Britain itself, and this reduction is likely to become more marked with the passage of time. Anxiety about this prospect has given rise to a deep and increasingly bitter debate over the future of British institutions and policies, and we shall refer to this debate in several later chapters.

THE CASE FOR THE CONSTITUTION

As we saw in Chapter 1, the British constitution was held in high regard by a majority of political scientists on both sides of the Atlantic until fairly recently. They counted among the British system's virtues:

1. Its ability to produce clear decisions and the opportunity to implement them more or less intact. The contrast with the U.S. system is particularly dramatic at budget time. When the British government proposes its budget plan, the minister explaining it to Parliament (the Chancellor of the Exchequer) makes lengthy introductory remarks until the stock markets close for the day, at which point he presents the government's intended tax changes. The reason for this procedure is that everyone knows that, although Parliament has to ratify the changes, they will go into effect immediately—and it is important to avoid the possibility of gyrations in the market or of giving anyone a chance to make a quick profit on the information. (One chancellor resigned when it became known that he had given a small scoop to a journalist friend while on his way to make the budget speech.)

    On the other hand, under the U.S. system, the president proposes, Congress disposes. At worst, a president's plan is dead on arrival on Capitol Hill, as happened with George Bush's budgets and also with Bill Clinton's budgets after the 1994 congressional elections. At best, the budget is subjected to prolonged and merciless remaking at the hands of the two houses of Congress, as happened during the first two years of Bill Clinton's term. There are very rare exceptions to this experience; in general, the intricately balanced structure designed by the constitution's framers was designed to encourage deliberation and caution rather than incisive decision-making.

    Consequently, no U.S. president, not even Franklin Roosevelt as he tried to pull the country out of the Great Depression, had the sustained freedom of action that enabled Clement Attlee's Labour government in the 1940s to enact major changes in the direction of socialism, or that enabled Margaret Thatcher's government in the 1980s to institute extensive privatization.

    What the British system does, in other words, is provide governments with a chance not only to present their ideas but to put them into effect over a period of time, and thus to determine whether or not they work and are acceptable to the voters.

2. The British voting procedure, with single-member districts and simple plurality winners (whoever gets one more vote than the runner-up wins the election), manages to produce stable governments. It is true that the system discriminates against minor parties, and usually gives the leading party many more seats in Parliament than would seem appropriate given its share of the vote in the country. But it is this very inequity that gives the government a

chance to govern without having to depend on the kind of shifting coalitions that have created such havoc in other democratic countries.
3. The British system clearly identifies who is responsible for the making of decisions. Harry Truman may have had a plaque on his desk in the Oval Office proclaiming "The Buck Stops Here," but that kind of policy is rarely enacted in reality. Decision-making in U.S. government is so fragmented that, when things go wrong, it is common practice for presidents to blame Congress, for each house of Congress to blame the other as well as the president, and for all of them to blame the courts or the state governments. In Britain there is very little ambiguity about who to blame when things go wrong, or who should get the credit when they go well.
4. The British system of party government provides the electorate in Britain with clearer choices than is the case in the United States. Although the two main parties, Conservative and Labour, do not represent far right and far left, and both usually move toward the center as election time approaches, the differences between them are more substantial than those between the Republican and Democratic parties in America. And the greater coherence and discipline of British parties ensures that their differences are, in considerable measure, translated into actual governmental policies.

   A cardinal feature of democracy is that it offers real choices, and British parties do a better job in this respect than their U.S. counterparts.
5. Despite the relative concentration and centralization of power in Britain, the checks and balances described above—the rule of law and the principle of democratic accountability—are potent constraints on the arbitrary exercise of power. Every Sunday, Americans can see a vivid illustration of how the British system works to make government accountable through C-SPAN's televised coverage of the twice-weekly "Question Time" in the House of Commons; usually the prime minister is pummelled with interrogation during these sessions. The U.S. president faces much less severe challenges in his press conferences or his interviews with Larry King.
6. The fact that the British constitution is largely unwritten is not a defect, but a source of strength. Codified constitutions are relatively inflexible. They express the ideas of one generation, only to tie the hands of their successors. Thus the U.S. constitution was devised to serve a predominately agrarian eighteenth-century society, and its framers, brilliant though they were, could not begin to envisage a world of computers, space exploration, and thermonuclear bombs. Of course, the original document has been considerably amended, but the procedure for amendment is elaborate and cumbersome.

So enormous energies and vast ingenuity must go into interpreting a single, rather brief document, and judges and armies of lawyers try to discover the "original intent" of men deliberating more than two centuries ago. Instead of debate on the contemporary merits of, for example, gun control, convoluted arguments must be addressed on whether the Second Amendment's "right of the people to keep and bear Arms" is unqualified or limited to the need for "a well regulated Militia."

In any case, written constitutions do not avoid the need to build over time a superstructure of constitutional conventions. Political parties appear nowhere in the U.S. Constitution. Nor do party primaries. Yet both are very much a part of U.S. constitutional practice, together with an array of customs and established practices comparable to those that undergird politics in Britain.

Finally, the real protection of the liberties of a people are not to be found in formal documents, however hallowed, but in the nation's political culture. Consider these statements from Article 125 of the 1936 Constitution of the Union of Soviet Socialist Republics:

. . . the citizens of the USSR shall be guaranteed by law:

(i) Freedom of speech;
(ii) Freedom of the press;
(iii) Freedom of assembly and rallies;
(iv) Freedom of street processions and demonstrations.

In reality many citizens of Stalin's USSR in 1936 found themselves in labor camps for having the temerity to exercise these guaranteed freedoms.

Even in the United States there have been periods when the protections guaranteed by the First Amendment have been far from secure. In the 1950s the House Un-American Activities Committee and Senator Joe McCarthy used Congress to ride roughshod over the rights of free expression of many U.S. citizens, and the Supreme Court did nothing to restrain them. In time the inquisitors overreached themselves, the temporary panic induced by the Cold War gave way to the longer-term, more open political culture, and Supreme Court decisions reemphasized the binding force of the First Amendment. Britain, without a bill of rights, has not experienced anything comparable to McCarthyism in its recent history.

In short, the British constitution is flexible enough to provide for sensitive responses to the emerging needs of each generation, yet authoritative enough to secure the rights and liberties of the citizenry.

PRESSURES FOR CONSTITUTIONAL REFORM

Until quite recently, the case for the British constitution commanded a broad consensus of opinion. But in the 1970s, and with gathering force in the 1980s, a clamor for constitutional reform has been heard. In part, as we indicated in Chapter 1, this has resulted from the fact that the fabled ability of the British system to produce and implement decisions has not prevented the country's relative economic decline. But there has also been dissatisfaction with the forms and procedures of the constitution, and the charge is heard that the checks and balances of the system are no longer sufficient. This charge has three components:

The Growing Supremacy of the Executive Branch

At one time, the British system was referred to as "parliamentary government." Then the erosion of the functions and stature of Parliament led many to the conclusion that the British system in reality was "cabinet government." Lately it has been argued that within the cabinet, power has shifted to "prime ministerial government." If this is true, Britain has moved toward a personalized form of leadership comparable to the American presidency—but without the competing institutions of power, for there are no independently elected legislative houses, no judicial power to overturn the laws passed by the subservient legislature, no states with their own reserved areas of responsibility.

As critics see it, debates and question-times in the House of Commons may provide lively theater, but they rarely succeed in exerting real control over the actions of prime ministers and cabinets, who have acted in an increasingly high-handed, arbitrary fashion.

Secrecy

Governments everywhere prefer to keep their processes from public view except when it serves their purposes. But in the executive branch of British government there is a veritable obsession with secrecy. All government documents are supposed to remain classified for 30 years under the Official Secrets Act (this representing a liberalization of an earlier 50-year rule). The national bureaucracy, the civil service, believes devoutly that the public should be given no more information than is absolutely necessary, and that complete confidentiality is essential for a well-run government. Prime ministers of both parties have agreed with them. In Chapter 17 we will see how a Conservative prime minister and government covered up the release of a radioactive cloud from a plutonium plant; how Labour prime ministers made decisions on nuclear weapon development that were kept even from most members of their cabinets; and how Margaret Thatcher took the passion for secrecy to even greater lengths than any of her predecessors.

In face of these displays of prime ministerial power, it has been the practice of the courts to accede to the executive's wishes whenever they are cloaked in the phrase "national security;" and much the same has been true of parliamentary committees.

A "Predominant-Party System"?

With so much authority vested in the government, more and more commentators were given to quoting Lord Hailsham's dictum that the British system was becoming an "elective dictatorship"; in other words, once a government has been elected to office it faced very few constraints on its power.

But at least there was the ultimate sanction of periodic elections. With the Labour and Conservative Parties alternating in power after 1945, each government always looked nervously over its shoulder at its potential replacement, and this would prevent its becoming too arrogant in its conduct of affairs.

Starting in 1979, however, there were four successive election victories by the Conservative Party. Thus the Conservatives had satisfied the criteria for what political scientist Giovanni Sartori has called a *predominant-party system,* in which one party has little fear of being defeated in elections for a long period of time.[3] Moreover, the Conservatives appeared especially dominant, for their fourth successive victory came in 1992 despite a bitter internal struggle culminating in the ejection of Margaret Thatcher from the party leadership and prime ministership and during the worst and longest economic recession since the 1930s. This led to a number of commentators asking the question: if the Labour Party could not win in those circumstances, what prospect was there of its ever winning again? Such apparent dominance by one party did not bode well for a properly balanced constitutional system.

By 1994 the conventional wisdom had changed again. The deepening unpopularity of the Conservative government and Labour's large lead in the polls suggested that elections might again produce alternations between parties in power. Even so, this outcome would not address another aspect of the complaint about the 15-year Conservative domination. It would have been difficult to contest the democratic legitimacy of the Conservative governments if the Conservative Party had won repeatedly with a clear majority of the people's vote. But in the four elections starting in 1979, they had never achieved more than 43 percent of the popular vote. So there was a 57 percent anti-Conservative majority in the country, but this majority was not reflected in the election outcomes—for two reasons.

First, the opposition was split between Labour on the left and one or more parties in the center. In 1979 the center was represented by the Liberal Party—formerly one of the two main parties, but a poor third to Labour since the 1920s. In 1983 and 1987, the Alliance was formed as an electoral combination of the Liberals and the newly formed Social Democratic Party. In 1992, there was one center party again, the Liberal Democrats. Each time the center group fought Labour as well as the Conservatives.

Second, the voting system was heavily biased against third parties. Because only a plurality, not a majority, is needed to win in each district, a third party may come in second in a large number of districts but first in very few. This has been the repeated fate of the Liberals in recent years, their most bitter experience in 1983 when, in combination with the Social Democrats, they gained approximately 25 percent of all the votes cast but only 23 seats out of 650 (see Table 3.1).

This result is vastly different than would be the case if Britain used any of the

TABLE 3.1 1983 Election results (percent)

	Share of Votes Cast	Share of Seats Won
Conservative	42.4	61.1
Labour	27.6	32.1
Alliance	25.4	3.5

systems of *proportional representation* that are employed in several other democratic countries. Under such a system, a coalition of parties opposed to the Conservatives might have taken office; if not in 1983 (for as we shall see, there were special circumstances operating that year that would have made cooperation between Labour and the Alliance impossible), then quite conceivably by 1992.

Defenders of the voting system argue that proportional representation breeds unstable governments. But there are many examples elsewhere—in Germany, the Scandinavian countries, the Netherlands, for example—of coalition governments that survive for years, and there is no reason that a two-party coalition in Britain would not be able to hold together.

Reform Proposals

At first the idea of constitutional change was associated mainly with the small Liberal Party (now the Liberal Democrats) and some academic specialists. Then in 1988, a group representing a band of opinion from the moderate left to the center presented a program for reform under the rubric *Charter 88*. Their ideas included a freedom of information law, an elected second chamber in place of the House of Lords, a reformed, more independent judiciary, and devolution of central power to subnational governments. And there were two even more fundamental proposals: The first was for replacing the present voting system by proportional representation; the second was for following the example of other nations by drawing up a bill of rights and a written constitution.

More radical even than these bold proposals was a Commonwealth of Britain bill offered by a leader of the Labour left wing in Parliament, Tony Benn. Among his suggestions were the establishment of a federal system; two houses of Parliament elected for a fixed four-year term, the upper house elected by the states; all constituencies returning one male, one female representative; the voting age lowered to 16; the abolition of the monarchy and all titles; the disestablishment of the Church of England; withdrawal from Northern Ireland.

Although Benn's bill as such will not be acted on by Parliament, several of the reforms put forth by Charter 88 have already entered the mainstream of political debate. The leadership of the Labour Party, after long hesitation, has now lent its support to a bill of rights, a freedom of information act, a reformed second chamber, and devolution of power to Scottish, Welsh, and English regional assemblies, and it has raised the possibility of a referendum on electoral reform. John Major's Conservative government opposes all of these, but it has started to make more information available to the press and public, and concedes that the time has come to make British government more open and more accessible to the citizenry.

CONCLUSION

Britain and the United States represent two contrasting approaches to the task of organizing democratic self-government. Both qualify as democracies by offering periodic elections conducted by rival parties and by providing a variety of limits on the power of the government, including a continuing barrage of public criticism.

Yet as we have noted, the constitutional foundations of the two systems are very different. The British constitution, being largely unwritten, is more flexible. The British party system is stronger than that in the United States. There are fewer checks and balances on the executive in Britain than in the United States and the British system has the capacity to produce change faster and more decisively than the U.S. system.

In the chapters that follow, we elaborate on these differences and examine their implications. Thus Part II, *The Party System*, might well be called *Party Government,* so integral are the parties to the functioning of the system. Part III explores the power relationships between the different branches and levels of government. And Part IV shows how, through their party system and governmental institutions, the British deal with the major public policy issues, domestic and international, of the day.

Throughout we shall be examining the arguments put forward by the advocates of constitutional reform: that too much power has been concentrated in the hands of the national executive, and that measures should be introduced which, while retaining the capacity for effective government, set limits to centralized power.

SOME QUESTIONS TO THINK ABOUT

Does constitutional government require a written constitution?
What do you think of the absence of separated powers in Britain?
Should the courts have the power to overturn acts of Parliament?
Are the limits on central government power in Britain sufficient?
What do you see as the relative strengths and weaknesses of the British and U.S. systems?
What do you think of the various proposals for constitutional reform?

NOTES

1. T. Erskine May (ed. Sir Charles Gordon), *Parliamentary Practice,* 20th ed., Butterworths, 1983.
2. Walter Bagehot, *The English Constitution,* Fontana edition, 1963, with introduction by R. H. S. Crossman.
3. Giovanni Sartori, *Parties and Party Systems: A Framework for Analysis* (Cambridge University Press, 1976), p. 196.

SUGGESTIONS FOR FURTHER READING

Walter Bagehot's classic *The English Constitution,* first published in 1867, was reprinted with an introduction by former Labour Cabinet minister, R. H. S. Crossman, by Fontana in 1963. More recent studies include Rodney Brazier, *Constitutional Practice* (Oxford, 1988) and *Constitutional Reform* (Oxford, 1991), and Philip Norton, *The Constitution in Flux* (Martin Robertson/Blackwell, 1982).

A prescription from the left has been presented by Tony Benn, *Common Sense* (Hutchinson, 1993), and a conservative reform proposal has come from Ferdinand Mount, *The British Constitution Now* (Heinemann, 1992).

PART TWO

THE PARTY SYSTEM

In which we demonstrate how much more central parties are in Britain than in the United States. We examine interest groups, voting behavior, party structures and policies, and election campaigns, and pose the questions:

- ✦ To what extent are British political parties based on class and interest groups?
- ✦ What are the major differences between the parties? How divided are they internally?
- ✦ To what extent do British elections differ from elections in the United States?
- ✦ Why have the Conservatives been the dominant party since 1979? Is this likely to change?

4

Groups and Voters

Organized and Mass Influences on the Parties

The British party system is not as completely dominated by two major parties as is the case in the United States, where there are usually only Democrats and Republicans in Congress, and where despite strong challenges from independents like George Wallace, John Anderson, and Ross Perot, the electoral system ensures that the White House will remain in the hands of one of the two giant parties.

In Britain there are Liberal Democrats and representatives of Scottish, Welsh, and Northern Irish nationalist parties in Parliament. Still the voting system strongly favors the big parties, Labour and Conservative, and governments since 1945 have been drawn entirely from one of these two.

Before we examine the structure and programs of the parties themselves we must look at their constituencies, the sources from which they draw their strength. First we explore their relationship to certain group interests, which provide most of their funding and organizational resources. Then we turn to the largest constituency of all—the electorate at large—and we review the segments of the public that tend to provide their voting base.

INTEREST GROUPS

The British, like the Americans, are a nation of joiners. They join a remarkable array of organized groups. There are organizations for the protection of children (the National Society for the Prevention of Cruelty to Children), and of the homeless (Shelter). The environment is passionately defended by a myriad of organizations including the Friends of the Earth, U.K. (with 200,000 members), Greenpeace (350,000), the Botanical Society, the Open Spaces Society, the National Society for Clean Air, the Ramblers Association, and the British Herpetological Society. There are more than 70 animal rights groups, including the Royal Society for the Prevention of Cruelty to Animals; and the Royal Society for the Protection of Birds has over 800,000 members. There are Campaigns for Nuclear Disarmament and Against Racial Discrimination. There is a Monarchists League, a Rolls Royce Enthusiasts Club, a Flat Earth Society.

There are groups to advance the cause of most religions, of veterans, of women, and of almost every conceivable sexual orientation. Each profession generates a number of organizations; so does every level of local government, and so does every kind of economic interest.

In Britain, as in the United States, membership in these organizations is predominately middle-class; many of those involved are college-educated professionals and managers. Thus some of the groups are concerned with middle-class "NIMBY" ("Not In My Backyard") causes, such as keeping roads and other developments from intruding into established communities. Yet there are more than 40 organizations dedicated to fighting for the poor.

Most interest groups at one time or another try to influence public policy, as we shall see in our discussion of various policy issues in Part IV of this book. The tactics used in Britain by these groups are similar to those used in the United States: unleashing barrages of letters, telegrams, faxes, and phone calls, sending delegations, holding public meetings and demonstrations, communicating to the public through media newsmaking and advertising. Some of these pressure tactics are directed at members of Parliament, but because Parliament has much less influence than Congress, the more serious pressure efforts are aimed at the executive branch, both elected officials and members of the bureaucracy.

With so many groups entering the political arena we would appear to have a perfect scenario for a *pluralist* analysis of power in Britain, which would propose that the process of making and influencing decisions is widely distributed and diffused rather than concentrated in the hands of a relative few. In fact, a leading American analyst of British politics, Samuel Beer, has argued that this process of diffusion has gone so far as to produce what he calls *pluralist stagnation*. The existence of so many organized groups, each of them fighting for its own narrow, short-run interest, prevents the shaping of policies that benefit the nation as a whole. "The outcome," in Beer's words, "has been incoherence and immobilism; drift not mastery . . . a paralysis of public choice."[1] This language sounds very much like that applied by political scientist James McGregor Burns to the U.S. system; Burns has argued that the U.S. system is one of deadlock and stalemate, that it suffers from "government by fits and starts . . . a statecraft that has not been able to supply the steady leadership and power necessary for the conduct of our affairs."[2]

However, as we saw in the previous chapter, the British system is clearly less prone to political stalemate than the U.S. system. Moreover, while there has been, as Beer argues, a major increase in the number and activity of interest groups in Britain—many of them created by the expansion of government programs—it does not follow that they tend to balance each other out. Some kinds of groups are more powerful than others. In particular, organizations speaking for *economic* interests command the largest resources and are the most persistently and deeply involved in the process of government. Among these, agricultural groups are able to exercise influence well beyond the number of farmers they represent. But less than 300,000 people now work on the land, mostly on farms of less than 50 acres, and agriculture is no longer a dominant force in Britain. Since the advent of industrialization, its place has been taken by business and labor, and we shall see that it is principally business and labor organizations, speaking for rival *class* interests, that provide the political parties with their organizational and financial bases.

Business

The scope of government in Britain is more extensive than in the United States. Nonetheless, Britain is still a predominately capitalist country, and considerably more people are employed in private businesses than in agencies of government. Thus a high proportion of the wealth of the country is under the control of the owners and managers of industrial and financial enterprises.

A variety of organizations speak for them, including the Confederation of British Industries, which represents larger corporations, and the Institute of Directors and the Association of British Chambers of Commerce, which speak for medium-sized and smaller enterprises.

Industry in Britain, as in the United States, has produced some very large corporations, in part through the use of mergers, holding companies, corporate raiding, and so on. A monopolies commission is charged with discouraging collusion and price-fixing; but its resources and punitive powers are considerably less than those of the U.S. Federal Trade Commission.

Because Britain is heavily dependent on foreign trade, it is not surprising that there is a large flow of investment into and out of Britain. There is a strong U.S. business presence in Britain, including Ford and McDonald's. Conversely, many large British companies are multinationals, and their holdings abroad include extensive investments in the United States. Thus the J. Walter Thompson advertising agency, Kool cigarettes, and Smith and Wesson guns, as well as various banks, department stores, airlines, food companies, and real estate holdings are owned by British companies. In 1987 alone, British firms spent over $30 billion in buying American companies, and the British today are the largest foreign investors in U.S. factories and property assets.

The emphasis on foreign trade and the history of empire have also made Britain an important financial center, with several large banks and investment firms located in the small area of central London known as the City. The Bank of England is also situated in the City of London. Though it is nationalized, and lacks the Federal Reserve Bank's independence from the government, it does not generally adopt positions hostile to those of its neighboring private institutions.

Business and the Conservative Party. Politically, the business and financial communities are overwhelmingly in the camp of the Conservative Party. A high proportion of the Conservatives' money comes from business firms, and there is no need for companies to resort to the creation of U.S.-style Political Action Committees (PACs) to make their donations, because unlike the United States, Britain has no laws forbidding direct political contributions from corporate funds. The law specifies only that the contributions be listed as such in the annual company reports and this requirement is not carefully monitored.

Conservative governments always include prominent businessmen. Others serve as advisers to prime ministers and cabinet members or are appointed to official bodies reviewing government programs. Conversely, a number of cabinet members have joined business and financial organizations after leaving the government. For example, Lord Young, a business executive who had been Secretary of State for trade and industry in the Thatcher government, and thus responsible for the privatization of the telecommunications industry, became chairman of the board of the privatized Cable and Wireless; and Peter Walker, the former Energy Secretary who had privatized British Gas, joined the company's board soon after leaving the government.

The Conservative position is further advanced by the fact that wealthy businessmen own the national newspapers. In particular, Rupert Murdoch, the Australian-Anglo-American media tycoon, owns five British national newspapers, including the *Times* and the biggest-selling daily and Sunday tabloids, the *Sun* and the *News of the World*, as well as a satellite TV network. Most British papers support the Conservative Party in their presentation of the news as well as in their editorial columns.

These facts are cited by Marxists and others of the radical left to support their belief that Britain is run by and for corporate capitalists and their allies in the Establishment. In the far left perspective, economic power controls political power; economic power in Britain is concentrated in the hands of a small number of great industrial and financial corporations; and the people are socialized and indoctrinated into supporting the system by capitalist control of the media.

Other facts may be cited to cast doubt on this analysis. British business is no monolith. The big corporations engage in collusion, but they also compete with each other, with smaller businesses, with U.S. and Japanese companies, and increasingly with European firms. They must deal with unions and (sometimes) with Labour governments. Even Conservative governments do not always please them: In the early 1980s many corporation leaders strongly critized the Thatcher government for allowing the recession to go on too long. As for their manipulation of public opinion, although the majority of newspapers support the Conservative Party, television news is quite evenhanded—and more people in Britain, as in the United States, get their political news from TV than from the papers. Moreover, business corporations cannot buy television time to influence elections because airtime is provided free to the political parties. Regarding the concern over the concentration of media ownership in the hands of a few giant corporations, the Conservative government announced in 1995 its intention to bar newspaper groups with more than 20 percent of total national circulation from owning a television license. This would inhibit further expansion in Britain of Murdoch's News International—whose papers had mostly provided strong support for the Conservative Party.

Just the same, business and financial corporations do represent a very large accumulation of economic resources; although their interests sometimes diverge they share similar economic and political values; and, to a much greater extent than in the United States, business is connected with one party—the Conservative Party. In the United States, the larger number of business leaders are Republicans. Yet the Democrats, too, pledge their allegiance to the free enterprise system; Democratic presidential candidates raise substantial sums from sections of the business community; and Democratic members of Congress, in the decades when they constituted the majority of incumbents, raised more money from business than their Republican challengers. In Britain there are individual businesspeople who are sympathetic to Labour. But, whatever their internal divisions, business entrepreneurs in Britain, large and small, support the Conservatives with their votes and with their money.

Trade Unions

If the Conservative Party is, to a large extent, the party of business, the Labour Party is to an even greater degree the party of the trade unions (the British phrase for labor unions).

Unions grew out of the need for workers to protect themselves against the harsh, sometimes brutal, working conditions and low wages associated with unregulated industrialization. They faced bitter hostility from most employers, an ideological climate that reflected Herbert Spencer's Social Darwinism, and government legislation that was designed to cripple the unions' effectiveness.

Ironically, it was the Conservative government of Benjamin Disraeli that began the process of establishing the unions on a firm footing. In 1875 and 1876, laws were passed making collective bargaining and peaceful picketing legal, and putting employer and worker on the same legal footing. In 1906, it was the turn of a Liberal government to help the unions by passing a law overturning a decision of the courts in the Taff Vale case, which made unions financially liable for the actions of their members.

The Unions and the Labour Party. Yet, as the union movement grew, its leaders were coming to the conclusion that they should not rely on either the Conservative or the Liberal Party to represent their interests. So in 1900, together with some socialist (but mostly non-Marxist) societies, they formed the Labour Representation Committee, which in 1906 became the Labour Party.

There has been no parallel development in the United States, where unions have been an important component in the Democratic coalition—especially since Franklin Roosevelt's New Deal of the 1930s—and have contributed money and organizational resources to the Democrats. But there have been no formal bonds between the unions and the Democratic Party of the kind that connect trade unions and Labour Party in Britain.

The relationship established from the party's creation was then formalized in a number of ways. Twelve of the twenty-nine members of the National Executive Committee of the Labour Party were reserved for union leaders. Ninety percent of the votes at the party's annual conferences were cast by union representatives, each wielding a "block vote" on behalf of their membership. The system established in 1983 for the election of the party's leader gave 40 percent of the vote to the unions. This special weighting of the union role reflected the fact that between 80 and 90 percent of the Labour Party's money came from union funds and that at election time, the party relied heavily on the unions' organizational resources.

With this backing from the unions, the Labour Party grew as a political force, was then twice able to form a coalition government with the Liberals in the 1920s, and by the 1930s had replaced the Liberals as the main alternative to the Conservatives. Still, the returns to the unions for their investment came slowly. In 1926 a general strike, called by the Trades Union Congress (T.U.C.) in support of the miners' refusal to accept a reduction of already inadequate wages, ended in total defeat after nine days. It was followed by the Conservative government's Trades Disputes Act of 1927, which declared general strikes illegal and prohibited the use of union funds for political purposes unless members "opted in" by a specific written approval.

It was the election of a Labour government with a large parliamentary majority in 1945 that at last brought the unions their reward for creating and supporting the Labour Party. The 1927 Trades Disputes Act was repealed, and programs nationalizing a number of industries and expanding the welfare state enacted policies long backed by the unions. Starting in the 1950s, even under Conservative governments the unions grew in numbers and strength. By the late 1970s their membership had increased to 53 percent of the workforce and unions had become highly successful in delivering higher wages and better working conditions for their members.

The Strike Weapon. A potent weapon in the unions' armory was the strike. Even Labour governments disliked strikes, for they were likely to infuriate the public and cause dislocations to the government's economic policies. But in 1969, when Labour prime minister Harold Wilson tried to set some mild limits to "wildcat" strikes, called against the wishes of the union leadership, he ran into furious opposition within his cabinet and his party as well as the union movement. The Labour Party, the offspring of the unions, could not be allowed to harm its parent.

The Conservatives suffered under no such inhibition, and in a confrontation with the mineworkers in 1974, prime minister Edward Heath declared a state of emergency and put the country on a three-day work week. The miners went on strike, and Heath called an election on the slogan "Who governs Britain?"—meaning, the unions or their elected government? Heath lost. The message seemed to be that the unions governed the country. Indeed, polls in the mid-1970s revealed that a majority believed the unions to be the most powerful force in the land.

The power of the unions was always somewhat exaggerated in the public mind. The T.U.C., which includes most but not all unions, is a loose confederation of organizations with a diversity of members and interests. Two of the biggest unions, the Transport and General Workers Union (TGWU) and the General, Municipal and Boilermakers (GMB), speak mostly for semiskilled workers and laborers—category *D* on the previously defined social class scale—though they also reach into the *C1* category of office employees. Others, like the Amalgamated Engineering and Electrical Union (AEEU), represent *C2,* skilled craft workers. UNISON, a 1993 merger of three unions, is the biggest British union, with 1.3 million members representing a wide range of staff members (over two-thirds of them women) in local government, health services, utilities, and higher education. And there are even unions for salaried employees in the higher social class grades: scientists, technicians, and senior civil servants. Interests so diverse will sometimes clash, and the clashes on occasion take the form of disputes over jurisdiction and fierce competition for members.

Moreover, the hold of the leadership of the unions over their members is tenuous. Leaders may call a strike, but members do not always respond. Conversely, the rank and file may go out on sudden wildcat strikes that embarrass the leadership. And, as we shall see, many unions members ignore the official union line on which political party to vote for.

The power of the unions is also limited by the resources available to business, much of the time backed by government. Business commonly gets better press than the unions, and the reason for this is not only because most of the newspapers are owned by businessmen. The unions' great public relations liability is the very weapon they use so effectively: the strike. Most strikes cause inconvenience to the public, and some can threaten public health and safety.

In fact, the widespread use of the strike weapon during the winter of 1978-79 proved to be ruinous to the position of unions in Britain. It was a particularly severe winter, and a series of public sector strikes left railway travelers stranded, garbage uncollected, and even bodies unburied in cemeteries. And this time it was not the Conservative government of Edward Heath but the Labour government of James Callaghan that proved to be helpless to restore industrial peace.

The extent of the disruptions was somewhat overstated by the media. But the pictures on television and on the front pages of the newspapers portrayed vividly what came to be called the *winter of discontent;* and the discontent was directed at the unions and at the Labour government they had helped to create. In the election of 1979 it was the inability of government to control the unions and their strike weapon that, more than any other single factor, led to the defeat of Labour and the election of Margaret Thatcher as prime minister.

Thatcher versus the Unions. For Thatcher, union power was a prime reason for Britain's economic decline. Moreover, she was determined that there would be no repetition of Heath's humiliation by the unions, and particularly by the miners. So she set about the task of breaking union power; and by the end of her tenure in 1990 she had succeeded in reducing that power considerably.

This was partly accomplished by legislation. Three bills on industrial relations were passed during the Thatcher administrations. They set limits to picketing; protected individuals who refused to join the unions under "closed shop" agreements; forbade "secondary" action through which striking unions could be joined by others that were not directly involved in a dispute; made unions financially liable for strikes found illegal under the new laws; and required secret ballots on strike action and on the use of union funds for political purposes.

The last of these requirements proved to be a disappointment to the Conservatives, who had hoped that union members would vote against the use of their dues for partisan politics, thereby stripping the Labour Party of its principal financial base. In fact, every union balloting on the issue voted to continue the political levy. But all of the other provisions of the Thatcher era laws proved to be effective in their purpose of undermining the power of union leaders.

No less important was the failure of key strikes during the 1980s. The printers' union was forced to capitulate to the newspaper owners' requirements for the use of new technologies. Teachers unsuccessfully demanded major salary increases. But the crucial defeat was the eventual collapse of a bitter year-long strike in 1984–85 by the miners, fighting against plans for the closure of a large number of mines declared by the National Coal Board to be uneconomic. This time there was no three-day work week, for the government had waited until coal reserves at the electric power plants were overflowing, and gross miscalculations by the union leadership played into the hands of an administration implacably opposed to compromise.

A third factor undermining the unions' position was the high unemployment accompanying the recession of the early 1980s. With close to 13 percent of the workforce out of a job, many union members were unable to pay their dues, and it was difficult to sustain strikes when there were so many people available to replace the strikers.

By the time the Thatcher prime ministership ended in 1990, union membership had fallen from 53 percent of the work force to 39 percent, and continued declining. The number of strikes decreased sharply; workdays lost in strikes fell from nearly 30 million in 1979 to 400,000 in 1994. Wage demands were much more modest than in the past. The Labour Party's leadership began to look into ways of loosening the bonds that tied them to the unions. The "block vote" at the annual conference was reduced from 90 to 70 percent, and was likely to be further reduced to 50 percent as a result of decisions ratified at the 1993 annual conference; the union share in the selection of the party leader was cut from 40 percent to one-third; and the union's ability to dominate the selection of parliamentary candidates was weakened by the introduction of a "one person one vote" system that favored individual party members rather than organizations.

To some extent these manifestations of the decline of union power resulted from longterm trends operating in all industrialized countries: the shift to service from manufacturing jobs (many of them going to poorer nations in a globalizing economy), and the huge increase in women and part-time workers. Thus in Britain over the past 40 years, employment in the manufacturing sector has fallen from 40 percent of the total to 20 percent, self-employment has risen from 7 percent to 12 percent, and part-time jobs have gone up from 12 percent to 25 percent. Unions have traditionally been strongest among full-time male workers in manufacturing industries, so each of these changes has made the task of union organizers more difficult. But if the longterm trends were inescapable no matter what the political climate, they were speeded up and intensified by the actions of the Thatcher government.

Here again we must set the fact of decline in a relative context. Compared with the peak of 53 percent in 1939, union membership falling below 39 percent appears disastrous. But compared with the United States, union leaders, with less than 16 percent of the workforce organized, can only envy the record of their British counterparts. Moreover, even though unions are far from loved by the British public, the erosion of their power means that they are no longer feared, and recent polls indicate that the great majority of the British public believe that unions are necessary to protect people's interests at work.

So unions in Britain are still a force to be reckoned with, and this would be even more the case if a Labour government were again to come to power with a clear parliamentary majority. The union's control of the Labour Party was clearly weakened by the decisions made at the 1993 Conference. Yet to secure the passage of the reforms in face of fierce union opposition, John Smith, Labour's leader, had to assure the union leaders that "these proposals do not in any way break or diminish the link between the Labour Party and the trade unions." For Smith was acutely aware of the continued financial and organizational dependence of his party on the unions.

Even so, Tony Blair, Smith's successor, has made it clear that any future Labour government might modify but would be unlikely to repeal most of the Thatcher union legislation. For the unions there will be no returning to the levels of power that reached their peak in the 1970s.

The Corporatist Connection

Because unions were created to defend the employees' interests against the employers, there is a natural tension and a normally adversarial relationship between these two groups. However, contending parties may also cooperate in some circumstances; despite the strikes and conflicting views on wages and working conditions, there was a good deal of cooperation between the unions and business in the post–World War II period. Moreover, the two involved government in their collaborative efforts—so much so that some commentators argued that understanding key public policy decisions in Britain requires understanding not only the formal constitutional provisions for allocating power, but also the informal, interlocking network of government, business, and union leaders. This network, critics complained, provided the framework for discussions between cabinet ministers, senior civil servants, and the two sides of industry which created agreements that were presented to Parliament as a fait accompli.

This kind of tripartite arrangement of power is known as *corporatism*. In its extreme form corporatism becomes fascism, and it is only on the farthest left that we find accusations that Britain is a fascist state. Keith Middlemas, who has written extensively on this subject, has instead identified a *corporatist tendency* in Britain.[3] An example of this corporatist tendency was the 1961 creation by Harold Macmillan's Conservative government of the National Economic Development Council (NEDC, or "Neddy," with corresponding "little Neddies" for individual industries), which brought the three centers of power together to discuss economic issues. Then there were efforts during Edward Heath's administration to set "incomes policy," or wage guidelines, and price controls. In the struggle to bring inflation down in the

1970s, the Labour governments of Wilson and Callaghan worked out a "social contract" with the unions, under which the unions promised restraint on wage demands in exchange for expansion of welfare programs and a commitment by government to bring pressure to bear on employers to limit profits. With respect to strikes, it was common practice for Macmillan and Wilson to bring employers and union chiefs together at 10 Downing Street (the prime minister's home) to try to reach agreement over beer and sandwiches. The larger consequence of this collaborative pattern was a blurring of the distinction between Labour and Conservative governments and the establishment of considerable areas of consensus in economic and welfare policies.

The corporatist tendency was not a consistent pattern. It worked best in times of economic growth and prosperity, when there was enough to provide a satisfactory share for all the participants. But when the economy slowed, tensions increased and hostilities between business and the unions flared.

The social contract of the 1970s was a last desperate effort to sustain a collaborative relationship. It broke apart in the "winter of discontent," and Margaret Thatcher was determined that it not be restored. She was adamantly opposed to the corporatist style. The unions must be brought to heel; although Thatcher was certainly pro-business, she made it clear that employers must stop looking to government to help them work out cozy deals with the unions.

Competition must be the watchword in place of consensus. There would be no more efforts to settle strikes over beer and sandwiches at 10 Downing Street. Of course, strikes in nationalized industries were of direct concern to government, and Thatcher herself made the policy decisions that broke the coal strike. But the coal industry was run by the semiautonomous National Coal Board, and the appearance was maintained that it was the chair of the Board who was in charge.

Thatcher's successor, John Major, adopted a more consensual style, and a few members of his cabinet, particularly Michael Heseltine, were known to be sympathetic to the kind of quasi-corporatist methods that were successfully employed in Japan and Germany. Yet Major ordered the termination of the NEDC, and given the decline of the third leg of tripartitism—the unions—it was evident that the corporatism would henceforth be much a much weaker tendency than it had been before the Thatcher era.

VOTERS

Parties may look to interest groups for ideas, money, and organizational help. But if they are to perform their functions of proposing and electing candidates for office, they must operate in a still broader context: the electorate at large.

As we have seen, since 1832 that electorate has been extended by a series of parliamentary laws so that it now includes everyone over the age of 18 except the monarch, peers, felons in jail, those convicted of breaking specified election laws, and people of unsound mind.

This universal franchise, taken in combination with a number of other favorable factors, ought to produce an informed, active citizenry. The British have compulsory education to the age of 16, with many going on for further and higher education. Seventy percent of adults read one or more daily newspapers, and both the BBC and commercial television provide extensive coverage of the news. There is an abundance of political organizations. The density of population in a rather small area makes communication easy. Yet the extent of political awareness and involvement by Britishers is usually not much greater than the generally low level prevailing in the United States.

Interest and Knowledge

Less than one-quarter of British voters know anything about their M.P.'s record in Parliament. When Gallup asks people to identify members of the cabinet from their photographs, only the more flamboyant members are recognized by more than half those polled. Yet the cabinet in Britain gets much more media attention than does the President's cabinet in the United States.

British election campaigns run for only three weeks. Yet Britons are just as likely as Americans to complain that they go on too long, and angry complaints are received by television stations whenever a favorite program is preempted by a political broadcast. Harold Wilson was very much aware of this during the close-fought 1964 campaign. He noted that the BBC, competing with the independent TV channel, had planned to lock its audience into its own election coverage by scheduling its most popular program, *Steptoe and Son,* for 8:00 P.M.—just before the polls closed. Wilson told the BBC's Director-General that this was unfair to his party, for the majority of the program's viewers were Labour voters, some of whom might stay home to watch the program rather than go out to vote. *Steptoe* was rescheduled until after the polls had closed.[4]

This and other evidence of low levels of interest in politics come despite the fact that the British are avid newspaper readers. It is true that the "quality" or "class" newspapers provide serious and extensive coverage of national and international politics. But it is the tabloids that have the mass circulations: the *Sun* leads the pack with over four million daily, whereas the *Mirror* has close to three million, and on Sunday the *News of the World* sells almost five million copies. The tabloids deal with politics to some extent; however, with the exception of election campaigns, politics is relegated to the inside pages and subordinated to lavish coverage of royalty, media celebrities, crime, and "human interest" stories.

The tabloid style is gaudy and often in excruciating taste. The *Sun's* headlines are particular noteworthy in this respect. The paper screamed its dislike of Jacques Delors, the European Union's president, with the headline, *Up Yours, Delors;* and during the Falklands war the *Sun* produced a huge, one-word headline on the sinking of an Argentine troopship with the loss of hundreds of lives:

GOTCHA!

Every day on page three the *Sun,* ignoring feminist complaints, carries a picture of a young, bare-breasted woman (although publisher Rupert Murdoch, blaming the feature on an editor who acted when Murdoch was away, concedes that: "Now it's getting a bit old-fashioned. One day it will come out."). And the tabloid coverage of the hapless behavior of the royal princes and princesses has been crude, unceasing, and merciless.

To the extent that the British are informed about politics, television plays the leading role. And even television's contribution has not been sufficient to contradict the findings of innumerable surveys by social scientists, which indicate that the majority of the British people are like the electorates in most countries: their pressing concerns are not built around the compromises and conflicts of politicians, and they pay close attention to politics only in times of crisis or particularly dramatic events, or when politicians are involved in sexual or financial scandals.

Of course, people are concerned about political issues like the state of the economy, education, crime, and so on. But David Butler and Donald Stokes, in their classic study of the British electorate, found generally low levels of sophistication in the understanding of issues. As they wrote in 1974: "Understanding of political issues falls away very sharply indeed as we move outward from those at the heart of political decision-making to the public at large."[5] Subsequent studies have not suggested a significant improvement since that time.

Involvement

Despite the presence of large numbers of political organizations, as well as the panoply of groups that enter the political arena periodically, the British generally "do not like to get involved. Commitment is not their thing."[6] Active participation in organizations, including political groups, is left to a small minority. Only 3 percent claim to have taken an active part in a political campaign, and 5 percent to have written a letter to an editor.

In one respect, however, the British have been considerably more involved than Americans. In national elections, more than 75 percent of the British population tends to vote, compared with the barely 50 percent turnout in recent U.S. presidential elections. This is partly related to the difference in the registration process: Britain, like most other democracies, does not require the citizen to take steps to register, but makes the registration process an official responsibility of local governments, which compiles a list of voters from a form sent to each household. Yet this does not explain all of the difference in turnout; British voter participation is clearly more healthy than the U.S. pattern in this respect.

Voters and the Parties

There is another respect in which British political attitudes differ from those in the United States. The British are considerably more likely to identify themselves with a political party. In the United States, as many as one-third of the electorate describe themselves as *independent*. The proportion in Britain is much lower.

There are plenty of parties to choose from. In addition to the Conservative and Labour parties, there are the Liberal Democrats, the Scottish Nationalist Party, Plaid

Cymru (the Welsh nationalists), three Northern Ireland parties, the Greens, the Communists, the neofascist National Front, and the Maharishi Ayur-Ved's Natural Law Party. Others include the Monster Raving Loony Party, headed by Screaming Lord Sutch. (One of its candidates, who likes to dress as Boss Hogg from *The Dukes of Hazzard*, has argued: "When you hear of the EEC feeding butter back to cows, you have to ask who are the real loonies.")

All of these parties put up candidates for national and local office, and some are represented in the House of Commons. But most of them are also underrepresented there because of the voting system which, as we have noted, is biased against all but the two biggest parties and especially against the Liberal Democrats.

To correct this bias, various systems of proportional representation have been proposed. Some, by dividing the country into multimember districts, would allow a third-place party to win at least one seat in the larger districts. Others, like the German "additional member" system, would retain single-member districts, the winner being elected on the simple plurality principle, but also award seats in larger regions on a proportional basis. The Plant Commission, established by the Labour Party to consider electoral reform, recommended (by a narrow margin) a Supplementary Vote (SV) system. This would allow voters to state a second preference; if no candidate gained more than 50 percent initially, the second preferences (for lower-ranking candidates) would be distributed among the two front-runners, and the one with more first and second preferences would be elected. But past governments, without any of these systems, have since 1945 merely alternated between the two big parties, as suggested by Table 4.1.

Class and Party. As Table 4.2 makes clear, class is an important indicator of voting behavior in Britain. We see from this table that Conservative strength rises as we move through each of the social class categories from *DE* to *AB*, while Labour strength rises at each stage from *AB* to *DE*. (The Liberal Democrats draw more evenly across the classes, though they are somewhat more concentrated in the middle than in the working classes.)

TABLE 4.1 Party alterations in power

Years	Party	Prime Ministers
1945–51	Labour	Attlee
1951–64	Conservative	Churchill (1951–55)
		Eden (1955–57)
		Macmillan (1957–63)
		Douglas-Home (1963–64)
1964–70	Labour	Wilson
1970–74	Conservative	Heath
1974–79	Labour	Wilson (1974–76)
		Callaghan (1976–79)
1979–	Conservative	Thatcher (1979–90)
		Major (1990–)

TABLE 4.2 Voting in 1992 election

	AB	C1	C2	DE	Union Member
Conservative	56%	52%	39%	31%	31%
Labour	19%	25%	40%	49%	46%
Liberal Democrats	22%	19%	17%	16%	19%

SOURCE: Adapted from MORI.

However, looking at class alone does not enable us to predict the outcome of elections. For, as we have noted, more Britons identify themselves as working class than as middle class; Labour is generally perceived to be the party of the working class and the unions; yet the Conservatives won the 1992 election. Indeed, since 1945 the Conservatives have won eight elections to Labour's five and have governed Britain more than twice as many years as Labour during that period.

The explanation, as Table 4.2 shows, is that the link between class and party, although important, is frequently broken. A considerable number of voters defect from their class voting patterns. In 1992 one-quarter of the *C1* group, and almost one-fifth of the *AB* group, voted Labour. But considerably larger numbers moved in the other direction, with almost two-fifths of the *C2,* and nearly one-third of the *D* and *E* categories and trade union members voting for Conservative candidates. In varying degrees defections from class loyalties have characterized all recent British elections.

Some of the reasons for these disparities between class and voting behavior are to be found in factors we have already discussed, particularly the longterm decline in class consciousness and the "embourgeoisement" of much of the working class. Other factors are more ephemeral in nature, related to the performance of governments, the quality of party leaders, the salience of particular issues, and the conduct of election campaigns. We shall be elaborating on these in Chapter 6.

But whatever the reasons, the consequences clearly have been more damaging to Labour than to the Conservatives; over the decades, the Labour share of the vote has fallen drastically. As we see from Appendix I, from 1945 to 1970 Labour received between 43 and 49 percent of the votes at each election, and in 1966, in the aftermath of its second successive victory, Labour began to talk about its being the natural party of government, favored to win most future elections. Yet in the 1970s Labour's share of the votes fell to between 37 and 39 percent. The nadir was reached in 1983, when Labour received 27.5 percent of the votes cast, barely preventing the Alliance from taking second place. Recovery since then has only reached the level of 31 percent in 1987 and 35 percent in 1992, both of which are below Labour's weakest performance in the 1970s.

Further evidence of Labour's decline is found in the size of its membership. In the early 1950s, there were close to one million individual party members, apart from those who were affiliated through their unions. By 1990, the individual membership was down to little more than 250,000; and although the party claimed that a recruitment drive had raised membership to almost 350,000 in 1995, it is noteworthy that this figure is less than one-third the number of subscribers to the Royal Society for the Protection of Birds.

The shift of population from the Labour strongholds in the north to the traditionally Conservative southeast is one more factor sapping Labour's parliamentary strength; there will be a reapportionment before the next election, which could cost Labour at least a few more seats.

So it was the Conservatives—not Labour—who, after their triumph in 1992, could claim to be the party most likely to continue winning elections and governing the country.

This claim in turn was subject to challenge when, within a year of their success in 1992, the Conservatives had suffered a precipitous decline in their standing in the polls, and conventional wisdom, now revised, began to predict a Labour victory in the next election. Should this prove to be the case, however, it will not mean that Labour can return to the optimism generated by its triumph in 1966; it will be forced to consider the trends of the last three decades that we have considered here.

CONCLUSION

The class basis of British political parties is made abundantly clear by the interest groups that provide most of their financial and organizational support: business for the Conservatives, the unions for Labour.

However, the relationship is less evident when we turn our attention to the voters at large. Although class is still a significant indicator of voting behavior, it is less so than in the past; and in most respects this decline appears to benefit the Conservatives at the expense of the Labour Party. This hardly guarantees a Conservative victory in the next election and, as we shall see, the deep split within the Conservative Party over Europe could damage the party's prospects for years to come. But whether and how Labour can compensate for the decline in its basic strength over the long run is a question to which we shall return after building a foundation necessary in our chapters on parties and elections.

SOME QUESTIONS TO THINK ABOUT

What are the advantages and disadvantages of the multiplicity of interest groups in Britain?

Are U.S. parties as closely identified with business and labor as are British parties? Is the close relationship established in Britain desirable?

How accurate are the pluralist and corporatist analyses of the British system?

What are the reasons for the British electorate's relatively low levels of knowledge of and involvement in politics?

Why is voting turnout higher in Britain than in the United States?

Why has class declined as a determinant of voting behavior in Britain? How important is class in U.S. voting?

NOTES

1. Samuel H. Beer, *Britain Against Itself: The Political Contradictions of Collectivism* (Norton, 1982), p. 2.
2. James McGregor Burns, *The Deadlock of Democracy* (Spectrum, 1963), p. 2.
3. Keith Middlemas, *Politics in Industrial Society* (Andre Deutsch, 1979).
4. Michael Cockerell, *Live From Number 10* (Faber, 1988), p. 107.
5. David Butler and Donald Stokes, *Political Change in Britain,* 2d edition (Macmillan, 1974), p. 277.
6. Jacobs and Worcester, *We British*, p. 164.

SUGGESTIONS FOR FURTHER READING

On groups, see NOTES above for works by Sam Beer and Keith Middlemas; also Jeremy J. Richardson (ed.), *Pressure Groups* (Oxford University Press, 1993). On business, W. Grant, *Business and Politics in Britain,* 2d ed. (Macmillan, 1993) and Leslie Hannah, *The Rise of the Corporate Economy* (Johns Hopkins University Press, 1976). On trade unions, see Robert Taylor, *Trade Union Question in British Politics* (Blackwell, 1993) and *The Future of Trade Unions* (Andre Deutsch, 1994), Ken Coates and Tony Topham, *Trade Unions and Politics* (Blackwell, 1986), and Martin Adeney and John Lloyd, *The Miners' Strike, 1984-5* (Routledge and Kegan Paul, 1986).

On voters and voting behavior, the classic study is David Butler and Donald Stokes, 2d ed. (Macmillan, 1974). More recent studies presenting varying interpretations include Richard Rose and Ian McAllister, *Voters Begin to Choose* (Sage, 1986); Anthony Heath, Roger Jowell, and John Curtice, *How Britain Votes* (Pergamon Press, 1985), and Anthony Heath *et al., Understanding Political Change* (Pergamon Press, 1991); Patrick Dunleavy and Christopher T. Husbands, *British Democracy at the Crossroads* (Allen and Unwin, 1985); Bo Sarlvik and Ivor Crewe, *Decade of Dealignment* (Cambridge University Press, 1983).

5

INSIDE THE PARTIES

Parties are highly unpopular in the United States today; they are somewhat less unpopular in Britain. Yet the existence of at least two parties is an essential and inevitable component of democracies.

Thus in the United States, even while George Washington was warning against "the baneful effects of the spirit of party," Federalists were lining up against Antifederalists. These were loose associations, or factions, rather than parties, but the conflict between them set a pattern from which our two-party system has emerged.

In Britain, too, there were factions before there were parties. In the seventeenth century two rival groups formed around the struggle between king and parliament. The Tories were the royalists, the Whigs defended the rights of Parliament. The issues over which they fought changed, but the Tory-Whig dualism survived into the nineteenth century, gradually taking on more of the organized characteristics of parties. With the broadening of the franchise that started in 1832 and began accelerating in 1867, the early parties became anachronisms and had to give way to parties that could speak for broader constituencies. Yet in Britain as in the United States the two-party model had been set by history and by the "single district, simple plurality" system. After Tory and Whig, the Conservative and Liberal parties alternated in power in the last decades of the nineteenth century, and in the twentieth century, as the Labour Party surged, it was necessarily at the expense of the Liberals, for there was only room for two parties at the top.

Today Britain is often cited as having a strong, or "responsible," two-party system. This model has two facets. The first is a well-organized structure with a network of local units linked to a national headquarters. The second is the articulation of policies and programs offering clear choices to the electorate.

Organizationally the British parties meet this standard. Individuals and groups join local constituency parties, pay annual dues—a portion of which goes to the national party—and may participate in the selection of candidates and the shaping of policy locally and nationally. This is in contrast with the situation in the United States, where the parties are very loosely organized, with only weak links between local and national levels.

Programmatically, too, British parties offer clearer alternatives than U.S. parties. However, there is debate over the extent to which parties in Britain satisfy the strong party model in terms of articulating and offering clear choices to the electorate. Although some analysts see wide differences in party programs, others argue that those differences have been exaggerated. In this chapter we examine this debate on the extent of the differences between the parties; we then go inside the parties to discuss their structures and their internal conflicts.

PARTY DIFFERENCES

Every year in the fall, each of the parties holds a national conference attended by delegates from its mass membership. Even a brief glimpse at the televised coverage of the Conservative and Labour Party conferences reveals striking differences between the two in how their delegates look and sound. The Conservatives are mostly better dressed than the Labourites. Conservative behavior is usually more decorous and deferential to the leadership. There are far more upper-class accents among the Conservatives, along with some regional dialects and middle-class accents. On the Labour side there is a much greater variety of speech patterns, with a few public school inflections, a larger number of middle-class intellectual accents, and a preponderance of Cockney, north country, and other regional dialects.

The Conservatives are also the wealthier of the two parties, with more individual dues-paying members than in the Labour Party, and contributions from business that exceed Labour's declining revenues from the unions. This Conservative advantage was narrowed after the costly 1992 election, which plunged the party into a large debt; at the same time Labour, through organizational economies and restructuring, was no longer caught up in its customary desperate struggle to pay the bills. Even so, Labour, compared with the Conservatives, had fewer resources and fewer paid agents with smaller salaries in the constituencies, and would continue to be outspent by the Conservatives in national election campaigns.

These class-related contrasts are reflected in differences over policy issues. In general, the Conservative policies are more representative of middle-class and business concerns; Labour policies tend to represent working-class and trade union interests. Consequently, Conservative rhetoric is replete with phrases praising business and the free enterprise system, whereas Labour, looking to government to protect working people against the power of business, speaks of state intervention, planning, and public ownership. Conservatives advocate restricting government spending and taxes; Labour supports public spending to favor the lower income groups and higher taxes on the affluent.

These differences permeate political speeches, TV interviews, and House of Commons debates. They are also apparent in the manifestos, or party platforms, which are published at the beginning of each election campaign. The extent of the manifesto differences varies from election to election. They were very clear in 1945, when Labour proposed to transform social and economic policy through nationalization and a major extension of the welfare state. The differences were unmistakable in 1979, when the Conservatives proposed restricting union power, cutting income tax at the upper levels, and reducing government controls, while Labour spoke of working with the T.U.C. to restrain inflation, imposing an annual wealth tax on the rich, and continuing the use of planning and regulation.

In 1983, the contrast was wider still. The Conservatives proposed to privatize industries that had been nationalized by Labour governments and to set more limits on the unions. Labour, on the other hand, advocated a "massive rise in public spending," a wealth tax, renationalization of industries privatized by the Conservatives, and the repeal of antiunion legislation; Labour also demanded withdrawal from the European Common Market, which Britain had joined in 1971, as well as various proposals outside the economic realm, including the abolition of the House of Lords and, in accordance with the left's antimilitarist stance, unilateral nuclear disarmament.

Even in 1992, when Labour had pulled back from these radical policies, and the Conservatives aimed at a more moderate tone than had been projected during the Thatcher years, the manifestos were recognizable even without the party labels. The Conservatives were still calling for tax cuts and the denationalization of more industries, while Labour urged raising the top rate of income tax on upper middle incomes and expanding government programs. Labour also put forward proposals for a number of constitutional reforms that were not matched by the Conservatives.

Despite the common assumption that politicians' promises bear no relation to their ability to deliver, much of what is contained in the manifestos is put into effect by the winning party. The Labour government elected in 1945 did nationalize several industries, and did bring about a sweeping expansion of welfare programs, including the establishment of the National Health Service. The Conservative government elected in 1979 did reduce government controls, cut income taxes, and pass antiunion legislation.

In fact, some critics complain that the incessant battling between the two parties creates an adversarial relationship that inhibits sensible policy-making. For example, toward the end of Attlee's Labour government, a bill was introduced nationalizing the steel industry. When the Conservatives took over, they stopped the idea in its tracks. As soon as Labour came back to power, they reintroduced and passed their bill. Later, the Thatcher administration in turn reversed the process again—and set out to repeal almost everything passed by the Attlee government. As these critics see it, with policy-making swinging back and forth as parties alternate in power, it is very difficult to assure sustained, orderly progress.

PARTY SIMILARITIES

The contrasts we see between British parties are sharper than those normally found between the U.S. Republican and Democratic parties, especially in the area of economic policy. Yet in the British system there are also moderating forces that tend, most of the time, to narrow the extent of disagreement between the Conservative and Labour parties.

Indeed, when political scientist Richard Rose poses the question: Do parties make a difference?[1], he answers: Yes—but not very much. Every so often, he says, one of the parties introduces programs that have been incubating over a period of time; when the other party comes to power, it modifies the changes but does not alter them fundamentally. So, according to Rose, a new consensus is established on that policy. It reflects change, so it is a *moving* consensus, but what emerges is an underlying pattern that suggests broad areas of agreement between the parties.

Thus, despite the example of the steel industry, most of the industries nationalized by the Labour government after 1945 were not denationalized by the various Conservative governments that held office from 1951 to 1974; in fact, Edward Heath's administration chose to nationalize Rolls Royce in 1971 rather than see it go bankrupt. The last Labour Chancellor of the Exchequer before the end of the Attlee Government was Hugh Gaitskell. The first Chancellor of the Churchill government that followed was R. A. Butler. The similarities between the budgets proposed by these two men were so great that they gave rise to the term *Butskellism*.

In Rose's analysis, this moving consensus characterized most of the issues, foreign as well as domestic, from 1945 to 1979. Then Margaret Thatcher launched a frontal assault on several aspects of that consensus and changed the previous direction on taxes, trade unions, and nationalization so effectively that any future Labour government would not be able to change them back again. But as Rose observes, even Thatcher had to accept some of the policies established by her predecessors, was frustrated by continued high government spending, and had only temporary successes in bringing inflation down and revitalizing the economy.

Why is it that the consensus changes so rarely—and even then, only in piecemeal fashion? The first reason is that running a government is very different from maintaining an opposition or writing a manifesto. Once in power, party leaders must work through the permanent bureaucracy, and no bureaucracy in the world is more adept at presenting arguments against change than the British civil service. Moreover, many of those arguments are not mere obstructionism. The cost of a new policy may have been grossly underestimated. Abolishing an existing program may be difficult for legal reasons or because it is supported by powerful groups or by a large majority of the public.

Then, too, on most issues the electorate tends to cluster around the center of the political spectrum, so parties that stray too far from that center put themselves at risk electorally. Governments must also keep their party behind them, and in a population as large as that of Britain, narrowing the range of choices principally to two parties means that each of those parties has to represent a broad coalition of diverse ideas and interests. So party leaders must be wary of taking steps that could alienate a major block of party opinion.

Finally, there are the constraints on any government's freedom of action dictated by the prevailing real world circumstances. Labour governments were required to cut back their spending on welfare programs as a condition of receiving needed loans from the International Monetary Fund. In the 1940s and again in the 1960s, Labour's desperate efforts to avoid the devaluation of the pound were defeated by the harsh verdict of the currency markets. That same verdict was later delivered against John Major's Conservative government when it was forced to drop the fixed exchange rate between the pound and the German deutschmark. When Conservative and Labour governments alike were brought to their knees in the 1970s, the immediate cause was striking unions, but the underlying cause was inflation generated by the sudden escalation of world oil prices.

So, Rose argues, Labour and Conservative governments can make marginal changes, but not much more. Struggles over nationalization and denationalization are secondary to the fundamentals of economic performance. There may be short-term fluctuations in prices and wages, but over the long term, inflation rose and unemployment rose, and the rates of increase were not much different under Labour or Conservative governments.

Governments have been no less constrained in their conduct of foreign policy. Try as they might to maintain Britain's international position, there was no escaping the reality of the loss of empire and their country's decline from the front rank of world powers. Britain could prevail against Argentina over the Falklands, but could not prevent the return of Hong Kong to China in 1997.

Between those who complain of excessive gyrations as parties alternate in power, and Rose's "moving consensus" analysis, other scholars argue a third position: that there was a moving consensus from 1945 to 1979, but that the Thatcher administration succeeded in overturning much of the consensus and overcoming the obstacles to change.

To fully explore this debate, and determine how much difference parties actually make, requires an examination of each of the main areas of public policy, which we shall undertake in part IV of this book. But here we must take note of the fact that differences over policy are argued as fiercely *within* as *between* the parties, and we turn now to an examination of the internal structures of the parties and the controversies that erupt inside those structures.

CONFLICTS IN THE CONSERVATIVE PARTY

From its earliest history, the Conservative Party has had to endure fierce divisions over policy issues. Under Prime Minister Sir Robert Peel, Parliament in 1846 repealed the Corn Laws, which had given agricultural protection to Tory landlords. This departure from its protectionist tradition broke the party apart, and led to almost 20 years of rule by a Whig-Liberal coalition.

Then in the 1930s, Winston Churchill led a small but determined group of Conservative M.P.s opposing the government's appeasement of Hitler and demanding stepped-up rearmament. Churchill's faction finally prevailed, but only after the Chamberlain government had failed not only in its pursuit of peace, but also in its conduct of the war.

Since the end of World War II, there have been further internal conflicts over foreign policy, and today the relationship with Europe has become the most deeply divisive issue within the party. Then on domestic issues we find a fairly consistent division among Conservatives running along one principal fault line. On one side of the divide have been the "progressive" Conservatives, those who follow the precept of the nineteenth century prime minister, Benjamin Disraeli, that Britain must be "One Nation," in which the advantaged sections of the community have responsibilities to the less privileged. This sense of *noblesse oblige* requires government to undertake measures of social reform, but also mandates that these be introduced gradually and with a proper respect for established procedures and traditions. On the other side, those on the right wing of the party argue for a relatively unfettered market system, holding down expenditures on the welfare state, strengthening law and order, and reasserting traditional morality.

In a coalition as broad as the Conservative Party there are, of course, many variations on these themes. Thus libertarians in the party favor little government intervention in the economy but are against capital punishment. "Corporatists" in the party advocate close relationships between government and business. Many others are not committed to any camp, preferring to find a middle ground between them.

But the terms of the central debate in the modern Conservative Party have been set by the moderate reformers and the right wing, and the contest between them has been fought in four main arenas of power.

Locations of Power in the Conservative Party

There are four main Conservative decision-making centers. First there is the Parliamentary Party: the Conservative members of the two houses of Parliament, particularly the House of Commons. Second, the Conservative Central Office is charged with directing the party's national machinery. Third, the National Union of Conservative and Unionist Associations coordinates the efforts of the local party organizations, made up of the ordinary, dues-paying members. Fourth, there is the annual national conference in October, to which all elements in the party send delegates to review the party's direction and debate resolutions on specific policies.

These four components are brought together in a highly centralized structure, for the decisive power is in the Parliamentary Party, and particularly in the hands of the party leader. The leader is elected by the members of the party in the House of Commons, which means that when the party is in power its leader is prime minister, and when it is out of office the leader is also the leader of Her Majesty's Opposition. Relationships are summarized in Figure 5.1; as indicated, it is the leader who appoints the chair of the Central Office; the leader exercises a great deal of influence in the National Conservative Association, for this is a party that has a strong tradition of loyalty; and the leader's positions usually prevail at the annual conference.

Even so, there is a clear potential for tension between the Parliamentary Party and Central Office on one side, and the National Association and Annual Conference on the other. The first two represent the professionals—the Members of Parliament and the party functionaries. The other two give voice to the amateurs, the most active of the rank and file members at the grass roots in the constituency parties. The

```
                    ┌─────────────┐
                    │ Party Leader │
                    └─────────────┘
                   ╱       │       ╲
                  ╱        │        ╲
┌──────────────────┐  ┌──────────────┐  ┌──────────────┐
│ National Union of│  │              │  │ Parliamentary│
│ Conservative and │  │Central Office│  │    Party     │
│Unionist Associations│  │              │  │              │
└──────────────────┘  └──────────────┘  └──────────────┘
         ↕
┌──────────────┐
│ Constituency │
│   Parties    │
└──────────────┘
```

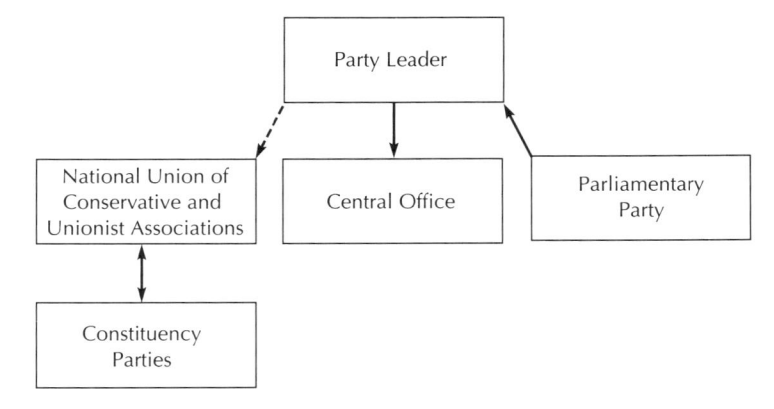

FIGURE 5.1 Organization of the Conservative Party

amateurs have tended to be on the right of the party. They are interested primarily in issues, and they have come into politics because they have strong feelings about the issues. So at the annual conferences, they have made deeply felt statements on issues of great importance to them: *For* capital punishment and holding on to the remnants of empire, and *against* trade unions and integration into Europe.

For many years the volunteer activists were held in check by the professional leaders, who were generally less ideological, more pragmatic and consensual. After all, the leaders insisted, they were responsible as legislators not only to their party but to the voters as a whole; and, unlike the volunteers, they must deal with the reality of being the nation's government, or at least the prospective government.

This tension between the careerists and the volunteers was essentially resolved when Margaret Thatcher was elected party leader. She shared the ideological fervor of the people at the grass roots of the party, and what later came to be called *Thatcherism* crystallized positions long expressed from the floor of the conference hall but repeatedly overridden by the leadership. There was criticism from the moderates, but they did not take their complaints to the floor of the conference. Even at the 1990 conference, just weeks before Thatcher was ousted from the leadership, her closing speech was acclaimed with a nine-minute standing ovation, and the only dissenting resolutions were those urging the government to go still farther and faster in the direction it had chosen.

This reluctance to express open dissatisfaction with the leadership, except for "fringe" meetings held outside the conference hall, was typical of Conservative Party conferences. There was always an undercurrent of fierce factionalism, but it remained an undercurrent because the Conservatives dislike airing their disagreements in public. So usually, conference resolutions are passed unanimously. (One year there was a single hand raised repeatedly in the negative, but it turned out to be a Communist technician working in the hall.)

Accordingly, there was general astonishment as viewers watched the proceedings of the Conservative National Conference in 1992. John Major had just led his party to an unexpected election victory, which should have been the prelude to a conference even more harmonious than usual. Instead there were furious denunciations of the government's policies on the economy and on Europe, and uproarious approval for a particularly bitter attack by Norman Tebbit, a former member of the Thatcher cabinet. It was all very un-Conservative. But even at that conference, no resolution critical of the leadership was approved. The surface forms of party unity were preserved.

When the schisms in the party over Europe and other issues became even more apparent during the following year, the 1993 Annual Conference was programmed to produce an effect of profound harmony, and roars of approval greeted speaker after speaker who produced variations on the conference theme: unity.

Leadership Contests

There is, however, one respect in which Conservative Party conflicts have broken repeatedly into the public view. This is the process by which the leadership succession is arranged.

Until recent years, the Leader "emerged" from a process of consultation among a few men at the center of affairs. Thus, when Anthony Eden resigned as prime minister in 1957, some 25 men in all—the cabinet members and a few party leaders—were consulted. The procedure was conducted by two elderly peers, Lords Salisbury and Kilmuir, and the choice was between two senior cabinet members, R. A. Butler (known to his friends as "Rab") and Harold Macmillan. Salisbury, with an odd quirk of speech sometimes found among members of the British upper class, put the question to each of the 25 in turn: "Well, which is it, Wab or Hawold?" It was "Hawold," and the queen sent for Macmillan.

In 1963, it was Macmillan's turn to step down. His decision was announced from his hospital bed in London while the party's Annual Conference was in session in the northern seaside resort of Blackpool. Supporters of the leading contestants for his job—Butler, Lord Hailsham, and Reginald Maudling—campaigned as energetically for their candidates at the conference as they would if they were at a U.S. party convention. Impervious to all the frantic activity, Macmillan was taking his own soundings among party leaders, and made the decision that he should be succeeded by his Foreign Secretary, Lord Home. The queen visited Macmillan in the hospital, received his recommendation, and named Home prime minister (for which purpose he had to give up his peerage and become Sir Alec Douglas-Home).

This was such a blatant example of the old boy network in operation that when the Conservatives lost the election a year later, Douglas-Home resigned as Party leader, and accepted a proposal that his successor should be elected by a vote of all the Conservative Party members.

Edward Heath was then elected as Leader on the second ballot. He remained the leader from 1965 until 1975, including four years as prime minister. However, his aloof manner made him increasingly unpopular in his party, and when he led the party to two successive defeats in 1974, there was a groundswell of opinion that he be replaced. The opportunity presented itself, for the rules had been amended to require that the leader stand for reelection every year. No challenger to Heath had appeared previously, but in 1975 he faced a formidable opponent in Margaret Thatcher.

Thatcher's Rise to the Leadership. On the first ballot, Heath came in second to Thatcher and he withdrew. On the second ballot, to general incredulity, the Conservative Party chose its first woman leader. The incredulity resulted not only from Thatcher's gender. As education minister, she was a relatively junior member of Heath's cabinet. Within the cabinet she had not adopted radical positions, but increasingly she associated with members of the party's right wing, placing her outside the Conservative mainstream that had produced all the leaders from Churchill through Heath. Moreover, Thatcher had become the right wing's candidate only because better-known leaders of the right had disqualified themselves by making politically outrageous statements in public.

So Thatcher was viewed as an accidental leader, who won because Heath, unaware of how unpopular he had become, insisted on running again, and as long as he was in the race, all of the other leading party figures (like William Whitelaw) were too gentlemanly to run against him. Consequently Thatcher received the first ballot votes of several who saw her simply as a temporary catalyst for anti-Heath sentiment until another, more acceptable candidate appeared. But by the time Heath withdrew, it was too late for any other candidate to overcome Thatcher's momentum.

Yet her success was not entirely the consequence of good luck. She and her associates ran a skillful campaign for the leadership, and she represented a force for change and energy when members of the old guard who had been running the party seemed tired and dispirited. In any case, talk of her being an accidental leader faded as she went on to become prime minister, to lead her party to three consecutive election victories, and to change the whole direction of public policy.

She was reelected leader—unopposed—every year from 1975 until 1989, dominating the government and the party. But at last, the schisms always present in the Conservative Party began to assert themselves. A backbencher with no pretensions to high office, Sir Anthony Meyer, threw down a challenge to the leader at the annual reelection procedure. He could not hope to win; but 60 Conservative M.P.s voted against Thatcher or abstained.

Thatcher's Fall. The rebellion of these 60 M.P.s was the precursor of much more profound trouble in 1990. Then, the man who threw down the gauntlet was no minor backbench figure but Michael Heseltine, a successful businessman and an attractive, effective speaker able to evoke huge ovations at party conferences, and popular among the general public.

On the first ballot Heseltine fell short, receiving 152 votes to Thatcher's 204, with 16 abstentions. So Thatcher had gained a clear majority. Yet she had not won. The Conservative Party's rules required more than an absolute majority, for the aim was to ensure that the leader would be a person commanding overwhelming support in the party. So the requirement for a victory on the first ballot was an overall majority plus at least 15 percent of the total eligible voters. With an electorate of 372, Thatcher needed a margin of 56. She fell short by four votes.

On the second ballot the rules called for no more than a simple majority, so

Margaret Thatcher disposes of Edward Heath
SOURCE: Copyright © Paul Delmar/Hulton.

Thatcher needed to hold on to only 187 of her first ballot total of 204. Yet the majority of her cabinet colleagues convinced her that there would be a drastic decline in her initial vote on the next ballot, and she withdrew, fearful that if she did not do so her archrival, Heseltine, would win rather than the man she had been grooming as her successor, John Major. On the second ballot, Major was well ahead of Heseltine and Foreign Secretary Douglas Hurd, and was declared the victor.

How could this have happened to the leader who had never been defeated by the electorate and who was still enormously popular among the activist rank and file in the Conservative constituency parties? It happened because she had been losing support among three vital constituencies.

First, she had alienated too many powerful Conservative leaders, men who had resigned or been dismissed from her cabinets over the years. They harbored resentments, partly based on her high-handed treatment of them, partly because of policy disputes, especially over her opposition to Britain's becoming more deeply involved in the European Community. Heseltine was among the leaders she had offended, and he had represented a threat to her position ever since he had literally walked out of the cabinet over a personal and policy argument. Yet he hesitated before issuing his challenge in 1990, for if she had won it would have ended his political career.

The event that precipitated his entry into the race was the resignation of Geoffrey Howe, who had served Thatcher faithfully as chancellor of the exchequer and foreign secretary, but who had then suffered being demoted. When Thatcher in Parliament poured scorn on the pro-European-Community views in which Howe believed, he left the government with a biting speech in the House of Commons rejecting Thatcher's European policy.

His onslaught sent shock waves through the House, for he had always been a mild-mannered man—so much so that Labour's Dennis Healey once said that being attacked by Howe was like being "savaged by a dead sheep." This reputation made his attack on Thatcher especially deadly and made her suddenly vulnerable. Now Heseltine had to take the plunge or continue to have the word *wimp* applied to him in the press.

The second constituency to turn against Thatcher was the decisive one, the Parliamentary Conservative Party. For whatever her standing in the constituency parties, the grass roots activists had no direct say in the matter. The votes were exclusively with the Conservative members in the House of Commons.

And despite Thatcher's 15 years as their leader and more than 11 years as prime minister, she had not converted a majority of her parliamentary colleagues to her doctrines. Perhaps one-fifth of the total were true believers in Thatcherism, but these were almost offset by the "progressives"—the group subscribing to the Disraeli version of Conservatism. The majority remained uncommitted to either camp. They would not easily desert their leader, for they were party loyalists, and loyalty was a high virtue for them. Yet loyalty could be pushed downward in the scale of values when survival was at stake. And reluctantly they had come to the conclusion that the prospects for victory at the next election were dubious as long as Margaret Thatcher remained as their leader. They had arrived at this judgment because all the opinion polls revealed that Margaret Thatcher had become deeply unpopular among the third and ultimate constituency—the electorate at large. Despite their having reelected her party three times under her leadership, the majority of the voters were still (as we saw in chapter 2) strongly attached to the welfare state and still obstinately unpersuaded of the merits of Thatcherism.

Moreover, a particular issue compounded her problems: the poll tax. This was her government's plan to replace the local property tax, the "rates," with a new assessment method based on individual residents instead of homes. The poll tax was widely regarded as monstrously unfair; and large numbers of middle- and working-class people faced much larger tax bills under the new system. But Thatcher refused to back down, her popularity plunged, and she found that the loyalty of the Parliamentary Conservatives was to the party rather than to her.

John Major and the Leadership Issue. For the moment it seemed that the selection of Major as leader would resolve the deep divisions in the party. He had been hand-picked by Thatcher and given remarkable rapid advancement in her Cabinet. Yet he was more low-key than Thatcher, more likeable, and more friendly toward Europe. The era of good feelings continued through the 1992 election and was reinforced by the Conservatives' victory and Major's high standing in the polls.

But then, with the deterioration of the economy and a series of blunders by the administration, Major's popularity plummeted. And although Thatcher had created him politically, Major found himself under bitter attack from the Thatcherite wing of the party (which was now probably larger than during Thatcher's term of office because of the influx of a number of young right-wingers elected in 1992). It was not enough for them that he continued Thatcher's policies on nationalization, health, education, and other areas. Nor were they mollified by his refusal to sign the European Union's social chapter, which favored the welfare state and the rights of labor (See chapter 18). The Thatcherites were adamantly opposed to any deeper involvement with Europe and Major had strengthened the European connection by signing the Maastricht treaty.

So once again, the party's leader had cause to be concerned about the process of annual reselection, and although no challenger was put forward in 1994, the party's low standing in the polls and disastrous local election results in the spring of 1995 made it almost inevitable that there would be a leadership contest before year's end.

Infuriated by persistent bitter criticism from the right wing of the party (including caustic comments in the media by Thatcher herself), Major launched a bold, preemptive strike against his tormentors. Instead of waiting until November, when the reselection process would normally take place, he abruptly resigned as party leader (although not as prime minister) and called a special leadership election, in which he would be a candidate, for July 4.

Initially he appeared to have underestimated the risk, for instead of being confronted by a stalking-horse candidate from outside the government (like Sir Anthony Meyer in 1989), Major was challenged by a member of his own cabinet, Secretary for Wales John Redwood, a right-winger who had headed Thatcher's Policy Unit from 1983 to 1985. Redwood had little chance of matching Thatcher's first-ballot lead in 1975. However, if he could garner enough votes to prevent Major winning clearly on the first ballot (a majority plus 15 percent), then the battle would move on to a second round, almost certainly without Major, in which it was assumed the choice would be between two other cabinet members, the pro-European Michael Heseltine and the Thatcherite Michael Portillo. This scenario loomed as a strong possibility, for a number of pro-Conservative newspapers declared Major's cause as good as lost, and Portillo's supporters were said to be setting up special telephone lines for their second-ballot campaign.

Yet just as Major confounded his critics in leading his party to victory in 1992, so he refuted the widespread predictions of his political demise in 1995. Of the total electorate of 329 Tory members of Parliament Major received the votes of two-thirds—218—to Redwood's 89, a much wider margin than the rules required for a first-ballot victory. The leadership issue appeared to be settled until the next election, and consciousness of the approach of that election would provide a powerful impetus to end the shrill discord of the past and contrive at least an appearance of unity.

But unity would not come easily. After all, one-third of the party in Parliament had refused to support their prime minister (89 for Redwood and 22 who had either abstained, spoiled their ballots, or not voted, for a total of 111). It was also clear that there were a number of others who had voted for Major not because he was their enthusiastic choice, but because otherwise they might open the way for his replacement by Heseltine (detested by the right) or Portillo (abhorred by the left). So if Major's victory was likely to subdue the clamor of his critics for a while, it could not close the deep fissures that divided Conservatives. Indeed, the very process of calling and waging the special election had made the public even more aware of the party's lack of unity.

It was all very different from the pre-Thatcher era. All the leaders from Churchill through Heath had come from the moderate mainstream of the party. In fact, so had all the candidates who had vied for the leadership. So each time the choice among the candidates had been made primarily on the basis of personal qualities, rather than policy. The personal factor is still important as the party decides on its leader, but with the election of Margaret Thatcher, the Conservative Party entered a period in which its policy divisions became more intense as well as more public.

CONFLICTS IN THE LABOUR PARTY

If open divisiveness is a relatively novel aspect of the modern Conservative Party, it has long been associated with the history of the Labour Party. This is a party, after all, that came into existence to transform British society in the direction of socialism. Clause 4 of the Labour Party Constitution declared that one of the party's goals was:

> To secure for the workers by hand or brain the full fruits of their industry and the most equitable distribution thereof that may be possible upon the basis of the common ownership of the means of production, distribution and exchange, and the best obtainable system of popular administration and control of each industry or service.

Despite this quasi-Marxist language, the Labour party was never really Marxist in its doctrine. Change was to come by persuasion and consent, not by revolution. Still, there was strong disagreement between those who wanted a rapid pace of change toward a fully socialist society and others who argued for a gradualist approach and to whom socialism meant little more than a reduction of inequality.

These positions were fought out as abstract principles until Labour came to the threshold of power. To cross that threshold in the 1920s meant collaboration with the fading Liberal Party. Twice the decision was made to enter a coalition with the Liberals, and each time in the party there was opposition to joining forces with members of the class enemy.

The second time proved to be a disaster for the party. Under Ramsay MacDonald, the coalition government formed in 1929 was unable to cope with an economic crisis. In 1931, MacDonald joined forces with the Conservatives and Liberals to form a new, national coalition. All but four of his Labour government colleagues refused to follow him, and the five were cast out as traitors to the party. An election was called, Labour was crushingly defeated, and in 1935 the Conservatives took over the leadership of the government from MacDonald.

In opposition, the Labour Party, despite the reduction of its parliamentary representation, still found issues on which to divide. Chief among these was the question of rearmament, which led to the resignation of the party leader, George Lansbury, a pacifist, and his replacement by a compromise figure, Clement Attlee. Then in 1940 Labour joined with Conservatives and Liberals under Winston Churchill to fight the war against Germany.

With Germany defeated, there were some in the party who favored continuing the coalition, at least until the war against Japan was won, perhaps even beyond that to deal with postwar reconstruction. But bitter past experience had left the great majority in the party unwilling to tolerate coalition governments in peacetime; an election was called, and Labour won a sweeping victory. The preelection arguments over what should go into the Labour manifesto were mostly won by the left, and when the Labour government succeeded in translating most of the manifesto promises into actual programs, they carried most of the party with them and presided over a relatively harmonious period of party history.

Yet the sources of conflict could not be indefinitely contained. The tension between the proponents of accelerated change on the left and the moderate gradualists on the right broke into the open in the last year of the Attlee government, and has remained on public display ever since. They have argued over an even wider range of issues than the Conservatives, including the extent of nationalization, the scale of spending on the welfare state, relations with Europe and the United States, and nuclear armament and disarmament.

Locations of Power in the Labour Party

There are three main arenas in which these arguments are fought out.

First, there is the Parliamentary Labour Party, from which the government is formed whenever Labour wins a general election. Second, the National Executive Committee (N.E.C.) is in charge of the party machinery outside Parliament. It consists of 29 members; 12 from the unions, 7 from the local constituency parties, 5 reserved for women, 1 each for the Young Socialists and affiliated societies, plus the party's leader, deputy leader, and treasurer. Third, the Annual Conference, held just before the Conservative Conference, brings together representatives of all segments of the party—the local constituency organizations, the trade unions, and various affiliated associations—to discuss and vote on the party's program. Resolutions passed by two-thirds of the conference votes are, according to the party's constitution, to be considered as party policy.

The potential for conflict between the professionals and the activists within this structure (see Figure 5.2) is even greater than in the Conservative Party. Whereas the Conservative leader appoints and controls the chair of the Central Office, in the Labour Party it is the National Executive Committee that elects the N.E.C. chair, not the party leader. And the Annual Conference has often challenged the leadership from the floor and overruled it. When it does so, it is typically from the left, for just as the Conservative local activists tend to be on the right of their party, so many of their Labour counterparts, especially those who are elected to the "management committees" that run the local party units, are more committed to strongly socialist policies than the parliamentary leaders.

This does not mean that the leadership is without power. Whenever Labour is in office, the leadership, being the government, does not usually allow itself to be instructed either by the N.E.C. or the conference. As prime minister, Clement Attlee was a master at making this position clear. In 1945 when the N.E.C. chair made speeches abroad on foreign policy that were well to the left of the foreign secretary, Attlee wrote him:

> You have no right whatever to speak on behalf of the government. Foreign affairs are in the capable hands of Ernest Bevin. His task is quite sufficiently difficult without the embarrassment of irresponsible statements of the kind which you are making. . . . I can assure you there is widespread resentment in the Party at your activities and a period of silence on your part would be welcome.[2]

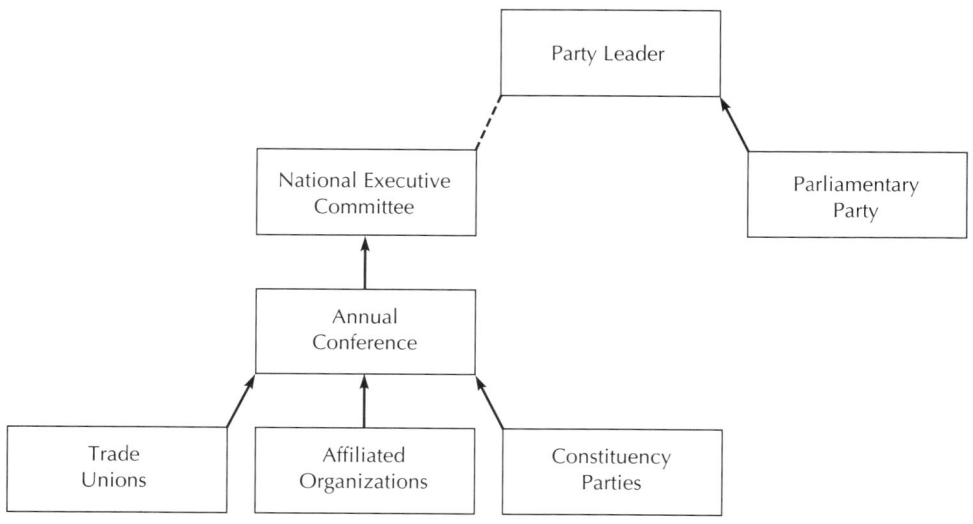

FIGURE 5.2 Organization of the Labour Party

As for conference resolutions, Attlee's position was:

> They are a guidance to the Parliamentary Party, not an absolute mandate. They couldn't be. You can't have a non-parliamentary body arranging things, saying, "You must do this. You mustn't do the other." What you do must depend on the circumstances. . . . You must always remember you are the Government of the country and act accordingly.[3]

Even when out of office Labour leaders have adopted this position, and although a two-thirds conference vote makes a resolution party policy, this does not mean that it will be included in the party manifesto at election time, and the manifesto carries much more weight than conference statements.

Moreover, for about 20 years after the war, the leadership was helped by the peculiar distribution of power in the Labour Party, particularly the remarkable weight assigned to the trade unions. As we saw in chapter 4, a few leaders of the biggest unions could hold up their voting cards, thereby executing a block vote which overwhelmed the votes of all the constituency representatives combined; and with twelve votes set aside for the unions on the N.E.C., plus other votes in their sway, they dominated that body, too. And usually the big unions sided with the parliamentary leadership.

But the power balance shifted dramatically when first in the 1960s and then in the 1970s some of the biggest unions moved to the left and sided with the majority of the constituency parties to challenge the parliamentary leadership.

The Rise of the Left

The party's left wing grew in strength throughout the 1970s, and became especially powerful after the defeat of James Callaghan's Labour government in 1979, which the left blamed on the government's failing to follow the party's socialist principles.

The several groups who joined in this attack on the party's leadership were dubbed the *outside left*, distinguishing them from (in soccer parlance) the other "forward line" positions—the more moderate *inside left* and their counterpart *inside* and *outside right*. Most of the media attention to the outside left was focused on the Revolutionary Socialist League or the Militant Tendency (after their newspaper, Militant). The Militants were followers of the late Russian Communist leader, Leon Trotsky, and since Trotsky had been exiled and then assassinated at Stalin's orders, they were no admirers of the subsequent Soviet regime. Yet their hostility to capitalism was no less deep than that of the Communist Party, and they were even more effective than the British Communists had ever been at the tactic of *entryism*—enlarging their influence beyond their very small numbers by infiltrating other organizations, including trade unions and the Labour Party. Their members had an almost cultlike commitment to the cause, including contributing most of their earnings and confining their social life to other members. Because they attended meetings faithfully and arrived earlier and stayed later than other people, they were able to gain a disproportionate number of leadership positions in the local party organizations and to be elected to some city councils in strong Labour areas.

The Militants were only one faction in the outside left, but they found willing allies in a number of more conventional radicals who were impressed with their energy and dedication. The combined efforts of the outside left forces brought them control of a few city councils and unions and even the sympathy of a minority of the party's M.P.s.

Among these sympathetic parliamentarians was Tony Benn—Anthony Wedgewood Benn, formerly Viscount Stansgate, who had succeeded in changing the law so that he could renounce his title and be elected to the House of Commons. He had served as a cabinet minister in the Labour governments of Harold Wilson and James Callaghan, but he had moved steadily to the left, and was now a hero of the constituency parties and the chief spokesperson for the outside left. Under Benn's leadership, the outside left succeeded in passing resolutions at the Annual Conferences in favor of more nationalization, withdrawal from the European Common Market, and unilateral renunciation of nuclear weapons. These positions were then written into the party's 1983 election manifesto.

At the same time left-wing leaders moved into key positions of power in the party. With support from some of the big unions, they won control of the National Executive Committee. In the name of "party democracy," they forced a change on the parliamentary candidate selection process by which every sitting member had to submit to readoption by the local constituency party before each election; this, the radicals believed, would make them more responsive to the volunteer activists than to the parliamentary leadership.

But there was still one more vital center of power to capture—that of the party leader.

Leadership Contests

Until 1981, the Labour Party leader was chosen by the Labour M.P.s. An absolute majority was required, so a first ballot lead was not necessarily enough to ensure victory. Thus when James Callaghan resigned as leader in 1980, Dennis Healey was well ahead on the first ballot, but when two others withdrew, Michael Foot won in a head-to-head race with Healey.

On the face of it, this was surprising. Although Foot was highly intelligent, a fine writer, and a stem-winding orator, he was almost 70, his health was frail, and his talents were better suited to opposition than leadership. He was not the first choice of the constituency parties or the unions, and a poll of Labour Party voters indicated a preference for Healey over Foot by 75 to 19 percent.

Yet the Parliamentary Party chose Foot, despite the fact that Healey was a man of considerable, if abrasive, leadership qualities and that his views were closer than Foot's to the majority of M.P.s. The reason was the ascendancy of the outside left in the party outside Parliament and the fear that if they chose Healey, from the right wing of the party, they would infuriate the left and might not be reselected by their constituency parties. Foot himself was an acceptable second choice for them, because he was seen as a member of the inside left rather than of the radicals, and because he had played a leading and responsible role in the Callaghan cabinet.

To the far left, Foot was certainly preferable to Healey. However, they were not satisfied. They wanted one of their own in the leadership. In particular, they wanted Tony Benn. But Benn was too far to the left ever to be elected as long as the choice was in the hands of the Parliamentary Party. So the choice had to be taken out of their hands, and the left succeeded in changing the selection procedure in 1981. Under the new rules an electoral college was created, with 40 percent of the vote going to the unions, 30 percent to the constituency parties, and only the remaining 30 percent to the M.P.s.

The first test of the new process came in the battle for Deputy leader of the party. Foot, eager to build bridges to the right, wanted Healey. The outside left wanted Benn. The result: Healey 50.426 percent, Benn 49.574. Just enough last-minute union votes had been secured for Healey to give him his hair-breadth victory.

Then in 1983, with the resignation of Foot—after he had led Labour to its humiliating defeat in the general election—came the first full test of the new system. This might have been a golden opportunity for the outside left, except for two factors. The first was Labour's lowest poll in any election since 1945, and it was fought on a far left manifesto that its critics defined as "the longest suicide note in history."

The second problem for the radical left was that while the new system was custom-made for Tony Benn, he was no longer eligible. Along with many other Labour M.P.s, he had lost his seat in the election. And even under the new system, the leader must still be a member of the House of Commons. The outside left had no other plausible candidate to put forward from their ranks. Once again they had to settle for someone from the inside left—Neil Kinnock.

The Decline of the Left

Soon it became clear that Kinnock, although personally well to the left on, for example, unilateral nuclear disarmament, wanted to wrest the party back from far left control. In its present condition, he concluded, the party was unelectable. Its policies were too far removed from the views of the great majority of voters. The takeover of the party machinery by the left had resulted in the departure of a number of Labour M.P.s, who joined a new Social Democratic Party headed by four former Labour cabinet members. That party had combined with the Liberals and fought the 1983 election as the *Alliance*, and it had come close to forcing Labour into third place.

So by the time Kinnock became leader, sentiment among the unions and the constituency parties was shifting away from the radicals. Reaching out to the right, Kinnock secured the election of Roy Hattersley as his deputy leader. The National Executive Committee majority shifted from the outside to the inside left. The N.E.C. undertook expulsion proceedings against some Militants, on the grounds that they were members of another party (and the Labour party constitution forbade dual party membership).

At the 1985 Annual Conference, Kinnock delivered a brilliant, scathing attack on the left. He was booed by a large section of the delegates and defeated on some key votes. But he also received rapturous applause from the floor and enthusiastic comments from around the country, and it was clear that his speech had made him a national figure with a dominant position in his party.

After that, Kinnock launched a series of reviews of party policies. The 1987 manifesto, though still to the left on nuclear policies, was considerably more moderate than the 1983 document. When Labour was defeated again, the move away from left-wing doctrine became still more pronounced. Unilateral nuclear disarmament was dropped. The party became pro-European Community. A mixed economy rather than all-encompassing socialism was seen as inevitable, and although Clause 4 remained in the party's constitution, there would be no new proposals for nationalization, not even for the renationalization of most of the industries Thatcher had privatized.

There was intense resentment on the left, and even from some moderates, at what they saw as Kinnock's heavy-handed, highly centralized decision-making process. But the result was the achievement of relative harmony in the party, and the uproar at the 1985 Annual Conference was not repeated in subsequent years. Although the leadership still suffered occasional defeats from the floor, Kinnock took the Attlee view that these would not necessarily be binding on a future Labour government.

All this was intended to make Labour look like a party of government with Kinnock as a potential prime minister. Indeed, the opinion polls before the 1992 election made it appear likely that Labour would win the largest number of seats and be able to govern either alone or in combination with the Liberals. But Kinnock, having taken his party to the borders of the promised land, was denied the chance to lead them in. There were many reasons for Labour's defeat in 1992; among them was the perception that Kinnock, despite his remarkable success as a party leader, did not have the qualities needed in a prime minister.

With the election over, Kinnock abruptly resigned the leadership, and Labour's electoral college, created to place the leadership in far left hands, elected on the first ballot by an overwhelming majority a man from the right of the party, John Smith. The flirtation of the unions and the constituency parties with the farthest left elements in the party was over. Now there was one overwhelming preoccupation: Conservative rule must be ended, and no internal party impediments must be placed in the way of Labour's coming back to power.

Any doubts on this score were ended when John Smith suddenly died of a heart attack in May 1994. Two months later the party's electoral college chose as Leader another proponent of "modernizing" the party and its programs, 41-year-old Tony Blair. Here was a public school and Oxford product whose positions could appeal to the middle class as well as the young (he had sung and played guitar in a band called *Ugly Rumors* while at Oxford) and who was articulate and highly telegenic.

Blair was elected by much broader constituencies than had been involved under Tony Benn's "party democracy" rules, which had placed power in the local parties in the hands of the activists elected to the management committees. John Smith

Tony Blair
SOURCE: Chris Davies Photography.

had pushed through at the 1993 conference a new "one person, one vote" process, which gave individual members of constituency parties and unions a voice in the process. Moreover, the voting balance for selecting the party leader in Labour's electoral college had been adjusted: Instead of 40 percent for the unions and 30 percent each for the constituency parties and the parliamentary group (M.P.s and Members of the European Parliament), each of the three segments was henceforth assigned one-third of the total vote. Under this new system Blair received clear majorities over two rivals in all three sections.

Blair moved ahead remorselessly with the effort to move the Labour party toward the center, and the issue he chose to symbolize the change from the past was the rewriting of Clause 4 of the party's constitution—the nationalization clause. Once before, a Labour Party leader—Hugh Gaitskell in the 1950s—had tried to repeal Clause 4, but was forced by outraged party members to drop the proposal. John Smith, fearing another bitter struggle, had been reluctant to reopen the question. But Blair, arguing that the great majority of voters now had no interest in nationalizing most of "the means of production, distribution, and exchange," called for a special party conference to redraft the clause.

After an intensive campaign on behalf of the change, Blair prevailed, receiving 65 percent of the votes at the conference, despite the opposition of the two biggest unions, UNICON and the T.G.W.U. Clause 4 was expunged from the constitution and replaced by more general language, including the commitment to "a community in which power, wealth and opportunity are in the hands of the many not the few," as well as to "a dynamic economy, serving the public interest, in which the enterprise of the market and the rigour of competition are joined with the forces of partnership and cooperation. . . ."

Now, with his party well ahead in the polls and apparently well positioned for the next election, Blar pressed for unity among his associates. This would be more feasible than in the past, for since Kinnock's time power had shifted back to the Parliamentary Party and the party's leader, and the N.E.C. was now controlled by "modernizers." Even so, ending factional struggles within the Labour Party, tantalized though they might be by the lure of coming back to power, could never be an easy task. Any large party is a coalition of many contending forces, and the Labour Party is an even broader coalition than the Conservative Party, bringing together unions (which themselves speak for many different kinds of trades and professions) with intellectuals (journalists and university teachers, among others) as well as rank and file members of various persuasions. And under recent reforms of the party's procedures, all of these elements must be taken into account in an elaborate policy-shaping process beginning with the preparation of proposals by the parliamentary leadership, followed by review and debate first in six policy commissions, then in the N.E.C., then in a 100-member policy forum, and finally in the annual party conference. So the party's leaders will always have a difficult time holding the disparate elements together.

Thus the unions had only reluctantly accepted the weakening of their block vote at the Annual Conference and the reduction of their share of the electoral college vote from 40 percent to one-third, and most of them had strenuously opposed John Smith's narrowly approved proposal to reduce the power of the unions in the selection of parliamentary candidates. Although the T.U.C.'s new general secretary, John Monks, was a "modernizer" like Blair, eager to find new, less confrontational roles for British unions, Blair could hardly avoid tensions with other union leaders. And although Blair aimed to make the Labour Party less obviously the party of the unions, this would be difficult to reconcile with the fact that it was the unions that provided the party with most of its money and organizational backing.

As for the left, they persisted in their argument that Labour had lost the last election not because it was insufficiently moderate, but because it was insufficiently socialist. The left complained bitterly that Blair and his supporters were overly impressed with Bill Clinton's victory in 1992 as a possible model for Labour to emulate, too obsessed with polls, images, and soundbites to the neglect of policies, and so eager to avoid offending anyone that they were ignoring the British people's readiness to put an end to Thatcherism. Even if, like Clinton, Labour were to win an election, its policies in office would quickly be revealed as bankrupt, and—like Clinton's party—Labour would soon be forced again into ignominious defeat.

The repeal of Clause 4 was bitterly resented by the left. Though its full implementation had never been a practical possibility, the left held onto it as a statement of principle, a familiar expression of a deeply felt socialist faith. The left was not reassured by vague undertakings in the new clause to shift power from the few to the many and was furious that an acceptance of the "enterprise of the market" was now enshrined in the Labour Party's constitution.

Still, for the time being at least, the left's position in the Labour Party was marginalized. Many of the party's rank-and-file members who would have preferred to keep the old Clause 4 voted to accept Blair's argument that "the reason we have been out of power for 15 years is simple—society has changed and we refused to change with it." Now it seemed that the party was ready to change, and every effort would be made to keep any remaining disagreements from hurting the party's prospects as the next election grew nearer.

So after 1992, a role reversal had taken place between the parties, and it was the Conservatives, previously polite and decorous in their public behavior, who had become the more openly divided of the two.

THE LIBERAL DEMOCRATS

We have focused on the Conservatives and Labour in this chapter—even though, as we have noted, there are several other parties in Britain—because the context of this section of the book is party government, and these are the only two parties to have participated in governments since 1945. However, if we expand our scope to the entire period of the modern party system we must take note of the fact that one other contemporary party can lay claim to a most distinguished history. This is the Liberal Democratic Party in its former incarnation as the Liberal Party.

Since the middle of the nineteenth century, the Liberals had provided the main alternative to the Conservatives as a party of government, drawing their strength largely from a combination of industrialists and the newly enfranchised working class. Unfortunately for them, early in the twentieth century, the workers began to move to Labour, the industrialists to the Conservative Party. The Liberals were left without a solid class or geographic base, and by the 1930s the big party bias of the voting system left them constantly underrepresented in Parliament.

In the post–World War II era, the Liberal vote rose and fell with the extent of dissatisfaction with the two main parties. Even when it rose to 19.3 percent in the first 1974 election, the product in Parliament was 14 seats, 2.2 percent of the total. In most years they did quite well in local council elections, but this did not translate into success in national elections.

Periodically, a Liberal would achieve a sensational victory in a by-election to fill a parliamentary vacancy resulting from the death, retirement, or elevation to the peerage of a sitting M.P. But by-elections gave voters a chance between general elections to vent their hostility to current government policies without actually forcing the government out, and when the next election came along, the regular party patterns were resumed and the unfortunate Liberal victor decisively rejected.

Programmatically the Liberals, as the center party, would appear to benefit from the tendency of the electoral majority to congregate around the political middle ground. The Liberals were closer to the Conservatives in their support for competitive enterprise and their criticisms of union power, but closer to Labour on policies toward the welfare state. However, the big parties in most years also gravitated toward the center as elections approached; and the Liberals in their annual conferences displayed internal divisions that strengthened the general impression that this was not a party ready for power.

Despite these disadvantages, Liberal hopes sprang anew when the Labour Party split in 1981, and the Social Democratic Party (SDP) was formed with an enormous burst of publicity and an immediate strong standing in the opinion polls. The Liberals met with the SDP leaders, and the Alliance was born to fight the 1983 election jointly, each party agreeing to support the other's candidates after dividing up the seats between them. One poll showed the Alliance in the lead with over 40 percent support, and with unemployment at its highest level since the 1930s and the Labour party in the grip of the radical left, the Alliance approached the election with high optimism.

They did considerably better than the Liberals had done since 1945, but they had already passed their peak, and their 25.4 percent of the vote fell just short of overtaking Labour for second place, yielding them only 23 seats in Parliament. The Alliance tried again in 1987, but they slipped a little further to 22.6 percent.

One cause of their weakness was the attempt to fight an election with two parties and two leaders and somewhat different programmatic emphases. A proposal to merge into a single party was approved by majorities of both parties; however, there were unhappy minorities in both, and the SDP leader, David Owen, refused to participate, and persisted with a small separate SDP until its dissolution after the next election.

The new party, which finally settled on the name *Liberal Democrat*, elected Paddy Ashdown as its leader by a procedure more democratic than the other two parties: a vote of all the party members. Initially the party's poll standing, following the prolonged public display of bitter dissensions, collapsed into single digits; a gradual recovery brought them back to a respectable showing in the 1992 election; and subsequently they began again to do well in local elections and score remarkable by-election upsets against the troubled Conservative government.

Some observers believed that this time would be different, and the upsurge would be sustained into the next general election. But others held to the view that the only real hope for the party's future lay in its proposals for constitutional reform and particularly for a change in the voting system to proportional representation. If this could be achieved, two-party dominance would be ended and the entire structure of party government in Britain would be transformed. Under what conditions this could occur is a subject to which we shall return in the next chapter.

CONCLUSION

The fact that Britain has a mainly two-party system is only slightly less remarkable than the fact that the same is true of the United States. In the United States we divide the concerns of over 250 million people into just two categories, Republican and Democratic. Inevitably this means that both must be broad, somewhat incoherent coalitions of diverse, sometimes conflicting beliefs and interests.

Even in Britain's smaller population, trying to crowd most of the voters into two parties leads to deep tensions in each. The disparities within the British parties are not as great as in the U.S. system, especially in the Democratic Party. Even so, it is hardly surprising that periodically Labour erupts into internecine warfare, and that from time to time there are cracks in the Conservative facade of polite unity.

One consequence of proportional representation might be not only to strengthen the representation of the Liberal Democrats, but also to replace some of the existing party factions with viable new parties, thereby reducing the internal tensions within the presently dominant two parties. However, this would not necessarily reduce the degree of conflict within the system as a whole, as the experience of multiparty systems in other countries makes all too clear.

SOME QUESTIONS TO THINK ABOUT

Are the differences between the two main parties greater in Britain than in the United States? If so, why?

Would the United States be better served by more coherent, better organized parties, as exist in Britain?

How do British and U.S. parties compare with respect to their internal conflicts?

How much should British governments be influenced by party resolutions?

What do you think of the processes by which the Conservative and Labour parties choose their leaders?

Why was Margaret Thatcher ousted?

Would the British be better off with a multiparty system?

NOTES

1. Richard Rose, *Do Parties Make a Difference?*, 2d ed. (Chatham House, 1984).
2. Attlee to Harold Laski, 20 August 1945, cited in Francis Williams, *Twilight of Empire: Memoirs of Prime Minister Clement Attlee* (A. S. Barnes, 1960), p. 169.
3. Ibid., p. 91.

SUGGESTIONS FOR FURTHER READING

On the party system in general, see Robert Garner and Richard Kelly, *British Political Parties Today* (St. Martin's Press, 1992).

On the differences between the parties, Dennis Kavanagh in *Thatcherism and British Politics: The End of Consensus?* (Oxford University Press, 1987) agrees with Richard Rose's argument (see Notes) that differences between the Conservative and Labour parties were fairly narrow from 1945 to 1979—but he disagrees with Rose about the extent of the differences after 1979.

On the internal politics of the Labour party, see Dennis Kavanagh (ed.), *The Politics of the Labour Party* (George Allen and Unwin, 1982), and Eric Shaw, *Discipline and Discord in the Labour Party* (Manchester University Press, 1988), and *The Labour Party Since 1979: Crisis and Transformation* (Routledge, 1994). On the outside left effort to take over the party after 1979 see David Kogan and Maurice Kogan, *The Battle for the Labour Party* (Fontana, 1982) and Michael Crick, *The March of Militant* (Faber and Faber, 1986). On the Conservative party, see A. Seldon and S. Ball (eds.), *The Conservative Party in the Twen-*

tieth Century (Oxford University Press, 1994), Zig Layton-Henry (ed.), *Conservative Party Politics* (Macmillan, 1980), Robert Shepherd, *The Power Brokers* (Hutchinson, 1991), and Paul Whiteley, Patrick Seyd, and Jeremy Richardson, *True Blues: The Politics of Conservative Membership* (Oxford University Press, 1994). On Thatcher and the Conservative party see John Ranelagh, *Thatcher's People* (HarperCollins, 1991), Alan Watkins, *A Conservative Coup* (Duckworth, 1992), and three important articles: Ivor Crewe and Donald D. Searing, "Ideological Change in the British Conservative Party" (*American Political Science Review*, vol. 82., no. 2, June 1988), pp. 361-384; Philip Norton, "'The Lady's Not for Turning' But What About the Rest? Margaret Thatcher and the Conservative Party 1979-89" (*Parliamentary Affairs*, January 1990, vol. 43, no. 1), and "Choosing a Leader: Margaret Thatcher and the Parliamentary Conservative Party 1989-90" (*Parliamentary Affairs*, vol. 43, no. 3, July 1990). On the Liberal Party and its successors, see J. Stevenson, *Third Party Politics Since 1945: Liberals, Alliance and Liberal Democrats* (Blackwell, 1993) and Jeremy Josephs, *Inside the Alliance* (John Martin, 1983).

6
ELECTIONS IN THE TELEVISION ERA

An American visiting Britain during a general election campaign would find a number of differences from how campaigns are conducted back home. Yet most of these differences are matters of procedure, and once the visitor had become accustomed to the different procedures, he or she would find the general style and techniques of British campaigns remarkably reminiscent of elections in the United States. Let us look first at the differences.

DIFFERENCES BETWEEN BRITISH AND U.S. ELECTIONS

Brevity

When a government calls an election, Parliament is dissolved, and a polling date is named—usually about a month after the announcement. Counting back from the date set for the election, three weeks are allowed for campaigning, and no money may be spent on the campaign before the three weeks begin.

In a real sense, of course, the campaign for the next election in Britain begins the day after the last one, and debates and Question Times in the House of Commons, along with political speeches and interviews, are intended and interpreted as influences on the next election.

Still, the mere three weeks of actual campaigning—though perhaps interminable to many members of the public—stand in merciful contrast to presidential election campaigns in the United States, which typically last at least one and often two years. (C-SPAN began its "Road to the White House, 1996" coverage early in the spring of 1993.)

No Primaries. However, the main difference in length between British and U.S. elections is not in the final confrontation between the two parties. In the United States, this does not really begin until its traditional launch on Labor Day, which allows two months of campaigning. Given the size and diversity of the United States, the difference between two months and three weeks does not seem disproportionate.

It is the nomination process, and especially the primary system, that makes for the seemingly unending spectacle of politicians appealing to U.S. voters for support. In Britain, as in most other democratic countries, the nomination of candidates is handled within the party organizations, and the voting is limited to those who join the party and pay their dues.

When Tony Benn and the Labour left proposed to change the method of choosing candidates and party leaders under the banner of "party democracy," their purpose was to shift the power from members of Parliament to the unions and to the activists who dominated the selection committees in the constituencies. When their opponents suggested that true party democracy would mean a mail ballot from all the paid-up members of the local parties, the left responded that it was reasonable to leave the responsibility in the hands of people who really cared about exercising their citizenship responsibilities, rather than with those who did little more than pay their party dues. But whatever the merits of the argument, a mail ballot would bypass the authority of the left's strongholds—the committees that ran the local parties. (Occasionally in this debate the word *primary* would be introduced, but there is no serious support in Britain for this manifestation of direct democracy. In fact, to British students of U.S. government, party primaries are difficult to reconcile with the clear intention of those who framed the U.S. constitution to create a representative rather than a direct democracy.)

No Paid TV or Radio Commercials

The British are not bombarded with 30- and 60-second political commercials during campaigns because viewing and listening time is not purchased for political purposes even on the commercial channels.

Instead, airtime is provided free for "party political broadcasts," which run usually for 5 to 10 minutes. Labour and the Conservatives are given an equal number, the Liberal Democrats somewhat less. Smaller parties receive one broadcast apiece if they put up a sufficient number of candidates around the country. Thus in 1987, free airtime was provided to the Ecology Party, the far left Socialist Workers, and the neofascist National Front; and in 1992 the voters watched representatives of the Natural Law Party explain their manifesto promise to "create Heaven on Earth in the nation," followed by a rather unimpressive display of levitation.

Less Campaign Spending

Candidates for Parliament are by law strictly limited in the amount of money they can spend, typically around $10,000—an amount that would hardly cover the costs of staff lunches in a campaign for Congress. Local campaigning consists mostly of door-to-door canvassing of voters, a technique easier to employ in Britain's smaller and more compact constituencies than in the United States.

However, these limits on individial candidates do not apply to the parties at the national level. They can spend as much as they can raise, and they need substantial sums to run effective campaigns. Television time is free, but the production costs of the party political broadcasts are considerable. And if paid advertising is banned from TV and radio, it is heavily employed in full-page newspaper ads and billboards, such as those shown in Figure 6.1.

Then there are campaign staffs to be paid for and the expenses for travel by plane, train, and special buses. Altogether in 1992 the three biggest parties reported national outlays in the neighborhood of $30 million: about $15 million by the Conservatives, $11 million by Labour, $3 million by the Liberal Democrats.

These sums are much smaller than are lavished on American presidential campaigns. In 1992 Bush and Clinton each received $55 million in federal funds, and with monies raised by their parties and other supporters, the totals reported came to $180 million for Bush and $156 million for Clinton, along with $69 million for Perot. But if British campaigns cost less than their American counterparts, parties in Britain still find fundraising a difficult assignment.

Labour, with considerably fewer individual members than the Conservatives, must go cap in hand to the unions, whose own resources have shrunk considerably since 1980. The Conservatives' advantage in individual memberships has been eroding in recent years as the numbers joining the local parties has declined. So they have had to rely more on contributions from business and wealthy individuals. Some of the contributions come from abroad. Thus in 1991 a Greek shipping magnate gave the Conservatives over £2 million and there have been other large donations from Hong Kong. In 1992 the Conservatives conceded that they had received over £400,000 from Mr. Asil Nadir, a businessman who had fled the country after jumping bail on charges of theft from his bankrupt company.[1]

Even with contributions from abroad, the Conservatives have fallen on hard times. Campaign outlays and declining contributions from British firms left them with a deficit of £20 million after the 1992 election, and they were forced into severe spending cuts.

The dependence on business and union funds, and the lack of legal requirements for reporting of campaign contributions, have led to proposals for reform. Every other European country provides a measure of state funding for elections and closer accounting of campaign contributions and expenditures than is the case in Britain. A Labour government under Tony Blair might well introduce government funding of elections, for this would make the party much less dependent on the unions. However, John Major's Conservative government opposed the reform of campaign finances, and in 1994, a Labour proposal to ban donations from foreign firms

FIGURE 6.1 Conservative and Labour newspaper ads, 1992

SOURCE: Labour Party ad courtesy of the Labour Party. Conservative Party ad courtesy of Saatchi & Saatchi Advertising.

and individuals was voted down by the Conservative majority on a parliamentary committee.

No Debates

There have not been any face-to-face debates between the candidates for prime minister similar to those between U.S. presidential candidates. Serious consideration was given in 1983 to the possibility of a debate, but Thatcher was so far ahead that her campaign staff advised against it (although Thatcher would almost certainly have more than held her own against Michael Foot).

However, the candidates in Britain have already faced each other in a number of debates in Parliament, which have been televised since 1989. During the election campaign itself, the party leaders are subjected to several searching TV and radio interviews. Viewer call-in programs to the leaders, sometimes with the viewers on camera, have also been a feature of British campaigns well before they became a part of the U.S. election scene. On one such program in 1987 Margaret Thatcher was sharply challenged by a caller, and Thatcher, who tended to treat questions from professional interviewers rather abruptly, was obviously thrown off balance by having to respond with restraint to an ordinary voter.

A Larger Role for the Press

Although television is the most important source of news for Britons as for Americans, newspapers play a more prominent part in elections in Britain than in the United States. For one thing, the British are more avid newspaper readers than Americans. For another, all the leading British papers have national circulations, in contrast to the United States where newspapers, with the exception of *USA Today* and *Wall Street Journal*, serve primarily local markets.

The "quality" press—the *Times*, the *Guardian*, the *Daily Telegraph*, the *Independent*, the *Financial Times*, and on Sunday the *Sunday Times*, the *Sunday Telegraph*, the *Independent on Sunday*, and the *Observer*—provide thorough coverage of the campaigns. The *Times*, the *Telegraph*, and their Sunday counterparts support the Conservative Party; the *Guardian* and the *Observer* are anti-Tory, and the *Independent* tries to live up to its name. But all provide reasonably fair coverage, and the *Financial Times*, which is more or less the counterpart of the *Wall Street Journal*, actually endorsed Labour in 1992.

But fairness is not an attribute of the tabloid press. All except the *Daily Mirror* and the *Star* endorse the Conservatives at election time. And all, including the *Mirror* and *Star*, do not work very hard at sustaining a fundamental ethic of journalism: separating news from comment. As polling day approaches, political news, usually relegated to inside pages, finds its way onto the front page under blaring headlines. Sometimes the front page story indicates that this is presented as "comment" or "opinion," sometimes not.

On April 25, 1979, the Conservative Central Office sent out a press release under the heading "LABOUR'S LIES," followed by a list of twelve alleged Labour lies.

On April 26, the front page of the *Daily Mail* was completely taken up by a list of "12 big lies they hope will save them," under the banner headline:

LABOUR'S DIRTY DOZEN

There was no suggestion that the alleged lies were offered as commentary or interpretation. On the contrary, said the *Daily Mail*: "All are presented as facts."

On the same day the Labour-supporting *Daily Mirror*'s front page presented a picture of Mrs. Thatcher surrounded by large headlines proclaiming:

I'M GOING TO SPEND, SPEND, SPEND
(but who will pay the Bill, Maggie?)

(However, in this case there was the saving clause: "Page One Comment.")

In the 1992 campaign, the *Sun* did use the phrase "Page One Opinion," but its opinions were presented in its characteristic sensational style. The day before the election its headline was:

NIGHTMARE ON KINNOCK STREET

This was followed by eight pages warning of the "disasters" that would follow a Labour victory, such as the control of local building permits by lesbians and gays on left-wing local councils. The paper's psychic also revealed that in 1987, Stalin had told her that Mao and Trotsky would have voted Labour while Queen Victoria and Elvis Presley would have gone for the Conservatives. On election day itself the *Sun*'s front page showed Kinnock's head inside a light bulb, and the headline asked:

IF KINNOCK WINS TODAY WILL THE LAST PERSON IN BRITAIN
PLEASE TURN OUT THE LIGHTS

Apparently, if Kinnock won, everyone would be heading for the airport. Meantime, the *Daily Mirror* was declaring:

IT'S TIME FOR A CHANGE: 13 Tory years . . .
NOW look at Britain's misery

The *Star* avoided an endorsement and told its readers:

IT'S UP TO YOU

This did not prevent it from warning that a Labour victory would bring a huge increase in the price of football tickets, or from depicting Kinnock as Dracula rising from the tomb.

After the election, the *Sun* congratulated itself on the Conservative victory:

IT'S THE *SUN* WOT WON IT.

THE AMERICANIZATION OF BRITISH ELECTIONS

Evidently there are several aspects of British elections that a visitor from the United States would find surprising. Yet there are other, perhaps more fundamental aspects, that the U.S. visitor would find very familiar. These are characteristics resulting from the application of public relations and advertising techniques to political campaigns, especially through the medium of television.

These techniques are now used in campaigns everywhere, and today ideas flow in both directions across the Atlantic: Witness the British Conservative Party consultants invited to the United States in 1992 to advise the Bush campaign on how John Major had won his election. Yet the basic inventions in this field were pioneered in the United States. Though television was used in the British general election of 1955, it did not become a central feature of elections until Harold Macmillan's successful campaign in 1959. Seven years earlier, the Republicans had used television to build upon the enormous popularity of Dwight Eisenhower. ("To think an old soldier should come to this," Eisenhower complained after filming a campaign commercial.) So it was the United States that set the pace in this area and U.S. techniques that were adapted to the idioms and styles of Britain and other countries.

Television and the Projection of Personality

Despite its claims, it probably was not "the *Sun* wot won it" in 1992. The effect of the ceaseless pounding of Kinnock and the Labour Party by the tabloids almost certainly hurt the Labour cause. Yet the majority of Britons, like Americans, get their news primarily from television rather than newspapers.

Ever since the successful Macmillan campaign of 1957, it has been apparent that to be effective, party leaders must know how to project themselves and their ideas over television. This made it all the more surprising that Macmillan himself proposed Lord Home as his successor, for an election was due within a year, and Home, though an able and intelligent foreign secretary, was an embarrassingly bad speaker in person and even worse on TV. To make his final 15-minute broadcast before election day in 1963, it was necessary for him to spend most of two full days taping the program in 2-minute segments. Not surprisingly he came across as unconvincing and uncomfortable with the medium.

By contrast his Labour opponent, Harold Wilson, was a very effective performer. Although his opening appearance suffered from poor lighting and makeup (reminiscent of Richard Nixon in the first debate with Kennedy in 1960), he learned quickly, made all his subsequent programs in a properly lighted studio, and took his own makeup man with him. Although he preferred cigars to a pipe, he knew that cigars created the wrong image and worked successfully at projecting his competent, relaxed, pipe-smoking persona.

Wilson's successor, James Callaghan, was another effective television performer, conveying an aura of an experienced, trusted, avuncular leader. Margaret Thatcher, on the other hand, had to be taken in hand by the campaign professionals to broaden her appeal from constituency party activists to the electorate as a whole. Accordingly her hair and dress styles were changed to create a softer impression and the pitch of her voice lowered to make it less shrill.

These changes were entrusted to Gordon Reece, a public relations specialist who had moved to California but was called back to London whenever an election was imminent. He worked with Saatchi and Saatchi, the British advertising agency that went on to become one of the biggest agencies on Madison Avenue. Their task in 1983 was an easy one, for Thatcher, now the tested and decisive leader, was challenged by Michael Foot, who despite his impressive and appealing personal qualities looked old and frail, was hopelessly inept in the role of campaign leader, and progressed throughout the election period from one disaster to another.

The head of the Labour Party's staff tried to make a virtue out of the way they had conducted the campaign. The Conservative Party, he declared, had appointed as their chief campaign professional a man who had been in charge of advertising for Mars, a candy manufacturer, and who made no bones about the applicability of commercial selling to political campaigns. *Our* party would never demean itself by trying to sell candidates like candy bars, said the Labour man.

This was almost exactly what Democratic candidate Adlai Stevenson had said after his defeat by Eisenhower in 1952. Democracy, he argued, was devalued if political candidates were to be sold like breakfast cereal. Yet in 1956, to the disillusionment of some of the Stevenson supporters, the Democrats were aggressively resorting to the kind of techniques Stevenson inveighed against earlier.

Similarly in Britain, the Labour Party in 1987 enthusiastically embraced the methods they had so high-mindedly rejected in 1983. Foot had been replaced by a new, young, vigorous leader, Neil Kinnock. For his opening party political broadcast his campaign hired the maker of the hit movie, *Chariots of Fire*. The program opened with a seagull swooping over a cliff, and Neil and his wife Glenys walking hand in hand to the soaring strains of Brahms. Then Kinnock reminisced about his parents who had worked hard to give him his start in life. Next he was shown at a conference asking why he was the first Kinnock in a thousand generations to go to a university (Senator Joseph Biden's presidential bid in 1988 was aborted when he was found to have plagiarized Kinnock's line.) This was followed by a clip of him denouncing the outside left at Labour's 1985 annual conference. After testimonials to the young leader from the party's elders came the closing caption: "KINNOCK." The program was immediately acclaimed as a masterpiece of political communication and it sent shock waves through the Thatcher entourage.

The focus on Kinnock himself was a manifestation of the tendency of British elections to become more and more like U.S. presidential races, featuring a contest between prime ministerial candidates rather than between parties. The British have not adopted the U.S. practice of setting up personal campaign organizations outside of the party structures, so British parties are still directly responsible for running the campaigns. Nevertheless, the personalization of the campaigns has proceeded apace. As seen in Figure 6.2, the cover of the 1987 manifesto was given over to a photo of Kinnock, and the Conservatives followed suit in their 1992 manifesto, with a photo of John Major on the cover. (Similarly, Paddy Ashdown, the Liberal Democrats' leader, was featured on the party's 1992 manifesto cover.) However, in 1992, the photo of

FIGURE 6.2 Manifesto covers: Neil Kinnock in 1987, John Major in 1992

SOURCE: Labour manifesto cover courtesy of the Labour Party; Conservative manifesto cover courtesy of the Conservative Research Department.

Kinnock appeared on page three, perhaps because Kinnock was no longer seen as Labour's prime electoral asset.

Trivializing the Issues

This preoccupation with the candidates, the candidates' looks, and the candidates' families is only one aspect of the tendency of campaigns to become bogged down in secondary matters at the expense of serious discussion of the issues.

Consider the furor that erupted over one of the Labour Party broadcasts in 1992. The subject of the broadcast was serious enough—the alleged deterioration of the National Health Service under the Conservative government. Two cases were chosen to illustrate the problem: Two young girls needing an ear operation, one getting it quickly because her parents were able to pay for private care, the other—Jennifer—suffering a long delay under the nationalized service. The program made a skillful emotional rather than rational appeal, but this could be justified as presenting a complex problem in human terms. However, the argument that followed over "Jennifer's ear" was concerned not with the issue of health care but with the question of whether or not Jennifer's parents had given their consent for the program (the mother had, but the father had not) and who had made Jennifer's name public (she was not identified in the program). And it was these peripheral matters that fascinated the media for several days after the program's appearance, distracting the voters from the central issues on which they had to decide.

The Polls

The British media are no less obsessed than the U.S. media with opinion poll findings during elections. Most of the newspapers, the television channels, and the parties have their separate surveys.

Polls have played a part in campaigns since 1964, but since 1979 they have become increasingly so central to media reporting that they crowd out much of the content of the campaigns, injecting a "horse race" mentality into the reporting. Thus in the 1992 campaign coverage on TV and radio: "Next to policies and personalities the most frequent theme in the news was the horse race. This took up more time than anything except the economy and the taxation issue."[2]

As polling day approaches, in fact, the clamorous newspaper headlines appear to reduce the contest to a battle of the polls rather than of parties and candidates. The polls battle because much of the time their results disagree. Thus there is fierce competition to see which of them comes closest to the final result (despite their disclaimers that polls are not intended to predict, only to provide a current snapshot of opinion).

Dismay was rampant throughout the industry in 1992 when *none* of the late polls, taken within a few days of the actual voting, indicated that the Conservatives were likely to win by a substantial margin. Gallup showed the Conservatives ahead, but only by 0.5 percent, compared with their actual final lead of 7.6 percent. A composite of the four polls published on election day itself showed a Labour lead of 0.9 percent.[3] The exit polls, taken for television news after voters had actually cast their ballots, were closer to the mark, indicating a 4 percent Conservative lead. But the TV newscasters and analysts were so impressed with their earlier opinion polls that it was some time before their reporting revealed what was really happening.

What accounted for the polling errors? According to a postmortem analysis by the Market Research Society in 1994, there was a last-minute swing to the Tories; then there were a number of "shy Tories"—"don't knows" or "won't says" who were really Conservatives all along; and some of the polls were guilty of sampling errors, such as overestimating the proportion of council tenants in the total population. Yet much of this was speculation, and there was no assurance that, even if these factors were compensated for in future polling, other sources of error might not creep in.

Despite these sobering thoughts, the polls, which were closer to the mark in most previous elections, have become so embedded in political calculations that politicians, journalists, and academicians will continue to exhaust the findings of opinion surveys, and it is too much to hope that future election coverage will be any less obsessed with the polls than in the past.

IN DEFENSE OF BRITISH ELECTIONS

The account given here leaves the conduct of election campaigns in Britain open to the same charge leveled at elections in the United States: The emphasis on personality and the polls crowds out the real policy issues, and that when the issues are discussed, they are trivialized, sloganized, oversimplified, and distorted.

Indeed, British elections clearly fall far short of the democratic ideal of a rational exploration of public policies. However, it is still possible to make the case that British election campaigns serve democratic ends, albeit in a somewhat crude fashion.

Manifestos Matter

Despite the increasingly glossy formats and the focus on the party leaders, manifestos still deal mostly with the presentation of policy issues. By and large they make the differences between the parties clear; and, as we indicated earlier, their proposals reflect at least in a general way what the parties do when they are in power.

Communication Skills Are Relevant

In criticizing the excessive emphasis on media personality, we should not ignore the fact that the ability to communicate effectively over television is an essential attribute of contemporary leadership, one that voters should properly consider as they choose not only a party but a prime minister. Moreover, repeated exposure over television provides revealing insights into the character and qualities of the candidates.

Thus if Sir Alec Douglas-Home came across on television as aloof and lacking in the common touch this was because his life experience was, in fact, remote from that of ordinary voters. He was an aristocrat, selected for his job undemocratically, and, notwithstanding his considerable abilities, unsuited to the job of top democratic leadership.

Labour's Michael Foot also failed to project himself as a decisive leader; but this was because, in fact, he was not decisive and was long past his prime. As the late left-wing M.P. Eric Heffer put it: "Michael Foot . . . should never have been leader. He ought to have continued doing what he did best, making good speeches in the House and in the country, writing and lecturing on people like Paine and Hazlitt and reviewing books."[4]

In 1992, John Major hardly came across as a charismatic figure. On the other hand, he was likeable and low-key, and this was regarded by the electorate as a desirable contrast to the abrasiveness that had finally made Thatcher so unpopular. So in personal terms he had the advantage over Kinnock who, despite a strong effort to take on the *gravitas* required of statesmen, was still widely perceived as too garrulous and not sufficiently solid. This perception of Kinnock may have been heavily influenced by the prolonged abuse he received from the tabloids. Yet it was not an impression gleaned during three weeks of an election campaign, and the public had ample opportunity to judge his qualities in almost nine years as Labour's leader.

Leadership Preferences Are Not Necessarily Decisive

Skillful media performance, though important, is far from being the sole determinant of election outcomes. Edward Heath won in 1970 despite the fact that his style was stiff and cerebral; despite the fact that he was a yachtsman and classical organist (not hobbies of the masses); and despite the fact that he could not be pictured with wife and children, for he was a bachelor.

When Margaret Thatcher won in 1979 it was not because of her new coiffure or better-modulated voice, for, despite these improvements, polls indicated that in personal terms Callaghan was preferred to Thatcher by 44 to 25 percent. In fact, the Liberal leader, David Steel, was preferred to both of them; and Steel was one of a succession of Liberal leaders who scored very high in media terms but still came in a poor third on election day.

Television News Is Important and Balanced

TV coverage of British elections does not consist only of party political broadcasts and the staged scenes carefully contrived by the campaign managers to appear on the evening news. Television also provides substantial coverage of the campaign issues. Both sides usually complain that the coverage is biased against them, but independent researchers find these complaints are mostly unjustified. And because the majority get their news from television rather than the newspapers, TV acts as a useful corrective to the blatant biases of the tabloids.

Campaigns Rarely Decide

If the candidates' carefully constructed TV personalities and communication skills are not the primary influences on election outcomes, nor in most cases are any other aspects of the campaigns.

The evidence suggests that most voters make up their minds before the campaigns begin and are impervious to the three weeks of frenetic activity by the candidates and their advisors. So the campaign is directed toward the floating minority, who can be influenced by the skills of public relations and advertising staffs. This minority can control the result only in very close elections; when the parties are running neck and neck almost anything, including a superior campaign, can make a difference. In 1964, for example, Labour beat the Conservatives by 44.1 percent to 43.4 percent, so it is not unreasonable to assume that Wilson's personal advantage over Douglas-Home was decisive.

For the rest, measuring the impact of a campaign depends on readings by opinion pollsters, and we have seen that these may be fallible. Still, indications of substantial changes probably indicate movement in the direction suggested by the polls, and it is likely that Labour narrowed the gap during the 1979 campaign and that the Conservatives widened their lead in the 1983 campaign. Although these changes could have made a difference on the size of their majority in Parliament, in neither case did they affect which party was to form the government.

The 1987 election provides us with a classic case of the limited impact of campaigns. By all accounts, the Labour campaign that began with Neil and Glenys Kinnock walking on the beach was superior to the Conservative campaign—so much so that it caused some days of panic in the Conservative camp and a complete reorientation of their strategy. Yet Labour was decisively defeated, and the poll indications were that any improvement in its position during the election period came at the expense of the Alliance rather than the Conservatives. Again in 1992, there was general agreement that the Conservatives ran a much weaker campaign than Labour, yet prevailed nonetheless.

Evidently the conduct of campaigns makes only a marginal difference to the election results. So we turn to factors other than the actual campaign that determine voting behavior.

WHAT DETERMINES ELECTION RESULTS?

Voting behavior is determined by both long- and short-range considerations.

Longterm Factors

Long before an election date is set, powerful trends have been in play irrespective of politicians' speeches or factional struggles.

Social Change. The factors we discussed in chapter 2 are the prime influences here. Social class is still a major consideration, but as its importance has declined, other factors have come into play increasingly, including changes in the extent of home ownership, the regional distribution of the population, educational level, ethnicity and race, and religion.

Party Affiliation. Voters' party identification is closely related to the social change factors listed above. We have seen that there are significant class differences between the parties. Through family tradition and early loyalties, many people continue to vote in accordance with their class origins even as they move up or down in the social scale. Others, however, shift from their initial partisan attachments as their social status changes, or because, like the upper-class Communists we discussed in chapter 2, they develop new ideological convictions.

In chapter 3, we saw that most of these long-range forces tend to favor the Conservative Party. The working class is shrinking and undergoing *embourgeoisement*. Home ownership has increased, which tends to make people more receptive to Conservative positions on private property and taxes. Conversely, the numbers renting public housing units from the local councils have declined, and public housing projects are mostly Labour strongholds. In Table 6.1, we see this clearly from the 1992 voting distribution.

TABLE 6.1 1992 Voting by housing tenure

	Conservative	Labour	Liberal Democrat
Owner-occupier	49%	23%	19%
Council tenant	23%	58%	14%
Private tenant	38%	37%	19%

SOURCE: Adapted from Gallup postelection survey.

Population movement has been mostly from Labour areas in the north to Conservative bastions in the south. Trade union membership has declined. And the aging of the population tends to favor the Conservatives. As we see in Table 6.2, Labour held a modest lead in 1992 among the 25–34 age group, but among those over 45, and especially among the expanding group over 65, Labour was well behind the Conservatives. Finally, party loyalties have weakened, undermining Labour more than the Conservatives.

There are some long-range factors apparently favoring Labour. The growing racial minorities tend to vote Labour. The increase in public employment, especially in local government, generally favors Labour as the party of expanded government. The rapid growth of higher education, especially in the newer universities, has expanded the number of young, left-leaning faculty. The decline of religion that we noted in chapter 2 hurts the Conservatives, for they are more likely to draw from voters strongly committed to religious values, especially within the Church of England. Finally, there is the attachment to communitarian over economic individualist values, which we discussed in chapter 2 and which apparently persists despite the challenge of Thatcherism. However, given the erosion of the Labour vote over the years, it would appear that the balance of longterm forces operating in the British political system tends to favor the Conservative Party (unless, as Labour's radical left argues, these long-term forces are transformed by a prolonged crisis of capitalism bringing crippling levels of unemployment among white-collar as well as blue-collar workers).

TABLE 6.2 1992 Voting by age

	Conservative	Labour	Liberal Democrat
Under 25	38%	35%	22%
25–34	37%	41%	18%
35–44	38%	38%	21%
45–64	44%	35%	19%
Over 65	49%	33%	14%

SOURCE: Adapted from Gallup postelection survey.

Shorter-Term Factors

Important though these longterm considerations are in influencing election outcomes, the fact that several of them are being subjected to powerful impulses for change diminishes their reliability as indicators of voting behavior. This opens the way for a variety of temporary influences that may sway the voters this way or that, making for a more volatile electorate.

The Salience of Particular Issues. The issues that are high on the list of public concerns tend to change rather rapidly, and the emergence of a potent issue on the list in the months or weeks before an election may very well determine its outcome. Thus in February 1974, the three-day work week made the ability to handle the unions the central question of the campaign. Again in 1979, when the election followed the "winter of discontent," unions and strikes were uppermost in the minds of voters. In 1983, the Falklands victory of the previous year continued to reverberate among the electorate.

Government Performance. To a considerable extent, elections produce judgments on how the government has been performing. Usually the verdict is rendered in the context of the year or so before the election: Hard times early in a government's life tend to be forgotten if a strong recovery has been achieved by election time.

Mostly voters judge governments by their performance on domestic and foreign policy issues, although scandals of the kind that rocked the last year of the Macmillan administration and the Major administration in 1994 may sap confidence in a government, and so may a series of blunders indicating sheer political ineptness.

Some elections have clearly constituted a vote of confidence in government performance, whereas others have just as strongly registered a negative judgment. Harold Wilson's Labour government was given an enlarged majority in 1966 because it was believed to have performed well in the preceding two years. Booming economies brought resounding victories to Harold Macmillan in 1959 and Margaret Thatcher in 1987. In 1951, however, the voters decided they'd had enough of austerity and controls, and turned Labour out. The Conservatives in 1974 and Labour in 1979 were dismissed because the electorate concluded they had failed to handle the unions.

The Credibility of the Opposition. Even if the electorate is strongly dissatisfied with the performance of the government, they may still re-elect it if they believe the main opposition party would do even worse.

In 1992 the economy was caught in a recession deeper and more prolonged than that which led to George Bush's defeat in the United States, and the polls indicated general disenchantment with the government's management of the economy. Moreover, Labour lost even though it was strongly preferred on several of the most salient issues in the election, as indicated in Table 6.3.

Although the Conservatives came out ahead on inflation and taxation, these were listed as important by far fewer people than listed health, jobs, and education.

TABLE 6.3 Issues and voting in 1992 election

Issue	% Saying Issue One of Top Two Affecting Their Vote	% Saying Issue Important and Best Handled by Conservatives	% Saying Issue Important and Best Handled by Labour
Health service	41	29	60
Unemployment	56	32	63
Education	23	27	57
Inflation	11	77	14
Taxation	10	85	10

SOURCE: Adapted from Gallup postelection survey.

However, it may be that Labour was more seriously hurt by its proposal for a tax increase on upper-middle incomes than people were prepared to admit to the pollsters, and if the evidence on this point is inconclusive, there is less ambiguity about another finding of various surveys: despite the government's weak economic record, Labour was trusted even less than the Conservatives to handle economic affairs.

The key question Gallup put to respondents was: "With Britain in economic difficulties, which party do you think could handle the problems best—the Conservatives under John Major, or Labour under Neil Kinnock?" All the way through 1991 and into 1992 the Conservatives held a clear lead on this question, and in the final preelection poll the margin was 52 percent to 31 percent. And in all likelihood, this perceived weakness of Labour was but one dimension of Labour's general inability to reestablish its credibility as a possible governing party after the convulsions that tore it apart after the 1979 election.

Consequently, Thatcher would have beaten Labour in 1983 even without the Falklands victory, and the brilliant Labour campaign of 1987 never had a chance of succeeding. Even by 1992, after several years of reform, moderation, and newfound unity, the electorate was not ready to entrust its future to Labour.

The Qualities of the Party Leader. Although the verdict in British elections is based largely on the performance of the government as a whole, the role of the prime minister or opposition leader can take on particular significance in some instances.

Earlier we discussed the ability of party leaders to communicate effectively on television. Yet the electorate judges leaders not only on their speaking skills but on their performance on a broad range of leadership qualities. In the case of Margaret Thatcher, this judgment was favorable in 1983 and 1987; although the polls indicated she did not inspire affection among the public, she was respected as a strong leader.

By 1990, however, the opinion of many of her parliamentary colleagues was that she had become an electoral liability—so much so that their party could win without her, but not with her, as leader. Their judgment appeared to be confirmed when her replacement, John Major, led his party to an unexpected victory.

Conversely, it is likely that Kinnock's leadership had a negative impact on Labour's chances in the election. The polls showed that Major had a clear lead over Kinnock on the question of who would make a better prime minister. The suggestion that Labour could have won had Kinnock stepped down before the election in favor of John Smith is doubtful given the size of the Conservative margin over Labour. Still, it is entirely plausible that the gap would have been narrower—possibly even to the extent of denying the Conservatives a clear majority in Parliament—had Labour changed its leadership in time.

The Fluctuating Fortunes of Other Parties. Whenever an election gives one party a large parliamentary majority, the minor parties are reduced to insignificance. But when the result is a narrow margin in Parliament, the British are reminded that they have somewhat more than a two-party system.

The *Liberals* have been the most frequent interlopers in this respect. Reduced from their once proud position in the system to a mere 2.5 percent of the national vote in 1951, their vote varied thereafter between less than 3 percent and 11 percent, until they sprang back in the two elections of 1974 with 19 percent and 18 percent. The second of these two elections gave them 13 seats in Parliament, far below their fair proportion, but enough to compel James Callaghan's Labour government, which lacked a clear parliamentary majority, to enter for a time into a "Lib-Lab pact," whereby Labour would withhold legislation unpalatable to the Liberals in return for their not voting to bring down the government. However, the Liberals pulled out of the arrangement when they decided it was doing nothing for them, but the 1979 election did even less for them, reducing their share of the popular vote to 14 percent.

The Liberals' next lease on life came with their formation of the Alliance with the Social Democratic party, but as we have seen this fell short of breaking through the two-party dominance. Disappointment came again in 1992, when the Liberal Democrats, despite the predictions of many experts, did not gain enough seats to bring about a hung parliament with the prospect of their inclusion in a coalition government. Yet subsequent successes by Liberal Democrats in by-elections and local elections revived talk of a possible electoral alliance with Labour.

The *Nationalist parties* have also been a factor to consider in the 1970s and again in the 1990s. The October 1974 election gave the Scottish Nationalist Party 11 seats, the Welsh nationalists (Plaid Cymru) 3, and the Northern Ireland parties 12. These were enough to give them bargaining power with the Callaghan government after the Lib-Lab pact collapsed, and it was only when Callaghan had no more concessions to offer them that the Scots joined the Conservatives and brought Labour down. Precipitating the 1979 election proved to be a less than brilliant move by the Scottish Nationalists, for their numbers in Parliament were reduced to two, and they could return no more than three in 1992.

The Irish nationalists did better, however. Their deal with Callaghan increased the representation of Northern Ireland from 12 to 17. And when John Major's government, with an overall majority of only 18, was faced with the threat of defections from his own party on his European policy, there was an unspoken understanding with some of the Irish nationalists that gave him a more comfortable margin.

Prospects For Future Elections

1992 and the "Predominant" Conservatives. In the light of the Conservatives' ability to hold on to power in 1992 in the depths of a severe recession, many commentators suggested it was overwhelmingly likely that the Conservatives would continue winning election after election, thereby reinforcing the concerns that Britain has become, in effect, a "predominant party system" containing few checks on the power of the ruling party.

These observers pointed to the fact that the most potent longterm factors we have examined favored the Conservatives, and that shorter-term influences had reinforced their advantage in four elections in a row, particularly the failure of the Labour Party and its leaders to present themselves as a viable alternative government and the inability of the other parties to gain enough strength to bring about a hung parliament.

Thus one leading political scientist found that Labour was still failing to adapt itself "to a radically changed political and social environment." Consequently, "Labour's electoral prognosis in the summer of 1992 was not good. If this prognosis proves correct, British government will remain one-party government into the next millennium."[5]

Then a major analysis of the 1992 election by Heath, Jowell, and Curtice[6] argued that Labour faced an uphill task in trying to convince voters that it could produce an economy strong enough to pay for the improved public services that the party advocated and the public wanted. Moreover, Labour was still seen as a party based in the working class; and the shrinkage in the working class meant it must attract more voters from the middle class. This suggested the need for moderate policies. Yet the study shows that by 1992, Labour was already perceived as moderate, so there was not much to be gained from the further steps toward moderation taken by Smith and Blair. Furthermore, these analysts warned, wooing the middle class too vigorously might involve policies that could alienate members of the party's working-class heartland; and the same authors had contended in a 1985 study that elections are not only "won and lost in the centre ground. They are won and lost in the heartlands as well."[7]

To gain a clear parliamentary majority, Labour faced the formidable task of securing a swing of 4.5 percent of the votes from Conservative to Labour since the 1992 election—a larger swing than any since the 1945 elections. Short of aiming for an absolute majority Labour might adopt the strategy of an alliance, or at least a tacit electoral understanding, between Labour and the Liberal Democrats. The idea attracted the support of a number of M.P.s on both sides. Still, skepticism was widespread. Many Labour M.P.s argued that, having come back from their nadir in 1983, moving up by close to four percentage points in each of the 1987 and 1992 elections, they needed only "one more heave" to win the next time. On their side the Liberal Democrat leaders knew that they could not promise to deliver their vote intact, for many of their supporters, seeing the Liberal Democrats tied to Labour, might switch to the Conservatives.

The Transformed Prospectus.   Within a year of the publication of the studies predicting a steep uphill struggle for the opposition parties, the outlook was dramatically transformed. The Conservative government, rocked by highly publicized blunders, internal discord, and a series of scandals, had plummeted in the polls, and John Major's standing had sunk even farther. By the end of 1994 Labour's advantage in the polls had stretched to leads of 30 or more points, and Labour had pulled ahead on taxes, economic policy, and crime—issues on which the Conservatives were traditionally favored. The 1994 elections for the European Parliament, and the 1995 local government elections, commonly seen as tests of the government's popularity, resulted in large gains for Labour and severe setbacks for the Conservatives. As we saw in chapter 5, John Major's dramatic confrontation with his Conservative critics in 1995 resolved the leadship issue for the time being but could not heal the divisions in his party. And the selection of Tony Blair as Labour Party Leader appeared to end the disadvantage that the Party had suffered in 1992 with respect to the personal appeal of the respective Party leaders.

So it no longer seemed implausible for Labour to make that "one more heave" and achieve the large percentage vote swing needed to give them a clear majority in the next election. Moreover, by-election and local election results suggested that the Liberal Democrats were now firmly establishing a strong challenge to the Conservatives in some of their previously secure areas in the south. Thus, even if Labour's lead in the polls were to be cut significantly an electoral arrangement with the Liberal Democrats, however informal, could seriously threaten the Conservatives' hegemony. As we have seen, the Conservative share of the vote in the last four election had never risen above 43 percent. They would have had a difficult time against a united opposition in 1992.

So as 1995 began, the *Economist* magazine declared that "voters currently despise this government on a scale unprecedented in modern history;" and that the Tories were about as likely to win the next election as pigs were to fly.[8] Evidently, the short-term factors had swung sharply away from a party which had been so long in power that it had become prone to the mistakes that come from exhaustion or arrogance.

Continuing Uncertainties.   Still, the Conservatives were not ready to concede defeat at this stage of the electoral cycle. Under the British system the incumbent government decides when, within the five-year limit, the next election will be held; their five-year term did not need to end until the spring of 1977, and (unless they lost a confidence vote in Parliament) they were likely to hold on as long as possible in the hope that the economy would continue to improve and change their party's abysmal standing in the polls. The government could also produce a popular pre-election budget offering a cut in income taxes. As for Labour, they would have to spell out their policies in more detail as the election approached, and this could make them vulnerable to counterattack.

But even if the various short-term factors hurting the Conservatives were to lead to their defeat at the next election, this would not necessarily bring to an end their status as the *normal* or "predominant" governing party. Any Labour or Labour-Liberal Democratic government would have to demonstrate that it could govern more effectively than the Conservatives, most particularly that it could improve the social services at a cost tolerable to the middle classes, and that it could sustain its appeal to the middle classes without losing its working-class support. Otherwise the long-range factors favoring the Conservatives could reassert themselves and give the Conservatives another long tenure in office.

CONCLUSION

Election campaigns in Britain, as in the United States, satisfy the criteria for a viable democracy only in the most minimal way. It is disappointing that, given the educational opportunities and the abundance of available information in both countries, elections should fall so far short of offering reasoned debates on the central issues to enable the citizenry to make sensible choices.

Yet some comfort can be gleaned from the fact that much of the nonsense thrust at the voters during election campaigns is ignored by the majority, and that the outcome of most elections is determined by more fundamental considerations. Moreover, the very clamor of the campaigns reflects the competition between parties and the openness of debate that are essential conditions of democratic systems.

Developments after the 1992 Conservative victory have also modified some of the concerns about Britain's government becoming an essentially one-party system in which elections have very little meaning. Even if the Conservatives do not lose the next election, they will certainly approach that election with great respect, if not fear, and will recognize the occasion as a supreme test of their fitness to rule.

SOME QUESTIONS TO THINK ABOUT

What are the main similarities and differences between U.S. and British elections?

Should Britain adopt primaries?

Would you support providing political candidates in the United States with free television and radio time and banning the sale of political advertising?

Are campaign finance reforms needed in Britain?

Would the British benefit from debates in general elections?

How important an advantage is the press to Conservatives?

Do election campaigns in Britain suffer from the same kind of shortcomings as U.S. elections?

What determines election results in Britain? How important are short-term compared with long-term influences? What do you see as the long-term prospects for the Conservatives? For Labour? For the Liberal Democrats?

NOTES

1. See Justin Fisher, "Donations to the Conservative Party," *Parliamentary Affairs*, vol. 47, no. 1, January 1994.
2. Martin Harrison, "Politics on the Air," in David Butler and Dennis Kavanagh, *The British General Election of 1992* (Macmillan, 1992), p. 168.
3. See Butler and Kavanagh, *British General Election of 1992*, p. 135.
4. *New Statesman and Society*, 29 March 1991, p. 19.
5. Anthony King, *Britain At the Polls, 1992* (Chatham House, 1993), p. 246.
6. Anthony Heath, Roger Jowell, and John Curtice, *Labour's Last Chance?* (Dartmouth, 1994).
7. Anthony Heath, Roger Jowell, and John Curtice, *How Britain Votes* (Pergamon Press, 1985), p. 159.
8. *The Economist,* 24 December 1994-6 January 1995, p. 76.

SUGGESTIONS FOR FURTHER READING

After each election (including the 1975 Common Market referendum) David Butler authors or coauthors an analysis, the latest being the 1992 work cited in the text (see NOTES). Other studies of the 1992 election are the Heath, Jowell, and Curtice book, *Labour's Last Chance?* (see NOTES) and Anthony King (ed.), *Britain at the Polls, 1992*, both of which are referred to in the text. Coverage of elections since 1945 is provided in David Butler, *British General Elections Since 1945* (Blackwell, 1989), and Frank Conley, *General Elections Today* (Manchester University Press, 1990).

Rodney Tyler, *Campaign: The Selling of the Prime Minister* (Grafton, 1987) gives a detailed account of the campaign techniques used during the 1987 election.

PART THREE

THE INSTITUTIONS OF GOVERNMENT

In which we discuss the institutions of British government—monarchy, prime minister and cabinet, civil service, Parliament, the courts and local governments—and pose the questions: Is the British system more efficient, more efficacious in producing decisions than the U.S. system? Does the British system contain enough protections against concentrated executive power?

7

The Monarchy Will It Survive?

1992, said Queen Elizabeth, had been an "annus horribilis." It had indeed been a dreadful year for the British monarchy. Day after day, the tabloid headlines had shrieked the news of a succession of royal family scandals, and even the *Times* and the *Daily Telegraph* had no choice but to carry extended stories on the sorry developments.

First, there were the accounts of the fraying marriage of Prince Andrew and his wife Sarah or "Fergie," which reached their nadir with a front-page photograph of her with another man sunning herself topless by the Mediterranean. Later in the year, the prince and his wife agreed to a separation.

A much more serious problem for the family and the monarchy raged around the heir to the throne, Prince Charles, and his wife Diana. Their dislike of each other became increasingly apparent as the year progressed. A book by Andrew Morton providing detailed allegations of his coldness and infidelity and her attempted suicides became an instant bestseller and was quoted extensively by every newspaper and magazine. Next the tabloids published a tape apparently made from an intimate telephone conversation between Diana and a male friend and another between Charles and his longtime friend Camilla. The conversations were more than friendly and in Charles's case, sexually explicit. The unhappy pair followed the example of Andrew and Sarah, and established separate households—after which a continuing stream of embarrassing revelations poured out through press leaks, books, and TV interviews, and the tabloids blared QUEEN MUM SAW DI SUICIDE ATTEMPT, DIANA

HAS BETRAYED ME, THE CAMILLA CONSPIRACY. The furor continued through 1994, as Charles tried to justify himself in a TV interview during which he admitted his adultery, and then in an authorized book in which he complained about a miserable childhood and an unfeeling father.

THE EROSION OF ROYAL POPULARITY

The polls registered a drastic decline in the standing of the monarchy. This was supposed to be, in the phrase of nineteenth-century constitutional authority, Walter Bagehot, one of the "dignified," or ceremonial, elements of the constitution. Yet here its members were acting in a most undignified manner. The saga of the royal family had always been a kind of elevated soap opera for the British people. Now, said one of the tabloids, the monarchy had gone beyond being a soap opera to become a laughing stock; and this in the year marking the fortieth anniversary of the queen's accession to the throne, an event that had been proclaimed as the symbol of a "new Elizabethan age."

This was by no means the first time the British monarchy had been the object of public abuse. The *Times*' obituary of George IV in 1830 said: "There never was an individual less regretted by his fellow creatures than this deceased king." Of his successor, William IV, the *Spectator* opined that he was honest but "a weak,

A cartoonist's caustic view of the royal family
SOURCE: *The New Statesman & Society.*

ignorant, commonplace sort of person. . . . His very popularity was acquired at the price of something like public contempt." We can date the enormous mass appeal of the monarchy from the reign of Victoria, but her years of seclusion after the death of her husband, Albert, led to mounting dissatisfaction. She was failing to carry out the first requirement of the monarchy, which was to be seen by her people. As Queen Charlotte tells her reluctant children in Alan Bennett's *The Madness of King George*, "Smile and wave. Everyone smile and wave. That's what you're paid for"; and when Victoria failed for years to do what she was paid for, an angry republican movement grew rapidly, dying out only when she resumed her public duties.

The monarchy was again plunged into confusion and disrepute when Edward VIII, confronted with the choice of marrying a twice-divorced woman or keeping his throne, decided to abdicate in 1936. Fortunately for the institution, Edward's predecessor, George V, and his wife Mary, had comported themselves with meticulous dignity; and Edward's successor, George VI, and his wife Elizabeth, endeared themselves to the public by their exemplary conduct during World War II. So the coronation of the young Queen Elizabeth in 1952 prompted a vast outpouring of affection, and there were similar massive displays of approval when Charles was invested as Prince of Wales and when the royal children were married.

What, then, had caused the precipitous decline in the popularity of the monarchy? In part the problem stemmed from the queen's laudable aim of making the monarchy less remote, more accessible, more suited to a democratic era.

Television was enlisted in this cause. Against Prime Minister Winston Churchill's advice, the queen agreed to have her coronation televised, and its full panoply was watched by multitudes all around the world. TV cameras were also brought in to the Prince of Wales's investiture, and then to the weddings of the royal children, preceded by interviews with the happy couples. And in 1969 the queen arranged with the BBC for the making of a documentary, *Royal Family*, depicting Elizabeth, Philip, and the children at home, with Philip barbecuing and the family acting like any other ordinary family.

However, there were problems with this approach.

The Role of the Tabloids

Once the media had been invited in, the Pandora's box was opened. The tabloids, always obsessed with the royals as the ultimate supercelebrities, redoubled their efforts to intrude into the lives of the family members.

Any hint of departure from the impeccable respectability expected of the monarchy was seized with enthusiasm. The media had already feasted on the failed marriages of the queen's sister Margaret and her daughter Anne. Now there were the activities of Andy and Fergie, Charles and Di with which to titillate the public.

Periodically the queen pleaded with the press to leave her family a small zone of privacy. The editors would agree to do so, then once again the *paparazzi* would be dispatched with their photolenses to catch members of the family in unflattering poses.

Royalty and the Establishment

Despite their portrayal in the BBC's *Royal Family*, the royals live very differently from ordinary families.

They are at the very apex of the Establishment, with a social status far above that of even the most ancient peerages. And they are very wealthy. The queen owns some, but not the most costly, of her palaces and paintings. She is not at liberty to sell Buckingham Palace or the crown jewels, but the wealth in her family holdings has been estimated to be at least several hundred million pounds sterling; whatever she does not own in the royal domain is available for the personal use of herself and her family.

So the royals move between Buckingham Palace, Sandringham, and Windsor Castle, and up to Balmoral in Scotland in the summer. They travel on planes and a train set aside for their exclusive use. Large staffs, headed by the Lord High Chamberlain, ladies-in-waiting, royal equerries, and powerful private secretaries attend to their every need wherever they go. And their staffs insist that only the finest quality is appropriate for royalty. Thus it was reported that when the queen was to pay a state visit to France, the British ambassador called the palace to check on which wines to serve. Does the queen appreciate really fine wines, he asked? The reply: "How would she know? She's never tried anything else."

A portion of this affluent lifestyle is paid for by the civil list, which contributes to the expenses of the royal family, and there are other public appropriations to pay for the upkeep of the royal palaces, trains, planes, and so on. The civil list outlay in 1992 was about £10 million, and almost another £50 million was allocated for the other costs. Moreover, by an arrangement negotiated by George V and George VI, the queen paid no income tax, and Charles paid a special 40 percent tax on his £4 million income from the Duchy of Cornwall—after deductions for costs of official duties which included a staff of 62 and rent on a mansion.

In defense, it was argued that the cost to the public was more than recovered through the royals' attraction for tourists, through their effectiveness as trade emissaries (wherever they go they advertise "Buy British" campaigns and take people along with them to transact business deals for the nation), and through their sponsorship of charities (a royal name opens purse strings for any good cause).

But these arguments failed to stem a rising tide of resentment in 1992. The recession contributed to this: The spectacle of a lavish, untaxed lifestyle amid mounting unemployment and homelessness was bound to attract criticism. But there had not been the same furor during the deep recession of the early 1980s. What made the difference this time was that the royal children were living so well, largely at the public expense, and behaving so badly.

The uproar grew louder when a fire broke out at Windsor Castle and the government announced that, because the castle was a public property, the damage would be repaired at public expense. At last the queen responded to the criticism. The palace announced that she would henceforth pay income tax on her private income, that the civil list would be reduced to cover only a few core members of the family, and that parts of Buckingham Palace would be opened to tourists for a fee in the summer to help defray the costs of the repairs to Windsor. Later it was decided that the royal yacht Britannia was to be taken out of service and the Queen's Flight of three aircraft and two helicopters would be amalgamated with a Royal Air Force squadron. And an official publication was produced, *Royal Finances*, which provided a number of new details on the queen's income and outlays and claimed: "The royal household is run in line with modern business practice." The document also explained that, though the queen was now to pay income tax, the royal family would not be subject to inheritance tax because the monarch needs "an appropriate degree of financial independence in order to be constitutionally impartial."

Damage to the Monarch's Constitutional Standing

Royal Family had depicted a conventional, stable family. This was a valuable portrayal, for the family concept is an essential feature of a hereditary monarchy. Unfortunately the gloriously celebrated marriages of all the children who appeared in the documentary were to disintegrate, those of Andrew and Charles amid grotesque scandals. These events carried with them some damaging constitutional consequences.

For one thing, the monarch is the governor of the Church of England. The church has in the past taken the position that it will not remarry a divorced person as long as the former partner is still alive—the policy behind the forced abdication of Edward VIII. So if Charles were to divorce Diana he apparently could not be remarried in the church. Perhaps the Church of Scotland would be more obliging, or the difficulty could be removed if, as Charles hinted in a television interview in 1994, the Church of England were to be disestablished—that is, no longer recognized as the official religion. (He would be happy, said Charles, to be "defender of faith" rather than "defender of *the* faith.")

Still, although the idea of disestablishment has many supporters, it would not come without a struggle, and if it were seen simply as a way of dealing with Charles's marital problems, the reform could further damage the reputation of a monarchy whose reputation was already severely eroded by the scandals of 1993 and their continued reverberations.

And the royal reputation matters in the British system because the monarch's ability to perform her or his constitutional functions is heavily dependent on the maintenance of a high degree of public respect for the institution.

But what exactly are those constitutional functions?

THE CONSTITUTIONAL ROLES OF THE MONARCH

Ceremonial Duties

To begin with, the monarch is expected to undertake the ceremonial responsibilities associated with being head of state, and is thus the symbol and embodiment of the continuity of the nation. So the queen receives foreign dignitaries, makes formal tours abroad, visits hospitals and disaster areas, launches ships, dedicates buildings, and "smiles and waves" to the populace. In the United States, activities of this kind take up much of the time of the president. Although the British prime minister must also undertake some of these rituals, the larger number devolves on the monarch.

Dealing with Constitutional Conventions

The monarch is required by convention to perform certain governmental responsibilities. Most are formalities:

She reads the Queen's Speech from the throne of the House of Lords at the opening of each session of Parliament. The speech presents the government's proposals for the session and is written entirely by the government. The queen is expected to read it without any intonation expressing approval or disapproval, even though it may flatly contradict the Queen's Speech of a year earlier written by a previous government.

She signs any statute passed by Parliament. Presumably this could include a statute abolishing the monarchy.

After an election, she sends for the leader of whichever party or combination of parties that can form a majority in the House of Commons.

In effect, all of these are formalities, and for the most part the queen has no choice but to do whatever the elected government of the day tells her to do. However, there are circumstances in which a limited amount of discretion might be available to the monarch in the exercise of these constitutional conventions.

If No Party Wins a Clear Majority in the House of Commons. The monarch must then consult with party leaders to see which is most likely to be able to pull together a majority coalition.

There have been no coalition governments since World War II. However, after the February 1974 election, Labour won the largest number of seats but not an absolute majority. The outgoing prime minister, Edward Heath, approached the Liberals with a proposal for a coalition, which they rejected. The queen then sent for Harold Wilson to form a Labour government.

She had played no part in the negotiations. If she were to be involved, there would be only one question for her to consider. It would not be: Who do I think would make the best prime minister? It would be only: Who is most likely to be able to gain the support of a majority in the House of Commons?

If a Prime Minister Dies or Resigns and There Is No Regular Party Procedure for the Succession. As we saw in chapter 5, this is exactly what happened after the resignation of Eden in 1957 and Macmillan in 1963, for the Conservatives had no formal machinery in place to decide on a successor.

In both cases the queen was subjected to some criticism for not calling for wider soundings before the announcement of the new prime minister. Yet in each case the key party leaders were making the decision, and for the queen to insist on others being involved would have taken her beyond the bounds of the established convention. It was up to the party, not the monarch, to call for a more appropriate procedure, and since 1964, when the Conservatives put a new method in place, this area of potential royal discretion has been effectively closed.

If the Prime Minister Requests the Queen to Announce a Controversial Dissolution of Parliament. Constitutional scholars are divided on the question of whether the queen is absolutely required to grant a prime minister's request for a dissolution of Parliament and the calling of a new election. Suppose, for example, the request is made after a government defeat in the House, despite another leader's plausible claim to be able to gain the support of a parliamentary majority. Yet it is difficult to see how the queen could refuse to accept a prime minister's request without being drawn into a political maelstrom.

The Monarch as Head of the Commonwealth. Here we enter somewhat more ambiguous territory. The monarch is head of the Commonwealth, formerly but no longer the *British* Commonwealth. Must the queen, then, follow the advice of the *British* government in all matters pertaining to the Commonwealth?

This question has embroiled the queen in some public controversies. Each year she makes a Christmas address to the Commonwealth. The address reflects some of her own thinking, and, having visited the many countries in the Commonwealth since her childhood, she has developed a strong belief in the importance of its survival and the values she believes it represents.

So in her 1982 address she saw the Commonwealth as a model of multiracialism: "I believe that for those with a sense of tolerance, the arrival and proximity of different races and religions have provided a much better chance for each to appreciate the value of the others." This provoked an angry response from a right-wing former Conservative minister, Enoch Powell. The speech, he said, reflected more concern "for the susceptibilities and prejudices of a vociferous minority of newcomers than for the great mass of her subjects."

Then in her 1983 address the queen declared that the world's greatest problem was "the gap between rich and poor countries," and that to begin to close the gap we must "hear less about nationalism and more about interdependence." A furious Powell protested that the queen should see herself as "the British monarch to the British nation."

Palace sources responded that the queen was not bound by the British government's views on all Commonwealth matters. However, this view did not withstand a test that came in 1986. The *Sunday Times* reported that the queen was upset over Thatcher's refusal to go along with all the other Commonwealth countries in supporting continued sanctions against South Africa. She feared that the Thatcher policy would lead some of the Commonwealth countries to pull out of the forthcoming Commonwealth Games and even withdraw from the Commonwealth completely. The report also indicated that the queen was critical of the Thatcher government's policies toward the inner-city poor and of allowing the United States to use British bases for the bombing of Libya. The source for this story turned out to be a Buckingham Palace press officer.

There was talk of a constitutional crisis. Could the queen really bring to the public's attention her disagreements with her ministers? The answer came quickly in the form of denials and disavowals by the palace, followed by a long period of silence by palace press officers. No countries withdrew from the Commonwealth games or from the Commonwealth.

The conclusion is that in Commonwealth matters, the queen has a small area of autonomy in the phrasing of her Christmas address, and perhaps on which Commonwealth countries to visit and when. But on substantive Commonwealth issues she is bound to follow the advice of her British ministers.

Consultation

The monarch, it appears, is a titular head without power. She reigns but does not rule. Yet the absence of specific decision-making power does not preclude the possibility of exercising a less definable but still significant degree of influence.

According to Walter Bagehot's much-quoted formula, the monarch has three rights—"the right to be consulted, the right to encourage, the right to warn." She is well-situated to exercise these rights. She is appointed for life, typically outlasting several prime ministers. She has been trained since childhood in public affairs. She meets weekly with the prime minister whenever they are both in town; she talks with other cabinet ministers, the opposition leader, and with top politicians from other countries; she has access to all government papers. She commands enormous prestige. She is advised by a staff of highly experienced and politically sophisticated private secretaries.

So the institution carries with it a considerable potential for influence. In George Bernard Shaw's play, *The Apple Cart*, this potential is set before us in full force. King Magnus is a philosopher-king dealing with a cabinet of thick-headed blunderers. While appearing to conform to the constitutional niceties, Magnus manipulates his stupid politicians and runs the country.

The reality has been that, although the politicians may sometimes have been of questionable competence, there has been no King Magnus on the throne—not, at least, since Henry VIII and Elizabeth I. Even so, prime ministers will listen to monarchs with respect. Certainly this has been true of Elizabeth II. By all accounts, though she would rather spend her time with her corgis and horses than with politicians, she is intelligent and well-informed, and takes her constitutional responsibilities very seriously.

Prince Charles has already demonstrated the influence flowing from the prestige of royalty. Searching for a role during the decades of waiting for his ascension to the Throne, he has spoken out on subjects he feels passionately about. One of these is an intense dislike of most modern architecture, and when he attacked a proposed plan for an addition to the National Gallery in London, the plan was scrapped and replaced by one in a more traditional style. Then in public speeches and a television documentary, which he wrote and narrated himself, he turned to the protection of the environment. He has also expressed his concern about unemployment and the plight of the inner cities.

In so doing, he encountered two problems. The first was resentment by right-wing Conservatives that he was coming dangerously close to "a Labour Party solution." The second was that his speeches tended to be crowded off the front pages by a simultaneous public appearance of the beautiful Diana wearing a new dress or hairstyle, and bringing yet another public reminder of the tensions between them.

It was these tensions, along with all the dismal events of 1992 and beyond, that were raising serious doubts about the future of the monarchy. We have seen that the place of the monarchy in the British constitutional system is largely symbolic, yet not entirely inconsequential. Ceremonies must be presided over; constitutional formalities must be attended to; consultations with political leaders are a regular feature of the system.

But now questions were being raised from many quarters. Can present and future monarchs carry out their duties effectively in the shadow of the institution's fallen reputation? When the royal family is the subject of ridicule, how much does this impair the performance of their ceremonial duties and their governmental and consultative roles?

The intense public discussion of these questions has generated various ideas for changing the monarchy.

PROPOSALS FOR CHANGE

Restoring the Mystique

The essential attribute of monarchy, according to some analysts, is to be found not in rational dissections of its constitutional roles but rather in its mystical embodiment of factors better described by anthropologists and social psychologists than by political scientists. The crown represents the continuity of society ("The king is dead. Long live the king!") It projects history, tradition, the achievements of the past into the present. It speaks for patriotism and the nation above sectional interests and politics. It brings color and pageantry into our otherwise drab existence. It is a construct of myth and the mysterious, and as such it depends on maintaining a degree of remoteness from everyday life. As general de Gaulle observed: "Prestige cannot exist without mystery, for one reveres little what one knows well."

The mistake of the British monarchy, in this view, was that it allowed the veil of mystery to be pierced, exposing the prosaic and fallible behavior of the royal children. This mistake is not likely to be made by the Japanese, whose mass media accepted, albeit with reluctance and impatience, a news blackout for almost a year on Crown Prince Naruhito's search for a bride. When the bride was found the wedding was not televised; there would be no breach of the Japanese custom of excluding the public and the media from the marriage ceremony. Advocates of a restored mystique recognize that the British cannot go as far in this direction as the Japanese, but they argue that some effort must be made to repair the damage caused by the blinding light of too much publicity and to reestablish a proper distance between the crown and its subjects.

This does not appear to be a realistic prospect. No doubt a sustained period of discreet behavior by all members of the family could lessen the air of notoriety that surrounds some of the royals. But the tabloids will not pull back from their incessant probing into the daily lives of every member of the family. The British, even in a more deferential era, were never as respectful of tradition and authority as the Japanese (whose own press has lately begun to make critical comments about members of the Imperial family); and, as we have seen, there is much less deference in Britain today than in the past. The mystique, in anything like its pristine form, will not be restored.

Abolition

George Will, the American conservative columnist, became disgusted with the royal scandals, and the consequent demystification of the British monarchy. He drew a drastic conclusion. "The magic is gone," he said. "When the current occupant of the throne is done, they should turn off the lights at Buckingham Palace."[1] Then the *Economist*, the pro-free market magazine, declared that: "British thinkers have done more than those of any other nation to help create the modern idea of democracy . . . ," and that "it is hard to believe that monarchy is vital for the political health of such a nation. How ironic it is that the land of Locke, Hume, Paine, Godwin, and Mill should even think it desirable."[2]

Yet most British Conservatives continue to find the institution desirable. Usually the proposals to abolish the monarchy have come from the left. Although Labour Prime Ministers Clement Attlee, Harold Wilson, and James Callaghan were all staunch upholders of the monarchy, many other Labour leaders were less enchanted. Until recently, open attacks on the institution were mounted only by Tony Benn and a few others on the far left, the rest believing it a waste of time given the monarchy's enormous popularity in the country. But since 1992, a growing number of politicians and intellectuals of the left joined in the open questioning of the value of the institution.

Their problem was not so much with particular occupants of the throne (although Edward VIII was not only a frivolous playboy, but also an admirer of Hitler). Apparently Elizabeth got along at least as well with Labour as with Conservative prime ministers. When Labour Cabinet minister Richard Crossman asked a Palace aide "whether she preferred the Tories to us because they were our social superiors," the answer was: "I don't think so. The queen doesn't make fine distinctions between politicians of different parties. They all roughly belong to the same social category in her view."[3] Moreover, Elizabeth is no Thatcherite, and apparently neither is Prince Charles. They are, in other words, progressive conservatives of the Disraeli school, what Mrs. Thatcher would call *wets*. But given the royal family's upbringing, their lifestyle, and the people they surround themselves with, their biases will always be antithetical to the left.

But more important than the monarchy's potential for impartiality in dealing with any future government that the left might establish was the belief system that the monarchy symbolized. In the view of the left, the monarchy represented obsolete and antidemocratic values. It stood for the Establishment and for the continuation of class distinctions. It attracted the kind of groveling snobbishness expressed by a former editor of the *Times* on the occasion of the birth of Charles's and Diana's first son. His tribute to this infant began with "May it please your Royal Highness," and concluded with: "I am Your Royal Highness's most humble and obedient servant."[4]

The monarchy encapsulated for its critics a disabling nostalgia for a past grandeur that could never return. As historian David Cannadine put it:

> Is it healthy for a nation in Britain's current condition to be quite so proud of this essentially ornamental and anachronistic institution? Romance and escapism are all very well, but it may also be that these very attitudes—which the monarchy engenders, legitimates and depends on—impede any serious attempts to modernize a society that is desperately in need of modernization.[5]

So the left proposes that, after Elizabeth, the monarchy be abandoned and replaced by a president elected separately and for a longer term than the parliament and government.

Support for this position has been growing, for sentiment in the country has been moving against the monarchy, particularly in light of the family scandals. A poll published in January 1995 indicated that only one in three respondents believed that the monarchy would last another 50 years; that a little over one-third described themselves as "strong supporters" of the institution, with another third saying they are "not especially keen on it," and support it only because it is better than the alternative.[6]

Still, that left a little less than one-third favoring abolition. And political analyst Peter Hennessy, writing in *The Economist*, insisted that ". . . 25 years from now (and whatever arguments the editor of the *Economist* may marshall to the contrary) there will be a Windsor on the throne, and . . . his name will be Charles III or William V."[7] (After all, Charles and Diana have already performed their fundamental duty—they have produced legitimate heirs to the throne.)

Indeed, doing away with the monarchy could not be accomplished overnight even if the political will were there. Almost all actions of government are performed in the name of the monarch. Statutes are passed by the queen in Parliament; the government is the queen's government (and exercises the royal prerogative); the armed forces are Her Majesty's Services and she is Commander-in-Chief; and even the opposition is Her Majesty's *Loyal* Opposition. Disentangling all this from the constitution would be a complicated undertaking indeed.

Simplification

If not abolition, said the left weekly, the *New Statesman*, "Give us, *at least*, a modern monarchy."[8] Models for such modern monarchies are to be found in Europe. All of them are much less ostentatious and much less expensive than the British monarchy. On ceremonial occasions they all play their parts with the full pomp and circumstance required, but for the rest their lifestyle is informal.

The Dutch queen goes shopping in department stores and works as a designer and illustrator. The Norwegian monarchs have sometimes been seen walking and cycling through city streets. All the European crowned heads are extremely popular—none more so than King Juan Carlos of Spain, who was largely responsible for saving democracy from a threatened military coup. And outside of Monaco, there have been no royal scandals in recent years to compare with those in Britain.

So there is a powerful argument for a drastic scaling down and simplification of the British monarchy. Some movement in this direction is already occurring, such as the modest reduction in the civil list, and the payment of income taxes (as a *voluntary* act, it was emphasized, not as legal requirement).

Yet the palace is still reluctant to accept comparisons with other European monarchies. Of the 21 or so monarchies extant in the world, the British has the most imposing history and is the most prestigious. No Hollywood extravaganza can compare with the glitter and magnificence of a great British royal occasion. Those occasions have been festivals not just for the upper and middle classes, but for the working class, who have celebrated royal jubilees and weddings with festive block parties.

CONCLUSION

If the enthusiasm for the monarchy has been abating lately in Britain, it does not seem to have diminished in the United States, despite George Wills's pronouncement on the subject. Diana's picture has been on the cover of American magazines almost as regularly as in British publications. Socialites fight for invitations to banquets thrown in honor of even junior members of the royal family, and when they visit U.S. college campuses they are received with acclamation by huge numbers of students.

This is not altogether surprising when we consider that we invest our presidents with some of the same aura associated with the magic of monarchy. It was especially so during the brief "Camelot" years of the Kennedys. And in the Nixon and Johnson eras, the talk of the "imperial presidency" brought home to us the dangers inherent in not separating the roles of head of government and head of state.

That separation is part of the British constitution. Of course, the principle does not require a hereditary monarchy, for many other democracies accomplish the same purpose with a president elected separately from the prime minister. Moreover, the British monarchy comes at a price and with an array of trappings that seem increasingly incongruous in a democratic political system. So, if abolition is to be avoided, some further steps toward simplification seem likely over the next decades.

SOME QUESTIONS TO THINK ABOUT

Is monarchy compatible with democracy?

What are the constitutional roles of the British monarch? Could they be performed as well by an elected president?

Would we be better off if we separated the functions of *head of state* from those of *head of government*?

What are the sources of the British monarchy's popularity? How seriously has its popularity been damaged by the family scandals?

Should the British monarchy try to restore its former mystique?

Should it adopt a simpler style similar to that of the Scandinavian monarchies?

Should the monarchy be abolished?

Why is there so much interest in the British monarchy in America?

NOTES

1. *Washington Post*, 25 June 1992.
2. *Economist*, 22 October 1994, p. 69.
3. Anthony Howard, ed., *The Crossman Diaries* (condensed version, Magnum Books, Methuen Paperbacks, 1979), p. 298.
4. William Rees-Mogg, *Sunday Times*, 27 June 1982.
5. *New York Review of Books*, 12 June 1986, p. 17.
6. *Manchester Guardian Weekly*, 15 January 1995, p. 1.
7. *Economist*, 24 December 1994–6 January 1995, p. 79.
8. *New Statesman*, 18 July 1986, p. 3.

SUGGESTIONS FOR FURTHER READING

Christopher Hibbert, *The Court of St. James* (William Morrow, 1980) provides a general overview of the monarchy from Victoria to Elizabeth II. Robert Lacey, *Majesty* (Avon, 1977) and Anthony Holden, *King Charles III* (Weidenfeld and Nicolson, 1988) are biographies of Elizabeth II and Prince Charles by two chroniclers of the royal family. A less respectful analysis is found in John Pearson, *The Selling of the Royal Family* (Simon and Schuster, 1986); Tom Nairn, *The Enchanted Glass* (Radius, 1988) presents the case for republicanism.

8
Prime Ministers and Their Cabinets

When the queen invites a party leader to become prime minister and form a new government, a number of politicians will wait anxiously by the phone for a call from 10 Downing Street, the prime minister's residence. Most of them will be members of the House of Commons, with a few from the House of Lords. The call, if it comes, will tell them whether they are to be given one of the hundred or so positions in the new government, and if so which position.

The more experienced or ambitious among them will aspire to one of the slots, which in recent years has numbered between 20 and 23, in the most powerful and prestigious part of the executive branch—the cabinet.

Some of these positions are long established, others vary with the requirements of individual prime ministers. There will inevitably be two cabinet ministers assigned to international affairs, the foreign and defense secretaries. The top two financial officers will be the chancellor of the exchequer and the chief secretary to the treasury. Other economic portfolios in recent cabinets have been trade and industry, employment, transport, environment (responsible for local government as well as environmental protection), and agriculture. Social welfare positions have covered health, education, and social security. Law and order are assigned to the home secretary, responsible for the police, the courts, immigration and so on, and the Lord Chancellor, the chief judicial officer. Scotland, Wales, and Northern Ireland each have a cabinet representative. John Major's cabinet also included a secretary of state for heritage, covering the arts, sports, tourism, and other matters.

All of these preside over substantial departments of government. There are others, however, who do not have large administrative roles, including the Lord President of the Council, who acts as leader of the House of Commons; the Lord Privy Seal, who leads the House of Lords; the chancellor of the Duchy of Lancaster, a free-floating minister for special assignments; and the chairman of the governing political party. Some administrations have included a deputy prime minister. Geoffrey Howe was assigned this role as a face-saving gesture after his dismissal from the foreign secretaryship by Prime Minister Thatcher. On the other hand, John Major's designating Michael Heseltine in 1995 as first secretary of state and deputy prime minister was intended to give him high public visibility as a principal voice of the administration, and included responsibility for chairing several important cabinet committees. One further position whose critical importance to the survival of governments has increasingly been recognized by inclusion in the cabinet is that of chief whip, in charge of maintaining party discipline in Parliament.

Most of the cabinet members hold the title of secretary of state, and under them serve one or more junior ministers with the rank of minister of state and others at the level of undersecretary of state. Some cabinet positions, of course, are more important than others. The roles of chancellor of the exchequer, foreign secretary, and home secretary are commonly regarded as the vantage points from which their occupants aspire to the prime ministership. Others, however, such as trade and industry and health, may take on particular importance when their programs become the center of attention.

The cabinet meets once or twice a week, presided over by the prime minister, who also carries the traditional title *First Lord of the Treasury*. The nature of the relationship between the prime minister and the cabinet raises questions that go to the heart of the quality of democracy in Britain. Is the prime minister essentially the chair of a collegial group that makes decisions cooperatively? Or has power, which had already gravitated from Parliament to the cabinet, now become even more concentrated in the person of the prime minister? If the latter is true—if Britain now has prime ministerial rather than cabinet government—this raises serious questions about the survival of the constraints on power necessary for democracy, because a government focused on one person to that extent would establish a kind of presidential system without the separation of powers that so severely constrains the U.S. president.

To approach this perennial debate over prime ministerial versus cabinet government, it is necessary to examine each of the several powers that have been vested in the office of prime minister. As we do so, we shall see that in each case the power, though formidable, is nonetheless subject to certain limits. Following our analysis of these powers and limits we shall look at the experience of particular prime ministers and their cabinets to help us determine where the balance of power lies.

PRIME MINISTERIAL POWERS AND LIMITS

Relations with the Cabinet

The prime minister has three kinds of power over the members of the cabinet.
First, there is the power to *hire and fire*. It is in the prime minister's discretion to remove members of the cabinet from their positions, promote them to more im-

portant posts, demote them to noncabinet positions, or drop them from the government entirely. This power is exercised more frequently than in the U.S. cabinet, for the reshuffling of positions is almost an annual ritual in British government. Then, too, within the cabinet, prime ministers may select a small inner group that makes most of the key decisions, and which in some cases may not inform the cabinet at large about those decisions.

The prime minister also appoints the various committees which do much of the work of the cabinet. The prime minister decides which committees to create and which will be most important, and he or she may undertake to chair any of them directly.

A second kind of prime ministerial leverage over the cabinet is the *control of cabinet procedures*. The prime minister, working with the senior civil servant who is secretary to the cabinet, makes up the agenda for cabinet meetings, and is thus in a position to keep other members from discussing inconvenient matters. The prime minister, as chair of the meetings, can also open or close consideration of issues according to his or her interests. Furthermore, the minutes of the meetings are prepared by the cabinet secretary and reviewed by the prime minister, and may emphasize or deemphasize items as the prime minister directs.

Third, there is the constitutional convention of *collective cabinet responsibility*. This principle ordains that whatever disagreements exist within a cabinet, once a decision is reached, the entire cabinet—indeed all members of the government—are bound to support it in public, or, if unable to do so, to resign. Thus dissenting ministers are not allowed to take their case against the prime minister to the party or the public without forfeiting their jobs.

The Limits. In the United States, some cabinet members are drawn from the Senate or the House or from state governorships; but others come from senior positions in business and finance, universities, and the professions. And the president has a separate White House staff, some members of which may well be more powerful than any cabinet member.

In Britain, all members of the cabinet come from the world of politics. Two hold seats in the House of Lords, the rest in the Commons. All have their own power base, some from a different wing than the prime minister's, and several have ambitions to become prime minister themselves. And it is from among these powerful party leaders that a prime minister must select the cabinet; when changes are made in the cabinet's composition, a few replacements may be brought in from among the party's M.P.s, but usually the process consists mostly of a reshuffling within the core group rather than a wholesale introduction of new faces.

Unlike most of their colleagues, prime ministers do not have a department of their own. They are assisted by the staff of the P.M.'s office in 10 Downing Street, consisting of a number of civil servants, secretarial and other support workers, and a few policy and political advisers. But in total they have far smaller staffs than serve the U.S. president in the White House.

To sustain a position of strength in the party, then, the prime minister must take account of the various factions and try to establish a degree of balance between them in the cabinet. Not to do so is to run the risk of having too many powerful enemies sniping at the government from their seats in Parliament (for the prime minister can remove them from the government but not from their parliamentary seats).

We have already noted that this was a prime factor in Margaret Thatcher's ouster. John Major learned from her experience. In an indiscreet remark picked up accidentally by a live microphone in July 1993, he explained why he had not fired three members of his cabinet who were opposed to his European policies. He already had too many critics among the Conservative rank and file in the House of Commons, so "we don't want another three of the bastards out there." He went on to cite Lyndon Johnson's famous comment about its being safer to have your enemies "inside the tent pissing out than outside the tent pissing in." (One of the "bastards," John Redwood, went outside the tent in 1995 to challenge Major, unsuccessfully, for the leadership.)

The power to fire from the cabinet can also boomerang if used excessively. In 1962 Harold Macmillan, facing a severe decline in his government's poll standings, suddenly dismissed almost one-third of his cabinet. Instead of this being seen as an indication of strength and decisiveness, it was viewed as a sign of panic, and the poll ratings went down further still. (In the United States, a similar decline followed Jimmy Carter's effort to retrieve his collapsing popularity in 1979 by replacing one-third of his cabinet.)

In general, prime ministers may overreach themselves if their dealings with their cabinets are too high-handed. Ignoring or overriding the strongly held views of cabinet members, or excluding them from key decisions, or editing cabinet minutes too selectively, can cause cabinet revolts or individual resignations like that of Michael Heseltine from Thatcher's administration. Even collective responsibility can be breached by carefully placed leaks; indeed, most prime ministers (like most U.S. presidents) have angrily initiated investigations into leaks to the press from highly placed members of the government.

Moreover, the larger part of the work of the cabinet is not conducted in the meetings of the full cabinet, but in an array of committees and informal discussions. The prime minister cannot be involved in all of these other forums, and may not always be able to countermand proposals they produce.

Control of Parliament

The prime minister's ability to control Parliament and ensure passage of the government's legislative program far exceeds the U.S. president's power over Congress. The absence of a separation of powers is only part of the story. No less potent is the tight party discipline maintained by a small army of whips. The importance of the whips can be gauged by the cabinet rank commonly assigned to the chief whip, and by the fact that his office is located at 12 Downing Street, with connecting doors to the chancellor of the exchequer at no. 11 and the prime minister at no. 10. So it is not surprising that the whip's office provided an important stage in the progress to the prime ministership of Edward Heath and John Major.

Parliamentary debates and Question Times provide valuable opportunities to all cabinet members to build their reputations. But it is the prime minister who is usually assigned the starring role. In major debates the prime minister can decide whether his or her speech will open or close the occasion. And although the various heads of government departments take their turn at responding to questions in

Parliament, it is the 15 minutes of prime minister's Question Time every Tuesday and Thursday afternoon that is invariably excerpted on the evening television news, reinforcing the sense of a government dominated by one person.

The Limits. In chapter 10 we shall see that, although the control of the legislature by the executive is far greater in Britain than in the United States, it is not complete, and prime ministers in particular must handle their parliamentary relationships with care. If they do not, they face the possibility of rank and file revolts—a special danger when the government's majority in the Commons is small, as has been the case with John Major's administration. And Edward Heath's failure to cultivate his Conservative Party members in Parliament was one of the reasons for his being ejected from the leadership in 1975.

Moreover, the prime minister receives no special deference from the House of Commons. When the President of the United States enters Congress to present the State of the Union Address, everyone rises and he is given standing ovations even by his opponents. The entrance of the prime minister to the House of Commons is too regular an occurrence to justify any such acclaim, and murmurs of applause from supporters may well be countered by catcalls and cries of "Resign!" from the opposition benches.

Finally, the opportunities given the prime minister to shine in debates and Question Times are also potential hazards, for poor performance on such occasions may profoundly erode a prime minister's standing in Parliament and in the country.

Election Timing

Within its outside limit of five years, a government may dissolve Parliament and call an election any time. This gives a great advantage to the government, for, if it does not wait until the last moment, it can choose the time when conditions in the country are improving or before they deteriorate too far. The prime minister will consult with cabinet colleagues on this crucial decision, but in the last analysis this prerogative is in the hands of the prime minister.

When the timing proves to be correct, the prime minister's stature is enhanced. This was the case with Eden's reelection in 1955, Macmillan's in 1959, Wilson's in 1966, Thatcher's in 1983 and 1987, and Major's in 1992.

The Limits. Conversely, an error in timing leads to the end of a government and perhaps to the prime minister's career.

Thus Wilson called an election in June 1970 and lost, though his government's term did not expire until April 1971. Wilson was reelected four years later, probably because Heath called his election too late: had he set it four weeks earlier, the miners' strike, which crippled the economy, would not yet have started. Similarly, James Callaghan waited too long. Most of his colleagues and the entire press expected an election in the fall of 1978. Callaghan astonished them by delaying—and the "winter of discontent" and the end of Callaghan's prime ministership followed.

Influencing Public Opinion

The prime minister is not quite as ubiquitous a presence in the media as is the U.S. president, for in Britain the spotlight at the top of the system must be shared with the monarchy. Nonetheless, the prime minister makes more news than any cabinet minister.

The personalization of election campaigns, which we noted in Chapter 6, establishes the prime minister as a figure larger than life and more important than any cabinet member. Once elected, the 10 Downing Street press office ensures that this will continue to be the case. That office holds regular off-the-record meetings with the newspaper correspondents known as the "lobby." Under the direction of Thatcher's chief press officer, the formidable Bernard Ingham, the press office became an instrument not only for advancing the cause of the prime minister, but also for undermining the position of others in the cabinet.

Some prime ministers have been particularly adept at dominating the news. Churchill, of course, was an accomplished master in this respect. So was Harold Macmillan, who cultivated at the same time the personae of the laidback Edwardian gentleman and of the cartoonist's indefatigable *SuperMac!,* jetting around the world performing marvels of international diplomacy. Harold Wilson, too, puffing on his pipe, knowledgeable and articulate, made for good copy and useful sound bites.

The Limits. Not all prime ministers have been especially skillful in projecting themselves and their ideas to the public. Home was sadly lacking in this respect, and Major is depicted by caricaturists as very much the "grey" man, pleasant but colorless in style and speech. Whatever their strengths in working with colleagues in cabinet meetings, such shortcomings can prove to be a severe handicap.

But even those prime ministers who are superb performers in this respect may find that their very prominence makes them the prime target if their governments are not doing well. When the economy declined during the Macmillan and Wilson eras, the press, which had treated them so admiringly, became harshly critical of them. Whenever this happened, the speculation turned to which of their cabinet colleagues could best replace them; there are always other cabinet members, some with very strong public relations skills, and all with their own press offices, ready to take over immediately if the leader falls.

Making Foreign Policy

The prime minister, unlike the U.S. President, is not the constitutional commander-in-chief. Nonetheless, the "royal prerogative," enabling the executive to act in world affairs without formal ratification by the legislature, is available to the prime minister, and the prime minister is the most visible member of the government on the international scene.

Thus Churchill's strategic grasp and vast international reputation ensured that he would always be a force to be reckoned with in world politics. Before they became prime ministers, the experience of Eden and Home had been primarily in foreign relations. Macmillan and Wilson energetically pursued the idea of making Britain the intermediary between the United States and the Soviets. Heath took Britain into the Common Market. Thatcher cultivated the "special relationship" with Reagan, was a prime mover in shaping the west's policies toward the Soviets, and was personally responsible for the decisions that led to the Falklands victory. Major staked his reputation on his dealings with the European Community.

The Limits. Although the prime minister may be the government's principal foreign policy mover, the views of the foreign and defense secretaries can hardly be brushed aside. Even Churchill could not ignore the role of Anthony Eden, his Foreign Secretary. Thatcher, though with reluctance, was persuaded by her initial foreign secretary, Lord Carrington, to drop support for Rhodesia's white government and enable the black majority to take over. Douglas Hurd, Major's Foreign Secretary, was a prominent and well-respected player in international negotiations.

Prime ministers must also work with and through the international affairs bureaucracy, particularly the Foreign Office, which has its own ideas—shaped by long diplomatic experience—on the conduct of foreign policy.

Still, it is the prime minister who is the embodiment of the British government at summit conferences and who will be on the phone with foreign leaders during times of crisis. So here again, although successes add luster to a prime minister's reputation, the prime minister cannot usually foist the responsibility for failures onto anyone else. Macmillan suffered a personal humiliation when the summit meeting he had arranged between himself, Eisenhower, Khrushchev, and de Gaulle was aborted by the shooting down of an American U-2 spy plane over the Soviet Union. Harold Wilson's persistent efforts to try to negotiate an end to the Vietnam war produced nothing but Lyndon Johnson's contempt and angry dissension within the Labour Party.

But nothing could be more revealing of the special vulnerability of the prime minister to failure in world politics than the collapse of the Anglo-French-Israeli campaign to wrest the Suez Canal back from Egyptian President Nasser in 1956. The invading countries had been forced to withdraw when their action was condemned by the United States.

Prime Minister Eden had been the principal architect of the plan, which he had designed in concert with a small inner group of his cabinet. Harold Macmillan, as chancellor of the exchequer, had been a member of that inner group, and had supported the plan, changing his mind only when it became clear that the financial consequences of proceeding without U.S. support would be catastrophic. Yet it was Eden's reputation that was ruined; and when Eden's health forced his resignation, it was an untarnished Macmillan who succeeded him.

Patronage

The power to appoint to positions in the government is not the only kind of patronage available to the prime minister. Proposals for awards on the honors list we described in chapter 2 are reviewed by a political honors scrutiny committee of leading public figures; but many of those receiving the highest-ranking honors will owe their appointment to the influence of the prime minister. This is true of the lists issued at the New Year and on the queen's official birthday, and it is especially true of the prime minister's resignation list, a privilege available to every outgoing prime minister.

The Limits. A prime minister may amass a considerable store of gratitude from the recipients of major honors. Yet there may also be an accumulation of resentment from those receiving only a knighthood when they were expecting a peerage and from those left off the list entirely.

Moreover, a prime minister's reputation may be besmirched by the award of honors to people whose own reputations are questionable. This was the case with Harold Wilson's resignation list in 1976, which included knighthoods and peerages to property developers, financiers, and other businessmen of a kind not greatly admired within the ranks of the Labour Party. In fact, over 100 Labour M.P.s publicly dissociated themselves from the list, and the press was full of stories that the appointments had been influenced by Wilson's political secretary, Marcia Williams, who had become Lady Falkender in a previous honors list, and who might be in line for one or more directorships in the companies of those who had been honored.

Wilson, of course, had nothing further to lose politically. But the damage to his reputation may have been the cause of his failure to achieve his postretirement ambition—appointment as Master of an Oxford college.

In the light of this listing of the prime minister's powers and the limits on those powers, it is apparent that descriptions of the British system as either *prime ministerial* or *cabinet* government are oversimplifications. As we look at administrations since 1945, we find that all of them were combinations of both. In no case was the prime minister merely the first among equals. Nor did any prime minister establish one-person autocratic rule. However, there were significant variations depending on the individuals involved. Some administrations were closer to the cabinet model, whereas a somewhat larger number provided evidence of a stronger prime ministerial role.

To illustrate this further, it is necessary to look more closely at particular administrations. Two revealing examples are those of the Labour government under Clement Attlee and Margaret Thatcher's Conservative administration. The Attlee government approximated the cabinet model, yet the prime minister played a pivotal role. The Thatcher administration was dominated to a large extent by the prime minister, but not without important qualifications. We shall provide brief case studies of these two governments, then provide some further illustrations from other post-1945 administrations.

THE 1945 LABOUR GOVERNMENT

The Labour government of 1945–51 brought about far-reaching changes in domestic policy, including extensive nationalization of industry, major expansions of the welfare state and educational opportunities, and the inauguration of the National Health Service. Abroad, the government began to wind down the British empire by withdrawing from India. It was a period of activist, energetic, innovative government, responsive to the demand by a substantial majority of the electorate that the country not return to the inequities and upper class complacency of prewar Britain.

Yet the man who presided over this extraordinary period in British politics was the most colorless prime minister in recent history. Clement Attlee, who had held on to the position of Labour Party leader after his election as a temporary compromise candidate in the 1930s, was utterly lacking in charisma. Diminutive and homely in appearance and an uninspiring speaker, he was the butt of derisive comments such as Churchill's that he was "a modest little man, with a good deal to be modest about."

His cabinet, on the other hand, included several extremely able men with strong personalities and substantial followings in the Labour Party. Four of them—Ernest Bevin, Sir Stafford Cripps, Herbert Morrison, and Hugh Dalton—had served with Attlee in the wartime cabinet and were of prime ministerial stature. Others, without previous ministerial experience, quickly built their reputations in the Attlee administration, including the health minister, Aneurin Bevan, an idol of the left and a brilliant orator able to hold his own in parliamentary debates with Winston Churchill.

Surrounded by such a galaxy of talent, Attlee might appear in danger of being very much overshadowed. Indeed a Foreign Office official noted: "(Foreign Secretary) Bevin effaces Attlee, and at Big Three meetings he does all the talking, while Attlee nods his head convulsively and smokes his pipe."[1]

Here, then, we would appear to have the very model of cabinet government, one in which the prime minister hardly even qualifies as first among equals.

However, this is not an accurate assessment of Attlee's contribution. During the war, whenever Churchill was away conducting international negotiations, Attlee as the deputy prime minister quietly and efficiently presided over the business of the cabinet. When he himself became prime minister, cabinet meetings were run with a firm hand. Whereas Churchill at cabinet meetings loved to engage in long, rambling discussions of grand strategy, Attlee was all business. He would put the issue at hand to the meeting, asking in quick succession: "Does anyone have anything to add?" "Is anyone opposed?", and then moving on to the next item.

Unlike most other prime ministers, he did not shrink from the task of firing people from his government: "Sorry, have to ask for your resignation." "But why, Prime Minister?" "Simply not up to it, I'm afraid."[2]

He was adept at surviving the periodic efforts to replace him. After Labour won the 1945 election, some of the other Labour leaders met to discuss who might take over from Attlee and thus become prime minister. While they met, Attlee's wife drove him to Buckingham Palace, where the queen asked him to become prime minister, a fact he announced to his colleagues on his return. Then in 1947, when the government faced a severe economic crisis, Sir Stafford Cripps went in to see Attlee and politely suggested that he step down in favor of Ernest Bevin. But Cripps had not consulted Bevin. Attlee did so immediately, then laconically informed Cripps that Bevin had no intention of accepting the proposal.

Attlee still had to deal with the reality of being surrounded by leaders of con-

Clement Attlee flanked by senior cabinet members Ernest Bevin and Herbert Morrison
SOURCE: Hulton Deutsch Collection Limited.

siderable stature. He might fire junior members of his government brusquely, but he could not so easily dismiss the more powerful members. Far from punishing Cripps for his disloyalty, he promoted him to a new position overseeing the economy. Attlee's main contribution to his administration, in fact, was keeping so many disparate and strong-willed personalities working together for so long. When at last open conflict between rival factions erupted, and Bevan and Harold Wilson resigned from the government, Attlee had been in the hospital, unable to perform his usual mediating role.

So this administration is commonly referred to as the Labour government of 1945–51 rather than the Attlee government. Attlee's contribution was far more important than would appear from superficial judgments of his personality. Still, this was an administration corresponding more closely to the model of cabinet government, the key decisions being made by five or six members of the cabinet in concert with the prime minister.

THE THATCHER GOVERNMENT, 1979–90

Most accounts of the 1979-90 administration do not refer to it as the Conservative government of that period, but, unequivocally, as the Thatcher government. It was her vivid personality and strongly held ideas that set her mark on her time under the title of Thatcherism.

Like any "ism," Thatcherism lends itself to many interpretations. Clearly there is a strong domestic policy component, as we saw in chapter 5—economic individualism, strong enforcement of law and order, and the upholding of traditional morality. Then in foreign policy, Thatcherism conveys a fervent nationalism and a commitment to military strength. But along with these policy or ideological strands, there is another element—the assertion of strong leadership. Without assertive leadership, she believed, it would not be possible to achieve her policy goals, and those goals amounted to nothing less than the repeal of most of the policies that had been introduced by the Labour government of 1945-51 (and consolidated and expanded subsequently by Conservative as well as Labour governments).

The two strands of ideology and leadership style came together in her self-

Margaret Thatcher at the peak of her power, 1988
SOURCE: Courtesy C.O.I.

identification as a "conviction politician." As she said in 1983: "Yes I do believe things very strongly. Yes, I do believe in trying to persuade people that the things I believe in are the things they should follow . . . I am far too old to change now." Confronted with demands that she change her economic policies to reduce unemployment, she delighted a Conservative Party annual conference by insisting there would be no Heathlike U-turn: "You turn if you want to. The lady's not for turning!"

Her leadership style matched the intensity of her beliefs. She was an engaged, hands-on leader (in sharp contrast to the laidback approach of her ideological soulmate, Ronald Reagan). She was a classic workaholic. Her press secretary reported: "It is impossible to get Mrs. Thatcher to relax. If she has an afternoon off, she will say: But what am I going to do with it?"

Trained in science and then in law, she quickly mastered the material set before her, and was impatient with anyone who fell short in this respect. "But what are the facts?" she would demand of anyone who offered her only generalities. Though thoughtful and considerate to her immediate staff, she treated other politicians and senior civil servants with an impatient assertiveness that seemed to many of them harsh and overbearing.

All these traits were evident in her relationship with the cabinet. From the outset she made it clear from her conduct of cabinet meetings that she was in charge. As early as 1980, the press was providing accounts of her hectoring and bullying her cabinet ministers. From the beginning, too, she established her control over the central area of her concern, economic policy, by appointing mostly fellow-believers to the top economic posts and to the relevant cabinet committees. Those in the cabinet who were not true Thatcherites were disdained as "wets," too disposed to accommodation and compromise. They were not, in her phrase, "one of us." And those who were not—St. John Stevas, Carrington, Gilmore, Pym, Prior, Heseltine, Walker—were weeded out one by one, sometimes two at a time. She might not be as matter-of-fact about firing people as Attlee; but, as she said: "I'm not a good butcher, but I've learned how to carve the joint." At last all the members of her cabinet shared her own convictions, or at least owed their advancement to her.

Her dominant style in cabinet was matched by her behavior toward opposition leaders, television interviewers, and heads of European governments. By the mid-1980s critics were warning that she was becoming increasingly arrogant and autocratic. Her style, it was said, was far more imperious than the queen's. She had presided over the Falklands victory parade, a role usually reserved for the monarch, and had taken to using the royal "we."

But for all the regality of her style, her dominance over people and events was far from complete. Before her election she had insisted that she would choose a cabinet of people who believed as she did, for otherwise time and energies would be frittered away in internal wrangling. Yet once elected, she had no choice but to include a number of the men associated with her predecessor, Edward Heath, although she and Heath despised each other. She had held a relatively junior post in Heath's cabinet and initially needed to draw on leaders with more extensive experience; also, until she established herself more firmly, she was obligated to give representation to other powerful factions in the party.

Outside of economic policy, the presence of so many "wets" in the cabinet set limits to her authority, and slowed her plans to produce change in such controversial areas as policy toward the trade unions. The process of getting rid of the dissidents extended over a period of years. And as they left, no longer safely inside the tent, they became potential sources of danger.

The dangers increased when the departures from the cabinet began to consist of men who had been strong Thatcher supporters, including Chancellor of the Exchequer Nigel Lawson and, finally, Geoffrey Howe. Both resigned, as we saw in Chapter 5, partly because of policy differences, but also because of her abrasive treatment of them. And ultimately it was Thatcher's cleansing her cabinet of everyone who did not fully measure up to her requirements that led to her undoing, for the successful revolt against her was precipitated by ousted cabinet members.

The vulnerability of her position, as exposed by her sudden overthrow, has been used by some scholars to support the thesis that Thatcher was always very much less powerful than the appearance suggested. Her achievements in both domestic and world affairs fell far short of her aspirations. Her control of her cabinet and of crucial policies is brought into question by her own complaint that in 1987-88 Nigel Lawson shadowed the deutschmark (intervened in the currency market to tie the pound closely to the deutschmark) without her knowledge and in defiance of her position.[3] (Lawson has strenuously denied that she did not know what he was doing.) Polls showed Thatcher to be among the most unpopular of recent prime ministers, and the majority of the people remained unpersuaded by Thatcherism at the close of her more than 11 years in office.

Yet if this position is a useful corrective to the perception of Thatcher as an almost absolute monarch, it understates the extent of her impact. Although Thatcher did not succeed in resolving Britain's deep economic problems or restoring her country to great power status, her administration changed the direction of public policy in important respects and forced the Labour Party, as well as the Conservatives, to accept much of this change. No doubt the modification of past policies would have been undertaken by any other Conservative leader; but the pace and extent of change in economic policy, privatization, and labor relations are directly attributable to her.

Some have suggested that her being ousted proved that her power was always overstated; but even dictators have been overthrown in coups, and their fall does not prove that they lacked power until then. Thatcher was far short of being a dictator, and she could never fully transcend the limits on any prime minister's power. Yet she did succeed, especially toward the end of her tenure, in directing a system that had many of the elements of prime ministerial government.

OTHER PRIME MINISTER-CABINET RELATIONSHIPS

Of the other post-1945 administrations, two can readily be classified as cabinet governments, and two as prime ministerial.

The most clear-cut example of cabinet government was that of *Sir Alec Douglas-Home (1963-64)*.

Home's appointment by a patently undemocratic process had been resented by

Lord (Sir Alec Douglas-) Home: the last aristocratic prime minister
SOURCE: Courtesy C.O.I.

other leading candidates for the job. He then had to negotiate to get them into his cabinet, thereby becoming dependent on their support. Despite his having been an able foreign secretary, his poor performances in public and in Parliament further eroded his standing with his colleagues. Moreover, as an interim candidate, with an election due within a year of his appointment, there was little opportunity for him to establish himself as a strong leader.

Interim judgments on *John Major* (see photo, p. 100), elected by the Conservatives in 1990 and by the electorate in 1992, have also placed his administration in the *cabinet* category. Partly this is because he is not Margaret Thatcher. His personal style is low-key and courteous, and his conduct of cabinet meetings is collegial rather than confrontational. But within a year of the 1992 election, his position was also weakened by a combination of unfavorable circumstances. A prolonged recession and a series of governmental blunders reduced his initially high ratings to the lowest of any prime minister in polling history. His slim parliamentary majority was made precarious by a small group of Conservatives implacably hostile to his European policy.

He did take a number of bold steps to assert his prime ministerial authority. He forced the rebels into line with a parliamentary vote of confidence in 1992. He abruptly dismissed his close friend, Chancellor of the Exchequer Norman Lamont.

His bringing forward the leadership election process in 1995 won him a two-thirds majority in the parliamentary party, and he followed this immediately with a reconstruction of his cabinet that gave little ground to his right-wing opponents. Michael Portillo was given a modest promotion to defense secretary, a few other cabinet appointees were acceptable to the right, and the department of employment, long a target of right-wing hostility, was abolished. Still, the Thatcherites' nemesis, Michael Heseltine, became deputy prime minister (a reward for having backed Major against Redwood), and other non-Thatcherites advanced to important cabinet posts. Although the new foreign secretary, Malcolm Rifkind, was somewhat less enthusiastic about Europe than his predecessor, Douglas Hurd, who had just retired, the new cabinet lineup made it clear that the Europhobes had been marginalized.

Yet if Major had strengthened his hand with his leadership election victory, he still had to maintain a precarious balancing act, conscious of the fact that one-third of the Conservative members of Parliament had declared themselves opposed to him and his policies and would certainly not be mollified by the remaking of his cabinet, which they viewed with dismay as a sharp swing to the left.

With *Anthony Eden (1955-57)* we come to an unfortunate example of prime ministerial government.

As foreign secretary, Eden had been the very image of coolness, suavity, and skilled diplomacy. As prime minister he was nervous and tense, badgering cabinet

Anthony Eden: successful foreign secretary, failed prime minister
SOURCE: Courtesy C.O.I.

Edward Heath: better at controlling an orchestra than the unions
SOURCE: Hulton Deutsch Collection Limited.

ministers with detailed questions about affairs in their departments, unable to tolerate opposition.

The Suez fiasco was planned by him in consultation with a few cabinet colleagues. The rest of the cabinet was informed, and most went along. But this was a prime ministerial enterprise, and its collapse destroyed the career of its chief architect.

Edward Heath (1970-74) also established a dominant position in his government, as clearly in command of his Cabinet as he was when conducting an orchestra—one of his favorite leisure pursuits. Yet, after some early successes, he too saw his administration end in failure.

Heath came to power after a surprising election victory that was seen as a personal triumph. This placed him in a strong position in relation to his party and his cabinet. As a close student of the machinery of government, he introduced a number of changes in its structure, including the establishment of the Central Policy Review Staff.

At home, he retreated from his initial free-market approach, imposing controls on prices and negotiating personally with the unions on wage policies. Abroad, he succeeded where his predecessors had failed by gaining acceptance for Britain's entry into the Common Market, conducting the final stages of the negotiation himself.

He was very much in command until the sudden jump in world oil prices—and the consequent union demands for wage increases—created the economic crisis that overwhelmed him.

The rest of the governments since World War II are less easy to categorize, although the administrations of Churchill, Macmillan, and Wilson tend toward the prime ministerial side of the spectrum, and Callaghan's toward the cabinet side.

The administration of *Winston Churchill (1951-55)* would appear on the surface to be strongly prime ministerial, for Churchill himself was a charismatic world leader whose personal style was that of a benevolent but self-absorbed autocrat.

Oblivious to the heavy work schedules of his colleagues, Churchill would summon them to join him for discussions of grand strategy that continued into the small hours of the morning. He used his power of appointment to make excellent use of the available talents; his long experience in government and politics made him knowledgeable in many areas of policy; and he was still able to keep Parliament under his oratorical spell.

Yet he had come back to office at the age of 77. Though still energetic, he left domestic affairs largely in the hands of R. A. Butler and others; and even in foreign policy he had to contend with the sometimes conflicting views of Foreign Secretary Eden. In 1952 his health began to fail, and a severe stroke in 1953 incapacitated him for several months—a fact that was not revealed to the public. Although he slowly improved and was able to function in public again, the country was governed in his last year or more in office by members of his cabinet.

Harold Macmillan (1957-63) was the central, highly visible figure in his gov-

Winston Churchill: not quite as great in peace as in war
SOURCE: Courtesy C.O.I.

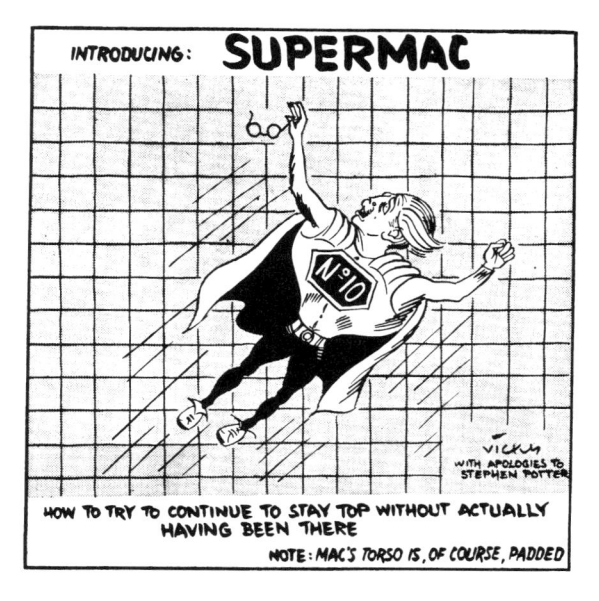

Harold Macmillan: "Supermac"

SOURCE: Vicky [Victor Weisz], *Evening Standard*, 6 November 1958. Cartoon Study Centre, University of Kent, Canterbury.

ernment, an activist leader despite his affecting the style of a languid Edwardian gentleman. In domestic affairs he enjoyed settling industrial disputes over beer and sandwiches at 10 Downing Street. In foreign policy he was "SuperMac," jetting from one trouble spot to another.

Yet his cabinet meetings, according to his colleagues, were constructive and even enjoyable occasions. He showed respect for the opinions of others, did not insist on his own positions if he encountered strong opposition, and sought to build a consensus.

Macmillan basked in high levels of popularity, inside and outside his cabinet, especially during the economic boom of 1957–60. After that, however, as the economy weakened, and he suffered some major foreign policy disappointments, his standing deteriorated. Then he was made to look foolish when he accepted the denial of his war minister, John Profumo, that he was involved with a call girl who was also sleeping with a member of the Soviet embassy staff. Profumo told the same lie on the floor of the House of Commons. Profumo was a gentleman, and Macmillan believed that gentlemen do not lie to the House of Commons.

Macmillan's resignation in 1963 was ostensibly on health grounds, but also because he was under a good deal of pressure to step down. Yet his power was still sufficient to enable him to override the claims of others and name his own successor.

Harold Wilson (1964-70 and 1974-76) was an even more activist leader than Macmillan.

Wilson believed that a prime minister must be knowledgeable about and involved in all major areas of public policy, domestic and international. As a wartime civil servant and former cabinet member, he was an expert on governmental structures. As an economist, he was at least a partner in financial decisions with his economic ministers, and even for a time assumed personal command of economic affairs. Like Macmillan, he became an arbiter of industrial disputes and made a number of efforts at international shuttle diplomacy. He was the paramount figure in his government, especially during his first years in office, making many of his decisions in consultation with one or two members of his cabinet or even unilaterally.

However, Wilson provides yet another example of the difficulty prime ministers have in maintaining their dominance indefinitely. As time passed, other cabinet members became increasingly unhappy with his practice of excluding all but a few favored leaders from his decision-making, and he was forced to set up cabinet committees to secure wider consultation.

Then the limits of his authority became painfully clear when he and his employment minister, Barbara Castle, tried to impose some mild limits on labor strikes. The debate on the proposal ran into furious resistance in the cabinet. One of the members of that cabinet, Richard Crossman, is among those who have argued that Britain has prime ministerial rather than cabinet government. Yet Crossman's account

Harold Wilson: more dominant, but less successful, than Attlee
SOURCE: Courtesy C.O.I.

of the confrontation in cabinet does not convey an impression of an all-powerful chief executive:

> It became clear that Harold's self-confidence, complacency, bounce and good temper were all breaking down. At one point he said, "Well . . . you are abandoning your cabinet commitments because they are unpopular, you're soft, you're lily-livered. If you do that, why shouldn't I?" . . . He was a little man, for the first time dragged down on our level. It was painful because in a sense he was sabotaged and utterly nonplussed.[4]

Wilson's standing never fully recovered from his defeat on the trade union proposal, and in his second administration he moved toward a more consultative style in his dealings with his cabinet.

Moreover, Wilson was a deeply insecure man, obsessed with the notion that others in his cabinet were conspiring to unseat him. Indeed, there were other members of his cabinet—notably George Brown, Roy Jenkins, and James Callaghan—with strong positions in the Labour party and with ambitions to succeed Wilson as prime minister. During 1968 and 1969, when Wilson's popularity had been severely damaged by the forced devaluation of the pound, his paranoid tendencies were grounded in reality. As one supporter of Jenkins put it: "Since Wilson believed that everyone was plotting against him even when they weren't, they thought they might as well do so."[5]

Wilson's method of protecting his position was to play his rivals off against each other, changing their roles periodically so that none would be established as his obvious successor. Yet a leader so preoccupied with protecting his power might not achieve very much with that power, and Wilson's critics have argued that, in fact, his administration accomplished very little. This judgment may be unduly harsh, for the Wilson years saw major expansions of higher education and individual rights, and his skillful handling was largely responsible for preventing a British withdrawal from the Common Market. However, Labour achieved much less under Harold Wilson than it had under Clement Attlee.

James Callaghan (1976-79) was Wilson's final choice to be his successor.

Callaghan seemed likely to survive only briefly in office, for his party lacked an overall majority in parliament, and Wilson had resigned just before the economy deteriorated and inflation began to soar. Moreover, Callaghan's previous record in holding top cabinet positions had been mixed, and he had to preside over a cabinet that included sharply diverging political doctrines.

Yet he succeeded in keeping his party in power for three more years. He held off parliamentary defeat by forging alliances with the Liberals and then with the nationalist parties. Within the cabinet he showed the same kind of skills that Attlee had demonstrated to keep a fractious group of strong personalities from breaking apart. Callaghan accomplished this by paying careful attention to the various ideological and policy positions represented in the cabinet. But he also used one other prime ministerial weapon: enforcement of the convention of collective responsibility. The doctrine was rigorously applied even to the most minor member of the gov-

James Callaghan: surviving without a majority
SOURCE: Courtesy C.O.I.

ernment, and speeches by cabinet members were personally reviewed in advance by Callaghan.

Callaghan has insisted that cabinet government still prevails in Britain, and his own experience was one in which he was dependent on the continued support of every member of his cabinet. Yet this apparent weakness was also a source of strength, for in the absence of a parliamentary majority, the prime minister's fate is interwoven with the fate of his party and his Cabinet, and Callaghan made brilliant use of this reality. So his government not only survived, but actually passed some significant legislation—until its acute vulnerability was exposed by the "winter of discontent."

CONCLUSION

British government clearly cannot be defined as rule by one person. There are checks and balances in the system. There have been no Hitlers or Stalins in 10 Downing Street.

Nor is the prime minister in the position of a U.S. president, who is able to operate key areas of policy independently of the cabinet. In our survey of British administrations since 1945, we have seen that any prime minister who tried to force the cabinet into his or her personal mold has come to grief sooner or later—sooner for Eden, later for Thatcher.

Yet our review also indicates that in most of these administrations, the prime minister has been the leading figure. The media's preference for covering individuals rather than institutions may overstate the prime minister's importance. Nonetheless, the very fact of their coverage contributes to the personalization of power in government and builds the status of the prime minister.

How much power is actually accumulated in the prime minister's office depends on the individuals involved and the circumstances of the time. The potential for power will be realized only to the extent that two conditions are satisfied. First, the prime minister must have very strong leadership skills, and the will and energy to use them. Second, the prime minister must have the backing of a substantial majority of the parliamentary party, which in turn will be heavily influenced by the degree of support among the electorate.

If these conditions are satisfied, a prime minister is in a position to establish, not dictatorial rule, but at least a marked tendency toward a concentration of personalized power, and this tendency has raised justifiable concerns about its appropriateness to the healthy functioning of democracy.

SOME QUESTIONS TO THINK ABOUT

What are the most important powers of the prime minister? In what ways, and to what extent, are these powers limited?

Would you classify the British system as prime ministerial government? Cabinet government? Neither?

Of the various prime ministers, which come closest and which farthest from the dominant prime ministerial model?

What are the similarities and differences in functions and powers of the British prime minister and the U.S. president?

NOTES

1. Cited in Henry Pelling, *The Labour Governments, 1945-51* (Macmillan, 1984), p. 120.
2. Alan Watkins, *The Observer*, 12 November 1979.
3. Margaret Thatcher, *The Downing Street Years* (HarperCollins, 1993), p. 699.
4. Anthony Howard, ed., *The Crossman Diaries* (condensed version, Magnum, 1979), p. 626.
5. Ben Pimlott, *Harold Wilson* (HarperCollins, 1992), p. 490.

SUGGESTIONS FOR FURTHER READING

On Prime Ministers in general, see Anthony King (ed.), *The British Prime Minister* (Macmillan, 1985), Peter Hennessy and Anthony Seldon (eds.), *Ruling Performance* (Blackwell, 1987), James Barber, *The Prime Minister Since 1945* (Blackwell, 1981), Bernard Donoughue, *The Prime Minister* (Cape, 1987), Peter Clarke, *A Question of Leadership*, and Michael Foley, *The Rise of the British Presidency* (Manchester University Press, 1993). On the cabinet, see Peter Hennessy, *Cabinet* (Blackwell, 1986), and John P. Mackintosh, *The British Cabinet* (Stevens, 1977).

Biographies of post-1945 prime ministers include Kenneth Harris, *Attlee* (Weidenfeld and Nicolson, 1984), David Carlton, *Eden* (Allen and Unwin, 1981), Anthony Sampson, *Macmillan* (Simon and Schuster, 1967), Ben Pimlott, *Harold Wilson* (HarperCollins, 1992), and Bruce Anderson, *John Major* (Headline, 1991). There are, of course, vast quantities of material about Winston Churchill, but most of it deals with the period before his peacetime return to power, when his health was deteriorating.

Margaret Thatcher is already the subject of a fullscale publishing industry. In addition to her autobiographical *Downing Street Years* (HarperCollins, 1993) and *The Path to Power* (HarperCollins, 1995), see Hugo Young, *The Iron Lady* (Noonday, 1989), or, in its British final edition, *One of Us* (Pan, 1993), Peter Riddell, *The Thatcher Era and its Legacy* (Blackwell, 1991), Peter Jenkins, *Mrs. Thatcher's Revolution* (Cape, 1987), Chris Ogden, *Maggie* (Simon and Schuster, 1990) and Dennis Kavanagh, *Thatcherism and British Politics* (Oxford University Press, 1987). On John Major's handling of the Thatcher legacy see Dennis Kavanagh and Anthony Seldon (eds.), *The Major Effect* (Macmillan, 1994).

After *The Crossman Diaries* (condensed version, edited by Anthony Howard, Magnum Books, 1979) was published in defiance of established British rules, two other Labour ministers, Barbara Castle and Tony Benn, also published detailed diaries of cabinet proceedings. Many others, both Labour and Conservative, have published memoirs of their experiences in government. Among the most interesting of these are Roy Jenkins, *A Life at the Centre* (Pan, 1991), Dennis Healey, *The Time of My Life* (Penguin, 1990), Ian Gilmour, *Dancing With Dogma* (Pocket Books, 1992), Nicholas Ridley, *My Style of Government* (Fontana, 1992) and Nigel Lawson, *The View From No. 11* (Corgi, 1992).

9
Civil Servants and Their Ministers

Downing Street, where the prime minister lives and works, is a short, unpretentious street off a much more impressive avenue: Whitehall. Along Whitehall, stretching from the Palace of Westminster, which houses Parliament, to Trafalgar Square, are located several of the longest-established departments of the national government. And working within these and other departments located in less prestigious areas are the bureaucrats—the members of the civil service, who under the general direction of elected ministers, are responsible for the detailed interpretation and execution of laws passed by the legislature.

In Britain this national bureaucracy extends farther into the governmental structure than the federal bureaucracy in the United States. An incoming U.S. president has at his disposal the power to appoint a White House staff of some 500 members, a larger number to the Executive Office of the President, and a much larger number still to the various cabinet departments. With thousands of people to hire, and the senior appointments constitutionally mandated to be reviewed by the senate, criticism is almost invariably directed at incoming administrations for taking so long to fill the available posts.

Such complaints are rarely heard in Britain. A new prime minister appoints about a hundred members of the government and a small number of policy advisors and consultants to the prime minister's office. In addition, cabinet ministers may each hire one or two political advisers. Because there are no constitutional requirements for legislative review of each of these appointments, the new administration is quickly in place.

Once established in their positions, the politicians must work out their relationships with their senior civil servants, headed in each department by a permanent secretary and one or more deputy secretaries and under-secretaries. The occupants of these positions constitute the 700 or so members of the Higher Civil Service.

This Higher Civil Service is a prestigious body. Typically, permanent secretaries are rewarded with knighthoods (although under new policies this will not be as automatic as in the past), and the most distinguished among them, dubbed "the Great and the Good," have been called back from retirement periodically to head up royal commissions.

The British civil service at large has a well-deserved reputation for integrity. Corruption scandals involving its members have been rare. Yet, for all its prestige and probity, it is the target of a good deal of criticism. The critics make two charges, one concerned with competence, the other with accountability.

THE COMPETENCE QUESTION

Recruitment to the "fast stream" of the civil service leading to the senior positions is an extremely demanding process. Applicants for the position of administrative trainee are university undergraduates who sit through a day of rigorous qualifying examinations testing verbal, numerical, and problem-solving skills. One in six qualifies for the next stage—two intensive days with the civil service selection board.

The board takes them through more written tests, requires them to participate in and chair group discussions, and subjects them to assessment by a psychologist. The reviewers judge the candidates' intellectual and personal qualities and their communication skills, and the applicants they qualify are passed on for a final interview.

Educational and Class Background

This method of selection of the prospective "high flyers," demanding though it is, has been faulted on two grounds. First, it favors candidates from Oxford and Cambridge: over two-fifths of those applying from Oxbridge passed the first hurdle in 1987, whereas only about one in ten passed who applied from other universities. The 1992 intake of these high flyers included 41 percent from the two universities.

At the top of the civil service, too, Oxbridge graduates predominate: in 1994, 14 of the 20 largest Whitehall departments were run by Oxford or Cambridge alumni. To be sure, Oxford and Cambridge offer an excellent education, but as we have seen, they draw disproportionately from the expensive public schools; in fact, 16 of the top 20 permanent secretaries in 1994 had gone to a public school. Three-quarters of them had made their entire careers in the civil service. And all 20 were men.

Efforts have been undertaken to encourage recruitment from other universities, and the civil service today certainly is not as unrepresentative as it was before the Northcote-Trevelyan reforms of 1854. These replaced entry by upper-class patronage with competitive examinations, causing Queen Victoria to protest that the result would be the admission of "low people without breeding or feelings of gentlemen." Yet even though appointment and promotion in the civil service is now based on meritocratic principles rather than family background, few of today's senior staff would have been considered ill-bred by Victoria. Despite a series of reports over the years, including that of the Fulton Committee in 1968, all of which urged that efforts be undertaken to broaden the strata from which top civil servants are drawn, the public school-Oxbridge background still predominates.

The Lack of Technical Expertise

The Fulton Committee's report identified a further problem. It pointed out that the qualities tested by the selection process do not encompass all of those needed by a modern state in a competitive, global economy.

By all accounts, British civil servants are superb at chairing committees, analyzing problems, and writing lucid memos. In foreign policy their exemplary tradition of cool, sophisticated diplomacy is admired internationally. Yet most of them do not have training in science and engineering or in professional fields like law and accounting which play such a large part in contemporary government. There is a separate recruitment process for lawyers, scientists, and other specialists, but they do not have the status of the administrative group or rise to the top civil service positions.

Thus the government ministers, who mostly possess the generalist skills of the politician, need the complementary expertise of specialists but instead find themselves working daily with people who are themselves outstanding generalists. This is one of the reasons why the Attlee government's program of nationalization was not entrusted to regular cabinet departments and thus was not supervised by the civil service, but rather by specially created public corporations run by people recruited from industry and the professions.

For Margaret Thatcher the problem was not how to bypass the civil service but how to cut its size and invigorate what was left. The cutting was severe: there were 730,000 civil service employees when she came to office in 1979 and 560,000 when she left in 1990. Much of the reduction was accomplished by privatization: government departments sent to private firms work that had previously been performed by themselves or other government agencies (so that many of those removed from civil service status were industrial employees). Other economies resulted from a series of reviews directed by industry leaders, notably Marks and Spencer's Sir Derek Rayner.

Invigoration came from geographic and administrative decentralization. In 1988, a government efficiency unit produced a report, *Improving Management in Government: The Next Steps,* which proposed radical civil service reforms. The principles of the report were put into effect by the Thatcher administration, and a major feature of the "next steps" was the creation of a number of agencies responsible for delivering government services. These agencies, each headed by a chief executive, were given a high degree of independence from their parent, policy-making departments, thus giving them much more flexibility than is commonly the case in civil service operations; and they were given targets on, for example, productivity and speed of delivery. Thatcher also encouraged the recruitment and promotion of people with technical and other specialized skills.

John Major continued the process. More cuts to bring the number of civil servants down below 500,000 were announced, and the government published a plan to tie salary increases to performance rather than civil service grade, as well as to step up the recruitment of midcareer outside specialists. Major also introduced and gave a high personal priority to the Citizen's Charter, aimed at making government services more responsive to the concerns of consumers. For example, travelers on British Rail were promised refunds if trains were persistently late. Moreover, the government published a proposal to bring more outsiders into jobs previously held by civil servants.

Supporters of the changes believed that at last the government was responding to demands for greater value for the taxpayer's money, and that the civil service needed to be jolted out of its complacency. In the age of Thatcherism there was no room for the view stated in 1973 by a former civil service head that the business of the civil service was "the orderly management of decline."[1]

Skeptics saw the changes as a systematic effort to reduce the scope and quality of government services, to replace what they called the *public service ethos* with the methods of market individualism, and to instill a permanent sense of insecurity among civil servants. The critics saw the Citizen's Charter as a naive exercise in public relations. And they believed that the public was not well-served by steps that could destroy the morale, and thus the effectiveness, of civil servants at all levels. Others doubted that the civil service hierarchy would take productivity targets seriously, or that they would allow privatization to proceed to the point at which it seriously threatened their control over the departments of government.

ACCOUNTABILITY

The second main criticism of the civil service concerns the relationship between the career officials and the elected government ministers, a relationship that is no less difficult to define than the distribution of power between the prime minister and the cabinet.

The Ethos of Subordination and Impartiality

Taken at face value, the traditional ethos of the civil service resolves the issue. Several senior civil servants have articulated that ethos in unequivocal terms. Sir Robert Armstrong, secretary to the cabinet during the Thatcher years, explained that "the civil service as such has no constitutional personality or responsibility separate from the duly elected government of the day," and that it is the duty of civil servants always to obey their ministers. For one of his predecessors the rule was "conviction politicians, certainly: conviction civil servants, no."

Was there no limit on this duty to obey? Another head of the civil service was asked whether he had ever considered resigning over an issue he felt strongly about. He admitted that, as a treasury department official at the time of the Suez crisis, he had disagreed with the government's policy and resented having been used as part of a cover plan to deceive the American State Department. So he wore a black tie until the operation was over. Asked if anyone had noticed he said: "one or two chaps noticed, yes. It was the equivalent of letting off steam. I now think it was rather a juvenile gesture . . ."[2]

The insistence on avoiding even the impression of guiding policy could actually be intensely frustrating to political leaders. Thus Edward Heath was furious when he asked Burke Trend, his secretary to the cabinet, for his advice on a complex policy matter, and Trend replied that it was not his job to do so. Trend's style was to pose a series of Socratic questions to the prime minister that he believed would help him make his own decisions. Sir Robert Armstrong, on the other hand, took the view that he was obligated to offer advice where appropriate to the prime minister. But he explained that he didn't mind in the least when his advice was rejected.

The ethos required that subordination must be combined with strict impartiality. Whatever the private opinions of civil servants, this must in no way affect their ability to serve the government of the day, whatever its political complexion. Thus as soon as the parties' manifestos are published at the beginning of an election campaign, the civil service prepares alternative programs for implementing the proposals of the main parties and presents the appropriate version to the victors.

While serving as secretary of state for health, Barbara Castle, a left-wing minister under Harold Wilson, was embarrassed when it was revealed that she—an opponent of setting aside beds for private patients in National Health Service hospitals—had herself been given a private bed for an emergency operation. One of her civil servants reassured her. He did not agree with her views on private beds, but the department would not have her hounded. "They were all so charming," Castle wrote later, "gathering round to defend me, that I wondered once again at the unique quality of the British civil service: the capacity of its top people to develop a genuine loyalty to a Minister who wasn't here yesterday and will be gone tomorrow."[3]

Civil Service Assets

Are the British civil servants truly subordinate? Are they completely impartial? Not according to those who have written most extensively on the subject. And the skepticism of scholars and journalists is shared by a broad public educated by two witty and highly popular television series, *Yes, Minister* and *Yes, Prime Minister.* Margaret Thatcher was a fan of the programs, which depicted the exploits of a minister repeatedly outwitted by his principal secretary. Of course, the series exaggerated the wiliness of the civil service and the haplessness of the politicians. Yet the literature on the subject and the testimony of many in government suggested that what was presented as farce had a strong basis in reality.

In fact, the British civil service is not a mere implementer of programs and policies of its political overlords. Although its senior members do not directly refuse to carry out instructions of which they disapprove, they have a number of assets at their disposal to delay or even kill initiatives that they believe to be contrary to the public interest.

Knowledge. Once established, civil servants have security of employment until the normal retirement age of 60. Those who reach the top will typically have served in at least a few different departments. But generally they will stay in each department long enough to become thoroughly acquainted with its agenda.

Ministers, on the other hand, do not have tenure. And the frequency with which prime ministers reshuffle their governments makes it difficult for cabinet and other departmental ministers to become experts in the field for which they are responsible before they are moved on to their next assignment. Thus they are placed in the position of amateurs, dependent on full-time professionals for access to the information without which they cannot function effectively. And how that information is presented to them may determine whether or not they can proceed with their proposals.

For example, Labour's education secretary was briefed by his permanent secretary about the promise contained in Labour's October 1974 election manifesto to "withdraw tax relief and charitable status from public schools." The civil servant presented a number of reasons why the minister should not take the initiative on the matter. There were a number of complex legal problems concerning the definition of public schools and the precise character of their charitable status. The responsibility for untangling these problems lay with three other departments, not the education department. So "I cannot think of anything we ourselves can usefully do in the interim."[4]

The permanent secretary was not inventing these difficulties. No doubt there were complicated legal and legislative hurdles in the way of following through on the idea. But the information was presented in a way that seemed to allow of no alternative but to forget the proposal. Were there no ways of overcoming the obstacles? Was the civil servant simply presenting the facts—or selecting those facts that supported his own dislike of the idea?

The Paper War. Richard Crossman, reflecting on his years as one of Harold Wilson's ministers, says: "Every department wages a paper war against its minister. They try to drown him in paper so that he can't be a nuisance."[5]

Every night, ministers must take home with them red boxes stuffed with papers on decisions that have to be made that night as well as briefing material for the next day's meetings. And, says Crossman, he had no chance of asserting his authority unless he carefully read the material and showed that he had done so by a written comment—at least a "yes" or a "no"—by the next day.

Staff Networks. Within each department a minister may bring in one or two political or policy advisers of his own, but together they will be greatly outnumbered by a civil service staff organized on a hierarchical basis with the permanent secretary at the top. Thus the rest of the staff owe their career prospects to the judgments of the permanent secretary rather than the minister, a fact that militates against the possibility that lesser staff members might propose ideas not favored by the permanent secretary. Even the private secretary assigned to the minister is a civil servant. Thus the rule that the private secretary should keep in strictest confidence everything that transpires in the minister's office will not always guarantee the minister's ability to keep anything from the permanent secretary.

Moreover, the collegiality of civil servants is not confined to their own departments. They keep in touch with their counterparts in other departments. Because a normal route to the top includes experience in the treasury department, its alumni who go on to senior positions in other departments remain in contact with the treasury, thereby forming a treasury network. This ensures that permanent and deputy secretaries are always well briefed on financial matters and always equipped to tell their ministers the budgetary obstacles in the way of any of their initiatives.

Then, too, civil servants often form their own committees to parallel cabinet committees. This enables the officials to form a common policy which each can recommend to their ministers, thus heading off the danger that ministers might come to a different conclusion among themselves. Crossman tells how his idea of substituting a local income tax for the existing system of rates, or property taxes, was stymied by such a committee. When the civil servants heard about his suggestion, they got together across departmental lines and hammered out a common position. Then: "before I could get to my colleagues and argue the case for the local income tax, every one of my colleagues had been briefed by his officials that there was no alternative to the rates."[6]

Interest Group Alliances. There are still further collaborations in which civil servants engage that may bolster their position vis-a-vis their ministers. Governments, even those that reject corporatist tendencies, must consult with relevant organized interests about proposals for new laws and regulations and then about interpreting and applying them. Politicians, of course, deal with interest groups as part of their trade. But government's links with a great range of organizations must be maintained on a continuing basis, and this inevitably involves the permanent officials, the civil servants.

So the civil service works day-by-day with the leaders of organizations representing business, labor, agriculture, the professions, local government, and so on, and thus builds its personal networks in the country. These contacts can be invaluable to the ministers—or may serve as stumbling blocks when the civil servants explain that proposals for change would be adamantly opposed by powerful organizations.

Ministerial Responsibility. Ministers are perpetually exposed to the harsh world of public criticism and are vulnerable to removal or demotion if they blunder too often. Civil servants, despite the possibility that ministerial blunders might be the result of recommendations from their officials, are much less exposed.

In fact, it is a convention of the British constitution that ministers are ultimately responsible for everything done in their name by the civil service, except for reprehensible conduct of which the minister knew nothing and disapproves. The exception does provide an escape hatch for ministers. But it is rarely used, and typically "the minister has to stand his or her ground under intense fire in the House of Commons" for actions that everyone knows were largely attributable to the civil service.[7] This problem may be intensified by the delegation of responsibility to the new agencies under the "next steps" reforms; for if these agencies, and their chief executives, are to have a large degree of autonomy from the department heads in Whitehall, how can ministers realistically be held responsible for decisions made by the agencies?

Is There a Civil Service Bias?

Given the fact that civil servants are not merely agents of the politicians, but are also influential in pressing their own ideas, the question arises as to whether their ideas reflect any particular political bias. Accusations that such a bias exists have come from both Labourites and Conservatives.

From the perspective of Labour, suspicion is bound to be aroused by the high proportion of senior civil servants with a public school-Oxbridge background. Cabinet Secretary Robert Armstrong was a product of Eton and Oxford. His successor, Robin Butler, was top of his class at Harrow, then played rugby for Oxford. Both served as committee secretaries to the Royal Opera House.

Then there is the tendency among senior officials, after or even before retirement from government service to find lucrative positions in business and finance—often in fields for which they were responsible in government. Even though senior British civil servants are better paid than their counterparts in the United States and continental Europe, and the £118,000 salary of the head of the civil service in 1994 was higher than the prime minister's, they still earned much less than many corporation CEOs, and there were senior civil servants in charge of huge budgets who were earning £52,000. So it is not surprising that a succession of permanent secretaries at the Department of Trade and Industry went on to become chairs or directors of large insurance and banking companies; senior treasury officials have assumed top positions in banks; an official in the Ministry of Power was appointed to a well-paid position in a consulting firm employed by major oil companies. Although the law requires a waiting period between leaving the government and accepting related private employment, exceptions may be made by a reviewing committee, and have been approved in several cases. With this kind of prospect in mind, the critics ask, is it not likely that civil servants will want to curry favor with private institutions they hope will be their future employers? So there is the assumption among many on the Labour benches in Parliament of a pro-business bias in the civil service.

On the Conservative side, there is a very different kind of doubt about the impartiality of the civil service. These are people, after all, who work for government, and whose career prospects expand with the growth of government functions and government budgets. So, Conservative critics charge, they enjoy engaging in social engineering—interfering with the economy and society rather than leaving them to private efforts. And, immune from the spur of competition by their lifetime security of employment, they have no understanding of or sympathy for business enterprise. Never was the civil service happier than during the Labour government of 1945-51, when its members could throw themselves into the tasks of socializing the system. Indeed, Attlee paid tribute to the indispensable role played by the civil service in putting through Labour's ambitious programs.

The civil service responds that these two contrary charges provide confirmation of its impartiality. If Labour says it is pro-business and the Conservatives see it as quasi-socialist, is this not clear testimony to its neutrality and its readiness to serve its political masters and mistresses, whatever their policies?

However, this brings us to a third line of criticism that is subscribed to by some on both the left and the right. On the left, Tony Benn sees the top ranks of the civil service not as closet Conservatives, but as people committed to a point of view that is above the partisan battle. This viewpoint may be nonpartisan, but it is a distinctive position. Located in the political center and committed to continuity of policy, the civil servants' doctrine is therefore hostile to the kind of radical change that Benn and his supporters advocate.

A similar objection is found on the right of the political spectrum. Margaret Thatcher detested the very notion of consensus. Yet it is precisely the pre-Thatcher era of consensus in British politics that defines the policy positions preferred by the civil service, which they played an indispensable role in maintaining. Indeed, the dogma of consensus was perfectly encapsulated in the comment that the civil service's job was "the orderly management of decline."

The Politicians' Assets

Ministers are outnumbered and outlasted by their civil servants. But they are not outranked by them nor are they always outsmarted. Although the armory of techniques available to the officials is formidable, ministers can draw on their own assets to prevent becoming captives of their staffs.

Civil Service Career Advancement. Although the government cannot fire civil servants for anything less than the most heinous misbehavior, promotions and transfers to the more prestigious departments are influenced by the ministers, especially the prime minister. Thatcher, because of her extended stay in office, was able to use this power to a greater extent than any other recent prime minister. In general, her litmus tests for advancement were less ideological than stylistic; she looked for people with vigorous personalities, even, in a few cases, older men with the courage to stand up to her. For example, she chose Sir Anthony Parsons, a retired foreign office official, as a personal foreign policy advisor. Earlier he had impressed her by his analysis of a problem at a meeting, and by his comment: "Prime Minister, will you please not interrupt me until I have finished and, in the meanwhile, will you please stop scowling at me." However, it is unlikely that Thatcher would advance people she believed to be hostile to her views, and the philosophical tilt of the senior civil service has probably been to the right as a result of her time in office.

Political and Policy Advisers. To counteract the civil service's command of information, ministers may make temporary appointments of political and policy advisers. Usually there is a total of about 30 advisers in the government, mostly one to a department, with treasury and the foreign office getting two apiece, and two or more in the prime minister's office. These outsiders typically face a good deal of tension in their relationship with the permanent officials. An extreme example of this tension occurred in the Thatcher government, when statements appearing in the press by Thatcher's personal adviser on economic affairs, Sir Alan Walters, were at odds with the position coming out of the treasury department. The minister, Chancellor of the Exchequer Nigel Lawson, expressed the frustration of his department by handing in his resignation (which was followed by Walter's own resignation).

Prime ministers, in their search for alternative sources of information and analysis, have set up special policy units outside the regular departmental structure. In 1970, Edward Heath created the Central Policy Review Staff, a "think tank" charged with making studies of various areas of policy without regard to departmental boundaries and with the help of outside consultants. This body was retained by the Labour governments of the 1970s, but they relied more on a policy unit that consisted of a small group of Labour Party researchers with offices in 10 Downing Street. Thatcher abolished the Central Policy Review Staff in 1983, but made extensive use of a restructured version of the policy unit. In her early years as prime minister she also looked for ideas to the Center for Policy Studies, established in 1974 as a think tank for leaders of the right wing of the Conservative Party.

Constitutional Authority. Sir Robert Armstrong's words, "the civil service as such has no constitutional personality or responsibility separate from the duly elected government of the day," are not an empty pronouncement. All senior civil servants will pay at least lip service to this view; and in the final analysis, they will defer to the authority of ministers *as long as this is clearly and strongly asserted.*

But that is the key. Ministers must establish their position in the first place by working hard, mastering their briefs, and reading, understanding, and initialing the documents in their red boxes. Then they must select a small number of positions at a time on which they will concentrate, for they cannot dissipate their energies over the entire range of policies for which their departments are responsible. Above all, they must firmly assert their authority.

A number of cabinet ministers have been successful in gaining the committed support of their officials in bringing about change. The evidence for this is to be found in those departments in the Attlee government that created the National Health Service and nationalized a number of industries (despite the fact that the industries were not to be controlled by the civil service); in the departments that organized the privatization of those same industries in the Thatcher era; and in the various departments between those periods which, for example, transformed secondary and higher education, set up and later abolished price controls, and reformed the laws relating to divorce and homosexuality.

Richard Crossman claimed that he was able to prevail on a least a few key issues over an extraordinarily able permanent secretary, Dame Evelyn Sharp, by persistence, diligence, and assertiveness. Others described his brand of assertiveness as bullying and abrasive, and suggested that, especially because he defined himself as a socialist, he might have accomplished more by being a little nicer to his staff. But whether the style be gracious or harsh, determined ministers have been able to establish their authority over officialdom.

Certainly this has been true of some prime ministers. Attlee (Major Attlee in World War I) had no difficulty in this respect. An official who had been private secretary to both Attlee and Churchill found that of the two, Attlee was brisk and decisive in the management of his staff, whereas Churchill tended to be hesitant and uncertain. Harold Wilson, a former civil servant himself, and highly knowledgeable on the issues, was not one to be easily manipulated by his officials.

As for Margaret Thatcher, she established herself very quickly and unmistakably at a dinner to which all the permanent secretaries were invited. It was a memorably unpleasant occasion for them, for she made it clear that change was in the air and that she would accept nothing from them but their fullest cooperation. Evidently she got their cooperation, even in severely reducing the size of the civil service, and in the moves toward decentralization and privatization that were continued under John Major.

There were times during her prime ministership when she accepted the advice of her officials. For example, Sir Robert Armstrong appears to have persuaded her to undertake a new initiative on Northern Ireland and to take a leadership role in addressing the problem of AIDS. Yet on things that really mattered to her she was impervious to his advice, and he accepted without demur a personal public humiliation by testifying in the hopeless cause of trying to get an Australian court to ban *Spycatcher.*

In fact, Armstrong's willingness to accept this role is part of a pattern of taking on essentially political functions that come into conflict with the civil servant's claim to political impartiality. Thus Heath's cabinet secretary, Sir William Armstrong, was so actively involved in policy-making during the last fatal months of Edward Heath's administration that he was perceived in Whitehall as the "deputy prime minister." Thatcher sent Sir Robert Armstrong to speak for her not only in the Australian courts, but also before a House of Commons committee looking into accusations that she had engaged in a cover-up of her government's misbehavior on the Westland affair in 1986 (see chapter 10). In 1994 Sir Robert's successor, Sir Robin Butler, engaged in a fierce public exchange of correspondence with the editor of the *Guardian* newspaper in which Butler exonerated a government minister of conflict of interest charges. The civil servants in these cases were criticized for allowing themselves to be dragged into a public role on issues that were the subject of fierce contention by the opposition, and so engaging in the party political struggle.

Acting on a report by a House of Commons select committee the government addressed this issue in a set of proposals announced in January 1995. A code of ethics for civil servants was to be drawn up with an independent appeal procedure. Among other things, this would help protect civil servants from being pressed into inappropriate actions by their political overlords.

CONCLUSION

Ministers and civil servants taken together constitute the executive branch of government. Thus the constitutional debate about the power concentrated in the executive, which we discussed in chapter 3, treats the two elements as parts of a single, centralized structure of power that operates in a culture of secrecy, dominating Parliament and all other aspects of the British system.

We shall continue to examine that debate throughout this book. In this chapter, we have drawn attention to the fact that there are complicated issues to be examined in the relationship between the two sets of institutions within the executive branch.

On the one hand, we have reviewed the special advantages of the career officials, and shown that ministers who are not very diligent, skillful, and persistent can become little more than mouthpieces for the bureaucracy. This danger may increase as the making of policy, in the context of Europe as well as Britain, becomes ever more technical and complex. So the politicians will find it increasingly difficult to keep on top of some of the emerging issues, and will tend to lean more on whatever sources of expertise they can find in the civil service.

On the other hand, we have shown that ministers, particularly prime ministers, have the ultimate constitutional authority, and on occasion have even used that authority to force the civil service into the party political arena. We should also keep in mind that, though its skills and resources enable it to exercise considerable influence, the British civil service does not determine policy to anything like the extent of its counterparts in, for example, Japan and Italy. In those countries political instability, with frequent changes of government, has left a large measure of power in the hands of the only element of continuity—the bureaucracy. Britain, with its relatively stable system, still leaves the ultimate control in the hands of elected politicians—as long as they have the competence and energy to exercise it.

SOME QUESTIONS TO THINK ABOUT

Would the U.S. system be better off if, as in Britain, fewer top appointments were political?

How important are the skills prized by the British civil service?

Are other kinds of skills more important today? Should there be less emphasis on an Oxbridge background?

What advantages do civil servants have in their dealings with government ministers? How similar are the techniques used by bureaucrats in the United States and Britain?

What should politicians do to maintain their control over policy?

Should bureaucrats always be impartial? Is the British civil service impartial?

Do civil servants need protection against demands by ministers to engage in inappropriate or unconstitutional actions?

NOTES

1. Cited in Peter Hennessy, *Whitehall* (Fontana, 1990), p. 76.
2. Ibid., p. 164.
3. Barbara Castle, *The Castle Diaries* (Weidenfeld and Nicolson, 1980), p. 130.
4. Cited in Peter Kellner and Lord Crowther-Hunt, *The Civil Servants* (MacDonald, 1980), pp. 279–280.
5. Richard Crossman, *Inside View* (Cape, 1972), p. 74.
6. Ibid., p. 73.
7. Hennessy, *Whitehall,* p. 505.

SUGGESTIONS FOR FURTHER READING

Peter Hennessy, *Whitehall* (referred to in the text) is a lively, comprehensive treatment of the civil service. The earlier work cited, Kellner and Crowther-Hunt, *The Civil Servants,* is another useful source. See also Gavin Drewry and Tony Butcher, *The Civil Service Today* (Blackwell, 1991), and Jonathan Lynn and Antony Jay (eds.), *Yes, Minister* (BBC, 1982), based on the scripts of the TV series.

10

Parliament

✦ ✦ ✦ ✦ ✦ ✦ ✦ ✦ ✦ ✦ ✦ ✦ ✦ ✦ ✦ ✦

Does It Matter?

The full name of the British Parliament is "the Queen in Parliament," for it is composed of the monarch, the House of Lords, and the House of Commons. All three come together once a year for the state opening of Parliament, and the queen, wearing her crown and full, regal apparel, reads a summary of the government's program for the coming year to the assembled members of the Lords and Commons. It is a vastly impressive occasion, redolent with the traditions emerging from hundreds of years in the life of the "Mother of Parliaments."

Yet it is purely ceremonial. The monarch, as we saw in chapter 7, does not make the laws; the speech she reads is written for her, word for word, by the government ("My Government"). The setting is the Lords' chamber, and the Commons members stand at the bar of the chamber before the seated lords in their ermine robes (even though most of the real legislative authority is with the Commons rather than the Lords). And, as we noted in the last chapter, even the House of Commons has seen the larger part of its power subordinated to the prime minister and cabinet.

So the question is posed: Does Parliament matter very much any more? Has it been reduced to one of Bagehot's "dignified" elements of the British constitution, leaving the "efficient" responsibility in the hands of the executive branch? Certainly, if we compare the British Parliament with the U.S. Congress, this would appear to be the case.

Superficially, it is true, the two legislatures have much in common. Both consist of two houses, and no bill becomes law until (as depicted in Figure 10.1) it has

House of Commons

First Reading: no debate

Second Reading: principle debated on floor

Committee stage: clause by clause review in standing committee

Report stage: amendments discussed on floor

Third Reading: final version debated on floor

House of Lords

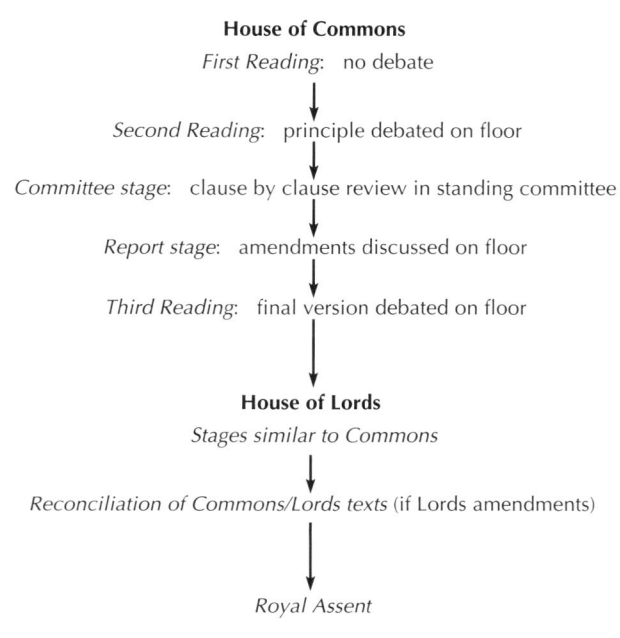

Stages similar to Commons

Reconciliation of Commons/Lords texts (if Lords amendments)

Royal Assent

FIGURE 10.1 How a bill becomes law

completed a successful passage in the two houses of several stages of close scrutiny, debate, and amendment on the floor and in committee.

Moreover, in both Britain and the United States, the lower house is elected from single-member geographic districts using a plurality voting system (i.e., the winner is whomever gets the largest number of votes). Both lower houses are organized on political party lines, very few independent candidates are elected, and two parties have dominated most of the time despite the presence in the British parliament of several smaller parties.

Yet the contrasts between the legislatures are more striking than the similarities. In fact, nothing more sharply differentiates the U.S. and British systems than the character of their legislative branches. This will become apparent as we look at the various aspects of the British Parliament, reviewing first the House of Commons and then the House of Lords.

THE HOUSE OF COMMONS

Representation

Legislatures represent—and the lower chamber is commonly seen as the house of—the people, reflecting the character of the electorate on a more or less egalitarian basis.

Accordingly, the United Kingdom is divided into 651 districts or constituencies, each returning one Member of Parliament (M.P.), and each supposedly containing roughly the same number of voters. In fact, there are considerable variations. The population of districts in Scotland and Northern Ireland is somewhat smaller than in the rest of the United Kingdom. And very large disparities can appear as a result of population movements—especially, in recent years, from north to south.

The distortions are corrected periodically by a redrawing of boundary lines. In the United States, this is undertaken, by constitutional mandate, every 10 years. In Britain, the intervals are sometimes considerably longer. On the other hand, under the U.S. system, state legislatures engage in fierce reapportionment battles every decade, with the parties contending to control the outcome, whereas the process in Britain is in the hands of a nonpartisan boundary commission. Of course, a matter so fraught with significance for politicians can hardly be removed entirely from partisan controversy. Thus the 1970 election was fought on the old register because Labour M.P.s followed the lead of their government and voted against the boundary changes proposed by the commission, and after the 1992 election the Conservatives pressed the commission to redraw the lines before the next election, for the Conservatives believed they would gain at least a few seats from the process. (In drawing up the new boundaries the commission proposed increasing the number of constituencies from 651 to 659.)

We have already noted that the drawing up of approximately equal districts is not sufficient to provide proportional representation of parties, for the voting system in both countries is heavily biased against the smaller parties. A further departure from the principle of equal representation is found in the social composition of the House of Commons, for it is heavily white, male, and middle class. Of the 651 winners in the 1992 election, 60 were women, 6 were black or Asian.

The key social class factors of education and occupation were distributed as follows in the Parliament elected in 1992:

TABLE 10.1 Social class in the House of Commons, 1992 (percent)

	Conservative (n = 336)	Labour (n = 271)
Education		
Public schools	39	14
Oxbridge	45	16
All universities	73	61
Occupation		
Professional	39	42
Business	38	8
Miscellaneous (white collar, politics, journalism, farmers)	22	28
Manual workers	1	22

SOURCE: Adapted from David Butler and Dennis Kavanagh, *The British General Election of 1992*, pp. 224, 226.

To some extent these figures suggest a polarization of parties, for a considerable number of the Conservatives come from an upper- and upper-middle-class, public school background, whereas one-fifth of the Labour members have been manual workers and over half were sponsored by a trade union. However, the trend in both parties is toward the middle of the social class scale. The upper-class proportion of Conservatives in Parliament has been falling. On the Labour side, the manual worker share of 22 percent (mostly skilled workers) was down in 1992 from 29 percent in the previous Parliament, and more and more of those sponsored by unions are white-collar or professional workers with a university education.

In terms of social class, then, the House of Commons has more people with a blue-collar, working-class background than does the House of Representatives, yet both institutions are largely middle-class in their composition. However, there is a different distribution of professionals in Parliament and Congress. Parliament has more teachers: about 15 percent (28 percent of the Labour contingent), compared with 10 percent in Congress. On the other hand, lawyers in Parliament comprise less than 14 percent of the total (mostly Conservatives) as compared with more than 40 percent of Representatives and almost two-thirds of Senators.

Resources

There is a vast gap between the resources available to a Member of Parliament and a member of the U.S. Congress. Although the M.P. salary has increased significantly in recent years, and is now linked to civil service pay, it is still among the lowest in industrialized countries. Thus, at £33,170 in 1995 (about $52,000), it was less than half that of members of Congress and well below the salaries of legislators in Italy, Germany, France, and Holland.

Provision for secretarial help has also been increasing and covers the cost of about one-and-a-half staff positions (some of which are filled by M.P.s' spouses). The norm allotted to each representative in the U.S. House is a staff of 18, and a staff of 40 is the norm in the Senate. M.P.s also receive travel passes and a very modest expense allowance.

Every M.P. has a desk in an office within the Parliament—the Palace of Westminster—or in an adjacent office building. But the majority share two or more to a room—again, a dismal contrast to the spacious suites provided each member of Congress.

Thus, there is not much money or space for research assistance. Many M.P.s manage to afford part-time assistance out of their secretarial allowance or from support provided by business organizations or unions. Some also draw upon the free help provided by students from the United States, engaged in field work for credit provided by U.S. universities. In 1985 a report by a House of Commons select committee charged that many of these students wasted the time of library staff by "asking questions of a sometimes disconcertingly uninstructed character," doing academic work rather than serving their M.P.s, and tearing pages from books and magazines. However, the report provoked a number of letters to newspapers from M.P.s delighted with the students' help. One Labour M.P. insisted that the report was "a collection of prejudice, half-truths, and innuendo," and a former Conservative leader of the House of Commons testified that he had employed 10 young Americans over the years and that "without exception they have given me splendid and dedicated service."[1]

Interest Group Influence

At one time or another Parliament will hear from most of the interest groups discussed in chapter 4. In fact, many of these interests are already represented within the legislature, for, as we noted above, 38 percent of the Conservatives are businesspeople, over half of the Labour M.P.s are sponsored by unions, and all the party delegations include a high proportion of professionals. In addition, in recent years there has been a rapid growth in the number of M.P.s—now close to one-third of the total—who act as paid parliamentary consultants, many of them working with professional consultancy firms.

M.P.s are required to list their outside connections in a Register of Members' Interests, and to declare any such connections in the course of parliamentary debates (though not during Question Time). Then there is a good deal of pressure applied from the outside by representatives of interests likely to be affected by legislation. However, there are no laws similar to those in the United States that require lobbyists to register or to list their expenditures other than in their companies' annual financial reports. Nor is there any requirement for those research assistants of M.P.s who are paid for by outside interests to register their affiliation with lobbying organizations.

The absence of any such requirements, together with the relatively low level of pay and other resources provided for M.P.s, might appear to invite abuses of the system. Indeed, there have been such problems periodically, with exposures of individual Conservative and Labour M.P.s using their influence in exchange for money or lavish gifts and entertainment. One flagrant abuse came to light in 1994, when investigative journalists from the *Sunday Times* posed as businessmen and paid two Conservative M.P.s £1000 each to put down a written parliamentary question. The two men were suspended from their unpaid posts (as parliamentary private secretaries to government ministers) and the House of Commons Committee on Privileges undertook an inquiry into the affair. Yet it appeared that the two M.P.s had broken no laws, and to many of their colleagues they had been guilty only of naïvete in being fooled by the *Sunday Times* reporters.

These and other alleged abuses of the public trust led to the government's setting up an inquiry into "Standards of Conduct in Public Life" under a senior judge, Lord Nolan. In its unanimous report the Nolan committee proposed substantial reforms of parliamentary and government ethics: M.P.s should no longer be allowed to accept pay from lobbyists to influence Parliament; the financial value of members' outside interests should be registered; standards should be monitored by an independent parliamentary commissioner; and former cabinet ministers should be subject to vetting by an independent committee for two years after leaving office before they may take jobs in industry or finance.

The Nolan report insisted that the abuses needing correction did not characterize British public life in general but were limited to "a minority that fall short" of acceptable standards. Some critics perceived much wider corruption in the system and argued that British politics had fallen far from its earlier reputation for integrity. Nonetheless, it is clear that malfeasance by M.P.s has been much less common than the scandals tied to members of the U.S. Congress and involved very modest sums of money. It would be tempting to suggest that the sole reason for this is to be found in the incorruptibility of most British M.P.s. However, there are other reasons that are more institutional than personal. First, because M.P.s are not allowed to spend much money on election campaigns, they are not as incessantly engaged in raising campaign funds as are members of Congress. To the extent that fundraising may taint the election process, problems exist at the level of national parties but not at that of local candidates. Second, party discipline is much stronger in Parliament than in Congress, which serves as a counterweight to the blandishments of outside groups.

Third, and most important, there is usually not much point in trying to corrupt the individual M.P., for he or she is not able to deliver much in return. The M.P. can state the case for an organization in debates and questions from the floor, and intervene on its behalf with bureaucracies. On a few issues, where the government of the day is undecided, organized pressure applied to the rank-and-file members can make the difference; for example, a well-financed, high-pressure campaign directed at Parliament and the public succeeded in persuading Churchill's Conservative government—despite the prime minister's doubts—to break the BBC's monopoly of television and allow the inauguration of commercial TV in 1954. However, most areas of policy are controlled not by the M.P.s but by the executive branch. In the United States, Congress, elected separately from the president, has a large degree of autonomy, and serving on an important committee can give the individual member of Congress a vantage point from which to exercise considerable leverage on behalf of constituents or organized interests. Committee service in Parliament carries with it no such advantage. Members of Parliament, as we shall see, serve a number of useful functions. But if they aim at exerting real power they must secure an appointment to the government.

Making (and Breaking) Political Reputations

In the United States, the Senate (though not usually the House) is one of the prime sources for producing candidates for the presidency. But so are state governorships and, as in the case of Dwight Eisenhower, high military office may qualify. Moreover, as we have noted, the President's cabinet may be drawn from a variety of backgrounds. In Britain, only the House of Commons serves as the recruitment base for prime ministers and for all cabinet members except the few drawn from the House of Lords. Thus individual performance on the floor of the House becomes a critical test for political advancement.

This does not mean that the best orators and debaters inevitably rise to the top. The qualities under scrutiny include negotiating skill, coolness under fire, and general character, and these are tested in committees and in many contexts behind the scenes. Still, without at least some demonstrated capacity to handle oneself in the hurly-burly of verbal exchanges in public sessions, there is little prospect of advancement to positions of political leadership.

Moreover, once in a leadership position, the testing is continuous and unremitting. Reputations are damaged as readily as enhanced by parliamentary performance. For example, Neil Kinnock, who performed brilliantly at Labour Party conferences, was much less comfortable as a parliamentarian, and his standing in the country was weakened by his usually being outmatched in confrontations with Margaret Thatcher.

At one point, indeed, his inability to rise to the occasion allowed Thatcher to escape from a particularly dangerous situation. In January 1986, Michael Heseltine had walked out of her cabinet, accusing her of dictatorial behavior in refusing to allow discussion of a helicopter contract awarded to a U.S. firm by the Westland company instead of to a European consortium. It was then suggested that criticism of Heseltine, which subsequently appeared in the press, came from an unauthorized leak of a confidential letter to Heseltine from the attorney-general. The leak was traced to a young official in the department of trade. But who had authorized the leak? It was alleged that two of the Prime Minister's close advisers had been involved. Had Mrs. Thatcher herself known about it? Then the secretary of state for industry resigned. Had he done so to protect Mrs. Thatcher?

The question was to be debated on the floor of the House of Commons. The circumstances of the leak in themselves might constitute a rather minor affair. But the charge now was of a cover-up, a kind of British Watergate. Mrs. Thatcher approached the debate on the Westland affair privately confessing her fear that as of that night she might no longer be prime minister.

Her statement to the House, in which she conceded that her aides had known about the leak but that she had not, was generally regarded as one of her least convincing performances. Fortunately for her, Kinnock's attack was even less impressive. In the words of Britain's leading journalist, Hugo Young: "Verbosely ranting about the prime minister's incompetence, ruthlessness, and dishonesty, he never succeeded in rendering these generalities precise or freshly lethal."[2]

Whether Thatcher would have been forced to resign by a more competent attack is questionable. But her authority could have been severely shaken. For his part, Kinnock's reputation never fully recovered from his failure, and he admitted after his retirement from the Labour leadership that over and over he had wished to have that opportunity back again.

Relations with the Executive Branch

We have seen that the executive remains part of the legislature and dominates the legislature. Its control is maintained by ensuring the cohesion of the majority party.

Party is the central organizing principle of the British parliamentary system. It is the means by which government sets out to present and pass into law proposals on public policy, and by which the opposition seeks to amend or defeat those proposals and put forward its alternative ideas.

Party and the Design of the House. This principle is made visible by the physical layout of the House of Commons. Instead of the semicircular arrangement of most legislatures, the House is rectangular in shape, with rows of straight benches facing each other across a gangway. The government and its supporters sit on one side, the opposition on the other. The speaker's chair is at one end between the two, with the clerk's table in front of his chair, and the mace, the symbol of the House in session, suspended from the end of the table. The government members sit on the front benches facing this table to the speaker's right, with the leaders of the main opposition party on the other side of the table. The rank and file of government and opposition parties—the "backbenchers"—sit behind them.

There are no desks for individual members, nor even arm rests to divide the seats on the benches, and no assigned places for the backbenchers. In fact, there are only 346 seats for the 651 members, and room for 91 more in the side galleries. Thus on a major occasion, many members must stand behind the speaker's chair or in the gangways.

When the House was destroyed by bombs during World War II, consideration was given to rebuilding it on less inconvenient lines. At Churchill's insistence, the House was reconstructed on exactly the same lines as before. Any alternative would detract from the special character of the institution as an intimate debating chamber facilitating the cut and thrust of rival ideas presented by opposing political parties.

The Whips. Keeping the party members in line is the job of the whips' office. The U.S. Congress also operates through a system of whips; there, however, the available tools are mostly persuasion and patronage, and the individual members frequently disregard appeals for party unity if these conflict with their own convictions or with the interests of their constituents or of powerful pressure groups.

But in Parliament the instructions of the whips, on both the government and opposition sides, are less easily defied. Before each vote, members receive a notification from the whips' office. If this is underlined once, the matter is regarded as routine, and an absence is not regarded as especially serious. A two-line whip is sufficiently important to require attendance and a vote for the party line. A three-line whip sends a signal of urgency: the member had better be there for the vote, and *must* vote in accordance with the position established by the party leadership.

Refusal to do so is likely to result in one or more of a range of sanctions available to the leadership. A first offense will probably lead to a summons to the whips' office for a dressing down and a warning of more serious consequences if the behavior is repeated. Next, the member may be denied access to patronage at the disposal of the leadership: service on important parliamentary committees, appointment to delegations visiting continental Europe or the United States, even inclusion on the queen's honors lists.

More serious, dissident members may find their prospects for political advancement jeopardized. Winston Churchill persistently opposed the policies of the Conservative government toward Nazi Germany in the 1930s. Despite several reshufflings of the cabinet, and despite his extensive previous cabinet experience and or-

172 THE INSTITUTIONS OF GOVERNMENT

The House of Commons in session: Neil Kinnock challenging the Thatcher government
SOURCE: Courtesy of the Speaker's Office, House of Commons.

atorical prowess, he was conspicuously omitted from the government until the outbreak of World War II.

His grandson, Conservative Member of Parliament Winston Churchill, was the opposition spokesperson on defense when, in 1978, he voted to end sanctions against white Rhodesia instead of accepting the party's decision to abstain. He was immediately dismissed from his role, and, throughout all the government changes of the Thatcher years, he never once received an appointment to the administration.

Still other punishments are available for persistent rebels. Harold Wilson made this clear in a harsh warning issued at a 1967 meeting with Labour M.P.s who were threatening to oppose some of his government's policies. Defying the leadership once may be tolerated, he said, for "every dog is allowed one bite." But if the dog goes on biting, "he may not get his license renewed when it falls due."

Nonrenewal of the license, in this context, could be withdrawal of the whip. Although this may sound more like a reward than a punishment, its consequences for the individual are damaging, for it means exclusion from meetings of the Parliamentary Party—and in an institution built around political parties, to be denied the fellowship of other party members is to be reduced to a very lonely, powerless existence.

The step beyond withdrawal of the whip is expulsion from the party. This does not mean the immediate loss of one's parliamentary seat, for only the voters have that authority. But without the party label, the prospect of reelection is greatly diminished.

Denial of the party whip has been used only occasionally and is usually temporary. However, when nine Conservatives voted against their government's European policy in November 1994, they were all stripped of the party whip. Expulsions from the party are even more rare than denial of the whip. Yet this threat, too, is a constant presence, as became clear when two Labour M.P.s, charged with being members of the Militant Tendency, were expelled from the party during Neil Kinnock's struggle against the outside left in the mid-1980s.

Beyond these sanctions against individual members, there is one more weapon available to the government to keep its party together—the power to dissolve Parliament. This is an ominous possibility whenever a government has only a small parliamentary majority, or even none at all. In this situation, members of the governing party know that by refusing to vote with the government, they may bring about a defeat that leaves the government no option but to resign and ask the queen to dissolve Parliament. A dissolution means the end not only of the government but also of the tenure of all M.P.s, who must then defend their own seats in a general election.

Survival through the Vote of Confidence. The Labour government of James Callaghan from 1976 to 1979 provides us with a dramatic illustration of the ability of an administration without a majority to survive through the power of the whips.

The election of October 1974 had given Harold Wilson's government a bare majority in Parliament, with 319 seats out of 635. By the time Callaghan had taken over from Wilson in 1976, Labour had lost two by-elections, and its majority was down to 1. In November, a key division was called on the proposed nationalization of the shipbuilding and aircraft industries. The government prevailed by a margin of 1. The whips had brought members in from their sickbeds. If they were not well enough to walk through the division lobbies—electronic voting is not used in Parliament—they were allowed to sit in rooms opening onto the lobbies and nod their heads to register their votes. The same method was allowed a young Labour M.P., who voted while breast-feeding her infant son.

For two more years the government clung precariously to power. But more by-elections took away its majority completely, and in December 1978 the government faced another key test. This was on a motion opposing its policy of denying government contracts to the Ford Motor Company, which had granted its workers more than the 5 percent raise stipulated in the government's anti-inflation guidelines. The unions were hostile to the government's action, a number of Labour M.P.s sponsored by unions voted against the government, and the opposition motion was carried 285 to 179.

Callaghan did not resign. Instead he placed before the House a vote of confidence in the government. If this were lost, the government would be forced to resign and Parliament would be dissolved. The dissenters came back into line. Some of the nationalist parties abstained. The vote of confidence carried 300–290. Still it was clear that the government could not carry on against a united opposition. So Callaghan negotiated a number of deals. For a time there was an understanding with the Liberals known as the "Lib-Lab pact." When this broke down, Callaghan promised the Northern Ireland parties five more seats in future elections, and arranged referenda on devolution of power to Scotland and Wales.

However, the proposed devolution for Scotland and Wales went down to defeat in referenda on March 1, 1979, and Callaghan had nothing more to offer the nationalist parties. The government was worn down by its long precarious existence, and its popularity was badly hurt by the "winter of discontent" strikes. On March 28, 1979, the opposition put down a motion of censure. The whips cracked over the heads of everyone except four nonvoting officers of the House (the Speaker and Deputy Speakers). Three seats were vacant through death or resignation.

The government was supported by all 306 Labour members and 4 others. But there were 311 against them, and 7 abstentions. By a margin of 1 the government was defeated, Parliament was dissolved, an election was called, and the Thatcher era began.

Some Labour members complained that it need not have happened. The whips had not been ruthless enough to force a 72-year-old Labour M.P. from his hospital bed where he was recovering from a heart attack a week earlier. Had he been brought to the House the result would have been a tie; the Speaker would then be called on to break the tie, and it is an established convention that the Speaker, no matter what his or her own party affiliation, will not break a tie to bring a government down.

A further example of the use of the vote of confidence to overcome internal party opposition came in 1993, when the Conservative government's overall majority was only 18. John Major's policy toward Europe—particularly his signing the Maastrict treaty—aroused fierce opposition from a minority in his party. The Labour opposition supported Maastrict in general, but opposed the government's refusal to sign a "social chapter" of the treaty which would provide certain protections to workers.

Labour put down a motion to include the social chapter. Several Conservatives who opposed the social chapter, but were even more strongly opposed to Maastricht, crossed the floor and voted with Labour. The government was defeated 324 to 316, with 23 Conservatives opposing their own government.

Major then played the same trump card used by Callaghan. He tabled a motion of confidence in the government for the next day. All but one of the Tory rebels came back into line (he was then suspended from the party), and with the support of most of the Northern Ireland nationalists, the government prevailed by 339 to 301.

Roles for Backbenchers

Advancement for the rank-and-file M.P.s who sit on the back benches of the majority party takes the form of promotion to minor positions in the government, then to heading government departments, and from there to the top level of the government, the cabinet. For the opposition it means election or appointment to the "shadow cabinet," whose members critique the governing cabinet from the opposition front benches and hope that their turn at forming the government will come before too long. This accounts for a substantial proportion of the membership, for the government typically includes 100 or more positions. Still, it leaves a substantial majority on the back benches, and many of them are never promoted.

Some of these perennial backbenchers do not complain of their fate, for they are not eager for the burdens and responsibilities of office, and there are a number of important and useful roles for them to fulfill beyond simply keeping a government in power or providing support to the leaders of the opposition. As we examine each of these, however, we shall see why many M.P.s tend to become frustrated in the performance of their job.

Constituency Service. In legislatures with single-member districts, constituents expect service from their representative. In Britain, the demands on the time of M.P.s have been growing as the role of government has increased and with it the number of complaints against decisions by the bureaucracy. These must be attended to in writing and in the local *surgeries,* in which M.P.s meet with individual constituents after their week in Westminster is over. Consequently most M.P.s report working at least 55 hours a week, with two-fifths claiming a 70-hour week.

Yet no matter how many hours they work, the limited resources available to M.P.s make it impossible for them to deal with some of the more complex problems brought to their attention. It is true that M.P.s serve smaller numbers of people than members of Congress, for the 435 U.S. Representatives are elected from districts with populations of a half a million or more, whereas the population base of the 651 M.P.s averages about 85,000. But this difference is still far from proportional to the disparity in available funds and staff, and sometimes M.P.s have had to dip into their personal funds to handle correspondence with constituents.

Consequently, Britain has followed the Scandinavian model of the Ombudsman—an independent official charged with investigating grievances of individuals against the government. This is the charge of the parliamentary commissioner, and of a separate official for the National Health Service. M.P.s are not left out of the process entirely, for these officials take up a complaint only after it has been referred to them by an M.P. However, the very existence of the commissioners is an indication of the limited ability of backbenchers to deal with the bureaucracies.

Question Time. Every Monday through Thursday when Parliament is in session, the day begins with government ministers answering questions from the floor for slightly less than an hour. Each government department takes its turn in this procedure every three or four weeks, and on Tuesdays and Thursdays for about 15 minutes the questions are addressed to the prime minister.

Altogether about 40,000 Parliamentary Questions a year are asked, though there is time for only about five or six thousand of these to be answered orally, the rest receiving written answers. Each M.P. may put down two questions a day for verbal answer, plus an unlimited number for written responses.

According to Harold Wilson, ". . . no prime minister looks forward to 'PQs' with anything but apprehension; every prime minister works long into the night on his answers . . . to help him anticipate the instant and unpredictable supplementary questions that follow his main prepared answer."[3]

These "supplementary questions" typically follow an innocent-sounding initial inquiry, submitted in writing, about the prime minister's plans for the rest of the day. When the prime minister has explained that he intends to hold meetings with his colleagues, the speaker then invites the member responsible for the inquiry to follow up with the real question, which has not been put down in writing. (The ritual is for several members to submit the same question about the prime minister's plans; the prime minister responds with a standard phrase: "I refer the Honorable Member to the answer I gave a few moments ago"; the supplementary question follows.)

If an answer is not to the satisfaction of the opposition—which is frequently the case—the prime minister may be greeted with howls of derision, for the House can be a rowdy institution, and the stereotype of the reserved, polite English is regularly shattered, especially at Question Time. Repeatedly the Speaker's stentorian cry of "Order! Order!" will ring out in an effort to quell the hubbub.

The speaker will also remind members they may not step beyond the bounds of "parliamentary language." Thus an apparently inebriated member may be described

Betty Boothroyd, elected in 1992 as the 155th Speaker of the House (and first Madame Speaker)

SOURCE: Courtesy of the Speaker's Office, House of Commons.

as "tired" but not drunk. "Liar" is impermissible, and members may not even be accused of having "misled the House," but they may be charged with "terminological inexactitudes" or "carelessness with the truth."

Occasionally a member will be ejected for the rest of the day for ignoring the speaker's warnings or for such misconduct, engaged in by at least two members over the years, as dislodging the mace from the table. (One of these was Michael Heseltine, who picked up the mace and furiously waved it over his head when the Conservatives were in opposition. The second was a backbench Labour member who, forced to read a statement of apology written by officials of the House, kept interjecting "Grovel, grovel" into his reading.)

In this turbulent atmosphere, prime ministers and their ministerial colleagues had better not be easily unnerved. Some junior ministers have never risen higher because they were too easily rattled by their turn at Question Time. In one case the experience proved fatal: in 1983 the under-secretary for Wales collapsed and died while answering questions from Welsh Labour members.

Undoubtedly, Question Time is an important opportunity for backbenchers to probe government intentions and gain some publicity for their issues and for themselves, and ministers are usually happy when it is over. Yet adept ministers soon learn how to evade and stonewall and even turn matters to their advantage with a barrage of selective facts or a flash of wit.

Prime ministers especially are helped by the format of Question Time. Only the leader of the opposition is allowed two or three follow-up questions. All others may only put the one question, and each time the prime minister has the last word. Moreover, questions come alternately from the government side and from the opposition parties, and most of the government party questions have been planted to enable the prime minister to promote the government's programs. (Thus: "Would not the prime minister agree with me that the performance of the British economy in the past year has far outstripped any of our European competitors?") The government's backbenchers are also just as ready as the opposition to engage in noisy interruptions. Neil Kinnock was subjected to persistent jeers and barracking from the Conservative side, and Liberal Democrat leader Paddy Ashdown has had to face the same kind of derisive treatment whenever he gets to his feet.

Then, although the backbenchers are not allowed to read their questions or use notes—a furtive glance down at a scribbled note produces loud cries of "Reading!"—the prime minister may read his or her answers. Finally, there are several techniques prime ministers may use to avoid answering embarrassing questions. They may challenge the questioner's facts ("Surely the Honorable Member is not unaware of the latest government figures . . ."), or intelligence ("I should have thought that even the Honorable Member would have understood . . ."), or patriotism ("Why is it that members opposite always insist on putting everything British in a bad light?"). They can refuse to answer on grounds that it would harm the public interest or that the information is classified or confidential.

They may also claim that the requested information is available "only at disproportionate cost." Mrs. Thatcher was asked by a Labour member what was meant by disproportionate cost. She replied that this was up to each minister to decide, and that anything costing more than £200 must be "referred to the responsible minister before significant resources are committed." This led to the following exchange:

> Mr. Tony Banks asked the prime minister how many questions she had refused to answer since 1979 on the grounds of disproportionate cost.
>
> The Prime Minister: This information can only be supplied at disproportionate cost.

Committee Service. Traditionally the House of Commons has had two kinds of committees. Standing committees—A, B, C, etc.—do not specialize in any particular subject area, but review in detail the variegated bills assigned to them in their passage through the legislative process; each of these committees disbands after completing its work on a bill, and a new A, B, or C committee takes up the next bill. Select committees concentrate in specific fields, and the Public Accounts Committee and the Select Committee on Expenditure are long-established institutions with reputations for close and tough examination of the financial aspects of government departments.

In the 1960s, efforts were made by Labour Leader of the House, Richard Crossman, to add a new structure of parliamentary committees that would oversee the operations of the departments of government. Although these attempts were unsuccessful, the idea came to fruition in the early years of the Thatcher administration, when 14 new committees were established to parallel several of the departments. Since then, there has been keen competition among M.P.s to serve on the new committees, attendance at committee meetings has been high, and a poll of M.P.s in 1994 showed that 88 percent of them thought the committees were effective. Several have called ministers and civil servants to account, sometimes generating lead stories on the evening's television news. A considerable amount of information has been forced out of the traditionally secretive departments of government. And some have had a direct impact on government policies, including the trade and industry committee's success in forcing a delay in the Major government's plans to close a number of coal mines.

Here again, however, parliamentary committees are pale shadows of the committees of Congress. By comparison, resources in the Commons are pitifully inadequate: The committees' small staffs and part-time consultants can hardly compete with the masses of civil servants and computerized information available to government departments. And the merest mention of the magic phrase "national security" has been sufficient in most cases to dampen the investigative enthusiasm of committee chairs.

Debates. Although the committee stages of legislation are important, much more of the work of the House of Commons takes place on the floor of the House than is the case in the U.S. Congress. Before a bill reaches a committee in Parliament, it already will have been through its first two readings, and the second reading will have discussed the basic principles set forth in the bill. The second and third readings are the occasion for set debates. Other opportunities for major debates on the floor are provided by the Queen's Speech, which sets forth the government's proposals for the year; votes on motions of no confidence in the government; 20 days devoted to government motions on various policy areas and another 20 days on topics chosen by the opposition parties.

The key speakers in these debates are government ministers and opposition front bench leaders. However, the Speaker will always ensure that a number of backbench members will be heard from, especially those who are known to specialize in the subject being debated. So these occasions will provide ordinary members with forums to influence policy as well as to enhance their prospects for advancement.

There are also adjournment debates for a half-hour immediately following each sitting, at which time the member who has won the privilege in a ballot may make a speech on any subject (often a constituent's grievance), and a junior minister from a relevant government department will be called on to reply.

Private Members' Bills. Although most legislation emanates from the government of the day, backbenchers have some opportunities to introduce their own proposals for legislation on Fridays. Because far more members wish to do so than the schedule allows, they must enter their bills in a lottery.

Margaret Thatcher's career in Parliament was launched when her name came up in the lottery. She proposed a bill to compel local councils to hold all their meetings in public. The idea was naturally attractive to the press, which gave the proposal favorable coverage. More important, the bill was, with appropriate amendment, acceptable to the government, and it was passed into law. Had it been opposed by the government it would have had no chance of passage. In fact, when a Conservative backbencher introduced a bill to force more open government by reforming the Official Secrets Act, the Thatcher government put down a three-line whip to ensure that it would be killed.

Ten-Minute-Rule Bills. For several weeks each session, 20 minutes are set aside after Question Time on Tuesdays and Wednesdays for members to introduce bills, with 10 minutes assigned to the sponsor and 10 minutes to an opposing speaker. There is fierce competition to take advantage of this rule, but this is because the bills are brought up during prime time for the media, not because they have any real chance of becoming law.

Conscience Bills. On contentious issues of social policy such as divorce, abortion, homosexuality, and capital punishment, governments have preferred not to identify themselves with one side or the other, but to leave the decisions to the individual members. Usually, laws on these issues are introduced as private members' bills, and when they come to the floor for a vote, the whips send out no instructions.

Year after year, proposals to reintroduce capital punishment are demanded by the Conservative Party's annual conference and introduced into Parliament. Yet, even during the Thatcher years, when the prime minister made known her strong support for the proposal, the matter was left to the conscience of individual M.P.s; and every time it was presented, a sufficient minority of Conservatives joined a large majority of Labourites to vote the bill down.

Using Parliamentary Procedures. As in any legislature the rules of the House of Commons are intricate, and an experienced member can cause a government considerable frustration by using a variety of parliamentary technicalities. Although the possibilities for filibustering are more circumscribed than those in the U.S. Senate, one Labour member in 1983 spoke for over 11 hours on a bill. Parliament's devotion to tradition provides an abundance of other devices to force delay. Thus cantankerous backbenchers like Labour's left-wing Dennis Skinner or the Tories' right-wing Bill Cash may cause a 15-minute delay by shouting "I spy strangers," which compels the speaker to call a vote on whether to clear the public and press galleries. Then there is the raising of interminable points of order. (When a vote is being taken, members wishing to raise a point of order must be seated and wearing a hat, and a small supply of top hats is available for this purpose. On one occasion in 1993 there were more members raising points of order than there were top hats, and the Deputy Speaker, asked to rule on what kind of headgear constituted a hat, concluded that even a knotted handkerchief covering the head could be acceptable—but not the day's parliamentary order paper.)

The possibilities for disruption of the government's legislative program become much greater when parliamentary technicalities are used systematically by a group of members, or even by the opposition parties. The effective conduct of the business of the House depends on a good deal of consultation and cooperation with the main opposition party; and when in late 1993 the government tried to force the pace on a new budgetary procedure, Labour resisted. The labour whips refused to allow their members to "pair" (find a Conservative who would join them in missing a vote), and encouraged Dennis Skinner and other backbenchers to demand sudden "ambush" votes on arcane technical issues. The government struck back by applying the "guillotine" to cut off debate until at last more cooperative arrangements were restored.

Other Backbench Forums. In both parties a variety of groups form to give voice to backbench concerns. Several are based on ideological strands within the parties or spring up in relation to particular issues, so their definition tends to change over time. On the Conservative side, however, the "1922 Committee," in existence since the year of its title, is elected by all Conservative backbenchers, and the leadership is well advised to keep in touch with the views of its members.

An important forum on the Labour side when the party is in opposition is the election of the shadow cabinet by all of the party's M.P.s. The party leader can still decide what assignments to give to those elected, and can supplement them with a few personal choices. However, the party's rules oblige the prime minister to include the winners in his or her first government whenever Labour comes to power, and although cabinet membership after the initial appointments are essentially at the discretion of the prime minister, backbench opinion is never a trivial consideration in the formation of cabinets.

Defying the Whips. Despite the sanctions available to the leadership through the whips, refusal by individuals and even small groups to toe the party line are not unheard of. Indeed, in recent years there has been an increase in the number of rebellions.

This happened on a number of occasions during the Callaghan government's struggle for survival. Usually the issues were secondary, but we noted earlier the revolt against the effort to impose sanctions on the Ford Motor Company for ignoring the government's wage guidelines. The administration won the vote of confidence that followed—but canceled the sanctions. The government was also forced to retreat on a key clause in the budget in 1977 when two Labour left-wingers defected.

During the 1980s there was more leeway for dissenters, for Conservative majorities in Parliament were so large that there was no danger of the government falling because of a few defections. Although Margaret Thatcher did not easily countenance rebellion in the ranks, she was forced to retreat on a number of occasions because of backbench unhappiness. Thus in 1986, the government's proposal to allow more shops to open on Sundays was defeated when several Conservative backbenchers voted against the instructions of the whips. Moreover, the education secretary's proposal to introduce student loans rather than increase grants met with such furious opposition by M.P.s from middle-class constituencies that the government chose to back down rather than face defeat on the floor.

The final sanction of dissolving Parliament and calling new elections if backbenchers do not toe the line endangers the careers not only of backbenchers, but also of the government, which goes down with them. So the threat of mass political suicide can hardly be used regularly, and although John Major employed the tactic successfully over the Maastricht treaty in 1983, its very use was an indication of the vulnerability of his government to pressure from dissident backbenchers.

In fact, according to some commentators, the battle over Maastricht was "without parallel in parliamentary history" as a case study in parliamentary dissent. The rebels carried out "a campaign of parliamentary obstruction that broke new ground in terms of both legislative and organization skill and sheer endurance," forcing the government to accept several amendments and to suffer a humiliating defeat on a key vote. This proved to be possible because the government had such a small majority, and the rebels actually connived with the opposition parties to embarrass the government (in one case infuriating the government whips by smuggling into the House, with Labour's collaboration, a member presumed to be in a sickbed hundreds of miles away). But the other critical element in the effectiveness of the revolt was the fact that the rebels had no personal ambitions for promotion to government positions, and so had nothing to lose (except their seats should the government call an election).[4]

Subsequently the rebels kept up their campaign against their government's European policy even after they had been stripped of the party whip, and in January 1995, the government was able to win approval of the European Union fisheries policy only through the support of six Northern Ireland Unionist M.P.s. Then in April 1995, five months after the whip had been withdrawn from the rebels, the government capitulated and brought them back into the fold.

All this evidence of increased M.P. resistance to the orders of the whips has led some observers to suggest that the House of Commons, formerly classified as an institution that merely ratified and legitimized government decisions, might now be viewed as a full partner in the legislative process.

This overstates the extent of the change. What can be said is that backbench M.P.s can no longer be taken for granted as mere voting fodder. Their concerns must be considered, and they must persuaded and not merely bullied into submission. For the whips to be effective they must do more than issue instructions; they must listen to backbenchers and communicate M.P. concerns to the leadership. So M.P.s exert significant influence on a number of issues, influence that may be too subtle to measure and too informal to be reported. In one respect, indeed, backbenchers on the Conservative side have ultimate power, for it was they who voted Margaret Thatcher, one of the most powerful prime ministers of the century, out of office.

Nonetheless, most of the time Parliament remains a subordinate body, weaker by far than the United States Congress and weaker than most other democratically elected legislatures. Many issues are dealt with on a noncontroversial, bipartisan basis; but whenever the House is divided, well over 90 percent of the voting is on strict party lines. This compares with 60 to 70 percent among congressional Democrats, and 70 to 80 percent among congressional Republicans. The situation in the House of Representatives in 1993, when the Democratic chief whip led the opposition to the Democratic president's bill ratifying the North American Free Trade Treaty, would be utterly inconceivable in the British Parliament. The unanimity of the Republicans in opposition to the Clinton budget in 1993, and in passing some of the "Contract With America" provisions in early 1995, was astonishing because it was such a departure from the past. In Britain, 100 percent unity in party voting is still the rule rather than the exception.

Furthermore, the already secondary role of Parliament in the system of power is likely to be still further reduced as Britain becomes more involved with the European Union. Parliament has established new committees to deal with legislation relating to Europe, and the workload of the entire body will increase steadily in response to the flow of rules and directives emanating from the various European agencies. But more work will not bring a sense of more power; and the frustration now felt by energetic younger M.P.s, and by those who have served in the House for many years but have never been appointed to a position in the government, is likely to grow more intense.

THE HOUSE OF LORDS

A Weak Chamber

The fact that after its passage through the House of Commons, a bill must go through a similar series of stages in the House of Lords gives the Lords the appearance of a coequal branch of the legislature. Until the twentieth century this was not far from the reality. However, with the broadening of the franchise, it was inevitable that a nonelected chamber made up of a hereditary aristocracy could not indefinitely be left with as much authority as the Commons. So in 1911, when there was a deadlock between the two houses on the budget, the Liberal government introduced a bill to limit the Lords' power to a two-year delay for general legislation and only one month for a money bill.

The Lords vetoed the bill. Asquith, the Liberal prime minister, then went to the king and got his agreement to create enough new peers to swamp the opposition if they did not give way. Reluctantly the Lords surrendered. Their power was further reduced by legislation in 1949, cutting their delaying power to nine months to a year. This can be a significant factor only in the last year of a government or when the government is trying to push through a heavy legislative agenda.

Today, then, the House of Lords can hardly be compared with the U.S. Senate or, indeed, with the second chambers of most other democracies. Its members receive no salary, though they are entitled to a modest stipend for expenses for each day they attend; their staff, accommodations, and other resources are extremely limited. (Perhaps this explains why, according to evidence to a Lords committee in 1995, members of the upper house had—like the two accused members of the Commons—taken money from lobbyists to put down questions to government ministers.)

So the House of Lords is often derisively dismissed as an obsolete, ineffectual body, a retirement home for over-the-hill public figures, or even "life after death."

Remaining Functions

The House of Lords does perform some useful functions. Its Judicial Committee, made up of the Law Lords, constitutes the highest court of appeal in Britain. Through its process of scrutiny and review it provides further opportunities for correcting deficiencies in the drafting of legislation.

The Lords' style is much more decorous than that of the Commons (which made it all the more startling when a group of lesbians, incensed by what they regarded as anti-gay attitudes by some of the Lords, descended by ropes hung from the spectators' gallery onto the floor of the chamber to make their displeasure known). But if the debates in the Lords are often subdued to the point of somnolence, there are times when they attain a level of quality rarely matched in the Commons. This is largely because the House of Lords is no longer exclusively hereditary. In a chamber of close to 1200 members, some 400 are life peers—appointed for their lifetime without the right to pass their title to their heirs. Many of these life peers are former government ministers. Others are drawn from the sciences, industry, the professions, and the arts; religion is represented by the "Lords Spiritual"—bishops of the Church of England. Thus the Lords can draw on resources of expertise that can be of considerable value in improving legislation and enriching debates.

The Party Line-up

The addition of the life peers has also affected the partisan makeup of the Lords. Predominantly the hereditary peers are Conservatives. But they are less likely to attend and vote than the life peers. Altogether, of the 1,200 members, less than 500 participate regularly. Of these, about half are Conservatives; the rest are drawn from Labour, the Liberal Democrats, and independents or "crossbenchers." Moreover, many of the Conservatives are not Thatcherites; and party discipline in the Lords is normally much weaker than in the Commons. In consequence, during Margaret Thatcher's tenure her government suffered over 100 defeats in the Lords. Most of these were on relatively minor matters, but they also included rejections of the privatizing of public housing for the elderly and of the expansion of government wiretapping authority.

Yet on fundamental questions of economic policy, the Conservative bias of the Lords has not been shaken. When Thatcher's massively unpopular poll tax came to a vote in the Lords, the whips went to work, peers who had not set foot in the House for years appeared from all directions, and the opposition was overwhelmed.

PROPOSALS FOR PARLIAMENTARY REFORM

Concern over the subordination of the legislature to the executive in Britain has led to a great many proposals for reform of the two houses of Parliament.

The Commons

The Schedule. The present meeting hours, which do not begin until 2:30 P.M. (other than Friday mornings) and entail many late-night (even all-night) sessions, are inconvenient for many members, especially women with young children. So the possibility of morning meetings has been under consideration.

Increasing M.P. Resources. M.P.s' salaries, though still below those of legislators in several European countries, have been improving, most recently as a result of backbenchers forcing concessions from the Thatcher government. But without more staff and office space, M.P.s cannot increase their effectiveness in reviewing legislation and serving their constituents.

Tightening Ethical Standards. The Nolan committee proposals, aimed at ending the more gross conflicts of interest among M.P.s, were accepted in principle by Prime Minister John Major. However, he faced strong resistance from a number of Conservative M.P.s, who complained that having to disclose earnings from consultancies would eliminate "professional middle class" representation in the House of Commons, for members of this class would not be able to live on their parliamentary salary alone. For their part, the opposition parties welcomed the Nolan recommendations; but some members (including a minority on the committee itself) called on the committee to inquire into the sources of party political funding. Moreover, the Labour leadership proposed to end trade union sponsorship of M.P.s.

Strengthening the Committees. Here, too, more staff is essential to improved performance. It is also suggested that a freedom of information act would greatly enhance the ability of the committees to gain access to the information needed to carry out their function as a watchdog over government policies and actions.

A Fixed Term for Parliament. Several other parliamentary systems set a specific period of years for the life of a parliament, thus avoiding the unfair advantage given the incumbent government by its power to manipulate the election calendar.

Electoral Reform. Proportional representation (PR) would result in a multiparty system, thus breaking the control that one party has on the entire system between elections. Several different versions of PR have been debated within the Labour Party, and the majority of a special commission appointed by the party has proposed the "supplementary vote," under which voters would register a first and second preference, and if no candidate received a majority, the second preference of the lowest candidates would be distributed among the leaders until a majority was obtained. However, party policy still goes no further than support for a referendum on PR.

The Lords

In the 1960s, the Labour government was close to an agreement with the Conservative leadership in the Lords over a sweeping reform that would have gradually removed the hereditary peers from the Lords, and in the meantime would have given the vote only to the life peers. The delaying power would have been reduced to six months. However, a combination of the Labour left, who wanted total abolition, and the Conservative right, who were against any change, killed the proposal.

Efforts have subsequently been made to revive reforms aimed at removing the power of the hereditary members. But the most widely discussed proposals currently focus on the principle of an elected second chamber. The Labour Party is now committed to the abolition of the hereditary principle in the Lords and the eventual replacement of the Lords by an elected senate.

CONCLUSION

The British Parliament, like the U.S. Congress, has fallen sharply in the public's esteem in recent years. Partly this is due to the wave of disenchantment with politicians that has been sweeping through most industrial countries. But in Britain it also reflects an awareness of the diminished role of the legislature in the total governmental system.

Placing the prime responsibility for public policy-making in the hands of the executive branch is not in itself incompatible with the democratic principle. However, democracy requires that power not be excessively concentrated, which means that the executive should have to deal with a legislature equipped to review, amend and, if necessary, challenge the executive's proposals. The British Parliament is not incapable of doing this on occasion, as the Conservative government found to its detriment over the Maastricht treaty and over the defeat of a proposed increase in the tax on heating fuel in December 1994. But these were exceptional circumstances, and if Parliament is to fulfill its roles consistently, reforms of both houses as suggested above are needed.

However, such reforms will be difficult to achieve, for any government composed of only one party is unlikely to support proposals that may weaken its dominance over Parliament. Some procedural and scheduling changes may be acceptable. But more resources in the hands of individual M.P.s and committees would make the government's life more difficult; fixing the term of Parliament would take away a valuable advantage; proportional representation would almost certainly destroy its ability to govern without a coalition partner; and an elected second chamber, even with a further limitation on the power to delay, would be endowed with a prestige and legitimacy that could enable it to challenge the government more effectively than the patently archaic House of Lords.

So major changes, especially for the House of Commons, seem unlikely as long as one party is able to secure the support of a majority in the Commons. Still, the Labour Party has joined the Liberal Democrats in forcing issues of reform onto the public agenda, and any future election that does not produce a majority for one party could provide the impetus for change.

In the meantime, there is at least a modest potential for M.P.s and their committees to assert themselves more strongly even in the absence of greater resources. The decline of deference that has characterized British society at large needs to be more sharply reflected in Parliament. Committee chairs do not have to be intimidated by the government's mention of national security. And even less subservience to the Whips on matters that do not involve the survival of the government could bring a new energy to Parliament and help to restore the institution's sadly fallen status with the electorate.

SOME QUESTIONS TO THINK ABOUT

How representative is the House of Commons compared with the U.S. House of Representatives?

Why are interest groups less influential in Parliament than in the U.S. Congress?

What do you think of the degree of party discipline in the House of Commons? Would you like to see more in Congress?

How effective is Question Time?

Should the role of backbenchers be increased? By what means?

Should M.P.s be given more resources? Should the select committees be given more resources?

What do you think of the Nolan committee proposals to reform ethical standards in the House of Commons?

What would be the consequences of a fixed term for Parliament?

Should the British change their voting system to some form of proportional representation?

Why has the House of Lords survived in its present form? What functions does it perform? Should it be reformed? Should it be replaced by an elected senate?

NOTES

1. *New York Times,* 24 March 1985.
2. Hugo Young, *The Iron Lady* (Farrar Straus Giroux, 1989), pp. 454-55.
3. Harold Wilson, *The Governance of Britain,* p. 132.
4. David Baker, Andrew Gamble, and Steve Ludlam, "The Parliamentary Siege of Maastricht," *Parliamentary Affairs,* vol. 47, no. 1, January 1994, pp. 56-57.

SUGGESTIONS FOR FURTHER READING

For general coverage of Parliament see Philip Norton, *Does Parliament Matter?* (Harvester Wheatsheaf, 1993), J. A. G. Griffith and Michael Ryle, *Parliament* (Sweet and Maxwell, 1990), Andrew Adonis, *Parliament Today* (Manchester University Press, 1993), and Paul Silk, *How Parliament Works* (Longman, 1987). See also Jack Brand, *British Parliamentary Parties* (Oxford University Press, 1992). On the Lords see Donald Shell, *The House of Lords* (Harvester Wheatsheaf, 1992).

11
THE COURTS AND CRIMINAL JUSTICE

British courts of law, with their bewigged and robed judges and barristers, and their archaic titles (Queen's Bench, Chancery, Master of the Rolls, and so on), are more redolent with history, and more formal in their procedures, than their counterparts in the United States.

For our purposes, however, there is a much more important distinction: courts in Britain are not as directly a part of the system of government and politics as in the United States, where we speak of the courts as a third branch of government, their status identified in Article III of the Constitution; and although the intent of the Founding Fathers on the question is not entirely clear, the Supreme Court, beginning with *Marbury v. Madison* in 1803, established its authority to declare acts of Congress null and void.

No such power rests with the British courts. Nor do appointments of judges require parliamentary approval, or involve the kind of intensely political public hearings accompanying proposed appointments to the U.S. Supreme Court.

Even so, the courts in Britain are very much involved in applying the laws passed by Parliament to particular cases and in determining whether the executive is acting within those laws. In doing so, the courts have a significant impact in several of the policy areas discussed in Part IV of this book—especially property rights, civil liberties, race, and gender—as well as the main issue considered in this chapter, criminal justice. So, as institutions contributing to the shaping of public policy, the courts will be considered here as important elements in the British system of governance. We will also review the role of the police, and explore the controversies that have emerged in recent years over the decisions of judges and the behavior of the police in the administration of the criminal justice system.

THE STRUCTURE OF THE COURTS

The British have evolved a complex system of courts for criminal and civil cases, with a somewhat confusing array of titles.

The great bulk of criminal cases, subject to a maximum six-month prison sentence, are disposed of in *magistrates' courts.* Most of the more serious cases are heard by one of the 100 or so *Crown Courts,* with appeals going to the *Criminal Division of the Court of Appeal.* From there a further appeal may be made to the *Appellate Committee of the House of Lords,* a panel of five to seven members drawn from the Lord Chancellor, "lords of appeal in ordinary" (life peers appointed for this purpose), and others who have held high judicial posts.

On the civil law side, minor cases are dealt with by *county courts.* More substantial ones go to the *High Court,* which consists of three divisions—*Queen's Bench* (common law, including some appeals on points of criminal law from the Crown Courts), *Chancery* (contracts, partnerships, bankruptcy, etc.), and *Family* (divorce and custody). Appeals from county courts and the High Court may go to the *Civil Division of the Court of Appeal* and from there to the House of Lords. Figure 11.1 outlines the structure and stages of this process.

In addition, the growth of the welfare state and of government intervention in the economy has led to the creation of a number of tribunals, which hear and settle disputes in a broad range of areas involving highly technical and specialized issues, such as industrial relations, immigration, welfare benefits, transportation, tax assessments, patents, and performing rights. Tribunals are less formal in their style and procedures than courts, but they are essentially an extension of the judicial system, handling caseloads that otherwise would overwhelm the regular court structure. Appeals on points of law from tribunal decisions may be made either to a special appellate tribunal or to the High Court or Court of Appeal.

There is yet one further stage which the litigation process may take beyond the Court of Appeal or even the House of Lords. The European Court of Justice was created to interpret provisions of the European Union treaties and subsequent decisions. The court has usually upheld the superiority of European Union law over the law of the constituent nations on a steadily widening range of issues. In general its rulings have been accepted by national courts, and the British courts have been no exception.

THE JUDICIARY

Presiding over the British courts are a mixture of part-time and full-time officials. Magistrates' courts are run by unpaid justices of the peace, except in bigger cities, where there are full-time "stipendiary" magistrates. Crown Court cases are heard by

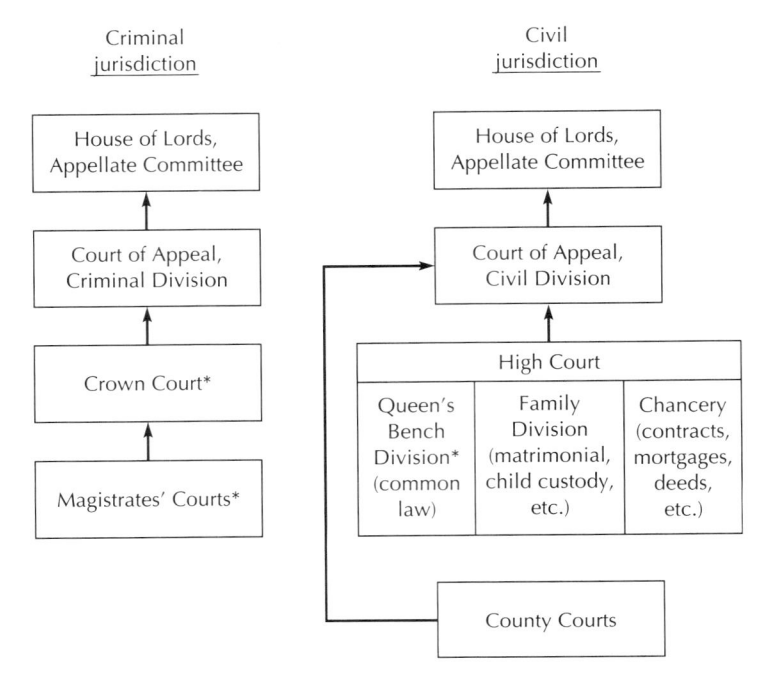

```
                    Criminal                          Civil
                   jurisdiction                    jurisdiction

              ┌──────────────────┐            ┌──────────────────┐
              │  House of Lords, │            │  House of Lords, │
              │Appellate Committee│           │Appellate Committee│
              └──────────────────┘            └──────────────────┘
                       ▲                               ▲
              ┌──────────────────┐            ┌──────────────────┐
              │  Court of Appeal,│            │  Court of Appeal,│
              │ Criminal Division│      ┌────▶│  Civil Division  │
              └──────────────────┘      │     └──────────────────┘
                       ▲                │              ▲
              ┌──────────────────┐      │    ┌────────────────────┐
              │   Crown Court*   │      │    │     High Court     │
              └──────────────────┘      │    ├──────┬──────┬──────┤
                       ▲                │    │Queen's│Family│Chancery
              ┌──────────────────┐      │    │Bench │Division│(contracts,
              │ Magistrates' Courts*│   │    │Division*│(matrimonial,│mortgages,
              └──────────────────┘      │    │(common│child custody,│deeds,
                                        │    │ law) │  etc.) │ etc.)│
                                        │    └──────┴──────┴──────┘
                                        │              ▲
                                        │    ┌──────────────────┐
                                        └────│  County Courts   │
                                             └──────────────────┘
```

*Additional appeal routes on points of law may be available from Magistrates' and Crown Courts to Queen's Bench, and from Queen's Bench directly to House of Lords.

FIGURE 11.1 Structure of the courts (England and Wales)

a High Court judge, a full-time circuit judge, or a paid but part-time recorder. The High Court, the Court of Appeal and the House of Lords Appellate Committee are, of course, made up of full-time judges. Tribunals are sometimes presided over by judges, but usually the chair is a barrister or solicitor or even a nonlawyer.

At the apex of their judicial profession are the *Lord Chief Justice,* who heads both the Criminal Division of the Court of Appeal and the Queen's Bench Division of the High Court; the *Master of the Rolls,* who supervises the Civil Division of the Court of Appeal, and the *Lord Chancellor,* who is a member of the prime minister's cabinet and the Lords' Appellate Committee, as well as the presiding officer of the House of Lords and nominally the president of the High Court's Chancery Division.

The facts in criminal cases and in some civil cases are decided on by juries. However, judges in Britain commonly play a more direct and active role in trials than is the case in the United States, and their conduct of cases and their instructions to the jury on the application of the relevant law tend to have a powerful impact on the decisions.

Judges are appointed nominally by the crown, in fact by the government, with the Lord Chancellor as the prime mover. The varied roles of the Lord Chancellor in the cabinet, the House of Lords and the court system breaches the separation of the judiciary from the other branches of government, and might appear to infringe on a fundamental principle of the rule of law: the independence of the judiciary. Yet judges in Britain enjoy a high degree of independence. Once appointed to the High Court and above judges may not be removed from office until the retirement age of 75 except by action of both houses of Parliament, and Parliament has never so moved. However, Circuit Court judges and recorders may be removed by the Lord Chancellor for misbehavior or incapacity, and although this power has been used very rarely until now, new guidelines were issued in 1994 under which judges, stipendiary magistrates, and tribunal chairs could face disciplinary action, including dismissal, for misbehavior, including drunk driving ("drink-driving" in Britain), and "behavior which could cause offense, particularly on racial or religious grounds, or amounting to sexual harassment . . ."

THE LEGAL PROFESSION

Lawyers in Britain are divided into two categories: solicitors and barristers. There are 57,000 solicitors and 11,000 barristers; solicitors perform the great bulk of legal work. With respect to litigation, solicitors may appear in the lower courts, and reforms are under way to allow them to participate in some of the superior courts. But most of the higher court litigation is still argued by barristers who, by tradition, may not be approached directly by a client, but must depend on solicitors to act as go-betweens.

Among the barristers there is a further division between the Queen's Counsel (Q.C.) and "junior" barristers; when juniors apply to "take silk" (Q.C.s wear silk gowns), 20 to 30 percent are successful. Appointment as Q.C. brings status and access to major cases. However, it does not automatically bring higher incomes. In fact, status and earnings are not necessarily linked in the legal profession; hourly fees of solicitors in City of London commercial firms are the highest in the world, and many of them earn considerably more than all but the most distinguished Q.C.s.

THE POLICE

Despite the trends toward the centralization of government in Britain, there is no national police force. There are, in fact, 52 local police forces, each headed by a chief constable, except for the London police, directed by a commissioner operating out of New Scotland Yard under the general supervision of the home secretary. Every local force other than London is watched over by a police authority with a strong representation of local councillors.

Because the police are the principal wielders of official force, limits on their power are an essential condition of the rule of law. A number of such constraints are provided in Britain, evolving under the common law as judges' rules, and then codified in the Police and Criminal Evidence Act of 1984.

Thus the police must, except in extraordinary circumstances, obtain warrants for searches and seizures; provision may normally be made for bail; the police must repeat a prescribed "caution" when making an arrest; questioning after arrest is regulated; there is a right to sue for false arrest. Unlike police forces in most countries, the British constabulary have been armed with truncheons, being issued with guns only in situations where they are likely to be facing armed suspects. This policy was supported by a survey of all British police officers in 1995; four out of five rejected the suggestion that they carry a gun routinely.

However, the truncheons are now being replaced by American-style batons; there are more occasions on which guns are being issued to police, particularly in the big cities; and the same survey of police that rejected their being armed routinely also revealed overwhelming support for an increase in the number of officers trained in the use of firearms. The reason is that crime has been on the upswing. The extent of the increase is uncertain, for statistics on crime are notoriously unreliable; but estimates of the increase in crime between 1980 and 1992—varying from at least 50 percent to well over 100 percent—gave credence to a pervasive sense of weakening law and order. This anxiety was not lessened by official reports of a slight decline in crime in 1993.

The greatest alarm was provoked by an increase in violent crimes, including a doubling in the rate of homicides between 1969 and 1992. The increase in the murder rate was especially disturbing to the public, for the media accounts were not so much of the classic English murders—poisonings for money by genteel doctors and solicitors—as of brutal, random killings.

Even with this increase, the total number of murders in Britain in 1992 was less than half that of New York City alone. But comparisons abroad were less impressive to the British than the contrast with their own recent past. In any case, cold statistics did not have the impact of the media's reporting in 1992 of the case of a two-year-old led away from a shopping mall and bludgeoned to death by two boys, ten and eleven years old.

The tabloids reacted predictably to the increase in the crime rate. Unless crime can be brought under control, said one, ". . . the government will have to recognize that people must have the right to defend themselves, their loved ones, and their property . . . by whatever force is necessary."[1] Said another: "We must drop the squeamish liberal concern for prisoners, which mirrors the similarly misplaced concern for the perpetrators of crime rather than its victims."[2]

These comments reflected a widespread public attitude, paralleling the mood in the United States, that crime had become pandemic, and that the system of justice had become too preoccupied with the rights of the accused at the expense of the protection of society at large.

THE CRITICS OF THE CRIMINAL JUSTICE SYSTEM

Despite the elaborate hierarchy of courts, the independence of the judiciary, and the restraints on police powers, the British system of justice has been the target of some leading specialists in the study of public law. In Chapter 17 we will discuss their complaints in the context of national security, free speech, protest groups, and other civil liberties issues. Here we focus on issues related to criminal justice in the context particularly of police powers.

Class and the Judges

For some of the critics, notably Public Law Professor J. A. G. Griffith, the principal target has been the judiciary. Formal independence from government, says Griffith, does not mean that British judges are truly neutral in their attitudes toward government policies and the use of government power. The trend in Britain, as in all modern states, is toward a "conservative and reactionary" authoritarianism; and the judges, in his view, are allies of the state and pillars of conservatism. The main reason for this is that "judges are the product of a class and have the characteristic of that class"—that is to say, they come from well-to-do families, went to public schools and Oxbridge, then spent 20 to 25 years as successful barristers before being appointed to the bench by the Lord Chancellor on the advice of the senior judiciary. "This is not the stuff of which reformers are made." The result, says Griffith, is that on questions of the powers of the police, as on every other major social issue, "the judges have supported the conventional, established and settled interests;"[3] and law and order and protecting the rights of property will come before individual liberties and the rights of the accused.

In fact, not all of the senior judges come from upper- or upper-middle-class backgrounds. Lord Denning, an extremely influential judge who was Master of the Rolls from 1962 to 1982, was the son of a draper and complained that: "The youngsters believe we come from a narrow background—it's all nonsense—they get it from that man Griffith."[4]

Still, the figures are with Griffith. Well over two-thirds have come from upper- or upper-middle-class backgrounds and have been successful practitioners at the bar before being appointed judges. This means, says Griffith, that they will be predisposed to support conservative, even reactionary, doctrines and to put law and order first, and the rights of the accused a distant second.

Problems with the Police

Since the 1960s, criticisms of the police have been joined to complaints about the judges. Previously there was a close relationship with the police in most communities, and the British "bobby" on the beat enjoyed a highly favorable reputation. To some extent this reputation has been tarnished in the public mind.

Partly this has been because, despite large increases in police numbers and pay since 1980, the proportion of crimes solved has dropped sharply; the reported "clear-up rate" of crimes other than murders (most of which are solved) fell from two-fifths to barely one-quarter in 1993. But there have been other, even more damaging, developments contributing to a loss of confidence in the police. The British police traditionally had a reputation for integrity, in sharp contrast to the conduct of police departments in several U.S. cities. But since the 1960s there have been revelations of corruption, in some cases even involving middle-ranking officers in Scotland Yard taking payoffs from owners of London gambling houses. Racism in the force has been charged and proven, and confrontations between the police and racial minorities has been a precipitating factor in the riots that erupted in a number of British cities in the 1980s. The deaths of prisoners in custody and the beating up of demonstrators has led to accusations of police brutality. And, as we shall see, there have been recent revelations of gross malfeasance by some police officers in the form of forced confessions and fabricated and concealed evidence.

Nonetheless, although the poll ratings of the police force have fallen in recent years, they remain higher than those of most other institutions—considerably higher than those of the government and Parliament. And polls in late 1993 indicated that four-fifths of the public put much of the blame for rising crime on the police "not having enough powers" and on lenient sentencing.

The Thatcher government generally agreed with this view. Although the passage of the Police and Criminal Evidence Act of 1984 was an effort by the government to give some recognition to the concerns about police misconduct, it was clear that law and order was the highest priority in the minds of Margaret Thatcher and her cabinet colleagues. Thatcherism, after all, included a strong belief in law enforcement and Thatcher herself was ardently pro-police. She looked to them to control crime and terrorism, and she was especially dependent on them for breaking the 1983–84 miner's strike. In the course of that strike, nearly 1,400 police officers and a larger number of strikers were injured, several local police forces were effectively coordinated from London, and special elite groups of police, trained in the aggressive use of crowd control, were formed and deployed.

The Major administration continued to employ a strong law and order rhetoric. Home Secretary Michael Howard brought the 1993 Conservative Party conference to its feet by promising to build more prisons and get more criminals into them by more effective policing, longer sentences, and weakening or even abolishing a number of long-established protections for the accused. These ideas were then embodied in the Criminal Justice and Public Order Bill of 1994, which, among other provisions, proposed restrictions on the right to bail, the extension of anti-terrorist provisions, more prisons—many of them privatized, more central control of the police and magistrates, and an increase in the maximum fine for possession of cannabis from £500 to £2,500. The right to silence was to be significantly limited: Henceforth inferences could be drawn from a suspect's refusal to say anything.

On the other hand, while following through on this Thatcherite approach, the Major government could not ignore a certain tension between the government and the police that was implicit in Thatcherism. For Thatcherism encompasses not only a belief in strong law enforcement, but also a thrifty approach to government spending and a demand for the efficient use of public resources. This did not seem to square with the rising crime rates and lower clear-up rates that were occurring despite sharply increased outlays on the police. Consequently John Major's administration set up a commission that proposed extensive changes in police organization, including a sharp reduction in middle-management positions; some reforms were then instituted, although the commission's recommendations were modified in the face of angry reactions from police associations.

For the more radical critics of the police, however, inefficiency was not the principal problem. They argued that more restraints on the powers of the police were needed. These limits had never been as far-reaching as those that prevailed in the United States beginning in the era of the Earl Warren Supreme Court. British courts have been somewhat less stringent than U.S. courts in reviewing confessions and searches and seizures, and there is no exclusionary rule that automatically throws out evidence obtained illegally, other than for the most flagrant of abuses. Moreover, the judiciary has shown a general disposition to rely on the testimony of the police; this has led to some grave miscarriages of justice, particularly in the struggle against the outrages perpetrated in England by the Irish Republican Army (IRA).

The IRA Cases

In October 1974, bombs exploded in crowded pubs in Guildford and London, killing and maiming several people. The following month more devastation was caused by explosions in pubs in Birmingham.

Three men and a woman—the Guildford Four—were arrested and charged with the first wave of bombings, and on the basis of alleged confessions they were convicted and sentenced to long jail sentences. Then in December 1975, three months after the sentencing of the Guildford Four, four members of the IRA were captured and confessed to the Guildford bombings, claiming that the Guildford Four were innocent. Nonetheless, statements included in the confessions of the Guildford Four led to the arrests of seven more people, the McGuire Seven; and traces of nitroglycerine said to have been found on the hands and gloves of the accused led to their conviction and sentences ranging from four years (for a 14-year-old boy) to fourteen years.

The Guildford Four appealed, claiming that their confessions had been beaten out of them. Then the McGuire Seven appealed, alleging a biased summing-up by the trial judge and gross errors in the chemical tests on their hands and gloves. The Appeals Court refused to overturn the convictions.

Yet publicity generated by an investigative journalist raised more and more questions about the conduct of the cases and especially about confessions obtained under the Prevention of Terrorism Act. This act, passed by a Labour government in 1974 and renewed and updated each year since then, empowers police to arrest without a warrant anyone suspected of an offense under the act and detain them without charge, and without access to a lawyer, for a period which, in some circumstances, can extend up to seven days.

This power had been used in the Guildford pub cases in ways that led a group including the Catholic Archbishop, two former home secretaries, and two former law Lords to press for a further review. The government refused to act at first, but further inquiries raised more doubts about the confessions, the police failure to fully investigate alibi evidence, and—the final blow—evidence in a confidential file of deliberate falsification by the police. In 1989, the Director of Public Prosecutions told the Appeals Court that the convictions were no longer sustainable, and the Guildford Four were freed. Attention now turned to the McGuire Seven, and in 1990 they were exonerated; however, all but one—who died in jail—had already completed their sentences.

A similar series of events transpired in connection with the November 1974 bombings of the pubs in Birmingham. Six men—the Birmingham Six—were arrested, convicted, and sentenced. They appealed on the grounds that they had been coerced into confessions and that scientific evidence used against them was unsound. Their appeal was rejected, but after a further referral to the Court of Appeal by the government, their convictions were overturned and they were released.

The eventual correction of such gross miscarriages of justice hardly represents a triumph of the British rule of law. Indeed, what was involved here was not merely fraudulent behavior by the police and shoddy work by prosecutors and defense counsel, but an obstinate failure by senior judges to act with impartiality and integrity. The initial summing-up by the trial judges conveyed nothing of the dubious nature of the evidence in all three cases. The IRA exoneration of the Guildford Four, said the Appeals Court, must be "wholly rejected as unworthy of credence," and "therefore gives rise to no lurking doubts whatever in our minds." In the case of the Birmingham Six, the Appeals Court, presided over by Lord Chief Justice Lane, insisted: "The longer the hearing has gone on, the more convinced this Court has become that the verdict of the jury was correct. We have no doubt that these convictions were safe and satisfactory."

Behind the certainties of these judges lay the fears expressed by Lord Denning when the Birmingham Six tried to pursue their case in the civil courts:

> If the six men win it will mean that the police were guilty of perjury, that they were guilty of violence and threats, that the confessions were involuntary and were improperly admitted and that the convictions were erroneous . . . This is such an appalling vista that every sensible person in the land would say: "It cannot be right that these actions should go any further."[5]

In these cases, it appears, the judges were more concerned with protecting law and order and the image of the criminal justice system than with dispensing justice.

SOME QUALIFICATIONS TO THE CRITICS' CASE

Griffith and his fellow critics make a powerful case against the British system of justice. However, defenders of the system argue that the critics cite their evidence selectively and overlook some important considerations.

Judges versus the Government

It is true that the judiciary gives special weight to the government's concerns with respect to the preservation of law and order (which, after all, is a precondition for any properly functioning society). But this does not mean they are mere agents of the policies of governments, and particularly of Conservative governments.

Thus there was a sharp confrontation between judges and John Major's home secretary, Michael Howard, over some of the proposals in the Criminal Justice and

Public Order Bill. A number of senior judges in the House of Lords, the Court of Appeals, and the High Court spoke out strongly in the press, insisting that building more prisons had failed to reduce crime in the past and was unlikely to do so in the future. Lord Lane, the former Lord Chief Justice who had been so ready to support the police and government in the Birmingham Six case, sharply criticized Howard's proposal that the release date of anyone serving a life sentence should be determined by the Home Secretary rather than the courts. Several judges also spoke out against abolishing or severely limiting the right to silence. Howard fought back in public statements but backed down on his proposals for exerting more central control over the police and magistrates, and was forced to accept a number of amendments to his bill in the House of Lords.

There were likely to be more such confrontations in light of the appointment of less conservative judges as Lord Chancellor, Lord Chief Justice, and Master of the Rolls, and these and other appointments led John Griffith to hope that the British judiciary might recover from its deeply tarnished reputation and "begin to rebuild its credibility."[6] Another commentator, noting the further appointments to senior positions of a number of extremely able reformist judges, suggested that the judiciary in the House of Lords "is as intellectually formidable and politically unsympathetic to a Conservative government as at any time ever."[7]

These changes at the top will take time to work their way through the judicial system, and in Chapter 17 we shall see that intemperate and reactionary comments by senior judges have not been limited to cases involving terrorism, but are also evident whenever a threat to national security or breaches of government secrecy are mentioned. However, this is not true of the great majority of criminal cases that come before British courts, for these do not involve terrorism or national security; by and large judges conduct these cases with scrupulous concern for due process and for the rights of the accused.

Moreover, where judges fail to do so, the accused may yet be protected by the jury system. Although juries did not help the Guildford Four or the McGuire Seven or the Birmingham Six, juries in some national security cases—as we shall see in Chapter 17—have ignored the judge's clear instruction to convict.

Expeditiousness

Despite the greater formality and apparent ponderousness of British trials, this system is less cumbersome and more expeditious than that in the United States. The relative simplicity of British trial procedures has been noted favorably by some U.S. legal scholars, together with the fact that—although British barristers do use the adversarial method—they are less prone than American lawyers to rely on tactics designed for wining at any cost rather than discovering the truth.

Moreover, the British press and television are under much more severe limitations than the U.S. media in their coverage of cases before the courts. For all the clamorous vulgarity and intrusiveness of the British tabloids, nothing resembling the media circus enveloping the O. J. Simpson case, with attorneys, witnesses, and even the judge giving newspaper and television interviews, would be possible in Britain. Once an arrest has been made there, the media may say nothing about a case, other than reporting the proceedings in court, on pain of being charged with contempt of court; and lawyers on either side may make no public comments on their case until the trial is over. Thus there is less danger in Britain than in the United States of defendants being tried by public opinion before a trial even begins.

It is true that in the United States we provide much greater protection for the accused in the form of interminable jury selection processes and repeated opportunities for appeal. Yet these advantages are usually more available to the rich than the poor. Moreover, as former Chief Justice Warren Burger observed in 1967: "The vastly greater efficiency of the British barrister (and I must add the greater efficiency of the British judge) enables them to try cases in much less time than we do in this country." If justice delayed is justice denied, then in this respect the British are less likely than the Americans are to deny justice.

And if by U.S. standards the British seem too ready to rush to judgment, it should be remembered that no one is executed in Britain because of inadequate procedural protection, for capital punishment has been abolished there since 1965. Bills to reintroduce the death penalty have been introduced in Parliament several times since then, and opinion polls have regularly shown overwhelming public support for the bills. Yet, as we noted in chapter 10, always the bills have been left to a free vote in the Commons, and every time, the proposals have been defeated decisively. Indeed, in 1994, at the height of the public anxiety about crime, the proposal to bring back capital punishment received its heaviest ever defeat in Parliament. Among those outside Parliament who opposed the death penalty were a number of senior judges (including Lord Denning, who had reversed his earlier opinion on the subject).

Reforms in Progress

Two kinds of reforms of the justice system are now being undertaken. First, in the aftermath of the overturned IRA convictions, the government accepted the recommendation of a royal commission on criminal justice that the responsibility for reviewing alleged miscarriages of justice be removed from the Home Office and assigned to a criminal cases review authority, which would be empowered to refer questionable verdicts to the Court of Appeal. Of 700 recent cases, the Home Office had referred only 10 for review, and it was assumed that the review authority would be more diligent in this respect (though it would still have to depend on the police to carry out its investigations).

Second, Lord Mackay, the Lord Chancellor appointed by Margaret Thatcher, has applied pressure to make the system less complex and less bound by archaic traditions. One result would be to reduce the cost of litigation; currently, going to court in Britain is even more expensive than in the United States, although legal aid for low income people is available from public funds. (Applicants must prove their income is less than £44 a week and that they have no more than £3000 in savings. However, several of the Lloyds of London "names" or partners ruined in a financial fiasco were deemed qualified under these rules by the Legal Aid Board, and the bankrupt sons of the late tycoon, Robert Maxwell, received millions of pounds in legal aid for their defense against charges of conspiracy to defraud.)

By 1994 Mackay's reform efforts had also enabled a number of solicitors to practice before higher courts and even be eligible to become judges; also, the procedures for selecting judges are under review in an effort to make them more open. It will take longer, however, before another proposal is accepted to reduce the intimidating formality of British trials by dispensing with the wearing of wigs by judges and barristers.

The European Court of Justice

One more factor that will have an increasingly important effect on the rulings and even the procedures of the British courts will be the European Court of Justice. We shall encounter in Part IV issues on which British law has been brought into conformity with findings of the European Court. There will be more such issues in the future.

CONCLUSION

Clearly the British trial system offers some important advantages over the way U.S. courts transact their business. However, the IRA cases, as well as others to be discussed in Chapter 17, raise troubling questions about the extent to which the rights of defendants are respected in the face of intense public anxieties about the breakdown of law and order.

Nor is the political reaction to the public clamor limited to the Conservative Party and government. Labour, as part of its process of moving toward the electable center, has decided to take a stronger line on the issue. Tony Blair became the Labour leader partly because of his espousing the cause of tougher law enforcement and his effective challenging of Conservative home secretaries in Parliament on their inability to prevent the rise in crime. He struck responsive chords on both the right and the left with his slogan: "Tough on crime and tough on the causes of crime."

"Tough on crime" until now has meant more police and more prisons. But as we have seen, more police has not meant less crime, and Britain already has a bigger prison population than any other European Union country, with overcrowding leading to periodic prison riots. As for being "tough on the causes of crime"—presumably unemployment, poverty, and the miserable conditions in the inner cities—these, as we shall see in chapter 14, will be even more difficult to solve with the resources likely to be available in Britain's foreseeable future.

SOME QUESTIONS TO THINK ABOUT

How would you compare the relative advantages of British and U.S. trial procedures?

Should the appointment of British judges be subject to review by Parliament?

Are the British giving too high a priority to the protection of law and order at the expense of the rights of the accused?

Was the Prevention of Terrorism Act justified in light of the IRA's campaign of bombings? Should it be repealed now?

NOTES

1. The *Star,* 31 August 1993.
2. *Daily Express,* 23 August 1993.
3. J. A. G. Griffith, *The Politics of the Judiciary* (Fontana, fourth edition, 1991), pp. 320-25.
4. Cited in Anthony Sampson, *The Changing Anatomy of Britain* (Random House, 1982), p. 159.
5. Griffith, *Politics of the Judiciary,* pp. 289-90.
6. *Judicial Politics Since 1920* (Blackwell, 1993), p. 191.
7. Simon Lee, "Law and the Constitution," in Dennis Kavanagh and Anthony Seldon (eds.), *The Major Effect* (Macmillan, 1994), p. 126.

SUGGESTIONS FOR FURTHER READING

In addition to his *Politics of the Judiciary,* J. A. G. Griffith has provided a historical perspective in *Judicial Politics Since 1920.* For a detailed description of the legal system see P. F. Smith and S. H. Bailey, *The Modern English Legal System* (Sweet and Maxwell, 1984). On the police see R. Reiner, *The Politics of the Police* (Harvester Wheatsheaf, 1992). Edmund Heward, *Lord Denning* (Weidenfeld and Nicolson, 1990) is a biography of an influential Master of the Rolls, and the memoir by Lord Hailsham, *A Sparrow's Flight* (Fontana, 1990), provides some insights from the perspective of a former Lord Chancellor.

12

Local Government and the Nationality Question

Whitehall (the national executive departments) and Westminster (the Parliament) are clearly the most important shapers of public policy in Britain.

Yet there is more to British government than those two locations. In fact, a large number of elected bodies operate below the national level, representing a strong tradition of local government in Britain. Close to three million people work for elected local bodies, and this number is not surprising when we consider their broad range of responsibilities. Local government agencies manage elementary and secondary school systems, libraries and parks, collect refuse, provide social services and bus transportation, maintain roads and sewers, build and operate public housing, and make rules affecting zoning and community planning. Fire departments, too, are a local responsibility, and so are the police, for there is no national police force in Britain.

The local government system has been remade periodically and is currently on the verge of another major overhaul. Briefly stated, the present structure is the product of the Local Government Acts of 1972 and 1985. The framework established by the 1972 act involved two kinds of governmental authorities: six metropolitan county councils, and nonmetropolitan or "shire" county councils. Under each of these was another level of district councils (those in the metropolitan areas having more responsibilities than the shire district councils); and within the district councils some minor functions were left in the hands of parish or community councils.

Then in 1985 the metropolitan county councils were abolished, leaving only one local government tier in the big cities and two in the less populated counties. Further changes are in prospect as a result of the establishment in 1991 of a local government commission, which has been examining the desirability of creating more single-tier councils, an idea favored by the Conservative government. However, in the face of strong local opposition, it appears that the commission will give the government much less than it wanted in this respect.

The commission's recommendations will relate only to England, for the structure in Wales is somewhat different—and in Scotland substantially different—from that in England; and Northern Ireland is a quite separate case. And in each of these three countries the pressures for change result not only from official commissions but from volatile political forces.

In this chapter we explore the tensions between the center and the localities, with special reference to the troubled relationships between the central government on the one hand and Scotland, Wales, and Northern Ireland on the other.

THE PULL OF CENTRALIZATION

Despite this multiplicity of local elected bodies and the great cultural diversity of the country, Britain, as we noted in chapter 2, is a small, urbanized, densely populated country, subjected to a number of standardizing forces including a national press and television. These forces are joined by several factors in the governmental and political system to weaken local control.

The Absence of Federalism

With Parliament sovereign, and no written constitution to reserve powers to bodies below the national level, local governments are the creation of the central government. Parliament gives authority to local governments for certain purposes, and what it gives it can take away. Each change in the structure or financing or responsibilities of local government is signaled by an act of Parliament—like those of 1972 and 1985—and those that will follow the recommendations of the commission established by Parliament in 1991.

The Loss of Functions

The trend of parliamentary and departmental activity in recent years has been to reduce the functions of local government. Until the 1940s, elected local bodies ran water, gas, electricity, and a considerable range of health services. Nationalization moved these responsibilities to public corporations, and denationalization has shifted them to the private sector. Some of the government departments that used to look to local authorities to implement programs now prefer to manage them directly through regional offices. Educational standards are being established nationally and local schools are subject to inspection by people appointed by the Department of Education in London.

Moreover, major functions like urban development, regional planning, and river transportation are increasingly under the jurisdiction of *quangos*: quasi-autonomous government organizations appointed by the central government. The word covers a great variety of institutions, from housing, education, and health agencies that spend huge amounts of government money to modest advisory groups on countryside preservation and the award of medals. But all are financed by government, and all are involved with matters affecting the public that otherwise would have to be handled directly by government departments.

In the 1970s, the Conservatives attacked the proliferation of quangos, which they saw as mechanisms by which Labour governments were spreading socialism without public debate or accountability. In the 1980s, the Thatcher government closed many of them down—but created a large number of new ones, such as national health service trusts, training agencies, regulatory bodies set up to monitor denationalized industries, and executive units formerly part of the civil service.

By 1990 quangos were spending over £40 billion a year—three times the amount when Margaret Thatcher became prime minister—and their budgets continued to increase in the 1990s. Government ministers make or renew 10,000 appointments a year to a total of 40,000 members of these public boards. Critics charged that many of these appointments were going to contributors to Conservative Party funds who might benefit financially, and the House of Commons public accounts committee documented a number of cases of corruption in the quangos. The government denied the charges indignantly, evoking the sarcastic comment from the usually friendly *Economist* magazine, "Thank heavens that the exclusive concern of all quango appointees, beyond a shadow of a doubt, is the public interest."[1] The government provided a partial response to this criticism in 1995 by introducing guidelines for appointments to quangos (paid positions would have to be advertised), together with a recommended code of conduct for quango members.

A more fundamental criticism of the growth of quangos has been raised by some writers on the constitution; one calls it a "new pattern of governance" that weakens accountability and undermines local government;[2] but the Major government declared that it saw no merit in this accusation.

Finances

In most industrialized societies, local units of government receive a substantial portion of their income from the central government. This is because national governments usually have access to a wider range of revenue sources than subnational units, and because the poorer localities look to the central government to redistribute national revenues in their direction.

This is certainly the case in the United States, and it is even more so in Britain, where underwriting from the departments of the central government rose steadily after World War I, and by the late 1970s had considerably exceeded local government revenues from taxes, fees, services, and loans. As a general principle, whoever provides the funds will have some say in how those funds are to be spent, and local governments have been compelled to accept a plethora of rules and regulations written in Whitehall.

Partisan Elections

Unlike national elections, local elections in Britain are for fixed, four-year terms, although not all local councils are elected at the same time.

Most of the candidates run under the banner of the national parties, and some, especially on the Labour side, see election to a local council as a stepping stone to election to Parliament. However, there are more opportunities for independents, and a few candidates from eccentric parties like the Monster Raving Loonies, who have no hope of winning parliamentary seats, get elected to district councils. Some councils, too, are run by Labour-Liberal or Conservative-Liberal coalitions.

Despite these differences, the results of local races are read by the national parties and media as symptomatic of changes in the mood of the country and portents of the likely outcome of the next general election. These interpretations are often misleading, for local considerations may crowd out national issues in council elections, and the Liberal Democrats, who have traditionally emphasized the importance of grass roots activities and issues, consistently do better in local than in national elections. Still, the national party system is more clearly reflected at the local level than is the case in the United States, and there is no counterpart in Britain to the nonpartisan local elections found in some of the western United States.

LABOUR AND CENTRALIZATION

Early Trends

In its early history, Labour Party intellectuals like Sidney and Beatrice Webb focused on municipal socialism. Labour was not yet a national power, so it was natural that it would be interested in building its strength from the grass roots up, even if this meant talking about such humble issues as better drains rather than grand economic policy. But once Labour had replaced the Liberals as the alternative governing party it could concentrate on national policies, and with its attainment of a majority in 1945, nationalization of industry and national economic planning came into vogue.

In adopting centralizing policies of this kind, Labour was being consistent with the general trend of ideas on the left. For socialists, the two major evils that must be attacked were the excessive power of the great business corporations and the gross maldistribution of wealth and income. In their view, only big government could countervail big business, and only the national government possessed the authority and the resources to reduce inequality.

Recent Shifts toward Decentralization

Recently there has been some modification of Labour's faith in centralization. One influence has been the "new left" perspectives that emerged in the 1960s, with their renewed interest in the local community and the belief in the virtue of smallness. But more important has been Labour's long sojourn in the political wilderness since 1979, its dislike of the centralizing policies of the Conservative government, and the fact that the only bastions of power remaining to it during this period have been local city councils. Consequently the Labour leadership has included in its newfound interest in constitutional reform a strong interest in devolution of power from the center to the regions and localities. Nonetheless, Labour has not given up on its belief in the importance of action at the national level, and its past policies reinforced the centralizing forces in government and the economy.

THE CONSERVATIVES AND CENTRALIZATION

If Labour's recent policies favoring the shift of power from the center reflect a departure from traditional positions on the left, the policies of the Thatcher government represent a still greater deviation from classical conservative doctrine.

In general, conservatives have decried the power of big government, and to the extent that government action is needed at all, they have preferred to assign it as close to home as possible. Thus conservatives in the United States fought the battle of "states' rights" to keep power out of the hands of the federal government, dropping the slogan only when it became identified with racial segregation in the south; and the Republican congressional majorities in 1995 were again talking about the need for federal monies to go directly and without strings to the state governments.

It is true that Margaret Thatcher was very much in the conservative tradition in her distaste for government intervention in the economy. She was also squarely in that tradition in her dislike of national bureaucracies, in the cuts she enforced in the size of the civil service, and in the measures of decentralization of the civil service from London to the regions. Yet, elected local governments were far from rejuvenated; their power was considerably reduced during Thatcher's tenure, and the erosion continued under John Major. There are three reasons for this apparent contradiction between conservative doctrine and practice.

Strong Leadership

As we saw earlier, economic individualism was only one of the strands that made up Thatcherism. Another important component was the belief in the assertion of strong leadership. This was necessary, she believed, to shake Britain out of its moribund complacency and to compel it to accept radical departures from policies she believed to be ruinous. The instrument available to her to achieve this purpose was the national government and she intended to use to the full the power vested in her government.

So, as Conservatives sustained an effective attack on the Labour Party for espousing the policies of the "nanny state," their opponents replied that Mrs. Thatcher was herself the ultimate British nanny, scolding the public for its past misbehavior, and laying down stern new rules for everyone to follow. Among those she considered delinquents were many of the local governments, and she set about the task of bringing them into line.

Money

If Thatcher was to achieve her goal of cutting government spending, she had to do something about local government. By 1979, over 60 percent of local government spending came from the national government, some of it for specific programs developed under national legislation, the larger part as a supplement to the local property tax, or "rates." The amounts involved were very substantial, for local governments accounted for more than a quarter of all government spending in Britain.

Politics

For Thatcher, the problem of high local government spending was compounded by the fact that the biggest spenders tended to be councils with Labour majorities. They spent more than others for two reasons. First, they had an ideological commitment to government as the representative of community—as opposed to private—values and as an instrument of helping the poor. Second, Labour had majorities on those councils because they were in metropolitan areas with a disproportionate number of low-income people; and low-income people need government services more than the affluent.

Then there was the enthusiasm of Labour councils under the sway of the far left to spend money on projects calculated to enrage the Conservative government. Liverpool and London were among the chief offenders in this respect. The Greater London Council, chaired by a fiery young leader, Ken Livingstone, spent over five million pounds on projects like Babies Against the Bomb, the Gay London Police Monitoring Group, and the Karl Marx Centenary. IRA leaders were welcomed to County Hall, and a royal wedding day was lampooned by releasing black balloons over London. One London borough council banned the use of the word "family" from council literature as discriminatory. Another changed its twinning (sister cities) program from France, West Germany, and Israel to the Soviet Union, East Germany, and Nicaragua at the height of the Cold War.

Only a small proportion of Labour councils were involved in programs of this kind. But the tabloid press devoted many headlines to what it called the *loony left,* and the national Labour leadership was placed on the defensive, for the radical projects were being paid for not only by local taxpayers but also by funds from the national government.

Thatcher, determined that no more of her money would be devoted to celebrating Karl Marx, supporting the IRA, and criticizing the police, began her attack on local government spending. First, her government cut the level of national grants and demanded that local councils privatize many of their functions by contracting them out.

Some of the Labour councils fought back. They increased the local rates and spent beyond the limits provided for by the national grants, believing that this would force the government's hands and make it provide more money. But they were dealing with Margaret Thatcher. She counterattacked by instituting "rate-capping"—a limit on how far local property taxes could be raised—and imposed penalties (fines and loss of office) on council members who voted to overspend.

An effort to get all the offending councils to unite in defiance failed. Most gave in; but Liverpool city council, dominated by Militant and other outside left members, continued the fight. First, as a grandstanding tactic, they sent out dismissal notices by taxi to most municipal employees. These they rescinded after Neil Kinnock expressed his outrage at the 1985 Labour Party conference—the first step in his fight to take the party back from the far left. Then the council, saddled with a huge overdraft, bailed itself out with a loan from the class enemy—a consortium of British, Swiss, and Japanese banks. Several council members from Liverpool and elsewhere were subsequently fined and ejected from office by the courts for their refusal to abide by the national laws introduced by the Thatcher government.

Still, the victory in Thatcher's mind was incomplete, for the big metropolitan councils were mostly still controlled by Labour. So in 1985 the metropolitan councils—the super-tier of government in the cities—were abolished. The value of this super-tier had been a subject of debate for many years. Some specialists on the subject had suggested that they represented an unneeded and costly layer of bureaucracy. Still, the political animus behind their abolition aroused considerable controversy. In particular, opposition erupted in response to the rushing of special legislation that would do away with the Greater London Council. Even Conservative members of the council protested, and the House of Lords voted to delay the bill. Ken Livingstone, formerly the *bête noire* of the middle class, now became a popular media figure, pluckily fighting to preserve tradition against the oppressive forces of centralization.

But the delay was only temporary. After one last splurge on a huge, fireworks-studded celebration, the Greater London Council joined the other metropolitan councils in oblivion. The borough councils remained—and a few of them still provided fodder for the "loony left" stories—but disowned by Kinnock and impoverished by Thatcher, the day of the left as a municipal resistance movement was over.

The Poll Tax

Thatcher had won. But she was still not satisfied. From the time she had become Conservative Party leader she had wanted to change the system of rates, which, like the property tax in the United States, was levied on homes and businesses.

Property taxes as the principal source of local government revenue have always been the subject of criticism, and the critics have come from all points on the political spectrum. This is no less true of the United States than of the United Kingdom, and it was outrage at the spiraling levels of the California property tax that sparked a massive tax revolt with repercussions throughout the nation.

For Margaret Thatcher there were two special reasons for opposition to the rates. First, in her view the system was unfair, for six people sharing a home placed six times the burden on local government services as one person living alone in a house next door, yet the tax on both houses was the same. Second, there were those high-spending Labour councils, who could raise much of their money from the central government and from rates on business and spend it on their low-income constituents.

So Thatcher looked for an alternative. This would not be the proposal put forward in the 1960s by Labour cabinet minister Richard Crossman to replace the rates with a local income tax, for cutting the income tax was a Conservative campaign promise on which she had already delivered at the national level. Instead she adopted a proposal presented by two junior members of her government for a "community charge," or what became known as a poll tax, for it was levied not on homes but on every individual. This, she believed, would be more equitable than the rates. Each adult would be required to contribute (with exemptions for the very poorest, and reductions for students); and because everyone would be paying something, the entire electorate would be made more aware of the cost of local government and thus of any unnecessary extravagance by the councils.

As we saw in chapter 9, Crossman's proposal had run into the barrier of civil service opposition. But this time the advocate of change was the prime minister herself, and the key civil servants minister provided her the "unswerving loyalty and commitment" needed to put the poll tax into effect.[3] So the 1987 Conservative Party manifesto contained the promise: "We will legislate in the first session of the new Parliament to abolish the unfair domestic rating system and replace rates with a fairer Community charge."

This produced expressions of concern from a number of Conservative members of local councils, some backbench M.P.s, and a few members of the cabinet, particularly the Chancellor of the Exchequer, Nigel Lawson; but the issue did not surface during the 1987 election campaign, nor was there much interest in it until the legislation was introduced in the House of Commons. Then the controversy began to build, and although the bill passed by a comfortable margin, 38 Conservatives defied the whips to support an amendment relating the tax to incomes. The resistance was stronger still in the House of Lords, where the whips had to bring out of the backwoods large numbers of peers who had rarely or never before voted in Parliament. But these were mere skirmishes before the storm of opposition that broke when the poll tax bills went out, first in Scotland, then in the rest of the country. The new system ran into a barrage of objections.

The first addressed the central rationale for the poll tax, its claim to be fairer than the rates. Suddenly the public learned that the Duke of Westminster was paying the same tax as a laborer who lived in a cottage on his property, and it was evident that the backwoods peers who had overwhelmed the opposition in the Lords had been motivated not by duty to their party but by financial self-interest, for they would pay much less in poll taxes than in rates. Moreover, the principle that everyone would pay the same was true only within a taxing district. Affluent communities, where the residents did not make many demands on council services, set a lower rate than elsewhere. So there were wide disparities, the highest tax being four times the lowest.

Still, the uproar would have been considerably less had the designers of the reform not seriously underestimated the size of the increases that would fall on very large numbers of voters, many of them in the middle classes. Insufficient account had been taken of the rate of inflation. Administering the program proved to be cumbersome and much more costly than had been predicted. And, because the bills were so high, a great many people in some communities were unable to pay or simply refused to do so. The courts became clogged with suits against the delinquents, some of whom were sent to jail (and are now suing the government for wrongful imprisonment). Moreover, a considerable number may have been dropped from the voting rolls by eluding the poll tax. While some experts have argued that this probably made little difference in the 1992 election, because most of the nonpayers were in safe Labour areas,[4] others have suggested that, had there not been so many lost poll tax registrants, "the Labour Party could have won as many as seven more seats in the 1992 general election, and the Liberal Democrats three"—enough, with by-election losses, to have deprived the Conservatives of their overall parliamentary majority by 1993.[5]

With so many nonpayers of the tax, the bills for the rest of the population had to be adjusted upward to compensate. Now it was not only the opposition parties who were attacking the poll tax. Many Conservative M.P.s, inundated with furious complaints from constituents, pleaded for the program to be scrapped or at least heavily modified, and there was increasing uneasiness in the cabinet. Thatcher accepted some minor changes. But there would be no retreat on the core of the plan. "You'll see," she told Parliament, "it will be recognized as a fair and just tax."

This was not, after all, the first time she had faced strong pressure to turn back or temporize. She had resisted the faint hearts who wanted her to change her economic policies during the recession of the early 1980s, and to make deals to end the miners' strike and the Falklands war. Each time she had persisted and each time she had prevailed. Surely she would do so again on the poll tax.

But this time she had miscalculated. Few would join her in seeing the poll tax as fair and just, and it was this issue that proved to be the final cause of her ouster. She had been highly successful in using centralized power to change the behavior of local governments. But then she had overreached herself and been brought down by what, in the U.S. context, would have been a purely local issue.

The Conservatives after Thatcher

John Major was Thatcher's hand-picked successor. But a first order of business when he became prime minister was to do something about the poll tax. As an interim measure, money was provided from the national treasury to bring down the levels of poll tax. Then the poll tax was abolished and replaced with a "council tax," which differed from the old rates system by assuming a two-person household, but then graduated the tax according to the value of the house.

Labour was critical of this system, too, for its top band was still well below the value of some expensive homes, and Labour proposed a "fair rates" system as a modification of the old rates method. Nonetheless, the differences between the parties were now within a consensual range. Thatcher argued in her memoirs that "the community charge, having been modified in several ways, was beginning to work at the very time it was abandoned. Given time, it would have been seen as one of the most far-reaching and beneficial reforms ever made in the working of local government."[6] But the more general verdict is that the poll tax is a historical curiosity, occupying a prime place in the annals of political fiascos.

It should be noted, however, that each of these alternative tax systems was imposed by the central government. In the United States the federal government influences local decisions through the monies that it provides for a variety of programs. Yet it is the states and not the federal government that set the procedures by which local governments may raise money.

So, despite the difference in their styles, John Major must be as deeply involved in decisions affecting local government as was Margaret Thatcher. Moreover, the Major government aggressively pursued a number of initiatives introduced by Thatcher that profoundly affect local governments, including the contracting out of government services to private firms and, as we shall see in chapter 15, the setting of educational policies. And the government applied pressure—with, as it transpired, very little success—on the local government commission to propose more consolidation into one-tier units.

THE NATIONALITY QUESTION

In chapter 2 we noted that local loyalties are especially marked in the three areas that are British but not English. Scotland, Wales, and Northern Ireland possess some of the cultural attributes associated with nationhood yet are not defined as nations in the full sense because they are subordinate to the sovereignty of the British Parliament. Although each operates under governmental arrangements somewhat different from those of English counties, they lack even the powers residing in the states or provinces of federal systems. Thus foreign, defense, and economic policies are run from Westminster and Whitehall; welfare benefits are the same throughout the United Kingdom; and although there are variations in the level of local taxes, the basis on which they are levied is uniform.

Given the strength of attachments to the symbols and customs of Scotland, Wales, and Northern Ireland, it is not surprising that periodically pressures have mounted to change the existing governmental relationships.

Scotland

The Act of Union of 1707 between England and Scotland did not prevent the development of a separate Scottish legal system, an official Church of Scotland, and an educational system that in many respects is superior to that of England.

These and other differences brought about the creation in 1885 of the Scottish Office under a secretary of state for Scotland who, most of the time, has been a member of the British cabinet. Many of the functions directed by other government departments are brought together under the Scottish Secretary, and most of the Scottish Office has been moved to Edinburgh.

Despite this special attention to Scottish concerns, there is a strong current of dissatisfaction with a relationship that is ultimately controlled from London. Although many Scots have achieved positions of power and influence in British government, business, and the professions, and some parts of the country have prospered through their proximity to North Sea oil, Scotland usually has had a higher rate of unemployment and poverty than England, and this has bred a sense of resentment at policies emanating from outside of Scotland. This resentment has engendered two proposals for change.

Devolution and Independence. The moderate proposal is for devolution for a number of domestic powers to a Scottish legislature while remaining within the United Kingdom and accepting British sovereignty over foreign and defense policy. The radical proposal, espoused by the Scottish Nationalist Party (SNP), is for complete independence—the establishment of a sovereign Scottish nation.

Both of these ideas gained wide support in the 1970s. The October 1974 British election returned eleven SNP members to Parliament. By 1976, when Callaghan took over from Wilson, the Labour majority in Parliament was gone, and Callaghan had to make deals with the small parties to survive. One of these deals was with the Scottish and Welsh Nationalist Parties. A referendum was to be held in each country on a proposal for devolution. If approved, Scotland would have an elected assembly with powers over such areas as health and land use.

However, the parliamentary bill to authorize the referenda ran into intense opposition, which resulted in the insertion of a provision requiring not only a clear majority in the vote but approval by at least 40 percent of the eligible voters. This provision proved fatal to the plan. A slight majority of Scots voting in the referendum approved the idea, but they were not enough to constitute 40 percent of all voters, for many abstained out of fear that devolution would be a step toward complete separation.

The referendum was held on March 1, 1979. On March 28 came the fateful vote of no confidence in the Callaghan government. The SNP vote against the government was the decisive factor. The consequence was almost as disastrous for the SNP as for Labour, for they won only two seats in the 1979 election. As Callaghan observed: "The minority parties have walked into a trap . . . It is the first time in recorded history that turkeys have been known to vote for an early Christmas."

However, the movement for devolution in Scotland did not die with the referendum defeat, and in the 1990s both Labour and the Liberal Democrats are strong advocates of the idea. Yet if substantial powers are to be delegated to a Scottish assembly, two questions have to be faced.

The first is the "West Lothian question," raised initially by Tom Dalyell—the longtime Labour member for the Scottish constituency of West Lothian—and relentlessly pursued by John Major: By what rationale should Scottish M.P.s be able to vote on English domestic affairs while English M.P.s would be excluded from Scottish domestic decisions?

The second question relates to the fact that currently Scotland is overrepresented at Westminster, for on the average its constituencies contain considerably fewer members than is the case in England. So if substantial powers are to be delegated to a Scottish assembly, does it not follow that Scottish representation in Westminster should be reduced? This would be damaging to Labour, because Scotland is one of its key strongholds. The 1987 election cost the Conservatives 11 of their 21 Scottish seats, whereas Labour, the decisive losers overall, won 50 seats in Scotland. The Conservatives won back one of the lost 11 in 1992, but Labour remained overwhelmingly the strongest party in Scotland. Without that margin, Labour's hopes of being able to mount a serious challenge to the Conservatives would suffer a severe blow.

Labour answered these questions by proposing that they would also devolve power to regional assemblies to be elected in England and Wales. The regions would correspond to the regional offices that recently had been set up by the Conservative government, and among other advantages they would serve, said Labour, to supervise the quangos, thus making them accountable to an electorate. Regional assemblies would also fit in with the trend among some European Union agencies to work directly with regions rather than nations. However, Labour faces the problem that in England, outside of London and the northeast, there is as yet no groundswell of support for a new layer of government at the regional level.

A further problem for the advocates of devolution is that it is not clear how much support exists for a Scottish assembly among British voters outside of Scotland. When the idea was injected by Labour into the 1992 election, John Major seized on the issue to make a passionate defense of the Act of Union; and some analysts have suggested this helped turn the tide against Labour.

The fourth successive defeat for Labour was particularly damaging to them in Scotland. In 1992 Scottish voters, blaming the recession on the Conservatives, could hope that a Labour government would be more concerned with their plight. But the Conservative victory in the depths of a recession was seized on by the SNP to support their view that Labour or any other party with its roots in England would never be in a position to help Scotland. So they pressed their case for total independence, control of the nearby North Sea oil, and membership in the European Community.

Their case was not helped by their failure to gain more than three seats in the 1992 election. Still, their share of the Scottish vote in 1992 was 21.5 percent, and by 1994 they had moved up to a full one-third of the votes cast in Scotland in the elections for the European Parliament. They were also winning hundreds of seats on local councils. Evidently the issue will remain alive as long as large numbers of Scots believe that Westminster and Whitehall are not responsive to their concerns.[7]

Wales

Wales has been bound to England longer and more closely than Scotland. Most of the rules and regulations coming out of Whitehall apply to England and Wales, whereas Scotland tends to be treated separately. The secretary of state for Wales is a cabinet member, but the secretary's areas of responsibility, though broadened in recent years, are not as extensive as those of the Scottish Secretary.

Wales does not, like Scotland, have its own legal system, and there is no official

Church of Wales (though the nonconformist churches are especially strong in Wales). And the Welsh have done particularly well in British politics, producing such leaders as Lloyd George, Aneurin Bevan, and Neil Kinnock.

Separatist sentiment is less widespread in Wales than in Scotland. The March 1, 1979 devolution referendum failed in Scotland only because of the inability to gain the required approval of 40 percent of all eligible voters. In Wales the proposal fell far short of a bare majority. Nonetheless, there is a strong concern in Wales for the preservation of the indigenous language and culture. Although Welsh is spoken only by a minority of the people, the interest is strong enough to have produced the allocation of a Welsh language television channel.

Moreover, throughout Wales there is a good deal of sentiment that decisions made in London do not give sufficient attention to their concerns. Wales, like Scotland, includes areas of high unemployment and deprivation, and although a considerable amount of money has been pumped into South Wales through the Welsh Development Agency, this has not been sufficient to offset the drastic decline of the coal and steel industries, or to cover the cost of repairing the 10 percent of homes in the area officially classified as unfit for human habitation. There is also resentment at the central government's decision to replace the existing system of local government with a one-tier system, and with the fact that the budgets of quangos in Wales now almost match those of all Welsh local councils combined.

Politically, Wales has been another area of Labour strength, the 1992 election sending 27 Labourites to Westminster, compared with 6 Conservatives and 1 Liberal Democrat. But the combination of economic grievances and cultural pride in Wales has also produced a nationalist political party, Plaid Cymru (Party of Wales). They have been represented in Parliament since a by-election victory in 1966, and in 1992 their 9 percent of the Welsh vote was sufficiently concentrated to yield four seats (three more than the Liberal Democrats who received over 12 percent of the votes). Plaid Cymru calls for the creation of a Welsh Parliament (for which they contend there is now a clear majority support in Wales) as a first stage toward independence. Like the Scottish Nationalists, they contend that independence would not mean complete separation from Britain, but interdependence within the European Union. Only through recognition of their national identity, they argue, can they avoid being lost in the larger British context and gain the attention to the needs of their people already given to other small nations such as Ireland and Luxembourg.

Beyond Plaid Cymru there are fringe groups who have resorted to extraconstitutional tactics against what they see as English domination and exploitation. Thus there have been bombings of vacation homes owned by English people. However, the homes have not been occupied when they were attacked, so there have been no casualties, and nothing has happened comparable with the deadly violence that for so long disrupted Northern Ireland.

Northern Ireland

On August 30, 1994, the clear possibility emerged of an eventual end to Northern Ireland's 25 years of bitter sectarian strife. On that day came an announcement from the Irish Republican Army: ". . . The leadership of the IRA have decided that as of midnight Wednesday, August 31st, there will be a complete cessation of military operations. All our units have been instructed accordingly." Should this, in fact, prove to be the beginning of the end of the struggle, it would resolve what had been the most intractable problem in British politics, bedeviled by a long and tortured history.

The Historical Legacy. The Irish still speak bitterly of Cromwell's Protestant army massacring the Catholic defenders of Drogheda in 1649, then settling large landed estates for English Protestants; of the exploitation of their tenants by their English (often absentee) landlords; and of English indifference to the mass starvation and emigration caused by the Irish potato famine of 1846-48.

Throughout the nineteenth century, turmoil and violence marked the campaign for Irish independence, and the issue overshadowed all others in Parliament until at last, after the suppression of a bloody uprising in 1916, home rule was granted in 1920 and the Irish Free States was established as an autonomous British dominion. Then in 1949 came complete separation from the Commonwealth, and the creation of the republic of Ireland.

But that was far from the end of the problem, for the 1920 settlement had partitioned Ireland into the overwhelmingly Catholic south and the six predominately Protestant "Ulster" counties, which remained as part of the United Kingdom. (See Figure 12.1.) Yet the south was not really reconciled to the division; and in Northern Ireland there was deep antagonism between the Catholic minority and the Protestant majority.

Religion was but one dimension of the tensions in the north. The Protestant settlers who had come from England and Scotland lived apart from the Catholics; and, as the Catholics saw it, segregation was accompanied by economic discrimination, for in general the Protestants occupied the best land and housing, held the better-paid jobs, and dominated the professions.

Northern Ireland's Parties. The religious and economic schism is reflected by Ulster's political parties, which are separate from any of the other British parties. Two Unionist parties speak for the Protestants, the Official Unionists and the Democratic Unionists. Most of the Catholics vote for the Social Democratic and Labour Party (SDLP), headed by John Hume, but there is also support for Sinn Fein (Ourselves Alone), the political arm of the Irish Republican Army (IRA), which advocated and practiced armed violence to force the reunion of Ireland.

Northern Ireland has 17 seats in the House of Commons. In 1992 the Unionists won 13 of these, the SDLP 4. Sinn Fein had won a seat in 1983 and 1987 (though the incumbent, Gerry Adams, never appeared at Westminster), but lost it to the SDLP in 1992, when a number of Protestants voted for Hume to get rid of Adams. The British Conservatives also entered the lists against the Unionists in 1992, but were decisively defeated everywhere. (The British Labour Party has not organized in Northern Ireland, but has been debating the desirability of setting up branches there.)

Until 1972, the Northern Ireland parties participated in elections not only for the House of Commons, but also for the Stormont, a legislature exercising a num-

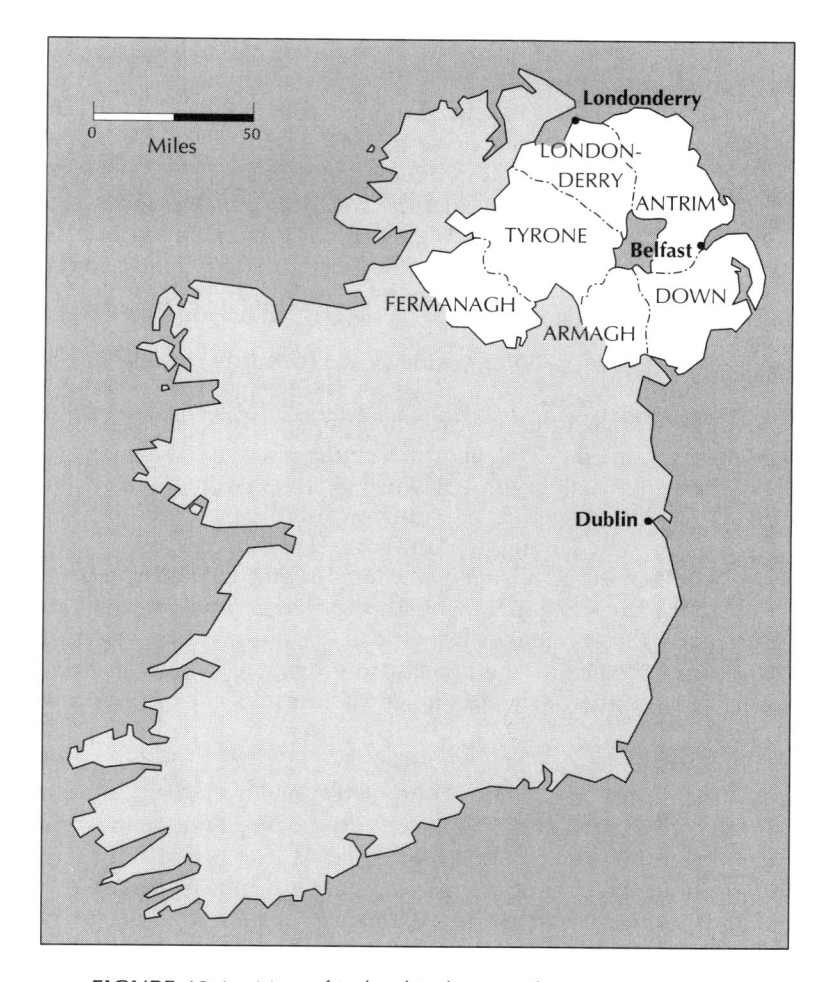

FIGURE 12.1 Map of Ireland indicating the six counties of Northern Ireland

ber of devolved powers. However, Stormont reinforced the sense of powerlessness of the Catholic community, for the Protestants always won about two-thirds of the seats and the Catholics had no representation in the government.

Violence and Counterviolence. As Catholic resentments intensified, a civil rights movement, inspired by the U.S. model, organized demonstrations and engaged in civil disobedience. Violent clashes erupted between Catholic and Protestant marchers which the police were unable to control, and the British sent in troops at the request of the Northern Ireland cabinet.

Initially the Catholics, on the defensive against larger forces of Protestants, welcomed the troops. But their mood changed as the army, working with the Protestant government, seemed to be acting more vigorously to control the Catholic protesters than the Protestants.

The IRA, which had by the late 1960s declined to the status of a small neo-Marxist sect, now had a cause that gave them wide support in the Catholic community, and they engaged in direct gun battles with the troops. This led to IRA leaders being interned without trial; the violence spread; the government of Edward Heath announced the abolition of the Stormont Parliament and the appointment of a secretary of state to manage Northern Ireland's affairs from London. Since then, Northern Ireland has remained under direct British rule and has a continued presence of British troops.

That presence did not bring peace to Northern Ireland. The troops were themselves drawn into a deadly struggle with the IRA, whose extremist wing carried the struggle to England itself, exploding bombs that killed several people and disrupted transportation. IRA violence met counterviolence from the police, the army, and Protestant paramilitary forces who, by 1993, were killing as many or more people than the IRA. Altogether more than 3,100 people have been killed in rioting, bomb explosions, and sniping in Northern Ireland since 1969.

The Labour governments of Wilson and Callaghan did little to resolve the issue. Callaghan's negotiations with the Northern Ireland parties increased their representation in Parliament from 12 to 17; but pressure against the IRA was intensified, and Callaghan visited Belfast to provide an assurance that Ulster would remain part of the United Kingdom unless a clear majority of its population wanted to separate.

The election of Margaret Thatcher did not appear to signal any relaxation of British control. As violence continued, a new round of internment (without trial) of suspected IRA leaders was instituted. Some of those imprisoned, demanding improvements in their conditions, engaged in a prolonged hunger strike, threw out their clothes, wrapped themselves only in blankets, and smeared the walls of their cells with their excrement to dramatize their sense of debasement. Thatcher would not yield, one of the strikers (Bobby Sands) died, and the IRA had a new martyr to the cause.

Thatcher's natural hostility to the IRA was reinforced by a number of other events. Two months before her election in 1979, Airey Neave, a close friend who had managed her campaign for the Conservative party leadership, was blown up in his car in Parliament's parking lot. At the 1984 Conservative Party conference in Brighton, a massive bomb devastated the main conference hotel, killing five people, including the wife of a cabinet minister, and seriously injuring the wife of Norman Tebbit, a close associate of Thatcher. Mrs. Thatcher herself escaped unhurt, having just left her bathroom before it collapsed. Then in 1990, Ian Gow, who had been her parliamentary private secretary, was killed by a bomb at his home. The IRA laid claim to all these disasters, along with a continuing series of attacks against targets in Northern Ireland and in England.

Thatcher's response was to clamp down still further on the IRA, forbidding Sinn Fein's appearance on British television except at election time, and suspending some of the rights of the accused in Northern Ireland, including the right to remain silent.

Negotiations. And yet Thatcher undertook a new negotiating initiative in an effort to break the deadlock. This was an agreement with the government of the republic of Ireland to bring them into the discussions on the future of Ulster. The introduction of this "Irish dimension" took the form of direct discussions between representatives of the British and Irish governments with a view to discovering some fresh approaches to the Northern Ireland problem. The Unionist parties were outraged and swore to boycott any further negotiations as long as the discussions with the Irish government persisted. But Thatcher, never one to back down under threats, persisted.

John Major (who had also been the target of an IRA bomb detonated in Whitehall) continued the initiative. The SDLP's John Hume and Sinn Fein's Gerry Adams had been talking, and were ready to offer some proposals to get negotiations started. At first Major declared he was not ready to talk to Sinn Fein (though later the government admitted that the British government had long maintained informal contacts with IRA members). But in December, Major met with Albert Reynolds, the republic of Ireland prime minister, and the two leaders issued the Downing Street Declaration, which was intended to establish the principles on which a negotiated peace might be achieved. According to the declaration:

> The British government agrees that it is for the people of the island of Ireland alone, by agreement between the two parties respectively, to exercise their right of self-determination on the basis of consent, freely and concurrently given, north and south, to bring about a united Ireland, if that is their wish.

Sinn Fein was invited to join the negotiations, but this was contingent on a cessation of violence by the IRA; this could be signaled, Major indicated, by a ceasefire of perhaps three months. Another eight months went by, and periodic shootings and bombings by the IRA and the Protestant paramilitaries stirred skepticism that the Downing Street Declaration would lead anywhere. But then came the dramatic IRA ceasefire announcement of August 30. Subsequently the Protestant paramilitaries announced that they, too, would suspend their armed counterattacks. By the end of the year, the preliminary stages of negotiations had begun, and in February 1995 Major and the new Irish Prime Minister, John Bruton, announced their *Joint Framework Document* as a basis for negotiated settlement.

Their proposal reiterated the principles that the future of Ireland, north and south, must be placed in the hands of their peoples; that a united Ireland must be one of the options available, but that any change must be subject to the clearly expressed will of majorities in both the north and the south. To put these principles into effect the Joint Framework, and an accompanying British plan for a new Northern Ireland constitution, proposed:

- a Northern Ireland Assembly, elected by proportional representation, with broad legislative powers over internal affairs
- "cross-border," North-South institutions of elected representatives of the Northern Assembly and the Irish Parliament

increased Dublin-London cooperation through an intergovernmental conference (without authority over the Northern Ireland Assembly)

guarantees by both governments to protect civil, political, social, and cultural rights

changes in British law to recognize the right of the people of Northern Ireland to decide their future, even if these meant accepting a united Ireland

removing from the Irish constitution its territorial claim to Northern Ireland

separate referendums in North and South, with a majority in both needed to endorse change

Agreement on these or similar proposals would not come easily in face of convictions long and passionately held by both sides. Thus the IRA from its beginnings had fought for one central purpose—the *reunification* of Ireland. Now Britain was accepting the possibility of unification—but only through what the Downing Street Declaration had called "self-determination on the basis of consent," and the Protestants quite certainly would not be giving their consent.

It is true that time may be on the side of the unifiers. When the partition went into effect in 1920, the Northern Ireland Protestants had a majority of two to one; but the margin was shrinking, for the Catholic population was growing faster. Within two or three decades the Catholics might equal or outnumber the Protestants, and then (on the uncertain proposition that the Catholics would all favor unification) consent to the end of partition could be freely given by a majority. But for the believers in the IRA cause, that would mean at least another generation of waiting.

Still, the initial Sinn Fein reaction to the Joint Framework Document was guardedly hopeful. The proposals for cross-border cooperation were a prominent feature of the Document, and out of that, Sinn Fein hoped, would come an increasing number of joint activities that could facilitate the movement toward unification in practical if not in formal terms. And the guarantees of minority rights in Northern Ireland could give the Catholics the kind of protection for which they had demonstrated in the early 1970s. So the cease-fire continued to hold, and in May 1995 a junior minister in the British government met with a representative of Sinn Fein to open exploratory talks.

Yet whatever gave encouragement to the Catholics was viewed with alarm by the Protestants. They, too, saw the cross-border institutions as the advance guards for a united Ireland. And in a united Ireland the Protestants, instead of holding their Northern-Ireland 57 to 43 percent majority, would be reduced to a small minority. This prospect was intolerable to them. They were no longer opposed to providing protection for the rights of the Catholics and even sharing some of the power that they had monopolized in the old Stormont. But, as British citizens in the full sense of the term, they could not accept the idea of being absorbed into a country whose political and social system, they believed, was alien to them, and dominated by the Catholic Church.

The Reverend Ian Paisley, the fiery leader of the Democratic Unionists, called the Downing Street Declaration "treachery . . . to buy off the fiendish Republican scum"; and when the Joint Framework appeared he told John Major: "You have sold out the union." By this time Paisley's influence was in decline; yet the larger Official Unionist party, which had been more supportive of negotiation than Paisley, also reacted negatively to the Major-Bruton proposal, fearing, as one of their leaders said, that "Ulster has been served with an eviction notice." And they professed themselves as not reassured by the repeated statements that no constitutional change would come without the Protestant's consent expressed through a referendum.

If this view held, it would represent a serious problem for John Major. With his slim and unreliable majority in the Commons, he needed the votes of the Unionist M.P.s. Moreover, while Sinn Fein seemed ready to accept the Framework Document, it was by no means clear that they (or the Protestant paramilitaries) would accept the British government demand that they surrender or destroy their weapons. Further cause for concern came with a riot in a Catholic area of Belfast in July 1995. The trouble was triggered by the early release of a British army private sentenced to life imprisonment for the fatal shooting in 1990 of a girl riding in a stolen car that ran through an army checkpoint. Sinn Fein denied that it had instigated the riot, but accused the government of releasing the soldier to appease Major's right-wing critics (the decision was announced the day before Major won the leadership reelection contest) and demanded the release of IRA prisoners.

Conceivably, then, it could all come to naught. This was not the first time high hopes of a settlement had been raised, for after the disbanding of Stormont in 1972, an arrangement had been agreed for the Protestants to share some of their power with the Catholics. But it had all fallen apart in face of intense Protestant opposition.

Nonetheless, circumstances had changed since then in some crucial respects. For one thing, disgust with the conflict had been growing among Catholics and Protestants alike, and thousands of them had joined in demonstrations against the violence.

Then, too, the British government could not overlook the severe burden placed on the British economy by the cost of maintaining troops and underwriting social services; altogether government expenditures per head of population in Northern Ireland cost the English government an additional 50 percent beyond comparable per capita expenses for England. In the past, such outlays might have been justified by Northern Ireland's role as a base protecting against Britain's vulnerability in the Atlantic; this was very much the case in World War II and could still have been a consideration during the Cold War. But today, as Major made clear, Britain has no strategic stake in Northern Ireland. Moreover, Major's initiatives for peace had the full backing of Labour and the Liberal Democrats. Labour, with its strong Catholic constituency in England, had long been pressing for movement toward a settlement. And all three parties were in accord with public sentiment in Britain, which was strongly in favor of disengagement from the Irish problem.

The U.S. Dimension. As long as the situation remains unresolved, the Irish question will be a matter of some concern to U.S. leaders. From the time of the potato famine of 1846–48, large numbers have emigrated from Ireland to the United States, with the result that some U.S. cities are heavily populated with Catholics of Irish extraction. Many of them have been strongly sympathetic to the IRA and have been among its principal sources of funds. A number of leading U.S. politicians, especially from Boston and New York, have spoken out in harsh condemnation of British policy toward Ireland. This has been strongly resented by the British government.

Moreover, President Clinton, after refusing at first to grant Sinn Fein's Gerry Adams a visa to visit the United States, changed his mind. This caused the British intense annoyance; but the visits of Adams and other Sinn Fein leaders were widely interpreted later as having contributed to the IRA ceasefire decision. Subsequently Clinton expressed warm approval of the British and Irish efforts to break the impasse and begin serious negotiations.

The Irish question is not among the most pressing issues for U.S. foreign policy, but reaching a settlement on Northern Ireland would remove a persistent irritant in the Anglo-American special relationship.

CONCLUSION

Trends toward centralization have become a marked feature of British government. On the one hand an increasing number of policies affecting Britain are being made by agencies of the European Union. On the other hand, local units in Britain have given more and more ground to the national government.

These changes have not come without resistance and charges that autonomy has been lost to remote centers of power. We have seen that this is a common complaint about Europe within the Conservative Party. No less do local councillors protest their loss of authority to Westminster and Whitehall.

In some degree the demand to devolve authority outside of London, especially to Scotland and Wales, is likely to be addressed—substantially by any future Labour government, much less so by the Conservatives. On the other hand, devolution to Northern Ireland is now part of the Conservative government's agenda. Indeed, the opposition parties will inevitably press hard on the apparent contradiction between Major's proposal for a Northern Ireland assembly and his adamant opposition to similar elected bodies for Scotland and Wales. (Advocates of electoral reform will also use Major's support for proportional representation in voting for the Assembly in Northern Ireland to bolster their argument that the same system should be used for the United Kingdom generally.)

Reaching a final settlement on the Northern Ireland problem remains a formidable undertaking. Yet, in an era in which deeply opposing groups have agreed to new dispositions of power in South Africa, it is no longer inconceivable that Protestants and Catholics could find a way of living together peacefully in Northern Ireland.

SOME QUESTIONS TO THINK ABOUT

What are the main centralizing forces in Britain? Is British government too centralized?
Should local elections be conducted on a partisan basis?
How justified was Thatcher in her efforts to weaken the powers of local government? What do you think of her argument for the poll tax?

What has caused the proliferation of quangos? Has there been a similar development in the United States?

Should more powers be devolved to Scotland and Wales? If so, should their representation in Parliament be reduced? Is there a parallel to the "West Lothian question" in the United States?

What are the causes of the Northern Ireland conflict? What solution would you favor?

Should the British pull their troops out of Northern Ireland? If so, would you attach any conditions? Why haven't the troops been pulled out before now?

NOTES

1. *The Economist,* 19 February 1994, pp. 67-68.
2. Donald Shell, "The British Constitution in 1993," *Parliamentary Affairs,* vol. 47, no. 2, April 1994, p. 298.
3. David Butler, Andrew Adonis, and Tony Travers, *Failure in British Government: The Politics of the Poll Tax* (Oxford University Press, 1994), p. 207.
4. David Butler and Dennis Kavanagh, *The British General Election Of 1992* (Macmillan, 1992), p. 232.
5. Anthony Heath, Roger Jowell, and John Curtice, *Labour's Last Chance?* (Dartmouth, 1994), p. 241.
6. Margaret Thatcher, *The Downing Street Years,* p. 642.
7. See Robert McCreadie, "Scottish Identity and the Constitution," in Bernard Crick (ed.), *National Identities: the Constitution of the United Kingdom* (*The Political Quarterly*, 1991).

SUGGESTIONS FOR FURTHER READING

On local government in general, see G. Stoker, *The Politics of Local Government* (Macmillan, 1991) and J. Chandler, *Local Government Today* (Manchester University Press, 1991). On the relationship between the United Kingdom and the various nationalities see Richard Rose, *The Territorial Dimension* (Chatham House, 1982), and Bernard Crick (ed.), *National Identities* (Blackwell/Political Quarterly, 1991). On the poll tax, the definitive study is the book by Butler, Adonis, and Travers, *Failure in British Government: The Politics of the Poll Tax,* listed in endnote 3.

On Scotland see J. Kellas, *The Scottish Political System* (Cambridge University Press, 1989). On Northern Ireland see Paul Arthur, *Government and Politics of Northern Ireland* (Longman, 1980), Brendan O'Leary and John McGarry, *Explaining Northern Ireland* (Blackwell, 1994), Tom Wilson, *Ulster* (Blackwell, 1989), and Padraig O'Malley, *The Uncivil Wars: Ireland Today* (Beacon Press, 1990).

PART FOUR

ISSUES IN PUBLIC POLICY

In which we apply the concepts established in Parts I, II, and III to some key public policy issues—the economy, the welfare state, education, race and gender, civil liberties, and foreign affairs—and pose the questions:

- ✦ Are the differences between the parties merely rhetorical, or are they implemented into public policies?
- ✦ How are the several institutions of government involved in the various policy issues?
- ✦ How does the British handling of these issues compare with the way we deal with them in the United States?

13

THE TROUBLED ECONOMY

At one time Britain, the advance guard of the industrial revolution, was the economic powerhouse of the world. Yet a constant theme by historians of the British economy is that Britain's initial lead over other industrial economies has been shrinking for the past century. Until World War II, the extent of Britain's declining world position was masked by her command of a huge empire. But in the aftermath of that war the empire began to break apart; Germany, Japan, and others recovered from the ravages of the war and started to forge ahead; and Britain's dependence on U.S. financial support made obvious her fall from economic greatness.

So since 1945, British governments have been hard-pressed to satisfy the economic demands of their electorates. As in democracies generally, these demands subject governments to two principal tests.

First, *how much does the economic system produce?* What is its gross domestic product (GDP—the sum total of goods and services generated within the country in a year)? Given increases in population and/or expectations, this test will be measured in the extent of *economic growth*.

Second, *how is that product distributed among the population?* Inherent in democratic systems is pressure to extend the benefits resulting from economic growth to all segments of the population—though not necessarily in equal degree.

These tests have been applied by British voters in their assessment of government performance, and in most elections have been a prime determinant of the outcome. This was especially apparent in the two "watershed" elections since the end of World War II, those of 1945 and 1979, both of which led to dramatic departures from the economic policies of previous governments. We will see that the 1945 Labour government inaugurated a new consensus on economic affairs which, with some variations, persisted until 1979; and that the election of Margaret Thatcher signaled a frontal attack on that consensus—and established what may prove to be in some respects a new consensus.

THE ECONOMIC CONSENSUS, 1945–79

The broad outlines of post–World War II economic policy were established by the programs introduced by the Attlee government of 1945-51. Although Labour was in power only half the time between 1945 and 1979, they provided the initial momentum for what Richard Rose calls the *moving consensus* between the parties. Butler and the Conservatives modified Labour's policies in various ways; although the result was known as *Butskellism*, it was actually Labour's Chancellor of the Exchequer Gaitskell who preceded Butler.

The central thrust of the Attlee government's economic policies was putting *redistribution first*. Their victory in 1945 was taken as a mandate to reject the prewar policies of the Conservative governments.

This rejection was not understood by most Americans. The reaction on this side of the Atlantic was incredulity at the defeat of Winston Churchill. How, it was asked, could the British be so ungrateful as to turn out of office the man who had saved them from Hitler? In fact, British survival had not been a one-man accomplishment, great though Churchill's contribution was. And the reason for his ouster was that he was the leader of the Conservative Party.

Churchill was not a typical Conservative leader, of course; he had been a rebel against the Conservative governments of the 1930s. But now he was inescapably at the head of the Conservative Party, a party held to be the representative and protector of a privileged upper class, and, fairly or not, that same party was blamed for the long years of economic depression, with millions unemployed living in squalid housing and acute deprivation.

The grim austerity of World War II had changed all that. Rations of food and clothing were slim, but everyone received a more or less equal share. One result was that on the whole the children of the working class actually were healthier during the war than they had been before. Here, then, was the message of the 1945 election as interpreted by Labour: Government policies must be directed to providing *fair shares for all*.

Consequently an extraordinary range of legislation moved through Parliament providing for a broad expansion of the welfare state: the National Health Service, unemployment insurance, old age pensions, family allowances, secondary education for all.

Britain's welfare state did not originate in 1945. Liberal and Conservative governments had contributed from early in the century, and much of the planning for the postwar programs had taken place during the war, with the full participation of Conservative members of the coalition government. Still, the scale and speed of the welfare state's enlargement that was undertaken by the Attlee government was unprecedented, and would not have been equaled had the Conservatives won in 1945.

But if redistribution of resources was the driving passion of the 1945-51 Labour government, this did not mean that it ignored the question of economic growth. Socialists believed that the capitalist system, which the Conservatives championed, was not only unjust, it was also inefficient. As they saw it, to the extent that competition was a productive force (and they had serious questions on that score) it was not allowed to operate in the most important areas of industry and finance, for there monopolies took over. Moreover, the old boy network that ran the country placed in the key economic positions people with no obvious managerial qualifications.

In place of unregulated capitalism, then, must come a *planned economy*. Planning today is very much out of favor in the aftermath of the collapse of the Soviet Union and the bankruptcy of its centralized command economy. But the inevitability of its failure was less obvious in 1945. In any case Labour was undertaking a different kind of experiment—democratic socialism, planning by consent and example, not by coercion. Moreover, for the time being at least, there would be a mixed economy, with wide sections of the economy remaining in private hands.

Still, even with democratic planning, the central levers of power must be in the hands of the government, which spoke for the community as a whole rather than merely for the owners of capital. This meant, first, the nationalization of certain key industries, those which occupied, in Aneurin Bevan's phrase, the *commanding heights* of the economy—energy, transportation, steel, and the Bank of England. Then there would be controls relating to foreign trade, the protection of the pound, and the supply of scarce materials. Rationing of some foods and clothing would be necessary until shortages were ended. And government tax and spending policies would be aimed at a carefully calibrated expansion of the economy.

When Harold Wilson became Labour's second Prime Minister of the post–World War II era he pursued the goal of the planned economy. But he added a rhetorical dimension designed to transform the concept of planning from mere restrictiveness to a bold adventure. His theme, as he explained it to Labour's annual conference in 1963, was to engage government in the task of "mobilizing scientific research in this country in producing a new technological breakthrough." Henceforth, he declared, "we are redefining and we are restating our socialism in terms of the scientific revolution." And a new Britain would be "forged in the white heat of this revolution."

On the surface, Britain seemed to have a strong potential for successful planning of the economy. The machinery of government was centralized. There was no separation of powers to set up roadblocks to decisions by the executive branch. The prevailing culture was much more accepting of activist government than was the case in the United States. And in several fields of science Britain was a world leader with a disproportionate number of Nobel Prize winners.

Indeed, these advantages made possible the remarkable transformation of the British economy brought about by the Attlee government. Yet, even before the defeat of the Labour government in 1951, its policies were running into severe problems. Those problems were to emerge in still more damaging form during Wilson's prime ministership, and were eventually to lead to the fall of the Callaghan government and the dawn of the Thatcher era.

Emerging Problems

Overloading the Economy. The expansion of social services engineered by the Attlee government contained within itself a powerful dynamic for still further expansion. The deprivations of the poor could be only partially ameliorated at first; once attention had been officially drawn to the problems of undernourished children and disabled pensioners more would have to be done. Moreover, it was not only the poor who were served by the welfare state. The *C2*, *C1*, and even the *B* social categories were among the beneficiaries. So well-organized pressures emerged to fight for increased government spending, and their arguments resonated with a wide swath of the voting public.

At the same time, Britain was spending more than any other west European country on defense. Even as the empire disintegrated, the legacy of imperial power kept British troops in the far east until well into the 1960s. Britain also made a substantial contribution first to the postwar occupation of Germany, then to the NATO forces facing the Soviet armies in Europe. And the Attlee government began the process of planning Britain's own stockpile of nuclear weapons.

These heavy outlays on social services and defense came on top of the urgent need to rebuild the stock of roads, railways, housing, and factories which had been neglected during the war. And World War II, coming only 20 years after another devastating world war, had drained Britain's overseas holdings and left the country impoverished.

Heavy though these demands on the nation's resources were, they might still have been manageable (after the initial help from a U.S. loan and the Marshall Plan) had the economy achieved a sufficient rate of growth. In fact, the pace of growth was quite creditable from the mid-1940s until the mid-1960s. But then it began to slow to a rate less than that of any other major industrial country. This meant that hard choices would have to be made among the accelerating demands on Britain's resources. Having to make those choices brought about a series of bitter conflicts between the left and right wings of the Labour Party, the first of which culminated in the breakup of the Attlee government over an increase in defense spending that coincided with some small cuts in the National Health Service. The conflict between military and health spending proved to be only a precursor of a larger struggle to pay for the welfare state and armaments and all the other demands on modern government from an economic system that, from the mid-1960s, was growing at a sluggish rate.

Problems with Planning. Planning did not prove to be the powerful engine for economic growth that Labour governments had hoped for. In fact, planning in the full sense was never achieved. In the nature of the case it could not be. For, even though decision-making power was heavily concentrated in the executive branch, the government could never be in full control of the economy.

The Mixed Economy. In the first place, despite extensive nationalization, the bulk of industry and finance remained in private hands; and this private sector included not only small retail businesses but also giant multinational complexes in such fields as chemicals and automobiles. Businesses on this scale might be subjected to government regulations and taxes, but if they are to exist at all, they must have enough freedom to make profits. They would therefore have the opportunity and the funds to oppose government policies, and in this effort they would have the support of most of the press. Financial institutions, too, would join industry in resisting full-scale planning, and although the Bank of England was nationalized, and never as independent of the government as the Federal Reserve Board in Washington, its directors were closely attuned to the private firms of the City of London. Consequently the mixed economy was unlikely to be merely a stage on the way to full-blown socialism, for it contained powerful business interests that would not easily give up their independence.

Then there were the unions. The union leaders believed in strong government. But they also believed in free collective bargaining. When Harold Wilson's government tried to introduce some mild restrictions on wildcat strikes the unions' fury was unbounded. Within the cabinet, the opposition was led by James Callaghan. This is not the Soviet Union, he insisted. Industrial relations cannot be controlled by government. But if there were to be no limitations, other than voluntary ones, on the freedom of action of labor, one of the prime elements of production, how could there be planning in any but the most general sense?

Moreover, if there were to be less than full control of the economy by the government, the imperatives of the market system would come into play. And the competitive market system tends to fluctuate over time, moving in cycles between accelerating growth with rising prices on the one hand, and contraction accompanied by rising unemployment on the other. So, despite the various kinds of government intervention after 1945, Labour and Conservative governments alike experienced this "stop-go" phenomenon in various degrees.

The International Context. Even if capital and labor could be controlled, no British government could really be master of its own destiny, for Britain lacked the capacity to build a high wall around its economy. This was a country that imported half its food, most of its raw materials except coal, and, until the North Sea discoveries in the 1970s, all of its oil.

In part, Britain paid its way by being an international financial center. But this also made it particularly vulnerable to the international market in currencies, and whenever the economy showed signs of weakness—that is, whenever it was not generating enough to pay for all the demands upon it—the pound sterling came under pressure. Wilson railed against the currency speculators and the multinational corporations. They were the "bailiffs," he said, with the power to control Britain's destiny.

In fact, both the Attlee and Wilson governments were forced to accept a devaluation against the dollar (which was then the dominant international currency). Each time they had tried desperately to save the pound by throwing millions of

Britain's reserves into the currency markets. Partly this was because a cheaper pound, while helping to make Britain's exports more competitive, also makes imports more expensive, and so heightens the risk of inflation. But the defense of the pound was also regarded as a matter of the nation's, and the government's, prestige. Labour was still in thrall to the country's past greatness. But the currency markets traded in current realities rather than past glories.

One way of avoiding or at least postponing devaluation was to borrow money abroad, usually from the International Monetary Fund (IMF). A condition for granting the loans was always a reduction in domestic spending, which mostly fell on the social services. Here again was a significant limit on the British government's ability to engage in economic planning.

Imperfect Knowledge. With so many diverse factors to take into account, precise planning must become essentially impossible, for economics is still an inexact science. Planning depends on accurate information, but time and again the key data proved to be incorrect. "Unfortunately," said Dennis Healey, Labour's Chancellor of the Exchequer when the Labour government came back to power in 1974, "I soon discovered that the most important numbers were nearly always wrong."[1] The budget deficit estimates given him by his experts in the treasury department proved to be much too low in 1974. In 1976, on the other hand, their estimate was much too high, and this helped bring on a crisis that compelled Healey to go cap in hand to the IMF and impose severe spending cuts and high interest rates as a condition of receiving a loan that might not have been necessary in the first place.

The Pull to the Center. A final set of limitations on the power to plan the economy was the gravitational pull of British politics toward the center. Planning is a thoroughgoing, comprehensive procedure; but the natural tendency of the British political culture is toward half-measures, compromises.

We have noted that the operating impulse of the civil service is to move the government of the day toward consensual, middle-of-the-road policies. This is especially true of the treasury department, operating through the treasury network. Harold Wilson tried to outflank this network by creating a cabinet Department of Economic Affairs (DEA), charged with coordinating and directing all economic policy. This was headed at first by George Brown, one of the top Labour leaders, and after Brown by Wilson himself. But the experiment was unsuccessful. The DEA could not match the treasury's resources and too much time was wasted in turf battles between the departments.

Nor was the public at large eager for permanent government limits on their economic lives. At first the habit of the wartime years made continued controls and rationing tolerable. But even a population as communally inclined as the British grew tired of austerity. Toward the end of the Attlee government Harold Wilson, as President of the Board of Trade, announced a "bonfire of controls." Economic rules and regulations no longer suited the tastes of a people starved for consumer goods and demanding more choices and higher quality.

Finally, there were the politicians themselves. In the Attlee government Aneurin Bevan spoke for the left, but the majority, though committed to major changes from the policies of the past, were practitioners of the politics of moderation. Had Labour won again in 1951 it is unlikely that there would have been great new strides toward socialism. As for Harold Wilson, he came to the prime ministership in 1964 after 13 unbroken years of Conservative rule, and with a very small parliamentary majority. He was never likely to lose sight of the need to avoid getting out too far in front of the electorate.

In any case, despite his constant invocation of the creed of socialism, Wilson was far from being a fervent ideologue. This, in fact, became the bitter complaint of the left. Thus the left-wing journalist Paul Foot protested that Wilson was guilty of "pragmatic socialism," which was not socialism at all. "*Pragmatism is not neutral.* It accepts the existing structure and values of society."[2] And Foot's critique was as applicable to Callaghan and Healey and the other leaders who set the tone for the Labour government in the 1970s.

So Labour governments made only limited thrusts in the direction of economic planning, and the dominant mode was economic intervention rather than planning. The guiding economic theory was drawn not from Karl Marx or any of his disciples, but from the Cambridge economist, John Maynard Keynes.

It was the theories of Keynes that had helped America recover from the Great Depression, and he had been the key economic negotiator for Britain before his death in 1946. His followers at Cambridge continued his influence in the postwar years. According to their analysis, full employment could be sustained without its unfortunate side effect of inflation through adjustments in government spending and taxes.

This theory, which required strong government intervention but not full-scale planning, was well suited to the temperament of most Labour leaders. It was also, with modifications, an acceptable framework for the Conservative governments which alternated in power with Labour. Churchill, Eden, Macmillan, and Douglas-Home all leaned toward more private enterprise and less government, but their differences from Labour were matters of emphasis only. In the 1970 election, Heath did promise a more radical shift toward private enterprise, but within two years he had reversed course toward heavy governmental intervention. So Keynesianism became the economic underpinning of the consensual politics that followed World War II.

Unfortunately, Keynesianism was less helpful when the demands on the economy began to outstrip the rate of productivity; and it fell short of explaining what governments should do in face of the sudden jump in oil prices and the surge in industrial strikes that destabilized the economy in the 1970s. Previously it might have been possible to make a tradeoff between unemployment and inflation: An increase in either one would be offset by a decline in the other. But in the 1970s both were going up at the same time, and the economy was mired in *stagflation*—stagnant output and employment combined with rising prices. There was nothing in Keynes' writings that addressed stagflation.

To sum up, the economic policies of the postwar period, with their Labour-inspired mix of redistributionism on the one hand and a mélange of diluted planning and Keynesianism on the other, served the country fairly well for about two decades. An impressive, compassionate range of social services was provided, and Britain made a reasonably strong recovery from the massive cost of war and the loss of empire. But then the policies began to fall short of their promise. In part this was because of the underestimated costs of their successes, and in part it was because the "white heat" of the scientific revolution had never been adequately translated into technology and industrial productivity.

Two governments fell under the pressure: first the Conservatives under Heath, then Labour under Callaghan. Both failed in their efforts to intervene in the economy and set limits to wage increases. Neither party, it appeared, could any longer successfully manage the policies of consensus.

CONSERVATIVE ECONOMIC POLICIES SINCE 1979

The Thatcher Administration's Policies

With the arrival of Margaret Thatcher in 10 Downing Street, the era of *Butskellism* was finally laid to rest. The economic policies of the postwar period, she believed, were responsible for the nation's continued decline. These policies were initiated by the Attlee government. But she held equally culpable the Conservative governments that had followed the general direction set by Labour. Among these the most egregious was the government led by Edward Heath, for he had broken his promise to remove the dead hand of government from business enterprise, and then committed his unpardonable U-turn to even more government intervention.

The task ahead, then, was to undo the mistaken work of the past quarter-century. Among all the areas that had to be changed, the top priority was given to economic policy. So, although her first cabinet had to include several of Heath's associates, she appointed a faithful ally, Geoffrey Howe, as chancellor of the exchequer, and made sure that all the other top economic posts and the key economic committees of the cabinet were in the hands of her strong supporters.

Thatcher and her allies did not proceed according to a detailed economic blueprint. Many of their specific policies were responses to political circumstances and opportunities as they emerged. But each policy was driven by two central themes: first, that economic growth, not redistribution, must be given priority, for only if the economy expanded briskly could there be enough to satisfy the needs of all, including the poor; second, that the principal agent of economic growth must be private business. Given these themes, the Thatcher government pursued the following policies:

Cutting the Size, Functions, and Cost of Government. This was to be achieved by holding down spending on social services; pruning the civil service; selling off nationalized industries, including British Airways, British Gas, British Petroleum, British Steel, British Telecom, Cable and Wireless, Jaguar, Rolls Royce, the Rover Group, and various electricity utilities; and eliminating or reducing government regulations on currency exchange, the stock market, and a number of other areas affecting business and finance.

Reducing Income Tax. The top rate on earned income was 83 percent in 1979. This was cut at first to 60 percent and later to 40 percent. However, Thatcher never accepted Ronald Reagan's erroneous belief that a sharp reduction in income tax would, by itself, generate so much additional economic activity that total government revenues would not decline. Consequently she accompanied her income tax reduction with an increase in VAT (Value Added Tax, a form of sales tax) from 9 percent to 15 percent.

Controlling Inflation. Price increases reaching almost 25 percent at one point in the 1970s must not recur. Inflation, for Thatcher, was the great economic curse, the enemy of healthy growth, which must be brought under control. Especially severe measures were required, for the increase in VAT actually caused an initial jump in the rate of inflation.

At first, the techniques of monetarism were used on the assumption that control of the supply of money was the prime instrument available for determining the price level. When the monetary indices proved unreliable, a range of other methods was employed, principally an increase in interest rates—a technique essentially in the discretion of the political leadership, for the Bank of England did not have the same degree of independence as the Federal Reserve Board in the United States.

So Thatcher and her chancellor of the exchequer, Geoffrey Howe, persisted in imposing interest rates that contributed to recession and 12 to 13 percent unemployment. Industry leaders pleaded with Thatcher to change course, 364 economists signed a condemnation of her policy, and she faced opposition within her cabinet. But she was implacable. The skeptics dubbed her "TINA" because of her insistence that "There Is No Alternative." The lady was not for turning. These were the only policies, she believed, that could squeeze inflation out of the system. The economy would slow down at first, but the foundation would be laid for longterm, sustained growth.

Attacking the Unions. As we saw in chapter 4, this involved the passage of new industrial relations laws. The first, which passed when James Prior, a Heath man, was employment secretary, was fairly mild. It was not tough enough for Thatcher, and stronger measures followed after Prior had been moved to another position.

No less important than the legislation was the defeat of major strikes, especially the year-long strike of the miners, and levels of unemployment throughout the first half of the 1980s that were the highest since the depression years of the 1930s.

Cooperating (Cautiously) with the European Community. Thatcher signed the Single European Act in 1986, and agreed to British entry into the exchange rate mechanism (ERM) in 1990. But her interest in the Single European Act was solely in its establishing a single market, not in the implied development of a single monetary system; she entered the ERM reluctantly as a means of controlling inflation by tying the pound to the German mark.

The Major Administration's Policies

When John Major succeeded Thatcher, there were some modifications of Thatcher's economic policy, particularly a shift toward less confrontational dealings with the European Community and increases in social service spending. There was also some increase in government-industry cooperation, strongly advocated within the cabinet by Michael Heseltine as trade and industry secretary. However, he was strenuously opposed by right-winger Michael Portillo, then the chief secretary to the treasury, who launched an attack on what he called "the assumption that it is government's proper task to intervene in the functioning of free markets." Although Heseltine's position would not easily be swept aside, he had himself accepted many of the changes pushed through by Thatcher, and the general outlines of Thatcherite economics remained in place.

Further sales of nationalized industries and services, including water, the railroads, the vestiges of the coal industry, and parts of the postal service (the Royal Mail) were undertaken or prepared (though Heseltine was forced to drop the plans to privatize the postal service by protests from Conservative backbenchers). More mines, deemed to be uneconomic, were closed. The National Economic Development Council and wages councils for low-paid workers were abolished. Still more legislation limiting union power was introduced. Another prolonged recession, with rising interest rates and high levels of unemployment, was accepted as the price of cutting inflation. Closer cooperation with Europe did not include acceptance of the social chapter, which would provide protections for unions and social services; and membership in the ERM was reluctantly abandoned.

The Results of the Thatcher-Major Policies

Judgments on the Conservative government's economic policies since 1979 will inevitably change as their impact becomes clearer with the passage of time; and in the short run assessments vary with the political bias or economic school of the observer.

As of this writing, most commentators suggest that in two areas—industrial relations and privatization—the Thatcherite purposes have clearly been achieved (though there are strong critics of the achievements). In other cases the results appear to have fallen well short of the aspirations.

The Unions. Cutting the power of the unions has been the most successful area of Thatcher's economic policies. Membership declined from 13 million to 9 million by 1990 and to 7.5 million by 1994 with a consequent fall in union (and Labour Party) income; the number of workdays lost to strikes was reduced to the lowest levels since early in the century; wage pressures on the economy weakened—these developments are all attributable in considerable measure to government policies since 1979 (although the longterm factors noted in chapter 4 have also contributed).

Privatization. The policy of selling off nationalized industries attracted international attention and became the most widely emulated feature of Thatcherism around the world.

In most cases, denationalization in Britain led to sharply reduced government subsidies, and an expanded number of small stockholders (though many of these quickly sold out at a profit); and greater efficiency with smaller workforces was accomplished in steel and some other fields. However, support for still more privatization had waned by the early 1990s. Water rates went up much faster after privatization than before, and complaints that government monopolies were not being broken up into smaller competitive units but merely replaced by private, regulated monopolies were put forward even by free market advocates. (Ironically, the government angered private betting firms in 1994 by launching a National Lottery.)

Inflation and Unemployment. After the VAT increase from 9 percent to 15 percent, prices moved up then came down as the recession took hold from 1981. Inflation jumped again after the expansive budgets in 1987 and 1988. (The Sun greeted the 1988 budget with: "LOTSA LOVELY LOLLY. We're in the money, folks.") Subsequently it required another steep recession to get inflation under control again. By 1994 the rate was brought down to not much more than 2 percent.

The new recession was blamed by many on Britain's membership in the exchange rate mechanism, which tied the pound to the deutschmark and thus to Germany's fierce anti-inflationary policies. Still, inflation remained low after Britain pulled out of the ERM in 1993, and there were indications that to keep prices down, the government would enlarge the role of the Bank of England in setting interest rates, thus reducing the danger that the politicians would manipulate them for electoral advantage.

Throttling inflation through recession had a particularly harsh impact on the unemployment figures. From 1945 to 1970 unemployment had reached 3 percent in only one year, mostly moving in the 1 to 2 percent range; a rate of 5 percent would have been regarded as politically ruinous. By the late 1970s the rate hovered around 4 to 4.5 percent. The 1983 percentage was 10.5—over three million people out of work, yet the Thatcher government easily won reelection, and won again in 1987 with unemployment at 10.3 percent. Again in 1993 unemployment reached the three million figure, then began to fall slowly to 8.3 percent by the spring of 1995.

There was some disagreement on the meaning of these figures. In 1985 the director-general of the Institute of Directors dismissed unemployment estimates of over three million as grossly exaggerated, for two million of these were merely "between jobs." But others pointed out that a growing proportion of the unemployed had been "between jobs" for more than a year, and that the official figures fell short of the true levels by a million or more because of periodic changes by the government in the statistical basis for measuring unemployment.

For its part, the government did not deny that unemployment was at painfully high levels, but contended that this was a problem experienced by all the industrial countries: in 1994 unemployment in France passed 12 percent, in Italy 11 percent, in Denmark 12 percent, in Germany 9 percent and still rising, and European Union President Jacques Delors was warning that unemployment in the EU countries could rise from 18 million to 30 million by the late 1990s. To bring unemployment down over the long run, the Conservatives argued, required consistent economic growth, and this could only be achieved if inflation were kept under control.

Table 13.1 shows that Thatcher and Major won reelection in years when unemployment was very high, but when the misery index, an indicator that politicians watch closely, was lower than it had been during the Callaghan administration.

Government Spending. The rate of increase in government spending was slowed, a number of programs were cut back or eliminated, and the proportion of the gross domestic product spent by government declined slightly. But continued high outlays on social services and unemployment compensation frustrated the hopes of producing a very large decline in public sector spending, as indicated by the following list adapted from HM Treasury: *Economic Trends*.

Government Spending as Percent of GDP (Selected Years)

1963-64	36
1979-80	44
1982-83	47.5
1989-90	39.75
1992-93	44.75

Taxes. The sharp reduction from the confiscatory upper levels of income tax encouraged incentive and investment. Of course, the previous 83 percent top rate had not been paid by many, as was evidenced by the continued existence of many very large fortunes; however, the cuts obviated the need to find loopholes in the tax laws that made for inefficient uses of capital.

For those at the lower ends of the financial scale, the redistributive effects of Labour governments were reversed. Increases in VAT and social security taxes offset income tax cuts for most of those in the *C1* and *C2* categories, and actually led to a net tax increase for the poor.

TABLE 13.1 Unemployment, inflation, and the Misery Index for selected years (percent)

	Unemployment	Retail Price Index	Misery Index*
1970	2.6	6.5	9.1
1975	3.0	24.1	27.1
1979	4.0	13.4	17.4
1980	4.8	18.0	22.8
1983	10.5	4.5	15.0
1986	11.8	3.4	15.2
1987	10.3	4.2	14.5
1989	6.4	7.8	14.2
1992	9.7	3.7	13.4
1994†	9.4	2.6	12.0

* Sum of unemployment and RPI rates
† Estimate
SOURCE: Adapted from HM Treasury: *Economic Trends*.

But much more damaging to the government were treasury figures in 1994 revealing that the *average* taxpayer would be paying a significantly higher proportion of his income in taxes than in the year before Thatcher came to power. Tax increases in the 1994 budget (the extension of VAT to domestic fuel and power, national insurance going from 9 percent to 10 percent, and cuts in mortgage tax relief and married couples' allowance) meant that the total tax bill of a married man with two children and average earnings would go up to 35 percent in 1994-95 and to 35.9 percent the next year, compared with 32.2 percent in 1978-79.

The Conservatives pointed out that average earners were paying a higher proportion of their incomes because average earnings were so much higher than they had been in 1979 and that Labour's policies would result in much higher taxes still. Just the same, the publication of these figures in the media had to be disconcerting to a party that had made much of its claim to having slashed taxes dramatically.

The Budget. Balanced budgets are a declared goal of any conservative administration, and the Thatcher government succeeded first in reducing budgetary deficits (the public sector borrowing requirement, or PSBR) and then—with the help of the sale of nationalized industries and public housing units—of running surpluses, which were applied to reducing the national debt.

However, as Table 13.2 makes clear, large deficits appeared again from 1991, and reached over 5 percent of gross domestic product in 1993. The 1994 budget started the process of reducing the deficit—at the cost of embarrassing increases in taxes.

Deregulation. The Thatcher government ended currency controls, so businesses could invest abroad unimpeded and tourists were no longer limited to a specific allocation for spending in other countries. Red tape that inhibited business was also cut, and the stock market was freed from most regulation.

Giving business its head, however, also resulted in some of the biggest financial

TABLE 13.2 Public sector borrowing requirement for selected years

	£billions
1979–80	8.9
1980–81	13.2
1984–85	10.2
1986–87	2.5
1987–88	−3.0
1988–89	−14.0
1989–90	−7.6
1990–91	−0.5
1991–92	13.7
1992–93	36.5

SOURCE: Adapted from HM Treasury: *Economic Trends.*

scandals in British history. Lloyd's of London, formerly an exclusive bastion of the Establishment, expanded its clientele and ruined thousands who were persuaded to become investors in a number of losing ventures with no limit on their liability. Prosecutions followed charges of share manipulation in the takeover of Distillers by Guinness. Small as well as large investors lost their entire savings in the sudden collapse of the Polly Peck empire, built into a multibillion pound conglomerate by a Cypriot businessman who had made large donations to the Conservative Party and who fled the country to avoid prosecution for massive fraud. Many more small businesspeople were bankrupted by the crash of the Bank of Credit and Commerce International (BCCI), which had been given a clean bill of health after an investigation by the Bank of England of charges of massive corruption. Publisher Robert Maxwell went overboard from his yacht and drowned as his overextended enterprises fell apart—but not before he had allegedly diverted hundreds of millions of pounds in union pension funds to stave off bankruptcy. And in 1995 the Barings Bank, a pillar of the British financial community for over two centuries, went bankrupt because one of its employees in Singapore was given free reign to speculate with huge sums of money in the derivatives market.

Moreover, unions complained that weak enforcement of health and safety standards in workplaces resulting from cutbacks in the Health and Safety Executive were increasing accidents on the job—a similar complaint to that levied against the Reagan administration when it diluted the enforcement powers of the Occupational Safety and Health Administration.

Productivity. Lower taxes, deregulation, weaker unions, and privatization produced a more invigorating, competitive climate. *The Economist* claimed in 1992 that "for the first time since the early 1970s, output per employee began rising faster than practically anywhere else," with productivity growing by an average of 4.7 percent a year throughout the 1980s compared with slightly under 1 percent from 1975 to 1980. Altogether, said The *Economist*, productivity grew during the 1980s by nearly a third.[3]

The *Economist* also pointed out, however, that much of this gain came from severe reductions in the number of people employed in manufacturing. Profitable companies laid off large numbers of workers. Inefficient firms unable to withstand the newly competitive atmosphere went under. The steel industry, heavily subsidized when nationalized, cut its workforce after privatization and became profitable. The coal industry, which had employed 700,000 in 1947, had fallen to 230,000 by 1979 and to 70,000 by 1990, with further reductions under the Major administration. Although some of the decline in manufacturing jobs was offset by increased employment in the service industries, there was concern about the extent to which a country so dependent on imports could flourish without a strong manufacturing sector.

Moreover, even with the improvements of the 1980s, The *Economist* conceded that Britain's productivity remained much lower than in the United States, Japan, and several other industrial countries. This view was confirmed by a report on world competitiveness rankings by the International Institute of Management Development and the World Economic Forum.

Table 13.3 lists the biggest 6 of the 22 industrial countries studied by the Project. Britain's overall ranking was 16th. This ranking is closely paralleled in the annual estimates of gross domestic product per head by the Organization for Economic Cooperation and Development (OECD). Britain had ranked 14th among industrial nations in 1979, but had slipped to 17th place in 1992. (The United States headed the list in 1992 with $23,215 per capita, compared with Britain's $16,340.)

It was not surprising, then, that in 1993 the international currency markets bet against the British pound, and forced Major's government to withdraw ignominiously from the Exchange Rate Mechanism.

The Balance of Payments. Large increases in overseas holdings brought in substantial income from abroad. The privatized British Telecom, operating under much more relaxed telecommunications regulations than those prevailing in the United States, joined forces with U.S. cable and phone companies, who believed the British would be the world's leaders in fiber-optic, computer-switched systems. The privatized British Airways also bought a major stake in the U.S. airline industry.

Nonetheless, even though Britain became a net exporter of oil just as Thatcher came to power, the nation ran substantial deficits in the balance of trade in some years, including over £19 billion in 1993. In other words, the country was spending beyond its means.

Summing Up the Thatcher-Major Economic Record. The Thatcher and Major years yielded improved productivity and management performance through an attack on inefficient practices, old-boy-network appointments, and union featherbedding. These changes, combined with the intensifying problems of Germany, Japan, and other competitors, led to hopes that Britain could produce a lasting upward trend in Britain's economic standing. As evidence for the increased attractiveness of Britain's industrial climate, the government could point to the Japanese firms

TABLE 13.3 World Competitiveness League, 1993

DE: Strength of the domestic economy at a macro level
IT: Participation in trade and investment flows
GP: Conduciveness of government policies to competitiveness
ME: Management of enterprises—innovation, profitability, and responsibility
ST: Scientific and technological capacity, success of basic and applied research
HR: Availability and qualification of human resources

	DE	IT	GP	ME	ST	HR
France	10	11	16	11	8	16
Germany	11	7	5	9	4	3
Japan	1	9	6	1	1	2
United Kingdom	19	10	9	16	13	18
United States	2	5	3	5	2	10

Excerpted from World Competitiveness Project: *World Competitiveness Report 1993.*

that have been building production plants in Britain in preference to other European countries.

However, even if Britain's relative economic decline was halted, it was not yet reversed. Britain still lagged in the international competitiveness league. Moreover, despite the statistical evidence pointing to significant gains in the standard of living over the past 20 years, opinion polls in 1994 revealed widespread dissatisfaction with economic conditions, and the government in Britain (as in the United States) was frustrated by the absence in the country of what was called the "feel-good factor."

It was also evident from the Thatcher-Major experience that no solution has yet been found for the problem of which British economists had long complained: the "stop-go" behavior of the economy, involving sharp alternations between recessions and overheated expansions.

OPPOSITION RESPONSES

If Conservative policies since 1979 have fallen short of their economic goals, they have had a profound effect on the Labour party. After Labour's third defeat in 1987, Neil Kinnock began the process of reexamining party policies, and one by one some of the cherished shibboleths were modified or abandoned. The Thatcher administration's laws requiring ballots for union elections and proposals for strikes would be retained. No more industries would be nationalized; even before the abandonment of Clause 4 of the Labour constitution calling for common ownership, the clause was essentially a dead letter. There would be no return to the levels of income tax inherited by the Thatcher government. The demand in the 1983 manifesto to pull out of the Common Market was dropped and replaced by a commitment to the Single European Act and even to the exchange rate mechanism, despite its evident purpose of holding down wage pressures.

The process of transformation continued when John Smith and then Tony Blair followed Kinnock as leader. It is true that Smith had proposed a moderate increase in the top level of income tax to pay for higher outlays on social services, and this may well have contributed to Labour's defeat in 1992. But this only intensified the leadership's determination to avoid giving offense to the middle classes. In 1993 Gordon Brown, Labour's chief economic spokesperson, promised that "the next Labour government will not tax for its own sake," and even hoped to be able to produce tax cuts.

Differences with the Conservatives on economic policy remained. Labour (and a substantial majority of voters) opposed Conservative proposals to extend privatization to the railroads, the London buses, and all or part of the post office. A return to industrial policy, with government investments in promising future industries, was indicated. A minimum wage would be introduced by a future Labour government. There would be more job-creating and training programs as essential elements in reenergizing the economy and accelerating growth through upgrading the labor force.

Labour also promised increased spending on the National Health Service, education, and other social programs. Many of the health and safety regulations being scrapped by the Conservatives would be reimposed, and controls would be tightened to prevent the kind of financial scandals that had multiplied in the scramble for profits in the 1980s. The social chapter of the Maastricht treaty, rejected by Major, would be signed if Labour were returned to power, for Labour argued that Britain's economic future could not be assured by entering into a contest with low-wage, unregulated third world countries. Labour was bitterly critical of the widening gap between rich and poor resulting from the Thatcher-Major policies. And loopholes that enabled the rich to cut their taxes or avoid them altogether would be closed.

These differences were not sufficient to satisfy the party's left wing, who bitterly resented Blair and his "modernizing" policies. Tony Benn and his supporters sought a return to the principles of the 1983 manifesto: renationalization, the repeal of all antiunion laws, centralized planning (for everyone except the unions), protectionism, and higher taxes on the rich.

Benn's outside left fraction was a spent force. There would be no return to the manifesto economics of 1983. Yet there were many others in the party who were uncomfortable with how far the party was distancing itself from the radicalism of the past. They wanted stronger assurances that the party leadership was committed to getting rid of unemployment and not replacing the goal of *full employment* with vaguer notions such as *a high level of employment*. And both inside and outside the party, the question was raised: how could the party's proposals for increased spending be financed without some increases in taxes? Indeed, given the range of programs to which the party remained committed, what was the point of actually suggesting the possibility of future tax cuts? (Since the Labour leaders were so impressed with Clinton's victory, the critics asked, did they not see the damage that could be caused by suggesting middle-class tax cuts that could not be delivered?)

Among those raising these questions were the Liberal Democrats under Paddy Ashdown. Like their Liberal predecessors, the Liberal Democrats praised the virtues of competition and criticized the trade unions. Yet, like Labour, they favored the Maastricht treaty's social chapter. And they were much closer to Labour than to the Conservatives on the need for more spending on the social services, even outflanking Labour with proposals to pay for the increased spending. In the 1992 election campaign the Liberal Democrats proposed a penny-on-the-pound income tax increase dedicated to education, and subsequently extended the idea of "hypothecated" taxes, earmarked for particular purposes—tobacco and alcohol taxes for health, car taxes for public transportation, and so on.

Labour, too, expressed interest in hypothecated taxes, and evidently there were some grounds for a joint approach to economic policy between Labour and the Liberal Democrats. Still their differences would make for some very hard and difficult bargaining if there were ever to be an electoral pact or a governing coalition between the two parties.

CONCLUSION

In Britain in 1979, and in the United States in 1980, governments were elected that set out to repeal the economic interventionism of their predecessors. Although the victories of Margaret Thatcher and Ronald Reagan represented mostly a negative verdict on the governments of James Callaghan and Jimmy Carter rather than mandates for radical change, both Thatcher and Reagan proceeded as though they had been given clear mandates, both were reelected, and both were succeeded by a leader of their own party.

Both achieved their economic goals only partially. Yet their success in reducing government's role in the economy was sufficient to impress the leaders of several other nations, and Reagan and Thatcher were influential missionaries for ideas that were taken up with enthusiasm in most of countries of the former Soviet Union, eastern Europe, and elsewhere in Europe, Latin America, and southeast Asia.

So in the 1990s, private enterprise is in the saddle. Yet this was not a newly discovered system. Largely unregulated private enterprise had been the rule in the United States and Britain until the 1930s. It had collapsed in the United States with the 1929 stock market crash and the Great Depression that followed, and it took the New Deal and a world war to make the economy boom again. In Britain, too, the 1930s brought economic stagnation and mass unemployment until the war and the subsequent Labour government brought government direction of the economy.

In both countries the economy responded quite well to the new interventionism. But eventually the impetus flagged, a generation that had viewed unemployment as the overriding economic evil gave way to another traumatized by high rates of inflation, and the voters turned again to the advocates of less regulation and less government spending and taxing.

The question for the free enterprise system today is whether, with the more sophisticated techniques available to government, it can generate sustained growth without repeating the disastrous experience of the 1930s.

Thus far the answer is uncertain. The verdict has yet to be rendered on whether the former communist countries can quickly acquire all the institutions and practices necessary for successful capitalism. The *Economist* magazine may be right when it argues that across Eastern Europe, "the possibility and desirability of creating capitalism has now been accepted, even by the laggards ... Countries escaping from communism have shown that they can indeed change the economic structure of their societies in as little as three years."[4] However, economic "shock therapy" in Russia had produced a dangerous backlash by 1993, and old-line communists were winning elections in eastern Europe (albeit under new labels and with moderately reformist policies).

In Britain, too, resistance has grown to continued privatization and other legacies of Thatcherism, and by 1994, for the first time since the Thatcher era began, polls indicated that a majority believed that Labour was more likely than the Conservatives to manage the economy effectively. However, Labour was yet to spell out its economic policies in detail; the evidence reviewed in this chapter makes it clear that any future government, whatever its party complexion, would find the task of generating sustained economic growth a formidable one indeed.

SOME QUESTIONS TO THINK ABOUT

What are the causes of Britain's low competitive ranking among industrial nations?
What are the prospects that the Thatcher-Major policies will, in time, improve Britain's ranking?
What should be Labour's economic program for the next election?

Given the situation in Britain today, which do you see as the greater danger—unemployment or inflation? Can you conceive of policies that could bring both under control at the same time?

Should government pursue policies designed to narrow the gap between rich and poor in Britain? What might these policies be?

How much further should privatization go in Britain?

NOTES

1. Dennis Healey, *The Time of My Life* (Penguin, 1990), p. 379.
2. Paul Foot, *The Politics of Harold Wilson* (Penguin, 1968), p. 332.
3. The *Economist*, "Survey of Britain," 24 October 1992, p. 9.
4. The *Economist*, 3-9 December 1994, p. 27.

SUGGESTIONS FOR FURTHER READING

An overview of the post-World War II period is presented in Alec Cairncross, *The British Economy Since 1945* (Blackwell, 1992), and Graham P. Thomas, *Government and the Economy Today* (St. Martin's Press, 1992). For Britain's economic decline, see NOTES to chapter 1, and John Eatwell, *Whatever Happened to Britain?* (Oxford University Press, 1984). The Thatcher period is covered in Christopher Johnson, *The Economy Under Mrs. Thatcher* (Penguin, 1991); Alan Walters, a Thatcher adviser, provides a conservative analysis in *Britain's Economic Renaissance* (Oxford University Press, 1986); and a transatlantic left analysis is presented in Kenneth Hoover and Raymond Plant, *Conservative Capitalism in Britain and the United States* (Routledge, 1989). A later assessment of Britain's economic position is provided by the *Guardian* financial editor, Will Hutton, *The State We're In* (Jonathan Cape, 1994).

To keep abreast of economic developments, see the *Economist*, the *Financial Times*, and the *New Statesman*, as well as the financial columns in the *Guardian* and the *Times*.

14

THE WELFARE STATE AND ITS CRITICS

In chapter 2 we noted that the British are generally more communitarian, less individualistic, than people in the United States. It is not surprising, then, that the British welfare state—providing government support to the less advantaged sections of the population—was introduced earlier and is more extensive than its counterpart in the United States. The first, tentative steps were taken in Britain in the first decade of the twentieth century, with a major expansion after World War II. Margaret Thatcher's governments questioned the assumptions on which this expansion was built and slowed its growth; however, spending on a variety of welfare services will be much greater in the year 2000 than it was in 1950.

We examine this phenomenon, and the fierce political battles that have surrounded it, in the context of social security programs, health, and housing.

SOCIAL SECURITY

Government support for the poor in Britain dates back to 1601, when the Poor Law made support for the destitute a responsibility of the local parishes. Administration of this law became particularly harsh with the Poor Law Amendment Act of 1834, which set limits on the amount of relief, provided penalties for vagrancy, and institutionalized many of the poor in the kind of "workhouse" described so poignantly in Dickens's *Oliver Twist*.

In 1908, the first step was taken toward the establishment of the modern welfare state with the introduction by the Liberal government of old age pensions for the very poor. Then in 1912, the Liberals inaugurated a government program of unemployment insurance for skilled workers, which was extended to the entire work force in 1922. In the 1930s, the insurance program was supplemented by public assistance for the unemployed who had not been able to contribute to the insurance program.

Yet unemployment remained at high levels throughout the 1930s, and the benefits provided by the government programs were at the barest subsistence level—sufficient to ward off starvation but not enough to take millions of people out of acute poverty.

During World War II, a consensus emerged that there must be no return in postwar Britain to the abysmal conditions that had afflicted such a high proportion of the working class. The coalition government asked the Liberal economist, Sir William Beveridge, to review and recommend changes in the social welfare system. In 1942 the Beveridge Report appeared, identified "the five giants on the road of reconstruction . . . Want, Disease, Ignorance, Squalor and Idleness," and proposed a sweeping reform of the system to attack these five giants. The report received an enthusiastic response from a public eager to hear about the prospect of a better world after the war; and the Labour government that came to power at the end of the war put most of the Beveridge plan, with some modifications and enhancements, into effect.

The Party Consensus, 1945–79

The Attlee government's social security legislation included a wide array of programs addressed to a great diversity of needs, and subsequently a succession of governments have amended some, replaced others, and added a plethora of new programs. But most have fallen under the four categories of *unemployment insurance, retirement pensions, childrearing benefits*, and *welfare* (*National Assistance*).

There is an important distinction between the first three and the last of these categories. The first three were *universal* benefits. The entire working population paid into national insurance programs to provide benefits in case of unemployment (including sickness and disability) and retirement. Every family, regardless of income, received an allowance toward the cost of raising each child. But National Assistance was a *targeted* benefit, limited to the very poor and thus "means-tested."

The distinction between universal and targeted benefits has defined the major debate over the welfare state. The left has argued for universality, for this principle emphasizes the common needs of all citizens, avoids the humiliation of being identified as one of society's failures, and builds broader political support than is possible for programs restricted to the very poor. For those on the right, however, government should target its efforts to those in greatest need, and not lavish public funds on those who can provide for their own needs through savings and private insurance.

In general, then, the Labour Party has preferred universality, the Conservatives have denounced it. But from 1945 to 1979 the differences were of degree only. The

Attlee government's programs were mostly provided to the entire population, with National Assistance available to supplement the universal benefits where these were not sufficient to lift particular individuals and families out of poverty. However, as the costs of the programs mounted, and economic growth slowed, later Labour governments set more limits to the universal benefits. Supplements in 1966 to the benefits for unemployment and sickness, and for pensions in 1975, were financed through additional payments related to earnings. (The 1975 program was called SERPS—the State Earnings Related Pension Scheme.) For those who did not earn enough to qualify, supplements to the core, universal benefits were available only after the application of a means test. For their part, Conservative governments set the limits more severely than Labour, but the main universally available programs survived.

Thatcherism

So the debate remained within a consensual range until the Thatcher government took office in 1979. Margaret Thatcher had grown up over her father's grocery store and inherited a strong belief in thrift, hard work, and individual responsibility. The huge expansion of the welfare state since 1945 was an affront to this belief in two respects. First, the huge cost required high taxes, which undermined people's incentive to work and their ability to provide for their own contingencies. Second, benefits provided on an unnecessarily lavish scale created a culture of dependency, in which individuals expected government to take care of them rather than taking responsibility for themselves.

To her critics Thatcher's attitude reflected an arrogant selfishness, a doctrine of Social Darwinism that left the less fortunate behind in a harsh struggle for survival. To her sympathizers, however, Thatcher spoke not for a narrow selfishness but for a fundamental moral code. Thus the late political philosopher, Shirley Robin Letwin, argued that Thatcherism is an expression of what she called the *vigorous virtues*. Individuals admired by Thatcherites are "upright, self-sufficient, energetic, adventurous, independent-minded, loyal to friends, and robust against enemies." These vigorous virtues are not incompatible with the "softer" virtues: "kindness, humility, gentleness, sympathy, cheerfulness." So for Letwin, Thatcherism is not a heartless or cruel dogma. It insists that government provide a safety net to ensure that none falls below a minimum level of the necessities of life. But Thatcherites see Britain today "as a place in which the softer virtues have been too much stressed and the vigorous virtues insufficiently regarded."[1]

These ideas became guiding principles for social security programs from the onset of the Thatcher era. Legislation in 1980 began the process of slowing down increases in unemployment and pension benefits. Nonetheless, total outlays for social security actually increased, mainly because starting in 1980, unemployment began to rise to levels not experienced since the worst days of the 1930s.

In 1982 the government think tank, the Central Policy Review Staff, prepared a study predicting that on current trends public spending would claim a higher share of the gross domestic product than was the case under the previous Labour government. The study went on to make recommendations for drastic reductions in the welfare state, including the end of all inflation adjustments for welfare benefits.

The study was clearly in line with Thatcherite precepts, and Thatcher wanted the cabinet to discuss its recommendations. But in 1982 the cabinet still included several of the "wets" so despised by Thatcher, and they forced the issue off the agenda. Then one of their number leaked the contents to the *Economist* magazine, and the roar of public outrage that followed the publication convinced Thatcher that she had better shelve the report.

In the years that followed, some social security budgets were trimmed, and the rate of growth on several programs was slowed. A major review of social security led to the 1986 Social Security Act, which intensified the emphasis on means testing and targeting of benefits, and made sharp cuts in a number of programs. But in the face of widespread public protest the government backed away from its plan to include in the act the termination of SERPS, the earnings-related pension scheme inaugurated in 1975. And with unemployment continuing to rise until mid-1986, and a steady increase in the proportion of the population moving into the retirement age group (see Table 14.1), total outlays on social security grew, in real, inflation-adjusted terms, from £46 billion in 1978 to £63 billion in 1990, and from 10.0 percent of gross domestic product to 10.7 percent.

However, public attention took less note of the expanded budgets than of the government's efforts to hold them down. And the polls indicated that the majority still favored the "softer" virtues, and judged Thatcher, to her great chagrin, to be lacking in compassion.

So there was a general expectation that John Major, who was perceived as a much nicer person than Thatcher, would shift the balance from the vigorous to the softer virtues. Indeed, the social security budget increased rapidly after he took over, rising from £65 billion in 1990 to about £84 billion in 1993, and from 10.7 percent to over 13 percent of gross domestic product. However, although this increase reflected some modest upward adjustments in a few programs, it was driven primarily by the prolonged recession and unemployment of more than 10 percent.

Increases on this scale, and projections of continued escalations, would undermine the economic policies of any government. But they were especially intolerable

TABLE 14.1 Age structure of the population (percent)

	Under 16	16–39	40–64	65+
1971	25.5	31.3	29.9	13.2
1981	22.3	34.9	27.8	15.0
1991	20.3	35.3	28.6	15.7
2001*	21.0	32.8	30.5	15.6
2011*	19.5	30.3	33.7	16.6
2021*	18.5	30.0	32.3	19.2

* projected
SOURCE: Adapted from *Social Trends*, 1994

to the unreconstructed Thatcherites in Major's cabinet, particularly Michael Portillo, the chief secretary to the treasury who became the employment secretary, and Peter Lilley, the social security secretary. In a number of speeches they berated the culture of dependency they believed had been created by the welfare state, and argued that much of the increase in the social security budget was attributable to Britain's high percentage of single mothers (at 10.1 percent, the highest in Western Europe). Accordingly a child support agency was established, charged with forcing divorced or separated fathers to contribute child support—especially where the failure to do so forced the mother on to welfare. And, Major (like Bill Clinton) announced that his government was considering the introduction of *workfare*, which would tie welfare to mandatory participation in work schemes.

Yet, however great the budgetary problems, however intense the ideological fervor, the political realities could not be ignored. Peter Lilley assured the House of Commons in 1993 that his government would stand by the Conservative Party's 1992 manifesto promises to preserve the basic pension and child benefit and protect them against price rises. And when a furious public reaction greeted an increase in the tax on heating fuel in the 1994 budget, the government hastened to provide assurances that pensioners would receive compensatory benefits.

The Labour Critique

From the opposition benches came a steady drumfire of opposition to the social security cuts imposed by the Thatcher and Major governments. The Labour Party, expressing the concerns of organizations representing the poor, the elderly, children, social workers, local government councillors and officials, and trade unions, charged that the Conservatives were trying to undo, step by step, the great social gains achieved by the postwar Labour governments. And the Liberal Democrats, harking back to the Liberal governments of the early part of the century and to the plans of the Liberal Sir William Beveridge, joined Labour on this issue.

Still, the opposition parties could hardly ignore the problem of financing the great expansion of the programs as well as the need for an administrative overhaul of programs that had grown piecemeal over four decades. Labour responded by setting up the Commission on Social Justice, charged with proposing the ethical, financial, and administrative principles on which the future of the programs should be based. The commission's report, which was strongly endorsed by Tony Blair, attacked the Thatcher-Major vision for Britain's future, which it defined as the *Deregulators' Britain*, in which public services are reduced, the urge for ever-cheaper production drives the economy, and "the rich get richer and the poor get poorer." On the other hand, the commission rejected the idea of *Leveller's Britain*, which focuses on redistribution to the neglect of growth and offers "policies for social justice independent of the economy." Instead, the commission's preferred model, which they called *Investors' Britain*, aimed at "combining the ethics of community with the dynamics of a market economy" and "redistributing opportunities rather than just redistributing income."[2]

Nonetheless, a central concern of the commission was that the maldistribution of opportunities resulted in a huge gap between those at the top and the bottom of the wealth and income scales. The data showed clearly that the distribution of income in Britain had become more uneven after 1979. The proportion of total income received by the bottom half of the population fell from one-third in 1979 to one-quarter in 1990; the share of those in the bottom tenth fell from 4 percent to 2.1 percent. In 1991, over 11 million people, one-fifth of the population, were living on less than half the average income (the EU's definition of the poverty line); in 1977, under the last Labour government, the comparable figure had been only 3 million.

Thatcher had not conceded that these figures were reprehensible. For her, inequality was inevitable and even desirable if incentives were to be provided. Further, she pointed out, the figures demonstrating the increase in inequality were all related to averages; and if the average goes up, then even those at the bottom, though receiving a smaller share of the total, may still be better off. And in 1990, many more people from the lowest income group had central heating, a telephone, and even a car than did those from the lowest income group in 1979.

Still, the extraordinary disparity between very rich and very poor remained a vulnerable point for the Conservatives. As in the United States, large numbers of people lived on the very edge of subsistence, some forced to live on the streets, while corporations rewarded their CEOs for less than impressive performances with millions of pounds in annual salaries, bonuses, and "golden handshakes" when they departed. Thus the chairman of British Aerospace received a payout of £3.2 million when he left in 1994 after serving for 18 months; and privatization of the water and electricity industries was followed by the granting of huge increases in salaries and pension plans, as well as share options, to the top executives of the privatized companies.

According to a study published in 1995,[3] income inequality in Britain was growing at a rate considerably faster than in any other major industrial country, including the United States. In the face of what the report called the *great divide* between the top and bottom of the British income scale, cutting a few pounds off the benefits of pensioners or the unemployed would seem unconscionably mean-spirited to the voting public.

THE NATIONAL HEALTH SERVICE

The first step toward the establishment of national health insurance in the United States was taken in 1965 with the inauguration of Medicare, an insurance program covering the elderly, retired population. More than a half-century earlier, the Liberal government in Britain, in the face of intense opposition from the Conservative Party and the British Medical Association, passed the National Insurance Act of 1911, which provided free medical treatment to most of the working population.

Although the provisions of the act were broadened by subsequent legislation, its benefits were not comprehensive and did nothing for the workers' families. Consequently a proposal for a free national health service covering the entire population became one of the central features of the Beveridge Plan. The proposal was supported by the coalition government of World War II, and was put into effect by the postwar Labour government following the passage of the 1946 National Health Service Act.

Inauguration and Minor Modifications, 1945–79

In its main outlines, the National Health Service (NHS) reflected the socialist ethos of Health and Housing Minister Aneurin Bevan, a brilliant orator and idol of the left in the Labour party. The program provided full medical care to the entire population free of charge, the total cost to be paid out of general taxes. The comprehensive array of services included visits to the doctor (chosen by the patient) and the dentist, hospitalization, prescriptions, eyeglasses, and dentures, the cost to be covered out of general taxes.

However, once again there was fierce opposition from the British Medical Association. Bevan held his ground on the central principles of the NHS, but accepted some compromises that allowed participating doctors to take private patients and NHS hospitals to set aside a limited number of private beds.

Further incursions into the socialist principle underlying the NHS came in 1951 when Labour Chancellor of the Exchequer Hugh Gaitskell, looking for savings to offset the increased defense spending for the Korean war, imposed some small charges for glasses and dentures. Bevan protested, then, accompanied by future Labour prime minister Harold Wilson, resigned, precipitating the breakup and subsequent defeat of the Attlee government.

Bevan's critics accused him of manufacturing a crisis over a trivial sum of money. His response was that once the principle of charging patients for any part of the service was accepted more and more charges would be imposed. This proved to be the case, and governments of both parties subsequently raised charges for prescriptions, dental care and other services.

There were hotly debated differences between Labour and Conservative on the size of the increases. Conservative governments pushed up the costs to the patients faster than Labour governments. Conservatives also favored setting aside more private beds in NHS hospitals, whereas Labour preferred to cut the number down. Yet these were differences of degree. From 1945 to 1979, the debate over the NHS is well described by Richard Rose's consensual model as described in chapter 5—a Labour government, acting on a proposal put forward by a Liberal government and endorsed by a multiparty wartime government, had created a program which, with minor variations, was administered and expanded by Conservative as well as Labour governments.

The Limited Impact of Thatcherism

If the Attlee government's social security programs ran counter to Thatcherite principles, this must be even more the case with the National Health Service. Despite all its modifications, the NHS was still firmly based on the socialist concept of a government-managed program, provided almost free of charge to the entire population, and paid from tax revenues. It was not surprising, then, that the Central Policy Review Staff's study of welfare spending in 1982 included a proposal to replace the NHS with private health insurance, as well as charging for doctor visits and substantially increasing the charge for drugs.

As we have seen, Thatcher withdrew the report in face of the uproar that ensued when it was leaked to the press; and no feature of that report provoked more outrage than the proposals on health. For the NHS, though the subject of innumerable complaints, had become a political sacred cow, a program that politicians could propose abolishing only at the price of destroying their political careers. Thatcherites might look across the Atlantic for their health insurance models. But the great majority of the British public was not amenable to abandoning the NHS in favor of a system such as that in the United States, which itself was the subject of widespread dissatisfaction.

So in the 1983 election the Conservatives assured the voters that "the National Health Service is safe with us"; and Mrs. Thatcher declared: "I have no more intention of dismantling the health service than I have of dismantling Britain's defenses." The 1987 Conservative election manifesto claimed that the Thatcher government had substantially increased funding for the NHS and promised: "We will continue to improve the NHS."

Nonetheless, the NHS was a bone in the throat of the Thatcher administration. They were acutely uncomfortable at having to administer a program to which they were ideologically hostile. And even though they were correct in claiming that they had substantially increased spending on health (in real terms NHS spending went up from £21 billion in 1979 to almost £30 billion in 1990), supply was not keeping up with demand, and the pressure for much higher outlays was insatiable. The population was aging, and older people need more medical care. New marvels of medical technologies could not be denied the population, but they were very expensive. AIDS was beginning to take its financial as well as human toll. Consequently, the complaints multiplied, and although life-threatening conditions were attended to immediately (and without questions about ability to pay), operations for painful but not urgent conditions might have to wait for months or even a year—in some parts of Britain, over two years. And the polls indicated that a majority blamed the Conservative government for these shortcomings, and agreed with Labour that the problem was primarily insufficient funding.

The government response was to continue increasing the funds for the NHS, but at levels well short of those demanded by Labour, and to propose, in 1989, a major overhaul of the program. This could not conceivably involve the abandonment of the NHS and its replacement by the private market system. Instead, the NHS was to be made more efficient—provide more value for the available funds—by employing another favorite technique of the Thatcher administration: introducing market mechanisms into government programs. Decision-making was to be decentralized to the full extent possible, and competition and choice were to be maximized. The purchasers of services (the health authorities) would be separated from the providers (hospitals and doctors). General practitioners with large practices would be encouraged to manage their own budgets. Hospitals would be urged to opt out of local health authority control and become self-governing trusts, free to sell their services to doctors and other health authorities, and to set up their own conditions of employment. There would be greater cooperation with the private sector, including the contracting out of services previously provided within the NHS.

The NHS Restructuring Controversy. Before her government could get far with these proposals, Thatcher was gone from the scene. However, the Major administration pressed ahead with the same ideas, and found itself under intense attack on the issue in the 1992 election campaign. Labour's Kinnock, despite repeated angry denials by Major, persisted with the argument that the Tory reforms were a prelude to complete privatization of the NHS. The introduction of market mechanisms, said Kinnock, was a trial run for ever-increasing inroads by the private sector. According to Kinnock, the argument that the proposed changes were driven by a need for greater efficiency was refuted, by the fact that the administrative costs of the NHS took a smaller proportion—as little as 3 percent—of total program outlays than any other nation's health system, and even with all the increases, NHS spending constituted barely 6 percent of GDP, compared with over 12 percent (14 percent by 1994) in the United States.

The ulterior purpose of the Tory policy, as Kinnock saw it, was to starve the NHS of funds, create longer and longer lines for service, cause more and more dissatisfaction, until people were forced to turn to private insurance. Then, if the NHS survived at all, it would be the lower part of a two-tier service: private care for the more affluent, the NHS for the poor. A universal benefit would become a stigmatized program targeted to the dispossessed.

The Liberal Democrats, under Paddy Ashdown, joined the attack; and there was strong criticism of particular aspects of the reorganization from representatives of some of the hospitals and from the organization that had been the main opponents of creation of the NHS—the British Medical Association.

Polls during the campaign showed that on this issue, the critics had the best of the argument. However, the government softened the public's dissatisfaction by substantially increasing NHS spending in the year leading up to the election, and just before election day, the government produced figures showing a large decline in the number of patients waiting more than a year for an operation (although statistics released later showed an increase in the numbers of those waiting up to a year).

In any case, the issue was not sufficiently salient to overcome the electorate's distrust of Labour on the economy and other policies, and, with their mandate renewed, the Conservatives were able to continue with their restructuring efforts. Before long, two-thirds of NHS hospitals had reorganized themselves as trusts; more services were being contracted out to private vendors; a growing number of doctors were managing their own budgets. Prescription charges went up (to the equivalent of about $7 in 1994), though pensioners and many others were exempted from the fee, and patients had to pay 80 percent of dental costs. The government published ratings of hospital performance including waiting times, speed of treatment, use of same-day surgery; proposals were presented to move increasingly to one-day operations, thereby significantly reducing the number of hospital beds needed. It was suggested that further changes might follow after a commission of inquiry, Health Care 2000, brought in its recommendations.

Still the NHS costs rose, and still the drumbeat of criticism of the government continued. Decentralization, it was said, could result in wide variations in service from area to area. Some of the doctors managing their own budgets might not take onto their lists patients who were poor and thus more likely to suffer from ill-health. The pressure on hospitals to buy and sell their services could lead to cuts in quality, and charges were made (and indignantly denied by the government) that elderly patients were being refused some kinds of treatment because of their age.

Even so, after 15 years of the governments of Thatcher and Major, the National Health Service remained as a nationalized, essentially socialized service. For a while in the 1980s there had been a spurt in the growth of private health insurance (some of it provided by U.S. companies), and some trade unions had bargained to include insurance in their members' fringe benefits. But although the numbers covered privately grew by two-thirds from 1979 to 1994, they accounted for only 11 percent of the population, the great majority continuing to rely on the service they were paying for with their taxes. Thus Britain for half a century has adopted a "single payer" health care system in contrast to the United States, where during the healthcare debate of the mid-1990s, those who advocated a much less comprehensive "single payer" approach made little headway against the U.S. fear of expanding the role of government.

HOUSING

British government began its heavy involvement in housing in 1919. It entered this arena because very many working-class people were crowded together in dilapidated, rat-infested slums. So, with underwriting from the central government, local governments began the task of tearing down the slums and replacing them with publicly owned, operated, and subsidized *council housing*.

Fluctuations in Policy, 1945–79

Only limited inroads had been made into the housing problem when the six years of World War II saw a halt to new construction and 700,000 houses were demolished or badly damaged by bombing. With servicepeople demobilizing and starting new families after the war, the incoming Attlee government faced an acute crisis. The response was a crash program, directed by Aneurin Bevan's department, which, despite the acute shortage of resources in the postwar period, produced over a half-million new housing units, 80 percent of them owned and managed by local government agencies.

This was still far short of meeting the need, and in the 1951 election campaign the Conservatives struck a responsive chord among voters by promising to build 300,000 houses a year. Under housing minister Harold Macmillan, the Conservatives made good on their promise. There was a shift of emphasis from Labour's approach, however. Increasing reliance was placed on the private sector, and home ownership, supported by mortgage tax relief, was encouraged.

Yet this was far from a total repudiation of the role of government. Half of all new units under Conservative rule from 1955 to 1959 were council housing; and though the proportion put up by private builders from 1960 to 1964 had risen to 62 percent, local governments still put up over a half-million units during this period. And though the rent controls on private housing imposed by the Labour government were eased by the Conservatives, they were not abolished.

With Labour back in power from 1964 to 1970 there was a shift to greater reliance on the public sector and to tougher rent controls. Yet just as the Conservatives had not completely reversed the previous Labour government's policies, so there was no way that Wilson's Labour government could ignore the private construction industry, and well over half the houses built between 1965 and 1970 were put up by the private sector.

So as Conservatives took over from Labour from 1970 to 1974, and as Labour returned to power from 1974 to 1979, policy fluctuated—the Conservatives favoring private efforts, Labour preferring council housing. But there were no drastic departures from the past, no profound challenges to the policies of previous administrations.

Thatcherism in Housing

Change came much more abruptly after the 1979 election. The 1979 Conservative manifesto, following through on resolutions from the party's national conference, had promised to give every council house tenant a right to buy his or her dwelling at a discount—a proposal that may well have brought the party a significant number of working-class votes in the election of that year.

Privatization. Thatcher was all too ready to follow through on this promise. On social security and on health, the thrust of Thatcherism had been blunted, the fullblooded doctrine contained in the 1982 Central Policy Review study had been ignominiously withdrawn. But in housing policy Mrs. Thatcher could give full expression to her doctrine. Council housing was government housing, making heavy demands on the national budget, and keeping a large segment of the population in a state of perpetual dependence on the state. The arguments for privatization of nationalized industries applied with special force to housing; there, property ownership took on immediate and tangible form. As Shirley Letwin put it, "this transfer of assets was being made in order to promote, through ownership, the vigorous virtues of self-sufficiency, independence, energy, and adventurousness in individuals and, equally, to promote the cohesion of the family as an association whose members are joint owners of common property both within a single generation and by inheritance from one generation to another."[4] A further consideration for the Conservatives was that council housing tended to be concentrated in areas whose local governments were in the hands of Labour, in some instances the left-wing Labour groups who were to defy Thatcher's efforts to cut spending at the local level.

So the Thatcher government proceeded to make council houses available for sale to the tenants. This was not an entirely new development. The option to buy had already been provided by a few local councils. But from 1980 the central government *compelled* local authorities to offer their units for sale to the occupants. Moreover, the offer included sharp discounts from market values and mortgages at below-market rates. Additional inducements to buy came from a policy of raising council housing rents.

A further element of Thatcherism, paralleling its use in the National Health Service, was to promote opting out from local government control of council housing estates to nonprofit housing associations and later to housing trusts. (However, opting out to the trusts required a majority vote of the tenants, and most of the votes went against the idea.)

As seen in Table 14.2, construction of new council housing slowed drastically and by the end of the 1980s was down to a trickle. Conversely the private housing industry was given strong encouragement by the government.

Moreover, rent controls were reduced as part of an effort to provide a larger private rental market, which had fallen to a small proportion of the total housing market, and suggestions that mortgage tax relief might be cut back were strenuously and effectively opposed by Thatcher, even though by the end of the 1980s this tax break was costing more than direct government spending in housing.

The results were very much to the political advantage of the Conservatives. By 1990, two-thirds of British homes were owned by their occupants. Home ownership had been increasing since the 1950s, but now the trend was augmented by the sale of almost a million and a half council houses units, and significant numbers of the former renters were voting Conservative as of 1983. Some analysts have suggested that many of these people were on their way over to the Conservatives anyway, for they were among the most prosperous of the working class. Still, council housing tenancy was among the best indicators of Labour voting, and a reduction in the number of council tenants could hardly be helpful to the Labour cause. (This was very much in the minds of the Conservative Westminster city council in preparing for the 1990 local elections; the district auditor accused them of selling off a number of council houses at a large discount to bring likely Tory voters into closely divided wards.)

At first, then, the Labour Party bitterly opposed mandating the opportunity to buy. In several cities, Labour argued, there were long waiting lists to get into the al-

TABLE 14.2 Public and private housing starts (in thousands of dwelling units)

	Private	Public	Ratio, private:local
1979	144.0	65.3	2.2
1983	172.2	34.6	5.0
1988	221.4	16.3	13.6
1990	135.3	8.5	15.9
1991	135.0	4.1	32.9

SOURCE: Adapted from HM Treasury: *Economic Trends.*

ready inadequate supply of council houses; now the Conservatives were deliberately reducing the supply further. But, as the Labour Party shook off left-wing control and worked to make itself more electable, it could not dismiss the evidence of the electoral appeal of the Thatcher housing policy. So Labour endorsed the principle of council house sales, arguing only that funds generated by the sales should be used for further construction by the councils, and (a position that the House of Lords forced on a reluctant Thatcher) that housing for the elderly should not be included in the sales.

However, Labour was clearly on the defensive on the issue, and the Major administration pressed home the Conservatives' advantage by proposing still more incentives to council tenants to buy, including further discounts and a plan to enable tenants to apply their rents toward partial ownership, leading eventually to full ownership.

Thus it appeared that, whereas social security and health were issues that helped Labour politically, housing had become one of the issues that favored the Conservatives at election time. Moreover, housing conditions for the great majority of the population have greatly improved since the beginning of the century. New construction, slum clearance, and the improvement of older dwellings have removed most of the severe dilapidation and much of the overcrowding, and only a small proportion of households lack basic amenities. Although most of the larger cities still have rundown areas, Britain has nothing as desolate as some of the ruined parts of New York and Chicago. And surveys indicate that a substantial majority of people are satisfied with their housing conditions.

Nonetheless, housing policy contains a number of unresolved problems that caused the Conservatives considerable difficulty in the early 1990s.

Continuing Problems

Problems for Homeowners. For the homeowning majority, the dominant concern is the level of interest rates and their impact on the cost of mortgages. This became a critical issue when interest rates soared starting in late 1988. When recession hit the economy again in the early 1990s, many people were unable to keep up their mortgage payments, with the result that 75,000 houses were repossessed in 1991, and nearly 200,000 mortgages fell six to twelve months in arrears. Moreover, housing prices, which had been rising at unprecedented rates during the 1980s, began a decline so steep that many of those who had bought at the peak of the market found themselves with properties worth less than their mortgage debt.

The situation improved when Britain dropped out of the exchange rate mechanism, interest rates and the cost of borrowing fell, and housing prices stabilized. However, the rate of repossessions had picked up again by 1995, and with home prices generally below the peak of the 1980s boom, mortgage holders had received a painful education in the fact that home ownership does not necessarily bring financial security.

Home ownership did bring an important advantage in providing tax relief for mortgages up to the value of £30,000. This represented a cost to the national exchequer of £4.3 billion in 1993. Facing a large budget deficit, the government began to move away from Margaret Thatcher's attachment to this middle-class subsidy, trimming the cost by lowering the rate against which the relief could be claimed to the bottom tax bracket of 20 percent; and even though mortgage holders represented the natural Conservative constituency, the government did not rule out further reductions in mortgage tax relief.

Problems for Renters. Though the majority of Britons say they are satisfied with their housing conditions, it remains the case that in housing, as in employment and material standards generally, a significant minority is not well situated. To be a renter in Britain today is to be largely dependent on public provision through council housing, for private rentals, which had once been the dominant form of housing in Britain, constituted only 8 percent of the housing market in 1988. Recently the proportion has been rising again in response to government policies allowing landlords to set market-level rents. Even so, the supply falls well short of the demand by renters. At the same time, as we have seen, the supply of council housing has declined.

Principally this is because of the policy of selling to tenants introduced by the Thatcher administration. But even before Thatcher, there were problems with some council housing estates. During the rush to build in the 1950s and 1960s, standards were lowered in some areas and there was a good deal of shoddy construction. The consequence is that today an outlay estimated at over £12 billion is needed to overcome serious problems of dampness and decay in council estates. Moreover, in Britain as in the United States, the cost of land in the cities led to the construction of high-rise apartments totally unsuited to the needs of large families. The result was that some of the projects degenerated into slumlike conditions with vandalism and high crime rates until the government saw no alternative but to raze them to the ground. (In the United States, too, the government has blown up some dilapidated high-rise public housing projects.)

This is not to say that most council housing in Britain was substandard. On the contrary, a high proportion were single-story units, hardly distinguishable in quality from the average middle-class dwelling, and therefore an attractive investment for those tenants who could afford to buy. And the fact that many of them could afford to purchase their homes is testimony to the difference historically between public housing in Britain and the United States. Here public housing is intended only for the very poor. There considerable numbers from the *C2* and even the *C1* social categories were council house tenants, and, helped by discounts and favorable mortgage rates, were delighted to become homeowners.

But this took much of the more attractive council housing out of the pool available for renting. The remainder were occupied predominately by the poor, the unemployed, single-parent families on welfare. Council housing in Britain, in other words, has been moving from a broad, though not universal, benefit, to a targeted program much closer to the U.S. model of public housing. Moreover, even for the poor there is not enough council housing. There has been very little new construction to replace the units sold to their tenants. Waiting lists and waiting times for the remaining council units in some cities grow longer and longer. And the shortage of public housing contributes to another ugly social problem familiar to Americans: homelessness.

Homelessness. In 1991 a total of 175,000 households, representing about 400,000 people, were listed as homeless. This does not mean they were all out on the streets.

The majority were either living temporarily with family or friends, or lodging in bed-and-breakfast or hostel accommodations paid for by local authorities. On the other hand, there were several thousand squatters and people sleeping rough who were not included in the official statistics.

The increase in homelessness stems from several causes. Demography is a major factor—more divorces; more poor, single mothers; more elderly people living alone, and so on. Then there are the New Age "Travelers," wandering around the country in groups, with a lifestyle—similar to that of the gypsies—deliberately rejecting fixed abodes and the confines of organized existence. And, as in the United States, many of the emotionally and mentally disturbed were moved out of hospitals into the community, but without sufficient community resources; many of them wandered the streets.

But these factors do not tell the whole story according to *Shelter*, the principal organization fighting for improved housing for the poor alongside an array of associations representing tenants, churches, women, the young, racial minorities, and charitable foundations. Their position, as summed up by the *New Statesman and Society*, is that the root of the problem is "the failure of the housing market to provide for those at its bottom end, so that even during a period when housing conditions for the majority of the people have been improving, the circumstances of the minority in greatest need have worsened."[5]

Nor, as it turned out, has this deterioration of the condition of the poor saved the government much money. It is true that, unlike the situation with social security and health spending, the Conservatives were able to achieve a steep cut in the budget for council housing by ending construction and by requiring rent increases. However, another item in the budget was for *housing benefit*, which contributed to welfare recipients' rents in council housing or elsewhere. So the saving in the housing budget was to a considerable extent offset by an increase in the social security budget.

On the whole, then, the Conservatives have gained some important political advantages on the housing issue. But homelessness and long waiting lists for council housing have created areas of vulnerability for the government.

CONCLUSION

Debates concerning the welfare state usually find the Conservatives on the defensive. On most of the issues the electorate accepts the arguments—put forward by Labour and the Liberal Democrats—that spending on social programs has been inadequate, and a majority even declare a willingness to support tax increases to pay for them.

Moreover, in addition to their problems with public opinion and opposition parties, the Conservatives must face well-organized and angry opposition from an extraordinary array of groups. As the welfare state has grown, it has generated interests committed to its defense and expansion; and the proposition of Sam Beer (noted in chapter 4) that Britain is in the grip of *pluralist stagnation* is in considerable part based on this perceived consequence of the welfare state. Although stagnation is far from an accurate description of the changes that Thatcher and Major have brought about, especially in the housing field, Beer's analysis does help us understand the difficulties encountered by the Conservatives in achieving more fundamental changes in social security and health.

But if Labour presently enjoys a political advantage on welfare state issues, this does not mean that it would continue to do so should it come back to power. The fundamental economic problem examined in chapter 13 remains—a rate of growth not fast enough to provide for all the demands on the system. Since 1949 the real (inflation-adjusted) cost of the various social security benefit programs has increased by 700 percent, and the welfare state's share of the national income has gone up from one-twentieth to one-quarter. As welfare costs continue to increase, it will be extraordinarily difficult to avoid imposing cuts—unless taxes are increased, and Labour has signaled its reluctance to impose any draconian increases.

Indeed, reductions in welfare programs are now being undertaken by other European countries, which have been among the leaders in providing welfare benefits. Germany, France, Italy, Belgium, and Denmark have all imposed at least modest reductions in some areas. Yet for Labour to follow these examples would be to throw away their greatest political asset and to reject the claims of the interest groups dedicated to the support of the welfare state—groups that are part of Labour's own natural constituency.

This is not to say that the task of maintaining a viable welfare state is impossible for Britain. For one thing, Britain—while spending somewhat more on the welfare state as a proportion of GNP (23 percent) than the United States (20 percent) or Japan (16 percent)—falls well below the levels of France (33 percent) or Germany (28 percent), let alone Sweden (39 percent). For another, a significant increase in productivity of the kind the Conservatives hope their policies will produce (and called for as well by Labour's Commission on Social Policy, albeit by somewhat different methods) could provide the necessary resources.

However, the funds required will be formidable, and the welfare state in Britain will be an arena of intense political controversy for decades to come. The health service in particular will be the focus of agonizing choices, as the increasing demands for new treatments will force doctors and hospitals to determine patient priorities (i.e., to ration patient care). Thus, whatever the party makeup of future governments in Britain, the issues discussed in this chapter will continue to be more sensitive and more politically explosive than seemed likely in the heady, creative atmosphere of the postwar Labour government.

SOME QUESTIONS TO THINK ABOUT

How would you compare the welfare state programs in Britain and the United States?

What do you think of the extent of inequality of wealth and income in Britain? How does Britain compare with the United States in this respect?

Why was it not possible for the Thatcher government to privatize the National Health Service? Would it be desirable to move to a private insurance program for the more affluent and limit the NHS to the lower income groups?

What are the arguments for and against the sale of council housing? Are the causes of homelessness the same in Britain and the United States? What should be done about it?

NOTES

1. Shirley Robin Letwin, *The Anatomy of Thatcherism* (Transaction, 1993), p. 33.
2. Commission on Social Justice, *Social Justice: Strategies for National Renewal* (Vintage, 1994), pp. 95–96.
3. *Income and Wealth* (Joseph Rowntree Foundation, 1995).
4. Letwin, *Anatomy of Thatcherism*, pp. 112–13.
5. Steve Platt in "Gimme Shelter," booklet included in *New Statesman and Society*, 2 April 1993, p. 5.

SUGGESTIONS FOR FURTHER READING

Studies on the welfare state include Rodney Lowe, *The Welfare State in Britain* (St. Martin's Press, 1993), and Paul Wilding (ed.), *In Defence of the Welfare State* (Manchester University Press, 1986). See also *Social Justice*, the 1994 report of the Commission on Social Justice, referred to in the text, and a proposal for fundamental reform of the welfare system by Labour M.P. Frank Field, *Making Welfare Work* (Institute for Community Studies, 1995). On poverty see Peter Townsend, *Poverty in the United Kingdom* (University of California Press, 1979), and Peter Alcock, *Poverty and State Support* (Longman, 1987). On housing see David Donnison and Clare Ungerson, *Housing Policy* (Penguin, 1982). On health see R. Klein, *The Politics of the National Health Service* (Longman, 1983).

15

EDUCATION

ACCESS AND QUALITY

In Britain as in the United States, "education is the answer" is a favorite catch phrase. Education, it appears, is the universal panacea for individual success, social harmony, and international competitiveness.

There is, of course, some truth in the assertion. But before we identify education as the answer, we must first see it as the focus of a number of questions. In fact, the debate about education takes us into many of the issues raised throughout this book—social class conflicts, public versus private provision, egalitarian versus meritocratic principles.

In the context of education, these issues illustrate contrasting perceptions, held by the rival British political parties, of what constitutes the good society. And once again we shall see that the party differences were held within a fairly narrow range from 1945 to 1979, but have become more contentious since then.

In our discussion of education we begin by exploring early, mainly secondary education, and then turn to higher education.

SECONDARY EDUCATION

Here we encounter two areas of political controversy—the first relating to the publicly provided state sector, the second to the private fee-paying sector commonly known as *public* or *independent* schools.

The State Schools

State-provided elementary education began in Britain with the Education Act of 1870; until then, there were only private and church schools. Another Education Act in 1902 gave local education authorities (LEAs) the power to create secondary and technical as well as elementary schools. Yet, despite further legislation, which made education compulsory until the age of 14, there were few secondary schooling opportunities for the mass of the people before the second World War. The minority who passed an examination at the age of 11 won a scholarship to go to a *grammar school*, usually to the age of 16. But the great majority of working-class children left when they reached 14.

The 1944 Education Act. The social ferment unleashed during the war led the coalition government to the passage of the Butler Education Act of 1944. Enacted by the Labour government elected in 1945, the Butler Act moved all students at the age of 11 into free secondary education in one of three kinds of schools—grammar schools for the high academic achievers, technical schools, and, for the rest, secondary modern schools. The act also provided public funding for church schools, the degree of government control depending on whether the schools were totally or only partially dependent on public support.

Following the passage of the act, the school-leaving age was raised—first to 15, then to 16—and the Labour government, and the Labour Party generally, had reason to be pleased with their accomplishment. The new structure combined the egalitarian, democratic principle of universal secondary education with the meritocratic notion of providing special opportunities to the talented. Yet disenchantment came with experience. Labour's base, the working class, was seeing its children continue at school until they reached 15 or 16; but most of them were in secondary modern or technical schools rather than grammar schools. Although the intent of the Butler Act was to give all three the same status, prestige adhered to the grammar schools, for they provided entry to white collar and professional careers. To qualify for a grammar school, the student must still pass the "11-plus" exam, and it was the children of the middle classes who, coming from homes with books and better-educated parents, made up the bulk of those passing the fateful exam.

Moreover, the assumption on which the exam was based was being brought under critical scrutiny. In particular, doubts were expressed about the findings of psychologist Cyril Burt, whose research had been used to justify the 11-plus exam. Burt's hypothesis was that intelligence is inherited, and that future potential can be determined with a high degree of accuracy at a very early age. Other researchers challenged Burt's view, which fell into disrepute when later investigations suggested that some of his data were invented.

The Comprehensive School. When a Labour government returned to power under Harold Wilson in 1964, a further transformation of secondary education took place. The *de facto* separation of working- and middle-class schooling was broken down by the replacement of most of the grammar and secondary modern schools with the *comprehensive school*, which is similar in concept to the U.S. high school.

The rise of the comprehensive schools at the expense of the secondary modern and grammar schools proceeded apace. Education Secretary Anthony Crosland, who had angered the left by insisting that socialism did not depend on nationalization, was anything but a right-winger on education. "If it's the last thing I do," he confided in his wife, "I'm going to destroy every ******* grammar school in England. And Wales. And Northern Ireland."[1] Accordingly, Labour governments required the LEAs to adopt the comprehensive model, and although Conservatives preferred to leave the decision to the localities, the transformation continued even when Margaret Thatcher was education secretary in Edward Heath's government. Today, the comprehensives teach over 90 percent of secondary school students in the state sector.

The Thatcher Policies. When she came to power in 1979, Margaret Thatcher was deeply unhappy about the state school system. She had been compelled as education secretary to go along with the LEAs' decisions to change grammar schools into comprehensives, but she had attended a grammar school herself, and her convictions told her that comprehensives promoted uniformity and, unlike the grammar schools, failed to nurture exceptional talent. Then, too, she disliked unions, and the teachers' unions were powerful, resistant to change, and constantly pressing for higher salaries—which would undermine the government's efforts to cut public spending. Moreover, many of the LEAs were dominated by representatives of the Labour party.

Finally, the performance of the state schools was deteriorating. This was not simply a Thatcherite perception; in 1976 Labour prime minister James Callaghan had spoken out against falling standards in the schools. International comparisons on math and science tests showed British children well behind those of other developed and developing countries—except the United States (see Table 15.1). Many explanations were offered; but Thatcherites, like conservatives in the United States, blamed the pernicious influence of John Dewey and progressive education.

Despite her strong feelings on the subject, Thatcher at first had other priorities to attend to, and during her first two terms there were only limited changes in education. The requirement on local authorities to change grammar schools to com-

TABLE 15.1 Scores on standardized math tests, 1990

	Age 13, Average Percent
France	64.0
Hungary	68.0
Italy	64.0
Korea	73.0
Switzerland	71.0
Taiwan	73.0
United Kingdom	59.5
United States	55.3

SOURCE: Adapted from National Institute of Economic and Social Research and *Financial Times*, 10 November 1993.

prehensives was countermanded. There were Education Acts in 1980, 1981, and 1986 that enlarged the influence of parents and gave them broader choice on where their children went to school. And strikes called by the teachers' unions achieved meager results in face of determined opposition by the government. But it was not until after her third election victory in 1987 that Thatcher turned her attention decisively to the issue of education.

The Education Reform Act of 1988 delegated decisions on budgets and enrollment size from the LEAs to the government body of each school and further broadened parental choice by setting up an open enrollment system. A still more radical option was available to parents: they could "opt out" of LEA control. This meant that, working with the headmaster, they could take over the governance of a school and still be "grant maintained" to the full extent by the government. An additional choice was made available by the act in the form of City Technology Colleges—secondary schools to be jointly funded by government and industry.

If these provisions of the 1988 act widened options at the local level, other clauses made clear the dominant authority of the central government in educational affairs. A national curriculum of ten subjects was to be inaugurated, and there would be compulsory national testing at the ages of 7, 11, and 14. Changes were also instituted in the process of testing performance at the completion of secondary education. Previously students worked to achieve "O-levels" in various subjects at the age of 16 (followed by "A-levels" for those who stayed on until they were 18). In 1988 the locally administered O-levels were replaced by a standard General Certificate of Secondary Education (GCSE).

The Major Administration. Thatcher's departure in 1990 came too early for the full implementation of her educational reforms. In fact, conservative analysts complained that local governments were hamstringing the process of opting out, and that educational administrators and academics were capturing the national curriculum for their own ideological purposes.

But if the opponents of Thatcher's educational ideas hoped that they would be shelved by her successor, they were doomed to disappointment. John Major took up with enthusiasm the notion that the central government must take vigorous steps to reverse the decline in the performance of the schools, that the keynote must be "back to basics," and that the basics could best be restored by a national curriculum, national testing, and the right to opt out. Each of these changes was the occasion of fierce controversy.

The national curriculum inevitably stirred strong arguments. Opponents noted that the British tradition was very different from that of France, where pupils were taught the same lesson in the same grade at the same time throughout the country. And agreement on a matter of such crucial importance must ultimately depend on a central government mandate. Nonetheless, the general alarm about the decline in standards, and the threat this represented to Britain's international competitiveness, led to a growing consensus that core subjects—English, math, and science—must be reemphasized in a curriculum that would also include design and technology, information technology, history, geography, modern foreign languages, art, music, and physical education (and in Wales starting in 1999, Welsh as a second language for students age 14 to 16). The Labour Party questioned the precise content of the curriculum but subscribed to this consensus, their education spokesperson conceding: "The national curriculum *is* a good thing. The Labour Party would have introduced it had we won the 1987 election; both parties should have done so in the 1960s as the comprehensive system was brought in."[2]

A more angry debate erupted over national testing. Critics protested that it was one thing to require the inclusion of Shakespeare in the national curriculum—including the study of three Shakespeare plays for 14-year-olds—and quite another to insist that 14-year-olds respond cogently to such exam questions as the following:

> In Julius Caesar act 2, scenes 2, 3 and 4, the audience is prepared for the dangerous and dreadful events to come. Show how the atmosphere of threat and tension is built up. How do Caesar's reactions to the other characters increase the suspense for the audience?

Moreover, the government proposed the publication of "league tables" comparing the performance of schools against each other. The critics argued that competitive tables were grossly misleading, for they did not take account of the differences in social background between advantaged and disadvantaged areas, between wealthy suburbs and poverty-stricken inner cities.

For some time the Labour Party included the fiercest critics. However, in the Tony Blair era, the party accepted the publication of results—as long as these included the social environment factor by focusing on the educational "value added" in each individual school. The government agreed to give consideration to this principle.

But then the practical problems of implementing the tests began to conflict with the government's plans; the six unions representing teachers protested that the administration of the tests imposed an intolerable burden on them and simply refused to perform them. Their position gained widespread public sympathy and even the support of some Conservative M.P.s. The government retreated and won the cooperation of the unions by simplifying the tests and reducing their number to the core subjects of English, math, and science (plus Welsh in Wales).

So the Conservatives had been compelled to modify their initial proposals and correct some errors in implementation, but had succeeded in forging a new consensus on the need for a national curriculum, testing, and the publication of test results.

However, opting out remained a divisive issue. For the Conservatives, the plan gave parents the opportunity to choose the best available education for their children and an opportunity to take control away from the LEA bureaucracies. On the other hand, Labour, most of the LEAs, and the teachers' unions saw opting out as a stratagem to enable middle-class parents to remove their children from contact with the working class and racial minorities, leaving many of the LEA schools composed almost entirely of socially (and therefore educationally) disadvantaged children.

Despite strong pressure from the department of education, the process of opting out progressed more slowly than the government had hoped, and parents in many areas voted against the proposal. However, by the end of 1993, the number of schools moving out from LEA control had exceeded 1,000. Then in 1994, Labour's opposition to the idea was undercut when Tony Blair and his wife decided to send their 10-year-old son to a grant-maintained Catholic school instead of a comprehensive school closer to their home in London. Many middle-class parents would sympathize with the wish to provide the best possible education for one's children, and the Blairs were in fact remaining within the state system, rather than choosing an independent, fee-supported school. Still, the party's opposition to opting out would not henceforth carry much conviction, and Labour's leadership moved to defuse the issue by indicating that, although a Labour government would give back to the LEAs responsibility for funding and regulating all state schools, grant-maintained schools would not be abolished, and both types of schools would be given a high degree of autonomy.

Consequently, in 1995 Labour concentrated its main educational attack on two of the party's prime issues—inequality and the underfunding of vital public services. The government announced a pay increase for teachers averaging 2.7 percent, and Tony Blair accused the government of doing nothing "about the head of a privatized utility awarding himself 70 times as much as a teacher . . . " Moreover, even the 2.7 percent would not be fully funded by the government, which offered an increase of only 1.1 percent to local education authorities. So Blair charged that the LEAs would have to lay off teachers and raise class sizes, and teachers threatened strikes against the imposition of larger classes.

Thus, the Conservative government had succeeded in muting the controversies over some of its educational policies, but, given its general economic and financial strategies, could not hope to remove its handling of the state schools from the partisan battle.

The "Public" Schools

Around seven percent of British children are educated outside the state system in one of about 2,250 fee-paying or "public" schools, some taking only boarders, some only day students, others accepting both.

The top boarding schools are extremely expensive. Harrow charges about £12,000 a year, Eton and Roedean (an all-girls school) almost as much. This money does not provide a life of comfort for the students, for public schools do not pamper their young charges, no matter how aristocratic their families. Though some look back to their public school days with nostalgia, a number of memoirs, plays, and novels have given us bitter accounts of harsh treatment and sadistic masters. Thus a headmaster at Eton in the late 1960s is reported to have greatly enjoyed inflicting savage beatings with strap or cane on the boys' bare backsides, once administering lashings to 20 students in his divinity class in a single afternoon. Then there was the Briton who had spent five years incarcerated in Iran on a spying charge, and explained on his release that he "felt quite at home in a Third World prison" having been educated at a British public school, then served in the ranks of the British army.

Though conditions in those schools have been reformed since that era, the experience they provide remains spartan.

The public schools in the top tier generally set the pattern for the lesser schools in the private sector, though they lack the exotic aura and tradition of the more famous institutions. And while others are somewhat less expensive than the elite schools, all, including the day schools, charge substantial fees. Cost increases in recent years led to a slight decline in private sector enrollment during 1993 and 1994. Even so, many middle-class and wealthy parents continue to pay the fees for various reasons.

First, although many of the comprehensive schools provide a first-rate education, others have suffered from the deterioration discussed previously; also, British private schools generally offer smaller classes, more resources, and no doubt a generally greater capacity to prepare students for the kind of Shakespeare test cited above. Second, the Thatcher tax and economic policies generated sufficiently higher incomes for a section of the middle class to enable them to afford the fees. Third, private education is higher-status education. This is especially true of the most expensive boarding schools; as we saw in chapter 2, Eton, Harrow, Winchester, and the rest carry vast prestige and enhanced opportunities to enter Oxbridge and the upper strata of the professions, finance, and politics. Indeed, as we saw in chapter 2, they are pivotal contributors to the survival (albeit in somewhat diminished condition) of the Establishment.

Party Policies.   This is one area in which there are no divisions within the Conservative party. The Tory grandees are mostly graduates of the most prestigious of the public schools. Thatcher was not. She is the product of a grammar school and has been withering in her attacks on many Establishment bastions. But she has been a staunch defender of the public schools, and so has John Major, another non-public-school type. Thus Thatcher and Major have supported the special, tax-exempt status of the independent schools. They also provided expanding support for the *assisted places scheme*, which made it possible for bright but impecunious students to attend an independent school. By 1993 this provided close to £100 million to pay the fees of some 30,000 students.

One would expect the Labour Party, on the other hand, to attack the public schools as embodying the system of class privilege the party was created to oppose. Indeed, animus toward these schools has always been widespread among rank-and-file Labour Party members, and has been expressed periodically within the party. Yet only in the quixotically radical party manifesto of 1983 did Labour officially attack the public schools. That manifesto, defining private schools as "a major obstacle to a free and fair education system" demanded the end of the assisted places scheme and of their tax exemption, and the imposition of VAT on their fees. Fees would, in fact, be phased out, and the schools would be integrated "within the local authority sector where necessary."

But that was 1983; the manifesto tone in 1987 was more subdued. The call now was only to "stop the diverting of precious resources that occurs through the assisted places scheme and the public subsidies to private schools." The 1992 manifesto continued the call to end the assisted places scheme, though it provided for a phaseout that would not affect students presently admitted through the program.

The assisted places scheme was a natural target for Labour. Originally propounded as a means of providing opportunities to the children of lower-income people, the program was supporting mostly the children of the middle class. Only 10 percent came from manual working-class families; 60 percent were from the white-collar and professional classes.

Yet the survival of the public schools did not depend on the assisted places scheme, and by 1987 it was *only* this scheme—not the system as a whole—that was being targeted by Labour. In part, this lack of ardor for radical reform might be explained by the fact that several Labour leaders have themselves been public school products. This was true of Clem Attlee and some of his top cabinet members, of Attlee's successor as party leader, Hugh Gaitskell, and of Richard Crossman among others in later Labour governments; Tony Blair went to a Scottish public school. On the other hand, Harold Wilson and James Callaghan went to state schools, as did Neil Kinnock and most of the people around him.

But after 1983, although there were few lingering loyalties to public schools among the Labour leaders, moderation was to become the keynote of the party's appeal to the public. The graduates of independent schools or parents of children attending them constituted a small segment of the public, but they occupied a number of key positions in the media and other institutions that could help or harm Labour. Moreover, Labour was increasing its support among the professional classes; and among them were several who either sent their children to independent schools or were thinking of it. They tended to be readers of the mildly leftish *Guardian* newspaper, and the *Guardian* carried advertisements for private schools.

So if the Labour Party comes to power again, the public schools may see the assisted places scheme cut or phased out. Conceivably their exemption from having to pay Value Added Tax (VAT) could also come under scrutiny. But when the possibility of repealing the VAT exemption was raised by the Labour education spokesperson, David Blunkett, in late 1994, he was publicly rebuked by Blair and forced to repudiate his statement. He had not discussed the idea with other party leaders, and Blair was unwilling at this stage to commit to any increase in taxes, even on the most privileged members of society.

However, with or without assisted places, and even if they have to pay VAT, most of the public schools will survive. Their importance may not be as great in the future as in the past. A study by Leslie Hannah, a professor of business history, has found that since 1979, the number of chairs of the top 50 business companies educated at public schools has been cut almost in half, while the number from state schools went up from 14 to 25, and 6 others came from grammar schools. "Britain," said Hannah, "used to have an unusually uneducated business elite, which may be one of the reasons for our poor economic performance." But that has changed and changed permanently: "There is no likelihood of companies going back to selection by the old school tie."[3] Even so, many affluent parents will continue to believe that sending their children to an independent school will give them an important advantage in life; and in the light of our earlier discussions of governmental and other institutions, that belief is still not at all unreasonable.

HIGHER EDUCATION

Even more than secondary education, *universities* were the preserve of a wealthy elite until well into the twentieth century.

When the century began, there were only twelve universities in the United Kingdom, the oldest and most prestigious being Oxford and Cambridge. Most of the universities' finances came from endowments—some of the Oxford colleges being especially wealthy—and student fees.

Of the 20,000 or so students attending, all but a small minority of scholarship students were the sons (for not many daughters went to college) of affluent parents. Some took their education seriously, others treated it as an amusing rite of passage, an opportunity for a year or two of wild partying before having to get down to the serious business of life. Evelyn Waugh's depiction of undergraduate life at Oxbridge between the world wars in *Brideshead Revisited* is partly caricature, but it is revealing nonetheless of a kind of upper-class hooliganism no less obnoxious than that later associated with working-class soccer fans.

Expansion

Yet the undergraduate culture Waugh described was already changing. Higher education was increasingly entering the aspirations of the middle class. Performance on rigorous entrance examinations was taking the place of family connection for university admission. And universities were becoming more dependent on government money.

After the second world war these considerations became increasingly potent. Oxford and Cambridge, with a few other leading universities, maintained their dominant position through their control of the university grants committee, which allocated the government funds. But newer universities—known as the *red bricks*, for they lacked the ancient spires and spacious lawns of Oxbridge—were expanding and growing restive at their less advantaged status and finances.

The expansion accelerated from the mid-1960s, and by the time Margaret Thatcher came to power there were 47 British universities. In addition there were 30 polytechnics—originally purely technical institutions, which had developed into degree-granting institutions covering a full range of subjects—as well as a number of teachers colleges. Altogether, by 1980 close to 600,000 students were enrolled full-time in higher education, with another 350,000 attending part-time.

Changes in Student Composition

With the increased numbers came a major change in the class and sex composition of the student bodies. Though Eton, Harrow, Winchester, and the other exclusive public schools continued to be disproportionately represented at Oxbridge, the student body at the leading universities was no longer overwhelmingly upper-class. And although there were still a few Oxbridge colleges with all female students, there were none for males only. In fact, enrollments by women were rapidly catching up with the numbers of men students. However, the democratization of the universities did not extend much beyond the middle classes. Some academically talented children of the working class did go on to a university, even to Oxbridge. Money was not a serious deterrent, for every British student accepted by a university had his or her fees paid by the government, and for most students financial aid was provided for living costs (the amount depending on parental income). Nonetheless, the proportion enrolled in higher education fell at each stage down the social class scale from *A* to *E*.

Even the Open University, invented by Harold Wilson's Labour government, had only limited success in attracting working class people. The Open University was designed to provide access to a university education for working adults through correspondence study supplemented by television and radio courses, summer residential institutes, and local learning centers. From the outset it was an extremely successful enterprise, emulated in several other countries, and attracting large enrollments to programs of high quality. Yet although a substantial number of those enrolled were blue-collar workers, they were considerably outnumbered by people with white collar jobs.

But if the middle classes were the prime beneficiaries of the expansion of higher education in the 1960s and 1970s, even their needs for higher education were far from satiated. Compared with the previous British experience, the expansion was impressive; but comparisons with several other European countries, let alone the United States, showed the British to be lagging far behind in the proportion of college-age students enrolled in higher education.

A compensating factor was quality. Even with the growth in numbers, universities in Britain remained highly selective and provided an elite education for their undergraduates. It is true that the students tended to be rather narrowly gauged. From the age of 16 most college-bound students in England and Wales (though not in Scotland) had to choose between humanities and science curricula. At 18 or so they sat for their "A levels" in their chosen fields, and the results of these written exams, combined with special entrance exams and interviews for the more selective institutions, provided the basis for university admission. At the university they specialized still further, concentrating in a narrow cluster of subjects without the breadth requirements of a typical U.S. university.

But within this severe limit the requirements were rigorous. Progress was tested not course-by-course but with periodic comprehensive examinations. Students were expected to graduate in three years within the institution that admitted them (for the absence of transferable course units made it difficult to move from one university to another). And graduation rates were considerably higher than in the United States and elsewhere.

This, then, was the system prevailing when Thatcher became prime minister. It was a system that had been shaped by bipartisan efforts. The expansion of the 1960s was spurred by a 1963 report commissioned by the Conservative government of Harold Macmillan and written by Lionel Robbins, a free-market economist. The report was acted upon by the Labour government of Harold Wilson; Wilson's administration inaugurated the University of the Air, which became the Open University; however, the Open University was still in its early developmental stages when Wilson lost to Heath in 1970, so much of the credit for the institution's survival and growth must be assigned to Heath's Conservative government and his Education Secretary, Margaret Thatcher.

Thatcher versus the Universities

As in so many other areas, the post-1945 consensus on higher education did not appeal to Margaret Thatcher as prime minister, even though as education minister she had played an active role in putting it into effect. She now saw the universities, especially Oxbridge, as a major element in the complacent Establishment that had presided over the country's decline. British university education, she believed, was extravagantly expensive, its administration grossly inefficient, its content—in the sciences as well as the humanities—largely impractical, its culture stuffy and elitist.

So she set about the task of shaking up academia. Government funding was reduced; the universities could make up for this, she proposed, by raising more money from alumni and business corporations, and by replacing a portion of student grants with loans. The University Grants Committee was abolished, replaced by a body not controlled by Oxbridge, and funds were to be allocated by new criteria related on the one hand to internal efficiency and on the other in response to national economic needs. Plans were prepared to end the status discrimination against polytechnics by renaming them as universities. Faculty tenure—lifetime security of employment after an initial trial period—was abolished for all new appointees. Instead there were fixed contracts renewable after a limited number of years.

The response was furious. Thousands of students marched in demonstrations against the shift from grants to loans; and Keith Joseph, Thatcher's ideological guru and education secretary, withdrew the proposal after bitter complaints from Conservative M.P.s responding to their outraged middle-class constituents. Faculty resentment, especially intense at Oxbridge, led so many to depart for greener pastures in the United States that people began to speak of a damaging *brain drain* from Britain.

The confrontation between academia and government took on a particularly harsh tone when the Oxford faculty voted to overturn an offer of an honorary degree extended by the university to Thatcher, who had graduated from Oxford with a degree in chemistry. The invitation had previously been extended to any prime minister who was an Oxford graduate, but the enraged faculty members refused to be bound by precedents—and the most vociferous in demanding the withdrawal of the invitation were the scientists, who had not previously been known for their political activism.

To some extent, Thatcher was bearing the brunt of resistance to changes that would have come about under any other political leader. British university education—especially Oxford and Cambridge's one-on-one tutorial method—was extremely expensive, and continued expansion would be possible only if costs came down. There was a good deal of room for improvement in university administration. Sooner or later student grants were bound to be supplemented by loans. (When the proposal was resubmitted later it passed with much less furor.) Alumni who had prospered after receiving a free education could reasonably be pressured to give something back to their university. Corporations whose managerial and technical staff had been educated by the universities, and which benefited from university research, ought to contribute comparably to their counterparts in the United States. A case could be made that the curriculum in the older universities tended to overemphasize the classics, and Britain was more successful in producing Nobel prize winners and cultivated diplomats than generating industrial innovations.

But if part of the resistance to Thatcher's policies was based on academia's reluctance to accept the inevitability of change, much of it was also a reaction to her confrontational style, the public disdain she poured on individuals and institutions of high and well-deserved reputations, and the philistinism of her scornful references to the allegedly impractical nature of much of the work of the universities. In the words of Shirley Robin Letwin, otherwise an admirer of Thatcher: "The fundamental commitment of Britain to promoting the vigorous virtues and a flourishing Britain does not imply that universities should be treated as a training ground for industry."[4]

Higher Education under Major

Under John Major (who did not go to a university) the government's relationship with the universities was not as abrasive as it had been under Thatcher. The broad outlines of her policies continued, however. Faculty tenure was not restored. In fact, starting in 1995, independent teams of assessors were to grade university departments on six criteria—including teaching—and teachers judged incompetent were to be given one year to improve or face dismissal; and, as is the case for secondary schools, "league tables" comparing the performance of universities were to be published.

Moreover, universities were encouraged to engage in vigorous fundraising from industry and alumni (and Oxford responded with successful efforts in Japan and the United States). Administrative efficiency and relationships with industry were still emphasized. The polytechnics became universities—though there was still a pecking order among universities, headed by Oxford, Cambridge, London, and Edinburgh. Student loans were in wide use, and demand would increase in response to a 30 percent cut in grants, to take effect over three years, announced in 1994. Loans must be repaid within five years of graduation unless the graduate is earning less than 85 percent of the average wage, and the government agency administering the loans estimated that by 1997 almost a half-million students might be liable to prosecution for defaulting on repayments.

One feature of the later Thatcher years was taken up with particular enthusiasm. She had pressed the universities to raise their enrollments by using their funding more efficiently. Major's administration, believing that Britain's ability to compete internationally was heavily dependent on expanded higher education, set about the task of securing a dramatic increase in enrollments. In 1979, only one in eight students went on from secondary to higher education. By 1991 the figure was one in five. The target set by Major's government, for the year 2000, was one in three. Progress toward this goal was so rapid that by the fall of 1993 the government was proposing to set limits that would prevent some qualified students from being admitted; and in 1994 there were 400,000 applicants for 270,000 university places.

Expansion on this scale could not be accomplished without major changes in the style of university education. Increasingly, higher education in Britain has been undergoing a process that some observers describe as Americanization—the use of modular courses and accumulation of course units, the preoccupation with grades, the adoption of a semester calendar, and the need by many students to take a job to pay their way through college.

CONCLUSION

Britain is faced with a number of urgent problems in the field of education. First there is the need to bring secondary school performance in the core subjects up to that of other industrial nations. Both the Labour and Conservative parties, while arguing over issues like the right of schools to "opt out" and assisted places for independent schools, accept the commitment to upgrading standards. There is agreement, too, on the need to provide universal nursery education as the foundation for elementary and secondary education (the Conservatives proposing to introduce this with a voucher system applicable to either public or private nursery schools).

The rapid expansion of higher education has also been achieved with bipartisan support. Thatcher's abrasive treatment provoked angry responses from the universities, but most of the changes she instituted have survived and are not subject to attack by the opposition parties. In Britain as in the United States, the problem will be how to move from elite to mass higher education without seriously compromising quality.

A consensus is also emerging that more effective programs must be developed to provide craft training for the majority that will not be going to college; only one-third of Britain's workforce have attained a vocational qualification, compared with Germany's three-quarters, and less than one-fifth have an intermediate qualification in Britain, compared with one-third in France and over one-half in Germany. Accompanying the needed vocational training and apprenticeship programs, a further expansion of Britain's already sizeable adult education programs will be needed to provide the continuous retraining and upgrading that the workforce of the future will require; indeed Labour's Commission on Social Justice argued that achieving the highly productive Britain they envisioned depended on transforming education into a process of "lifelong learning."[5]

Given the inadequate economic growth that was the main theme of chapter 13, it will be difficult to assign to education the additional resources that are clearly needed. Yet if these are not provided as the seed corn for Britain's future, it is questionable that Britain can maintain, let alone improve, her position in the global economy.

SOME QUESTIONS TO THINK ABOUT

How similar are Britain's secondary education problems to those in the United States? What are the causes of their problems?

Are there counterparts in the United States to the British proposals for a national curriculum and testing?

Do private schools in the United States perform a similar function to the British "public" schools? What do you think of the assisted places program?

To what extent is there a U.S. counterpart to Oxbridge?

Can the expansion of British higher education be accomplished without a decline in standards?

NOTES

1. Susan Crosland, *Tony Crosland* (Jonathan Cape, 1982), p. 148.
2. Jack Straw, "Education: The 'C' word appeal," *New Statesman and Society*, 24 July 1982, p. 15.
3. *Times*, 11 November 1993.
4. *The Anatomy of Thatcherism* (Fontana, 1992), p. 275.
5. Commission on Social Justice, *Social Justice*, pp. 119-50.

SUGGESTIONS FOR FURTHER READING

For the pre-Thatcher education system, see Maurice Kogan, *The Politics of Educational Change* (Fontana, 1978). The Butler act changes through the early Thatcher period are covered in P. H. G. H. Gosden, *The Education System Since 1944* (Martin Robertson, 1983). For the Thatcher changes, see S. Maclure, *Education Re-formed: A Guide to the Education Reform Act* (Hodder and Stoughton, 1989). Patrick Ainley, *Degrees of Difference: Higher Education in the 1990s* (Lawrence and Wishart, 1994), explores the uneasy status relationships between the former polytechnics and the older universities. For general coverage on education see the *Times Educational Supplement*.

16

RACE AND GENDER

❖ ❖ ❖ ❖ ❖ ❖ ❖ ❖ ❖ ❖ ❖ ❖ ❖ ❖ ❖

HOW MUCH DISCRIMINATION?

Two kinds of discrimination have become significant political issues in Britain, and are likely to become even more so in the years ahead. The first, directed at non-whites, is of much more recent vintage and involves smaller minority populations than in the United States, but has been growing in intensity nonetheless. The second concerns the majority of the British population, women, who have been making important gains economically and politically, but are still well short of achieving equality in several respects.

RACE

Immigration

Until the 1950s, there was no race problem in Britain. Racism, most Britons believed, was an American affliction. But if the British were not racist, it was essentially because there was only one race. There were very few blacks in Britain, though there are records of some having been brought over during the Roman occupation, and later small numbers of sailors from the West Indies and Africa settled in British coastal cities. But, except for Chinese who ran laundries and small restaurants, almost all the rest—descendants of Celts, Romans, Anglo-Saxons, Normans, and Jews—were white.

For the children of the British upper class, the conquest of empire opened up political, military, and commercial positions in nonwhite countries, and there racism was part of the everyday life of colonialism. But within Britain itself, most of the population had little if any direct contact with people of other races, and the stereotypes of black people came largely from Hollywood movies: shambling clowns, faithful slaves in *Gone With the Wind*, or cannibalistic African tribesmen. The only positive images were conveyed by African American musical stars like Duke Ellington and Louis Armstrong; but even there Britishers, like white Americans, doted on Al Jolson singing *Mammy* in black face.

Then starting in the late 1940s, numbers of nonwhite people began arriving in Britain. They came from the West Indies and Africa, and then from the Indian subcontinent—countries that had been part of the British Empire and became members of the Commonwealth as they gained independence. As citizens of the Commonwealth they had the right, confirmed by the British Nationality Act of 1948, to settle in the United Kingdom and become British citizens. Many of the West Indians, in particular, had fought in the British services during the war, spoke English, and identified with Britain.

At first there seemed a perfect match of supply and demand. The immigrants came from poor countries seeking jobs. And there was a labor shortage in Britain, so jobs were available on buses and the subway (the underground), as hospital orderlies, and in unskilled and semiskilled work in clothing factories and foundries.

Altogether there were only about 200,000 nonwhite immigrants by 1951. But then the influx began to increase, and concentrations of nonwhites appeared in a few of the major cities. The labor shortage eased. Competition developed among the working class not only for jobs but for scarce housing. Tensions grew, and in the Notting Hill district of London a race riot erupted in 1958. This was a warning sign of problems to come, for nonwhite immigration jumped suddenly at the end of the 1950s, growing from 20,000 in 1959 to 136,000 in 1961.

The Evolving Party Consensus. The first political reaction came when the Conservative government passed the 1962 Immigration Act. This restricted entry from Commonwealth countries to dependents of residents, students, or those with the promise of a job.

The Labour Party called the bill racist and promised they would repeal it when they came back to power. But in the 1964 election Labour's designated foreign secretary, Patrick Gordon Walker, was defeated by a candidate running on an anti-immigration platform. Gordon Walker ran again in a by-election; again the immigration issue was raised against him; again he lost. Two or three other seats in 1964 were lost on the same issue. The new Labour government, with a slim majority in Parliament, took alarm. Opinion polls indicated that 80 percent of the voters believed too many immigrants were being allowed to enter. The government announced that it would renew the Conservatives' law and intended to strengthen it. They did so with the Commonwealth Immigrants Act of 1968. This took away the automatic right of entry to anyone *who did not have a parent or grandparent born in Britain*. All others would have to apply for one of the 7,500 vouchers issued annually.

This established a clear distinction between the whites from Australia, New Zealand, and Canada (the "Old Commonwealth" countries), most of whom could claim the "patrial" connection, and the nonwhite holders of British passports from the "New Commonwealth" countries. Among those in the latter category, who would have to compete for the 7,500 vouchers each year, were Asians being expelled from the newly independent Kenya. The previous Conservative government had promised these Asians entry to Britain when the time came; Labour was now reneging on that promise. Further restrictions came in a 1969 law setting up cumbersome bureaucratic procedures governing appeals to those refused entry.

The Conservatives were anxious not to be outflanked on the issue, and raised no objection to Labour's repudiating the promise the Conservatives had made to the Kenyan Asians. However, Enoch Powell, a classical scholar and right-wing member of the Conservative front bench, went too far for the party's leadership with a speech complaining of "wide-eyed grinning pickaninnies," and citing the words of a senator of ancient Rome who raised the specter of the River Tiber "foaming with much blood." Powell called for voluntary, subsidized repatriation of the arrivals from the New Commonwealth. The Conservative leader, Edward Heath, expressed outrage at Powell's language and proposals and expelled him from the front bench. Right-wing groups in the Conservative Party rallied to Powell's support. So did a contingent of London dock workers, who went on strike and marched to Westminster to express their approval of Powell's position.

After that, although there was no talk by either party's leaders of sending the immigrants back, a further tightening came with the Heath government's 1971 Immigration Act. (This act, however, did allow British citizens expelled from Uganda to come to the United Kingdom, unlike those who had been thrown out of Kenya.) When Labour won again, it approved a slight increase in the number of vouchers, and halted the virginity tests imposed by the previous government on women seeking entry. But Labour's basically restrictive position on immigration had already been established in the 1968 legislation, and the differences between the parties moved within a narrow, essentially consensual range.

Even so, when Margaret Thatcher became Conservative Party leader, she voiced continued anxiety about the rate of immigration and spoke of bringing it completely to an end. She said in a television interview in 1978 that otherwise, "the British character . . . might be swamped." The left attacked her for what they saw as demagoguery. But the polls reflected strong approval of her position, and James Callaghan, in an interview before the 1979 election, hastened to assure the public that the Labour party was just as tough on immigration as the Conservatives.

Once in office, the Thatcher administration introduced stricter legislation and tightened administrative requirements. Henceforth there was to be a clear distinction between British citizens, who had unqualified rights of entry, and British overseas citizens from the New Commonwealth countries, with very limited entry rights. "Genetic" fingerprinting was used to establish the legitimacy of claims for entry; visa requirements were introduced for people from the Indian subcontinent and some

African countries; fines were imposed on airlines bringing passengers without proper papers. Then the 1988 Immigration Act removed the automatic right of pre-1973 immigrants to bring in their dependents. Now they were required to prove that they could house and support them. Grounds for appeal against deportation were severely limited, and all claims to British citizenship had to be established before traveling.

Labour attacked these measures, and in a 1980 statement promised a much more liberal immigration policy. Yet even in its radical left manifesto for the 1983 election, the party did not call for an end to immigration controls, only for some modest adjustments. And in their 1987 manifestos, the Conservatives called for "firm and fair immigration controls," Labour was for "firm but fair immigration controls," and the centrist Alliance asked that "immigration control . . . should be fair."

Within this "firm and fair" or "firm but fair" consensus there was room only for rather constricted areas of disagreement. First there were specific opposition complaints about harsh treatment of individuals by immigration officials and police. Thus in 1993 a Jamaican woman, ordered to be deported as an illegal immigrant, died after police officers restrained her with a leather belt, handcuffs, and a mouth gag. A furor erupted and three officers were suspended. But the reports in the tabloids echoed widespread anti-immigration sentiment. The *Daily Express* called the police suspensions "a victory for the mob," and *The Sun*'s comment on the dead woman was: "If she had complied with the deportation order she might be alive today."[1]

Then there were partisan differences over the Conservative government's legislation to offer British citizenship to 225,000 residents of Hong Kong fearful of the impending takeover in 1997 by the Chinese People's Republic. Labour claimed the plan was elitist, for it limited the opportunity mostly to business and professional people. (However, Labour was not proposing to extend the privilege to the rest of the Hong Kong population.) Labour protested again when the government announced in 1994 that the immigration laws would be amended to allow any foreigner willing to invest £750,000 in U.K. stocks and shares to live in Britain for a year.

The British also took steps to address the problem experienced by most of the world's affluent countries in the 1990s—the large increase in the number of seekers of asylum. In 1991, with applications running at the rate of 1,000 per week, an asylum bill was passed with the aim of cutting down on this potential new wave of immigration.

Finally, John Major's home secretary, Michael Howard, responding to pressures from Conservative M.P.s concerned over the weakening of internal border controls in the European Union, prepared new measures in 1995 to curb illegal immigration. Included were proposals (similar to those under consideration in the United States) to require employers to check the immigrant status of prospective employees; to deny welfare benefits, student loans, and free medical care to suspected illegal immigrants; and to tighten up still further on the right of asylum.

Race Relations

Despite the severe restrictions on immigration imposed in legislation from 1962 onward, Britain is no longer a single-race country. The proportion of nonwhites is much less than in the United States; still, there were more than one million immigrants from the New Commonwealth countries by 1970. Their natural increase, supplemented by the arrival of dependents and others, raised the numbers to over three million by the mid-1990s, about 5.5 percent of the total population of England, Scotland, and Wales.

It has been the common practice to define all those deriving from the New Commonwealth countries as *blacks* and to group them together for reporting purposes. Yet there are considerable variations among the populations from different countries. Table 16.1 suggests the diversity of the nonwhite population in contemporary Britain.

Those from the Indian subcontinent tend to have stronger families; Pakistani families, in particular, often work together in running small neighborhood grocery stores. And increasing numbers of Asians have been moving into the professional and entrepreneurial middle classes.

Still, the majority of nonwhites tend to be disadvantaged in several respects. Their income is lower than the average, a considerable proportion living below the poverty level. They are more likely than whites to work in blue-collar, lower-skilled jobs. The unemployment rate among those of West Indian and Indian backgrounds has been double the rate of white workers, and among people of Pakistani or Bangladeshi parentage, the unemployment rate is triple that for whites. Educationally, while those of African and Indian backgrounds are actually more likely than whites to stay in full-time education after the age of 16, Afro-Caribbeans are somewhat below the average for whites in this respect, Pakistanis still further below, and Bangladeshis far below the national average.

Moreover, the disadvantages of the newcomers are exacerbated by prejudice and discrimination. Although their numbers are smaller than in the United States, and there is none of the almost total racial segregation of many American cities, nonwhites in Britain are mostly concentrated in particular areas, especially in parts of the bigger cities. And they have arrived in a fairly short span of time amid a rather provincial population to whom the lifestyles and folkways of the immigrants seemed strange, disorienting, distinctly un-*British*.

In the past, Britain had been hospitable to refugees practicing oppressed religions, including the Huguenots from France in the seventeenth century and the Russian and east European Jews from the late nineteenth century. It is true that there

TABLE 16.1 Nonwhite British residents, 1994

	Percent of Great Britain Population
Black Caribbean	0.9
Black African	0.4
Other Black	0.3
Indian	1.5
Pakistani	0.9
Bangladeshi	0.3
Chinese	0.3
Other	0.9
Total	5.5

SOURCE: Adapted from *Social Trends*.

was a good deal of anti-Semitism among all classes of the population, and a virulent strain was injected by Sir Oswald Mosley's black-shirted Fascist Party in the 1930s. And there was even allegations that members of the large immigrant population from Ireland suffered from prejudice and discrimination; thus a London police inspector complained to an industrial tribunal in 1994 that he was blackballed for promotion because he was Irish. (The Commission for Racial Equality has proposed that the Irish be considered a separate ethnic group.)

But, whatever their ethnicity, all of these were *white* immigrant populations, and the resistance to them was relatively minor. The reaction to people of color, including large numbers of Muslims—who built impressive mosques and demanded special privileges for their religion—was of a very different order.

So racism grew, taking various forms, some of them particularly ugly. Soccer hooligans took delight in hurling racial epithets and sometimes rocks and bottles at black players. Nonwhites accused the police of discourteous, even brutal treatment. Given the very small numbers of nonwhites on the police forces, and the relatively high rates of crime in the inner cities, a lack of racial sensitivity was not surprising. The National Front, a successor to Mosley's Fascist Party, stirred up hostility to nonwhites and won two local council seats by a blatantly racist appeal. In 1993, another neofascist group, the British National Party, won a council city in a working-class district of London, building on resentments directed at the Asian immigrant population among unemployed whites—though the seat was lost to Labour in the next election. Government statistics in 1993 indicated a sharp increase in the number of racially inspired attacks on blacks and Asians. An opinion poll in 1991 indicated that Britain was viewed as a racist society by 79 percent of blacks, 56 percent of Asians, and 67 percent of whites.

The combination of material disadvantages and racial prejudice proved to be, in Britain as in the United States, an explosive mixture. Riots erupted in Brixton, London, in 1981, followed in later years by others in Manchester, Liverpool, Birmingham, Bristol, and Brixton again. Then in June 1995 Pakistani youths rioted in the northern city of Bradford. The upheavals were not exclusively racial, for often white youths joined the smashing of shop windows and looting. But predominately these were race-centered upheavals, and, as in the United States, they usually started with an incident involving the police trying to arrest a nonwhite person on a street in a depressed area.

After the first Brixton riot a prominent judge, Lord Scarman, was asked to undertake an investigation of its causes. His analysis put a large part of the blame on unemployment, poor housing, inadequate education, and discrimination. Rectifying the situation, said Scarman, would require active government policies and the use, at least for a time, of *positive discrimination* (a British version of affirmative action). The analysis and the recommendations were remarkably similar to those put forward in 1968 by the Kerner Commission in its report on the urban riots in the United States.

Labour and the Race Relations Acts.   There were two reasons why the Labour Party would subscribe to the kind of ideas presented in the Scarman report. First, even the party's moderate leaders were embarrassed by the readiness with which Labour, the socialist champion of the underdog, had vied with the Conservatives to shut out people of color from the poor nations of the Commonwealth. Strong denunciations of the National Front were hardly sufficient to satisfy their conscience.

Conscience was fortified by pragmatic politics. Once the immigrants were citizens they were potential voters; economically they fitted into Labour's normal voter profile; and in a small but growing number of constituencies, they were sufficiently concentrated to constitute a substantial proportion of the total vote.

So in 1965 Harold Wilson's government passed the Race Relations Act, which declared discrimination on grounds of "race, color, ethnic, or national origin" to be unlawful in public places such as hotels, restaurants, and transportation, and established conciliation machinery to deal with complaints of discrimination. This was strengthened by further Labour government legislation in 1968 (the year Labour tightened the anti-immigration laws) and 1976. These laws extended the antidiscrimination provisions to housing and employment; made it a criminal offense to publish or distribute material likely to encourage racial hatred; established the Commission for Racial Equality; and allowed individuals to take their case directly to a county court or industrial tribunal.

Initially the laws were criticized for having weak enforcement provisions and for the very low level of awards made to successful claimants. In time, however, the laws began to make a difference. Thus in 1993 an industrial tribunal ordered a textile firm, which maintained separate shifts of white and Asian workers, to pay the Asians over £200,000 because, unlike the whites, they were not paid for overtime, had fewer vacation days, and were given no promotion opportunities. And a county police force, failing to make good on a promise to eliminate racism after a tribunal had found it guilty of discrimination, was ordered to pay a Sikh police constable £25,000 for twice being denied promotion to sergeant.

These awards were far from convincing the ethnic minorities that the law was on their side. In fact, in 1994 Lord Taylor, the Lord Chief Justice, declared that the criminal justice system was failing blacks and Asians by tolerating racist attitudes and allowing minorities to believe they were outside the law's protection. Nonetheless, the race relations laws, together with a number of other administrative actions by Labour governments to protect minority rights, helped win the support of a majority of nonwhite voters. The 1987 Parliament included four nonwhites, all of them Labour; and of the six nonwhites winning seats in the 1992 election, five were Labour.

However, the race issue was not without its complications for Labour. In the early 1980s there was pressure from black activists in the party, supported by the hard left, for the establishment of a black section. This was resisted as separatism by the party's leadership, which would concede no more than the establishment of a black and Asian advisory committee.

A further source of confusion in Labour's ranks was the growth of Muslim fundamentalism, particularly in parts of northern England where there were substantial numbers of people of Asian origin. There were demands for greater responsiveness to the needs of Muslim religion and culture, especially in schools with preponderantly Muslim children. Then there was the controversy over Salman Rushdie's novel, *The Satanic Verses*. Iranian Muslim clerics declared this to be grossly blasphemous, and announced a "fatwa"—a multimillion dollar reward for Rushdie's assassination. Rushdie, a British citizen, was compelled to go into hiding, with protection provided by the government. Muslims in Britain protested the publication of the novel, threats were made against bookstores carrying the book, and in northern communities protest marches culminated in book-burnings. These outraged Labour intellectuals; but some of the northern Labour M.P.s expressed sympathy with the protesters, and even in literary circles there was heated debate about the desirability of a paperback edition (which at last was to be produced in the United States).

The Conservatives. Margaret Thatcher had little enthusiasm for the race relations acts, and funding for the Commission for Racial Equality and other equal opportunity agencies was held down during her administration. When the riots came, Thatcher's first response was for "the poor shopkeepers" (an echo of her own childhood living over her father's grocery store). Her diagnosis was different from Scarman's: Riots were simply criminal acts. Her environmental secretary at that time was Michael Heseltine, who toured the riot areas and promised government action and government money; Thatcher was not persuaded, and there was not much government action or money.

Yet she was interested in attracting the support of the growing nonwhite middle class. By 1987, almost a quarter of Asians were voting Conservative—compared with only one in ten in 1983. John Major continued the efforts to increase Conservative votes among blacks and Asians, and he issued a strong rebuke to members of a constituency Conservative Party who had complained in harshly racist terms against the adoption by the local party of an Afro-Caribbean candidate for Parliament. In the 1992 election that candidate was defeated, but 1992 saw the first Asian to be sent to Parliament under the Conservative banner.

The Liberal Democrats. The Liberal Party tradition of opposition to racism and discrimination was continued by the Liberal Democrats. However, local anti-immigrant sentiment could find its expression among Liberal Democrats, too. Party members in east London were accused of pandering to racism, and in the local council race won by the British National Party in 1993, Liberal Democratic council members sent out pamphlets with a clearly racist tone and language. This led to vigorous denunciations of racism by the party's leader, Paddy Ashdown, and by resolution of the party's annual conference.

Prospects for Nonwhite Candidates. In sum, nonwhites in Britain have made some gains politically. In addition to the election of six nonwhites to Parliament in 1992, a growing number of racial minority candidates were being elected to local councils in urban areas. On the other hand, the three main parties nominated only 25 nonwhite candidates for Parliament in 1992, 3 less than in 1987. And, as two analysts of the 1992 election results have suggested, " . . . whether the mainly white electorate is prepared to accept nonwhite M.P.s as readily as white ones remains in some doubt."[2]

GENDER

Women have come a long way in British politics. But they had a very long way to come, and still a long distance to go.

Early Discrimination

The vote came to women in 1918. This was partially the result of a prolonged campaign of civil disobedience by the suffragettes, and partially in recognition of the contribution women had made on the homefront during World War I. Even then, only women over 30 were considered politically mature enough to qualify; ten more years passed before women were allowed to vote at the same age as men.

Again, women made an indispensable contribution to the waging of World War II, and again hopes were raised of giant strides toward equality after the war. Yet this was not an area of much interest to the Attlee government, and until the mid-1960s there was no dramatic transformation of women's roles and power in the system.

Politics remained very much a man's world. A few women were appointed to government, but none to the key positions of power in the cabinet. This was not surprising, for the pool of women M.P.s from which government members might be drawn was so small. The 1945 election produced a record number of 24 women M.P.s. Their number had risen only to 29 by 1964. Most constituency parties were not anxious to nominate women, and many women who might have been nominated were discouraged by the conflict between raising families and fitting into a House of Commons schedule—starting in the afternoon and ending very late at night—designed for the convenience of men in the professions and business. In the civil service, Dame Evelyn Sharp, who kept Richard Crossman on his toes at the Department of Housing, was the only female permanent secretary.

Nor was the private sector a haven of opportunity for women. Few women indeed were to be found in the senior executive ranks of industry and finance. The Establishment clubs in London, where so much business was convivially transacted, accepted no women members. Among the professions, all but elementary teaching, nursing, and social work were overwhelmingly male. In the trade unions, too, despite growing numbers of women members, most of the top positions were held by men.

In the workforce, women earned considerably less than men. The income tax system treated the wife as the dependent of the male breadwinner. Divorce was stigmatized and difficult to obtain, except in cases of long desertion by the husband. (Another common practice was for a husband to prove infidelity—by hiring a prostitute and being photographed in a seaside hotel room by a private detective.) Abortion, though widely and often unsafely practiced, was illegal.

Changes since the 1960s

The government of Harold Wilson is usually said to have been far less productive than that of Clement Attlee. But in the field of gender relations the Wilson administration, and especially Home Secretary Roy Jenkins, pioneered dramatic advances. Under pressure from middle-class professional women, the divorce laws were finally liberalized in 1969.

Then a backbencher's private bill, accepted by the government, legalized sexual acts between consenting adults, including same-sex couples. Soliciting on the streets or in public places was still prohibited; but the law, which was the culmination of a long campaign by gay organizations and publications, brought to an end most prosecutions for homosexual relations.

Abortion. Common law and a series of statutes in the nineteenth century and in 1929 had made abortion a criminal offense. However, changing attitudes were reflected in a court decision in 1939 in favor of a respected surgeon who had performed an abortion "in good faith" intended "to preserve the life of the mother."[3] Still, abortion remained illegal except in extraordinary circumstances until David Steel, a young Liberal M.P., introduced a private member's bill which resulted in the passage of the 1967 Abortion Act—approved on a free, unwhipped vote in Parliament by 262 to 181 (20 Conservatives joined 234 Labour and 8 Liberal M.P.s to form the majority). Under the act, abortion was lawful if the mother's life, or the physical or mental health of the mother or her other children, was likely to be affected, or if there was a risk of a serious fetal handicap.

However, concerns expressed by doctors' groups, as well as opposition from the Roman Catholic Church and antiabortion organizations, led to the provision that, with certain exceptions, abortions were not to be performed after the 28th week—further restricted to the 24th week by the Human Fertilization and Embryology Act of 1990 (which allowed exceptions where there was a risk of grave injury to the mother's physical or mental health or a substantial risk of a deformity).

Antiabortion groups have continued to fight for repeal or modification of the legislation. In 1987, Liberal M.P. David Alton proposed to set the limit at the 18th week unless the mother's life were in danger, but he received no help from the Thatcher government and his bill was easily defeated. The government gave time for a debate on the issue in 1990, but when the pro-life lobby sent to each M.P. a life-size plastic replica of a fetus at 20 weeks the result was only an angry backlash. Subsequently *Rescue UK*, inspired by *Rescue America*, conducted aggressive demonstrations outside abortion clinics; some *Rescue UK* leaders were arrested, a visiting adviser from *Rescue America* was deported, and their efforts were disavowed by mainstream pro-life groups such as the Society for the Protection of Unborn Children (SPUC) and LIFE.

In general, then, abortion is a less contentious issue in Britain than in America; the fetus is not recognized as a person and has no rights until birth; and judges defer to medical opinion on such matters as fetal viability.

Women and Social Change. These changes in the law in part reflected a more permissive attitude stemming from the 1960s. But for women, other specific factors were becoming increasingly important. More and more women were entering the workforce, though a sizeable proportion worked part time. Their concerns about pay, working conditions and childcare intensified and found expression in the women's movement. There had always been large organizations representing women's interests; now, however, there was a greater militancy, and a number of feminist groups, inspired by the U.S. example, sprang up and learned how to get the media's attention.

As the 1970s progressed, women began to move into prominent positions in business, the professions, and trade unions. And in 1975, a woman became leader of the Conservative Party, the springboard for her ascension to the prime ministership in 1979. This was an especially startling jump, for although Harold Wilson had two popular and impressive women in his cabinet, Barbara Castle and Shirley Williams, no woman had yet held the power positions of chancellor of the exchequer, foreign secretary, or home secretary, and Thatcher herself had not previously risen above the position of education secretary.

Other than the election of Thatcher herself, the 1979 election did not seem to signal a political breakthrough for women. Nineteen women M.P.s were elected, eight fewer than in the previous Parliament, and the number rose only to twenty-three in 1983. However, a decisive upward trend came with the 1987 election, when the number jumped to 41, followed by 60 victorious women candidates in 1992—37 Labour, 20 Conservative, 2 Liberal Democrat, 1 Scottish Nationalist. (The number of women candidates in 1992 was 341, up from 243 in 1987.) By-elections brought the number up to 62 in 1994, and, with the assistance of *Emily's List UK* (the counterpart of the U.S. organization that raises funds to support women candidates), there was a strong prospect of another significant jump after the next general election. Many more women were also being elected to local councils.

Labour and the Liberal Democrats are committed to further increases in these numbers. Both parties require that the *short-list* (finalists) of potential candidates in each parliamentary constituency includes at least one woman. Labour's national executive committee, which requires that its membership include at least five women, has even mandated that in half of the constituencies where there is a good prospect of winning, the short-lists should consist *only* of women. Labour's Parliamentary Party also mandates that at least one of their women members sit on each parliamentary committee, and that at least three women be included in its shadow cabinet (with a proposed increase to four). And the party has indicated that a future Labour government would include a cabinet rank minister for women.

The Conservative Party's organizational and fundraising work in the constituencies depends heavily on women, and the party's programs continue to win women's votes. In contrast to the gender gap in the United States, where women are less likely to vote Republican than men, 44 percent of women voted for the Conservatives in 1992, compared with 41 percent of the men. Still, the Conservative Party has refused to follow the other parties in requiring that women be included on candidate short-lists.

On the other hand, since 1919, the Conservative Party's constitution has reserved 30 percent of constituency offices for women. Moreover, Conservative women M.P.s joined with the other parties in 1993 to launch *Women Into Politics*, an effort to recruit more women for Parliament. The inauguration included the unveiling by Lady Thatcher of a plaque to one of the suffragettes who had chained herself to the feet of male statues in Parliament. And among those speaking on behalf of *Women Into Politics* was Conservative M.P. Teresa Gorman. A right-winger on Europe and on economic issues, Gorman is nonetheless a libertarian who favors abortion, agrees with Tony Benn that each constituency should return two members (one male, one female), and once caused several men to walk out of a House of Commons debate because she had mentioned menopause. While some of the Conservative women M.P.s adhere to traditionalist views of the role of women, several others agree with Labour and Liberal Democrats that government should do more to help single mothers and to expand opportunities for childcare.

Women are also being appointed to prominent and powerful positions previously reserved for men. In 1992, Betty Boothroyd was elected speaker of the House of Commons, despite her being a Labour M.P. in a House with a Conservative majority. John Major, after facing a storm of criticism for having no women in his first cabinet, appointed two subsequently, and then appointed women as director-general of MI5 and director of public prosecutions. In 1991 he launched the Opportunity 2000 campaign to get more women into top jobs.

Outside of politics, there are now women judges on the Appeal Court and several women editors on national newspapers; the Church of England has admitted women to its priesthood; and the prospect of future advances by women in the professions is assured, because almost half the students admitted to universities and medical and law schools are women. Moreover, special administrative agencies such as the Equal Opportunities Commission were helping redress discrimination against women in the workplace; and the Sex Discrimination Act of 1986 applied to Britain European court judgments on equal treatment of men and women. Industrial tribunals, too, found against discriminatory practices. Thus in 1994, a woman broker who claimed she had been called a bimbo and sacked after rejecting her boss's advances was awarded £18,000 in compensation. Several financial awards were also made to women dismissed from the armed forces because they had become pregnant. (A tribunal's decision in 1993 attacked a common "reverse" stereotype: a male sewing machinist was awarded £1000 because he was turned down for a job on the grounds that men could not use sewing machines because they did not sit properly.)

There was also a further advance toward equality for gays in 1994, when Parliament, on a free vote, approved lowering the age of consensual homosexual sex to 18. However, for all others the age of consent was 16, and a motion by a Conservative backbencher to lower the age for gays to 16 was rejected.

The Remaining Gaps

Despite the advances of the past quarter-century, British women as a whole still suffer some major disadvantages compared with men.

Persisting Disadvantages. Although equal pay legislation has been on the statute books since 1975, a European Community survey in 1990 revealed that British women earned 68 percent of what men received, well below the levels of Italy, France, Denmark, and Greece.

Most of this differential resulted not because women received lower pay than men for the same work, but because women are predominantly employed in lower-paid fields. The concept of *comparable worth*—equivalent pay for similar levels of skills in different jobs or professions—has gained a foothold in Britain, for employers are required by law to pay the same for jobs that their own evaluation system assesses as equally demanding. But the idea is difficult to enforce in the courts; the Equal Opportunities Commission lacks the resources and enforcement powers to make much of a difference; and the small protection provided women by the Wages Councils has gone with the Major government's abolition of the Councils.

Easier divorce, brought about partly through the support of women professionals, led to the highest divorce rate in Europe—and women were usually left worse off financially despite legislation to enforce child support payments. Inadequate childcare facilities seriously limited the work and career prospects of many women; and a rising proportion of single mothers were on welfare.

The gains in politics, too, left a wide abyss to be traversed. Even the 60 women M.P.s elected in 1992 represented only about 9 percent of the House of Commons, while almost 52 percent of the electorate are women. In the Scandinavian countries, over one-third of the M.P.s are women; in the Netherlands one-quarter; Germany, Italy, and Spain all have higher proportions than Britain. (After the 1994 U.S. Congressional elections, women comprised 11 percent of members of the House and 8 percent of the Senate.)

The increase in women M.P.s that began in 1987 has undoubtedly begun to change the character of the House of Commons. Yet its afternoon and late-night schedule continues to present problems for women with families; the House still retains something of the atmosphere of an exclusive men's club; and many of the male members still regard topics like childcare as trivial.

The 1990s also saw the emergence of a reaction against the strides made by the women's movement. The appointment of women priests in the Church of England came over the bitter protests of a minority in the church, and the defection of some ministers and lay members to Roman Catholicism. The government, faced with a bipartisan uproar against decisions of the child support agency that required some divorced husbands to pay their former wives more than the divorce settlement in court had required, set limits to the size of future awards. Within the parliamentary Labour Party, the use of numerical targets to increase the representation of women in Parliament and in the shadow cabinet aroused considerable resentment, and some of the constituency organizations resisted the national party's requirement of women-only short lists for their parliamentary candidates. (The requirement would end, said Blair in 1995, after the next election.)

Controversy was also brewing over another issue that had already caused bitter dissension in the United States: the right of gays and lesbians to serve in the armed forces. Though Parliament has decriminalized homosexuality in the services, the Queen's Regulations, which spell out the military's code of conduct, still makes homosexuals liable to administrative dismissal. In 1994 the *Guardian* newspaper claimed that since 1990, 260 service personnel had been dismissed from the service, including army majors and captains, an RAF squadron leader and two chaplains, because they were gay or lesbian; and the Ministry of Defense maintained a "lesbian index" on its central criminal record computer. This policy, although upheld in a 1995 case in the British courts, could lead to a number of suits against the defense ministry in the European courts.

The Courts. Although the British courts are less likely now than in the past to treat charges of sexual abuse lightly, some of the older judges have continued to display a strongly male chauvinistic bias. Thus in a 1982 rape case, a judge opined that "women who say no do not always mean no," and that women hitchhikers are asking for trouble through "contributory negligence." In 1991 a judge, while sentencing a rapist to three years in jail, praised him because he "showed concern and consideration" in using a condom. Another judge was forced to resign from the bench in 1991 by the public uproar following his freeing a man who had twice raped his stepdaughter. The judge, taking note of the fact that the man's wife was pregnant, found this had led to "a lack of sexual appetite in the lady and considerable problems for a healthy young husband." And in 1993 another judge, sentencing a man to two years probation for raping an eight-year-old girl, declared that "she was not entirely an angel herself."

"Family Values." We have noted how some Conservative government ministers have denounced the breakup of the traditional family and, like their Republican counterparts in the 1992 presidential campaign, called for a restoration of "traditional family values." This theme received strong approval in the tabloids. "Bring back the family," the *News of the World* demanded, in place of "the designer single-parent family."[4] "What's the quickest way for a single girl to get a council flat?" asked the *Sun*. "Answer: become pregnant.... We should make parents pay for the sexual behavior of their offspring."[5] We have noted, however, that this campaign boomeranged against the government when some of its members were found to have transgressed the code they were espousing.

Margaret Thatcher and the Role of Women

The contribution of Margaret Thatcher to the advancement of women is an ambiguous one. For Thatcher was no feminist. While praising the suffragettes and insisting that "the home should be the center but not the boundary of a woman's life," she declared in 1982: "The battle for women's rights has largely been won," and "I hate those strident tones we hear from some Women's Libbers." As education secretary in Heath's government she had argued for a massive expansion of childcare. But as prime minister in 1990, she opposed "the idea that we might have a whole generation of creche children" and opined: "I don't think you can have a child in nursery all day."

In her personal conduct she adhered to traditional feminine roles. At 10 Downing Street she made her husband's breakfast most mornings. She took great care of her appearance, once showing off her wardrobe to television viewers; and even some Labour M.P.s, who disliked her policies and political conduct intensely, confessed that they found her physically attractive. Her femininity gave her an important advantage in her parliamentary encounters with Neil Kinnock when he was leader of the opposition: he was brought up, he has said, never to be discourteous to an older woman.

Yet in her political life Thatcher gave little recognition to the special claims of women. Except for the two-year appointment of Lady Young as leader of the House of Lords, no woman other than Thatcher appeared at the cabinet table during her eleven-and-a-half years as prime minister. Her leadership style was characterized by the assertiveness and aggressiveness commonly associated with male behavior. She rejoiced in the title of *Iron Lady* bestowed on her by the Soviets. When Ronald Reagan called her "the best man in England" it was intended, and no doubt received, as a compliment.

She succeeded, in other words, at outdoing the men at their own game. But politics was still essentially a man's world.

CONCLUSION

Many more years will pass before British women approach parity with men in the political system. Yet the prospect of further advances seems inexorable through the sheer number of women as voters, workers, and university students, and through the efforts of organizations fighting for women's interests with increased confidence and a record of past successes. And despite Margaret Thatcher's rejection of feminism, there have been testimonials even from women on the political left to the effect that she has served as an extraordinarily impressive role model, demonstrating the possibility of raising a family and yet becoming the most powerful individual in the country.

For people of color, however, the road to parity will be longer and more difficult. Even though their numbers are growing, taken together they constitute a small minority in Britain. They also include higher proportions of the poor, the unemployed, the undereducated and badly housed, the imprisoned and the crime victims, than the white population.

We have noted that not all of those of immigrant backgrounds suffer disadvantaged lives. Many are moving into the middle class; a 1993 list of the 200 richest Britons included four Asians; and a black man, Bill Morris, is the president of Britain's biggest labor organization, the Transport and General Workers Union. We should also keep in mind that immigrants and their children in Britain become vested with full citizenship rights—unlike Germany, where citizenship can be achieved only by heritage.

Moreover, Conservative leaders argue that hostility to immigrants, while still a problem in Britain, is much less so than in Germany or in France, and that this is because immigration to Britain has been so severely reduced, with only about 50,000 being admitted in 1991—mostly wives and children of residents—compared with 80,000 a year in the mid-1970s. Thus Britain has been less impacted by one of the great changes, still unfolding, of the late twentieth century—mass migrations of populations from poor and politically oppressed regions to more advantaged countries. So there is less of the anti-immigrant fever that emerged in the United States, particularly in the southwest, in the 1990s.

Still, if overtly racist organizations like the British National Party have only a tiny membership, and their political victories are unlikely to go beyond an occasional council seat in particularly depressed areas, their platforms represent in extreme terms the latent feelings of many white Britons.

In America racism is a legacy of the dark side of our history, slavery. Britain, too, now has a race problem, a legacy of its own history of colonialism. The problem is smaller in scale than in the United States, but there are all too many signs that it will not be healed merely by the passage of time.

SOME QUESTIONS TO THINK ABOUT

How does the racial situation in Britain compare with that in the United States?

What do you think of Britain's restrictions on immigration? Of the Labour Party's race relations legislation?

What were the causes of the British riots in the 1980s? What do you think of the Scarman Commission's proposals?

How would you compare the opportunities available for women in Britain with those in the United States?

Why is abortion a less contentious issue in Britain than in the United States?

What are the prospects for "traditional family values" in Britain?

How important was Margaret Thatcher as a role model for women?

NOTES

1. *Daily Express*, 5 August 1993; *The Sun*, 5 August 1993.
2. John Curtice and Michael Steed, "Appendix 2, The Results Analyzed," in David Butler and Dennis Kavanagh, *The British General Election of 1992* (Macmillan, 1992), p. 338.
3. *Rex v. Bourne*, 1939.
4. *News of the World*, 3 July 1993.
5. *The Sun*, 2 July 1993.

SUGGESTIONS FOR FURTHER READING

Zig Layton-Henry is the leading authority on race in Britain. See his *The Politics of Race in Britain* (Allen and Unwin, 1984), *The Politics of Immigration* (Blackwell, 1993), and, with P. B. Rich (ed.), *Race, Government and Politics in Britain* (Macmillan, 1986). See also John Solomos, *Race and Racism in Britain* (St. Martin's Press, 1993).

On women in politics, see Joni Lovenduski and Vicky Randall, *Women and Power in Britain* (Oxford University Press, 1993), and Vicky Randall, *Women and Politics* (Macmillan, 1982).

17
CIVIL LIBERTIES UNDER THREAT

No country has contributed more to the idea of the liberty of the individual than Britain. Classic statements on the subject came from John Locke, David Hume, John Stuart Mill. Through a process of slow evolution—not all of it peaceful—the arbitrary rule of kings was limited, then demolished; in time a rule of law was firmly established whereby no person was so exalted as to be above the law. Actions of governments were subjected to a constant barrage of criticism in Parliament and the press, at Hyde Park Corner, and in mass demonstrations.

So when Margaret Thatcher went to Paris for a summit conference, which coincided with a spectacular bicentennial celebration of the French Revolution, she expressed her disdain of that revolution—launched, she claimed, "in the name of abstract ideas, formulated by vain intellectuals." In contrast to the "murder, purges, and war" into which the French Revolution had degenerated she pointed to the "quiet revolution" of 1688 in Britain. Britain's Glorious Revolution, she insisted, typified the "English tradition of liberty," which "grew over the centuries: its most marked features are continuity, respect for law and sense of balance . . . ."[1]

And yet in several earlier chapters we have encountered reasons to question whether or not "the English tradition of liberty" is as secure in Britain today as Thatcher and others have suggested. Indeed, the legal philosopher Ronald Dworkin is among those who have argued that liberty "is ill in Britain," and that while many individuals and forces contributed to this illness, it was greatly aggravated by Thatcher and her government.[2]

THE THREATS TO LIBERTY

Various reasons are put forward to substantiate the charge that liberty in Britain is under severe threat.

The Paramount Executive

First, there is the dominance of the executive, which we have already discussed at length. Although Britain, as we have seen, is far from being a dictatorship, there are fewer checks on the power of the executive branch—particularly the prime minister, key cabinet members, and senior civil servants—than are found in most other democratic countries. Clearly Parliament, though exercising some influence and performing a number of useful roles, is very much a subordinate branch, and the constraints found in other systems resulting from a federal structure and a written bill of rights are notably lacking in Britain.

Secrecy

Second, as we noted in chapter 3, the practice of secrecy is close to an obsession in British government. Thus in 1957 fire broke out at the Windscale plutonium plant, which released a cloud of radioactive contamination with hundreds of times the iodine content of the Three Mile Island disaster. Harold Macmillan's Conservative government did not tell the public about the extent of the damage, and allowed contaminated lamb and milk to be sold for weeks after the fire. The coverup was apparently related to the fear of undermining confidence in the nuclear industry, of giving ammunition to the antinuclear lobby, and of damaging Britain's nuclear relationships with the United States. The story did not become public until 1987 because of the rule that all government documents remain classified for thirty years.

Labour governments were no less secretive than the Conservatives. The Attlee government's decision to embark on a nuclear weapons program was made without even the knowledge of most members of the cabinet. Harold Wilson's attitude as prime minister was summed up in a book he wrote on the workings of British government. He quotes with approval a statement of Harold Macmillan that matters pertaining to MI5 and other British security agencies should be left entirely "to discussions between the leader of the Opposition and the prime minister of the day." His chapter on the issue runs to slightly over one page, and concludes: "The prime minister is occasionally questioned on matters arising out of his responsibility. His answers may be regarded as uniformly uninformative. There is no further information that can usefully or properly be added before bringing this Chapter to a close."[3]

Yet no prime minister carried the passion for secrecy quite as far as Margaret Thatcher. Civil servants who leaked information to the press or to M.P.s were brought before the courts on criminal charges. When former MI5 operative Peter Wright's book *Spycatcher*[4] detailed a number of illegal activities by his agency, Thatcher fought a long, relentless battle at home and abroad to prevent the book's publication. Her government also repeatedly brought pressure to bear on television stations to refrain from presenting programs critical of actions taken in the name of national security. Thus Independent Television aired a program called *Death on the Rock* in 1988, covering the shooting deaths of three IRA activists on Gibraltar by members of a British counterterrorist group, the SAS. Allegedly the men had been about to explode bombs in cars parked some distance away; but the TV investigators found the men had been unarmed and charged they had been shot in line with a police "shoot to kill" policy. Thatcher and several members of her government issued furious denunciations of the program, and continued to do so even after a government-initiated inquiry had exonerated the program's producers. And when a *New Statesman* investigative reporter prepared a television series on national security, beginning with a program on a new British spy satellite, the police confiscated the tapes from a BBC studio and ransacked the *New Statesman* offices.

However, these examples of an adversarial relationship between government and the media run counter to the general agreement by the media, and especially the press, to cooperate with the government in a process of prior censorship whenever the national security is involved. A committee made up of people from the media and the civil service sends *D-notices* to editors requesting a ban on any subject that, in the committee's view, might affect national security, and usually the editors comply.

The legal underpinning for this degree of government secrecy was the Official Secrets Act of 1911—amended in 1920—which included a section prohibiting anybody in government from revealing anything said or done within government to any outsider without official permission. As time passed a consensus emerged that the act went too far: the wording was such that it could lead to the prosecution of a minor civil servant for revealing the menu of the department's cafeteria. So at last, in 1989, the Official Secrets Act was rewritten, and the obvious absurdities removed. However, the sections dealing with national security, defense and international relations were tightened still further; and though no prosecutions followed, the act was a constant reminder of the paramountcy of confidentiality in British government.

Nor was this act imposed by the elected government on an unwilling bureaucracy. A few lesser civil servants might risk their careers by breaking the rules. But at the top levels confidentiality was an article of faith, integral to the smooth running of government. Thus when the cabinet secretary, Sir Robin Butler, was asked what he thought of the proposition that the "convenience of secrecy" was designed to inhibit the release of embarrassing information, he replied, "You can call that a matter of convenience. I would call it a matter of being in the interests of good government." It was also Butler's view that, although deliberate misleading was not justifiable, "very often you are in a position where you have to give an answer that is not the whole truth, but falls short of misleading." Accordingly: "Half the picture can be true."[5]

Presenting half or less of the picture is common to governments everywhere, but among democratic governments is especially true of Britain.

The Law of Libel

London has been described as the libel capital of the world, a factor that has inhibited a good deal of comment about the rich and powerful. Thus publishing magnate Robert Maxwell notoriously used the libel laws to launch court actions against anyone making a public criticism of him, thereby inhibiting opponents who could not afford to match Maxwell's outlays on legal fees. In some cases, indeed, Maxwell would sue U.S. competitors in the British courts by taking action against their British branches of subsidiaries.

Then, too, the left-wing *New Statesman* was forced into a special fundraising drive to pay the legal fees incurred when John Major sued the magazine for publishing an article discussing a rumor that he had been involved in an affair with his caterer (though the article concluded the rumor was false).

Crime and Terrorism

In our discussion of the courts and law enforcement in chapter 11, we discussed the rise in crime which, though still modest by American standards, is enough to cause serious concern among the British public. Periods of high tension about the erosion of law and order are never conducive to the climate of openness and tolerance in which individual liberties flourish.

In chapter 11 we also noted how the prevailing sense of insecurity was intensified by the recurrent waves of violence unleashed by the Irish Republican Army in a number of English cities, with several people killed by bombs exploding in crowded pubs. Other bombs killed a relative of the royal family, Lord Mountbatten, and two of Margaret Thatcher's close associates, narrowly missed killing Thatcher herself, interrupted one of John Major's cabinet meetings, caused havoc in London's financial district, and repeatedly disrupted London's train and underground (subway) systems.

A Labour government was in power when the violence first moved from Northern Ireland to England, and it responded by passing the Prevention of Terrorism Act of 1974. This was to expire unless renewed in six months; but it was renewed in 1975 and has been updated every year since then (though in recent years Labour has called for modifications in its terms). In addition to the power it gives the police to arrest and detain without charge for up to seven days, the law includes a number of provisions infringing on individual rights: membership in organizations cited as *terrorist* is banned, meetings of such organizations are prohibited, donating money to them is proscribed, and any individual believed to be connected with their activities may be expelled from Britain. In a further effort to curtail the IRA's activities, the Thatcher government banned televised interviews with members of the IRA's political arm, Sinn Fein, except during election campaigns. (TV organizations partially circumvented this ban by showing Sinn Fein members being interviewed, but having actors dub in their voices; and the ban was lifted in 1994 after the IRA ceasefire.)

The Decline of Traditional Morality

As has been the case throughout the industrialized world, Britain has experienced the breaking down of many of its established norms of behavior and belief. Family structure has eroded. Britain has the highest proportion of one-parent families and of unmarried mothers under 24 of any European country. Divorce, which became much easier as a result of the Labour government's reforms in the 1960s, more than doubled in rate between 1970 and 1990. Explicit sexual references, once limited to elite art and literature, are now as much the common fare of the popular media in Britain as they are in the United States, if not more so. Intimate details of the sex lives of the famous, including members of the royal family, fill the tabloids. Mrs. Thatcher tried to counter the wave of sex and violence on television (especially in programs coming from the United States) by setting up a broadcasting standards council in 1988. But the council would not be able to prevent anyone with a satellite dish from receiving hard-core pornography broadcast from Europe.

Moreover, as we saw in chapter 2, the deference that marked British attitudes for so long and which provided guides to acceptable and "respectable" conduct has lost much of its force. There are hostile reactions to the loud music blaring through the night at "raves"; to the "Travelers" who move around the country in vans and mobile homes, making encampments on farmers' lands; to squatters illegally occupying unoccupied homes and buildings; and to the increasing number of aggressive panhandlers on the streets.

Government Policies in the 1990s

Under John Major, some steps were taken in the direction of greater government accountability and accessibility. The Citizen's Charter, designed to make government departments more responsive to the customers of their services, includes statements of the consumers' legal rights. The government minister responsible for implementing the charter is also charged with increasing the degree of openness in government. Henceforth, for example, he will make known the previously confidential membership of cabinet committees (though scholars and journalists had already been revealing most of this information), as well as rules on the behavior of Cabinet ministers detailed in *Questions of Procedures for Ministers*. Then in 1993 the press was able to report that "MI5 came in from the cold." For the first time in the history of the counterespionage agency, the name and photograph of its director appeared in print, and the agency published a 36-page brochure explaining its work.

Nonetheless, British government remains far less forthcoming than, among others, the governments of the United States, Canada, Australia, or New Zealand. Parliament has less oversight of MI5 or MI6 than does the Congress over the CIA. Thirty years must pass before most government files are open to scrutiny (though, as we shall see, that rule has been breached on a number of occasions).

A tougher posture on crime, we have noted, became a central theme of the Major government, and their fervor for longer sentences and more prisons intensified in the face of harsh Labour criticism of the rising crime rate. Major's government also condemned the changing moral climate, in part blaming the media for its sensational treatment of sex scandals and its gross invasions of the privacy of the royal family and other public figures. The government would not rule out the possibility that the Press Complaints Commission, set up by the press to review charges of irresponsibility by journalists, might be replaced by a statutory tribunal with extensive enforcement powers.

But the Conservatives' targets were not limited to the press. Major insisted that his theme of getting "back to basics" referred to education, the economy, and law and order. But some of his right-wing ministers, as we noted earlier, insisted on extending the concept to the realm of morality. They argued that the nation was in the throes of a serious moral crisis, and that this was largely attributable to the decline of the traditional family.

Labour Party leaders—while criticizing the Conservatives for stigmatizing single parents as preparation for cutting welfare spending—added their own voices to general concern about the breakdown of the conventional family unit. And the opposition parties greatly enjoyed the government's embarrassment at a series of revelations indicating that some government ministers were not fully committed to traditional family values. Resignations followed extensive media coverage of some rather gaudy extramarital affairs, two of them resulting in illegitimate births, and another followed by the suicide of a minister's wife.

Nonetheless, the Major administration proceeded with its campaign against the decline of the old moral order, underscoring exhortation with stronger legal sanctions. The 1994 Criminal Justice Act gave the police more powers to use against "Travelers," "raves," and "squatters," and increased the penalty for possession of marijuana. The act provoked large demonstrations, including one in which some marchers tried to climb the gates to 10 Downing Street—triggering tabloid headlines such as "SCUM STORM DOWNING STREET."

John Major's reputation for niceness was somewhat tarnished when in June 1994 he called for strict enforcement of the law against beggars, whom he described as offensive to tourists and shoppers. People, he declared, should be "rigorous" in reporting beggars to the police: "I think the law should be used. . . . It is an offensive thing to beg. It is unnecessary. . . . If people are in desperately straitened circumstances we have a social security net in this country which they can use."

THE ROLE OF THE COURTS

When a powerful government responds to the perceived concerns of its citizenry by stepping up its involvement in public order and morality, the always delicate balance between individual liberties and the security of society is likely to tip away from individual liberties.

In such circumstances it is natural for defenders of civil liberties to look to the courts for help. The great constitutional scholar A. V. Dicey had explained the centrality of the courts to the rule of law in his exposition of the British constitution in

1885. Any person, no matter how exalted, was not above the law and was subject to the jurisdiction of the ordinary courts. Further, nobody could be punished except after due process before the courts. Finally, the rights of free speech and assembly were "the result of judicial decisions determining the rights of private persons in particular cases brought before the courts."[6] Thus basic freedoms in Britain were safeguarded not by the kind of general propositions commonly found in written constitutions but by case law, and the primary burden of interpretation is placed on the judiciary.

Yet, as we saw in in chapter 11, some constitutional law scholars have been skeptical about relying on the British judiciary to preserve individual liberties. J. A. G. Griffith, for example, concedes that Britain "enables its citizens to live in comparative freedom," and that the judiciary "play some part" in this achievement. But the judges' contribution has been, he contends, limited and grudging. True to their class background, "on every major social issue which has come before the courts during the last 30 years—concerning industrial relations, political protest, race relations, governmental secrecy, police powers, moral behavior—the judges have supported the conventional, established, and settled interests."[7] And two other law professors, K. D. Ewing and C. A. Gearty, have argued that: "Civil liberties litigation has been dismally deferential to authority. . . . In the civil liberties area the courts seem to have come to regard themselves as partners of the executive . . . rather than as a separate, autonomous, and sometimes necessarily antagonistic branch of government."[8]

Support for these positions can be found particularly wherever the government invokes the need to protect the public order, and even more so when national security is brought into question. These are the justifications put forward by the government in making their case against leakers of state secrets, journalists, protesters, and industrial strikers.

Official Secrets

In cases involving breaches by government employees of the Official Secrets Act, British judges have mostly sided with the government against the accused.

Thus in 1983, the *Guardian* newspaper received some confidential government documents about the prospective arrival of U.S. cruise missiles in Britain and published articles based on the document. The government demanded the return of the documents, for this would enable them to trace the leak. The House of Lords, by three to two, agreed with the government, for discovering who had disclosed the documents "must be established in order that national security should be preserved."[9] The returned documents did indeed reveal the transgressor, and Sarah Tisdall, a clerk in the foreign secretary's private office, was sentenced to six months in jail.

The next year a much higher ranking official, Clive Ponting of the defense department, sent to a Labour M.P. a secret document that cast doubt on the government's account of the sinking of the *General Belgrano,* an Argentine troopship, during the Falklands war. The government, though conceding that the disclosure did not actually cause any specific damage to national security, prosecuted Ponting for "breech of confidentiality." The judge's instructions to the jury were tantamount to telling them to find Ponting guilty. However, the jury took less than three hours to deliver a verdict of not guilty, despite the fact that they had been especially "vetted" to ensure that no one of potentially subversive views would serve on the panel.

Then came the great legal obsession of the Thatcher years: the *Spycatcher* case. Peter Wright had been a member of MI5 and MI6 for 21 years until his retirement in 1976. He had moved to Australia and written a book alleging that there had been an assassination plot against President Nasser of Egypt; that foreign embassies, including the French, in London had been bugged; that members of MI5 had plotted to destabilize Harold Wilson's Labour government; and that a former director-general of MI5 was a Soviet spy. Although none of these charges implicated her government, Thatcher was furious at this breach of confidentiality by a man who had been a member of Britain's most secret agency and had broken the agreement made in writing by every member of MI5 and MI6 never to reveal their activities without specific permission.

Therefore, from 1985 to 1988, the government undertook a remorseless international effort to prevent the publication of the book or newspaper excerpts from the book. Their case was thrown out in the Australian courts. The book was published in the United States. But in Britain the courts, over vigorous dissents by some judges, supported the government's case and maintained injunctions against publication by several newspapers. In 1987, the *Economist* magazine published a review of *Spycatcher* in its foreign editions. In a box in the center of the page they carried this announcement: "The *Economist* has 1.5 million readers in 170 countries. In all but one country, our readers have on this page a review of *Spycatcher,* a book by an ex-MI5 man, Peter Wright. The exception is Britain, where the book, and comment on it, have been banned. For our 420,000 readers there, this page is blank—and the law is an ass."[10]

At last the House of Lords, having earlier sustained the injunctions against the newspapers, changed its mind. It was too late to stop or repair the damage. The book was available all over the world, except in Britain, and individuals were bringing copies from the United States and elsewhere. One British bookstore, forbidden to sell the book, gave it away with purchase of an encyclopedia. So the Lords allowed *Spycatcher* to be published in Britain, where it sold far more copies than if it had never been banned. Yet the courts had made it clear that the principle of confidentiality of government documents, especially in the hands of security agencies, must be given great weight, and was overridden here only because it was too late for the ban to make sense.

Journalists

In 1977 two U.S. journalists, Philip Agee and Mark Hosenball, were deported by order of the Labour government's home secretary in the interest of national security. Hosenball appealed, arguing that he had never been told the grounds on which he was found to be a security risk.

The case came before Lord Denning, the Master of the Rolls. Denning has been much lauded as a champion of the ordinary individual against the power of the state.

His biographer declares: "Denning's efforts from his earliest days aimed to protect the individual from the abuse of power from whatever source";[11] and he quotes this view of Denning by a great liberal judge, Lord Scarman: "His steadfast purpose has always been to strengthen the courts in the ordinary man's defence against abuse of power."[12]

Yet Denning found against Hosenball, with a justification that even the most conservative of American judges would find remarkable:

> There is a conflict between the interests of national security on the one hand and the freedom of the individual on the other. The balance between these two is not for a court of law. It is for the Home Secretary. . . . In some parts of the world national security has been used as an excuse for all sorts of infringements of individual liberty. But not in England. Both during the wars and after them successive ministers have discharged their duties to the complete satisfaction of the people at large. . . . They have never interfered with the liberty or freedom of movement of any individual except where it is absolutely necessary for the safety of the state.[13]

This view was not actually tested in the courts over the police confiscation of the BBC program on the spy satellite. The government, having succeeded in persuading the BBC to pull the initial program from the series for the time being (it was eventually broadcast), did not need to pursue its case in the courts.

Protesters

Peaceful protest is very much a part of British political life, and is periodically made dramatically visible with huge assemblies marching through the countryside toward their gathering place in Trafalgar Square, there to cheer a succession of speakers bitterly attacking government policy.

However, in the name of preserving the public peace and order, the courts have sometimes supported efforts by the police to circumscribe such protests, especially where the issue of national security enters the picture. This was true of some of the demonstrations against nuclear weapons organized by the Campaign for Nuclear Disarmament (CND). Thus in 1961, a sit-in in Trafalgar Square led to mass arrests. So did efforts to enter a U.S. airforce base and organize a sit-in to prevent planes taking off, and convictions followed under the Official Secrets Act. The House of Lords upheld the convictions, for the plan to immobilize the base was "prejudicial to the safety or interests of the State."[14]

Then in the 1980s, CND and other organizations marched and demonstrated against the deployment in Britain of U.S. cruise missiles. Several airforce bases were targeted for protest, the most sustained action being an encampment of women on Greenham Common. This time the government made no mention of the Official Secrets Act. Instead the police used roadblocks under the Road Traffic Act; the government passed new bylaws to long-existing legislation such as the Military Lands Act, which made it a criminal offense to "enter, pass through or over or remain in or over" the area of a military base; and the protesters' symbolic wirecutting of fences around some of the bases was dealt with as the offense of criminal damage. A considerable number of protesters were arrested and charged in magistrates' courts; several among them were found guilty and sentenced; the Appeals Court, while raising questions about the language of some of the laws under challenge, upheld the verdicts.

Property Rights

The one area, according to Griffith, in which the judiciary can be relied on to protect the rights of the individual against government is with respect to property. Thus the courts have tended to be punctilious in their scrutiny of government plans to condemn private property through the power of eminent domain. When the Labour-controlled Greater London Authority introduced subsidies to bring down the price of bus and underground transportation, the courts ruled that this was a burden that could not be imposed on the taxpayers: the authority's action was "thriftless" and in violation of their "general fiduciary duty."

And in adjudicating issues between business and the unions, the courts tended

Campaign for Nuclear Disarmament poster

SOURCE: Courtesy of the Campaign for Nuclear Disarmament.

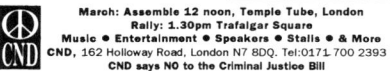

to side with business, establishing constraints on the right to strike (which were overruled by the Labour government's Trades Disputes Act of 1965), and upholding police limitations on picketing long before the Thatcher administration's legislation on the issue.

PROTECTIONS FOR CIVIL LIBERTIES

Despite the authoritarian impulses of British governments, and the general reluctance of judges to resist these impulses, civil liberties in Britain are not without institutional defenses.

Interest Groups

There exist a number of intensely motivated interest groups, particularly *Liberty* (formerly the National Council for Civil Liberties) and *Charter 88,* and these are joined on various issues by an array of organizations representing particular causes. For example, the battle against the 1994 criminal justice bill attracted such groups as *Friends and Families and Travellers Support Group, Advance Party* (speaking for ravers and festival goers), SQUASH (Squatters Action for Secure Homes), and *Release* (a 24-hour helpline for drug-related and other legal issues).

A demonstration against the bill in Hyde Park, starting in a peaceful, almost celebratory mood reminiscent of the 1960s, ended in a pitched battle between police and a militant minority among the demonstrators. Confrontations of this kind would tend to alienate middle-class opinion. Yet the 1990s have seen the emergence of angry protest movements in middle-class, perennially Conservative areas. Some of these were provoked by threats posed to established communities by proposed new highways or bypasses, or, as in the south of England, by a projected railway line from London to the Chunnel. But the most furious of the middle-class protests came in response to the shipment of live calves from England and Wales to the Continent under conditions regarded as intolerable by animal rights groups. The police, confronted by disruptive civil disobedience tactics, were nonplussed, for the protesters included a number of frail elderly women and sang such patriotic songs as "Rule Britannia" and the national anthem.

The Media

Then, too, the opposition parties are constantly on the lookout for examples of governmental tyrannies to expose. So are sections of the press (even on occasion the pro-Conservative tabloids), journals of opinion like the *New Statesman and Society,* and television. Moreover, despite the absence of a freedom of information act, it is becoming more and more difficult for British governments to keep secrets. Thus Richard Crossman's *Diaries of a Cabinet Minister* gave blow-by-blow accounts of discussions in Harold Wilson's Labour government that were supposed to have been shrouded in secrecy for at least 30 years. But despite government efforts to suppress publication, the courts lifted the ban in 1975, for almost 10 years had passed since the events described in the volumes. After that two other Labour ministers, Tony Benn and Barbara Castle, published similar diaries without hindrance.

The Courts

Recently, too, the courts have refused to accept some claims put forward by government under the protective cloak of national security. Thus when three directors of a joint British-Iraqi firm, Matrix Churchill, were prosecuted in 1992 for selling weapons-related material to Iraq in the late 1980s against government policy, they contended that government officials had informed them there would be no problem—government policy had changed. When four government ministers were called before the court to testify they signed "public immunity certificates" that enabled them, in the name of governmental confidentiality, to refuse to appear. The judge, convinced that the defendants' claim was justified, and furious that the government would have allowed the three men go to prison rather than admit their change in policy, threw the case out. The government was compelled to set up an inquiry into the whole affair under Sir Richard Scott, whose close questioning of a number of ministers and senior civil servants produced evidence that appeared to support charges that the government had deliberately misled parliament and the country and had then covered up its misconduct.

Moreover, where judges will not protect defendants accused of breaches of national security, juries may sometimes do so. It was a jury that freed Clive Ponting, and another jury infuriated a judge by ignoring his clear instruction to convict a group of anarchists accused of plotting a terrorist attack. (He detained them in the courtroom to observe his handing down a severe sentence in a subsequent case.)

Finally, there are the European courts. Whatever the disadvantages of the British system of justice, it is no longer the final recourse for aggrieved parties. In 1951 the United Kingdom signed the European Convention on Human Rights. This established the European Commission on Human Rights, which receives complaints of abuses from states and individuals, and, if it fails to resolve the complaints, refers them to the European Court of Human Rights.

In a case concerning contempt of court, the European Human Rights Court reversed a decision of the British courts. We noted in chapter 11 that once a case has gone to trial in Britain the media may say nothing about it beyond developments in the actual trial. This has served as a valuable protection for the rights of the accused. It has also, however, prevented the media from undertaking legitimate investigations. Thus in 1972, the *Sunday Times* published the first of a series of articles describing the plight of a number of children born with gross deformities that resulted from their mothers' using the drug thalidomide during pregnancy. Suits against the manufacturer of the drug had been instituted in 1968; some were settled out of court; others were still pending. The company asked the attorney-general to prevent any further publication on the ground that the issue was still before the courts and publication therefore constituted contempt of court. The attorney-general issued an injunction, which was upheld on appeal by the House of Lords. But when the question was taken to the European Court of Human Rights, the Court, on an 11 to 9 vote, ruled against the injunction as an infringement on freedom of speech, and the law was subsequently modified by the Contempt of Court Act of 1981. Then in 1986, corporal punishment in British schools was abolished as a result of a decision four years earlier by the European Court. And in 1995, the Human Rights Commission ruled that a man should be awarded compensation by the British government because he had been sent to jail for not paying the poll tax.

In addition, although the Court of Justice set up under the European Union thus far has dealt primarily with economic and environmental issues, some of its future decisions will inevitably have major implications for individual rights and liberties.

THE BILL OF RIGHTS CONTROVERSY

The various protections of civil liberties in Britain fall far short of satisfying the critics. Nor are the critics complacent about the decisions of the European Court of Human Rights. For one thing, the process of reaching the European Court is long, slow, and expensive: beforehand, all legal remedies within Britain must be exhausted. Then, too, the Human Rights Convention is subject to a wide range of interpretations, as indicated by the 11 to 9 vote in the thalidomide case. A still more serious shortcoming is that the convention is not binding on member states unless they decide to make it so, and the British have not. So although Britain has come into compliance in some cases, the Thatcher government refused to accept the 1989 European Court decision that went against the government power (under the Prevention of Terrorism Act) to detain a suspect without charges for up to seven days. And abolition of corporal punishment was barely upheld by the House of Commons on a free vote by 231 and 230 (and might have been voted down, had not several Conservative M.P.s failed to get to the House because of a royal wedding traffic jam).

So pressure has built across the political spectrum for the passage of a British bill or charter of rights, or, as an alternative, the incorporation of the European Convention on Human Rights into British law. Protagonists of each alternative see flaws in the other. A bill of rights passed by Parliament could, in the absence of a written constitution, be repealed by the next Parliament (though generally statutes dealing with fundamental constitutional matters have not later been overridden). The European Convention, once accepted as authoritative under an international treaty, would be more difficult to repeal; however, as a document covering a number of nations, it would not necessarily fit all of Britain's special circumstances. Still, either version would be responsive to one of the key constitutional proposals of Charter 88, as we saw in chapter 3, and different versions of the idea have been put forward by the Institute for Public Policy Research on the left and the Institute of Economic Affairs on the right, as well as by the Liberal Democrats and, at last, the Labour Party.

However, the Conservative government has continued to reject any version of a bill of rights or the incorporation of the European Convention into British law. Nor is the resistance confined to Conservatives. Griffith sees no advantages in a bill of rights that would inevitably be general and ambiguous and would therefore require interpretation by judges. And for Griffith, the problem *is* the judges. Without a transformation of the judiciary, involving a radically reformed system of selection and advancement, no document can protect the rights of the individual from the judges' preconceptions in favor of the established order.[15] Ewing and Gearty make the same point and go on to insist that the problem of civil liberties in Britain is much too serious to be treated "with a used Band-Aid . . . The need is for major surgery to the body politic to reduce the load on an overworked House of Commons and to introduce some real and effective political constraints on the power of the prime minister."[16]

But the Charter 88 group and other proponents of a Bill of Rights believe that, although reform of the judiciary is also necessary, a written guarantee of civil liberties would be desirable—even with the judges who are now on the bench. They point to the evidence of the United States and other countries that have such charters, and find that on balance they provide valuable protection against governmental intrusions into personal liberties. William Rees-Mogg, that pillar of the British Establishment, made the point for them when Mrs. Thatcher appointed him chairman of the broadcasting standards council. "One has to remember," he said, " . . . that the United States has a First Amendment and we don't."[17] And it was the First Amendment that the U.S. Supreme Court cited in its decisions forcing the government to accept publication of the Pentagon Papers.

CONCLUSION

Even without a bill of rights, Griffith agrees that the British system "enables its citizens to live in comparative freedom." Most of the time, most people feel free to express their views, including bitter disagreement with the government and its policies, without fear of legal or other retribution.

The late Peter Jenkins, a leading British columnist, believed that in Britain "the net flow of information to the citizen is both superior and greater" than in the United States. While agreeing that there had been "a narrowing of the freedom of speech" during the Thatcher era, Jenkins insisted that Britain did not compare unfavorably with the United States regarding civil liberties in general. To forbid the kind of raucous, sensational media coverage of trials commonly found in the United States is not, for Jenkins, a denial of free expression, but a proper protection of the rights of the accused. Then, too, freedom of speech in Britain "does not extend to the purchase of unlimited time on television in which to tell lies about your political opponents." On the whole:

> It is not obvious to me that as a result of the First Amendment the United States is a freer, better informed, or better functioning democracy than Britain with its parliamentary system . . . Americans certainly have more effective constitutional entrenchment of their liberties. If ultimate liberty is the test, they have more liberty. But when it comes to calculating how effectively liberties function in political life I would not be so certain.[18]

Jenkins's position depends, in the last analysis, on a perception of the British political culture that, even though less hostile to government than the prevailing attitudes in the United States, still prizes individual liberty. Support for this view can be found in the reaction to a consultation paper issued by the Major government for the introduction of identity cards. Everyone had carried an ID card during and after World War II, but their reintroduction, even on a voluntary basis, was fiercely opposed not only by civil liberties organizations and the opposition parties, but also by a number of Conservative M.P.s.

Moreover, the case for Britain as a free society would be further strengthened if the IRA does completely end its use of violence, for then the initial rationale for one of the principal infringements of civil liberties—the Prevention of Terrorism Act—would have disappeared.

However, to recognize that Britain is among the world's more open societies, and may even offer certain advantages over the United States in this respect, is not to dismiss the concerns expressed by Dworkin and others about the health of civil liberties in Britain today. Given the evidence we have reviewed in this chapter related to actions of the executive branch of government, the decisions and pronouncements of judges, and the public reaction to crime and terrorism, there is reason to be skeptical about the claims put forward by Margaret Thatcher as described at the beginning of this chapter. And, despite the dangers cited by Griffith and others, it may be that the time is approaching for the incorporation of an appropriate version of a bill of rights into the British constitution.

SOME QUESTIONS TO THINK ABOUT

Are civil liberties "ill" in Britain today?

Is there less government secrecy in the United States than in Britain?

What do you think of Jenkins' comparison between the United States and Britain?

In the light of the IRA bombings, was the Prevention of Terrorism Act justified? Should it be repealed now? Are there circumstances in which a similar law might be passed in the United States?

Does Britain need a bill of rights?

NOTES

1. Margaret Thatcher, *The Downing Street Years* (HarperCollins, 1993), p. 753.
2. Ronald Dworkin, "Devaluing Liberty," *Index on Censorship,* September 1988, pp. 7-8.
3. *The Governance of Britain* (Harper and Row, 1976), pp. 167-8.
4. Peter Wright, *Spycatcher* (Viking, 1987).
5. Richard Norton-Taylor, "Keeper of the Book of Golden Rules," *The Guardian,* 29-30 October 1994.
6. A. V. Dicey, *An Introduction to the Study of the Law of the Constitution* (Macmillan, 1959 edition, with an introduction by E. C. S. Wade).

7. J. A. G. Griffith, *The Politics of the Judiciary* (Fontana, 4th ed., 1991), pp. 320, 325.
8. K. D. Ewing and C. A. Gearty, *Freedom under Thatcher: Civil Liberties in Modern Britain* (Clarendon Press, 1990), pp. 12-13.
9. *Secretary of State for Defence v. Guardian Newspapers, Ltd,* 1984.
10. The *Economist,* 25 July 1987, p. 77.
11. Edmund Heward, *Lord Denning: A Biography* (Weidenfeld and Nicolson, 1990), p. 108.
12. Ibid., p. 217.
13. *R. v. Secretary of State for Home Affairs ex parte Hosenball,* 1977.
14. *Chandler v. DPP,* 1964.
15. Griffith, *Politics of the Judiciary,* pp. 324-5.
16. Ewing and Gearty, *Freedom Under Thatcher,* p. 275.
17. *New York Times,* 10 June 1988.
18. *New York Review of Books,* 8 December 1988, p. 23.

SUGGESTIONS FOR FURTHER READING

In addition to *The Politics of the Judiciary* by Griffith and *Freedom Under Thatcher* by Ewing and Gearty (cited in the text), see David Feldman, *Human Rights and Civil Liberties in England and Wales* (Oxford University Press, 1993). On laws aimed at preserving order against threats to national security, see Clive Walker, *The Prevention of Terrorism in British Law* (Manchester University Press, 1992) and Charles Townshend, *Making the Peace: Public Order and Public Security in Modern Britain* (Oxford University Press, 1993).

18

Foreign Policy

From Empire to European Union

"Great Britain has lost an Empire and has not yet found a role." This statement in 1962 by a former U.S. Secretary of State, Dean Acheson, aroused intense anger in Britain. Prime Minister Harold Macmillan retorted that "Mr. Acheson has fallen into an error which has been made by quite a lot of people in the course of the last four hundred years, including Philip of Spain, Louis XIV, Napoleon, the Kaiser, and Hitler."[1]

This recitation of past victories might bring consolation to the British, but it could not obscure, even to themselves, that in the latter half of the twentieth century Britain's standing in the international community was sadly diminished. The branch of the civil service that serves the foreign office still has a high reputation for skilled diplomacy, and given the huge increase in nation states since the end of World War II, the proliferation of summit meetings, and the great complexity of contemporary international relations, there has been no decline in the quantity of work assigned to the foreign service ministers and professionals.

Even so, the principal context of British foreign policy in the post-World War II era has been the process of adjustment from world power status based on a vast empire to the position of a middle-level power in the second rank of international politics.

We shall see that in some respects, British governments have made the adjustments necessary to finding a new and appropriate role for their nation. But we will also see that the transition has been slower and more wrenching than it might have been, because of a reluctance to face squarely the new and less exalted realities.

ADJUSTMENTS TO DECLINE

Two broad strategies were adopted by the British after 1945 in recognition of their reduced condition. First, they began the process of extricating themselves from their now burdensome responsibilities as an imperial power. Second, they developed associations and alliances with other nations in which they could play an important but not dominant part.

Empire to Commonwealth

Those countries that had been settled by British expatriates had already gained control over their own destinies through Dominion and then Commonwealth status. But progress toward autonomy had been much slower in countries whose populations were mostly nonwhite. Then Clement Attlee's Labour government in 1948 made good on a wartime promise to India of independence after the war, and in the same period Ceylon and Burma gained their freedom from British control. For their part the Conservatives under Harold Macmillan carried the process forward. "The winds of change" were blowing through Africa, Macmillan declared, and between 1960 and 1963 Nigeria, Uganda, Tanganyika, Zanzibar, British Somaliland, Kenya, and Sierra Leone gained their independence.

This is not to say that disengagement came painlessly everywhere. Following India's achievement of independence, over a million people were killed in the violence that erupted between Hindus and Muslims, until at last the country was partitioned into India and Pakistan. Before the British left Malaya in 1957, they had crushed a Communist guerrilla movement. Independence for Cyprus in 1960 did not bring the end of bitter conflicts between the Greek and Turkish communities, and Nigerian independence was followed by a ferocious civil war. White settlers in Kenya and Rhodesia did not give up their control easily. In Kenya their struggle was lost in 1963, but only after a bloody struggle with the indigenous Mau-Mau. And in the 1960s the Southern Rhodesian whites rejected the efforts of Labour Prime Minister Harold Wilson to get them to share power with the majority black population, declared their independence of Britain, and defied a leaky international oil embargo—until Margaret Thatcher's Foreign Secretary, Lord Carrington, negotiated a transfer to black rule, and Rhodesia became Zimbabwe in 1980.

So there were delays and disruptions before and after the end of empire. But nowhere was Britain forced out by a crushing military defeat, as happened to the French in Indochina, nor was there a dangerous struggle at home comparable with that which racked France before Algeria gained independence. Disengagement had been achieved mostly by mutual consent. The British Empire became the British Commonwealth of Nations and then, simply, the Commonwealth of Nations. The majority were republics, owing no allegiance to the British crown; and in 1993, when the Australian government raised the possibility that Australia might wish to become a republic, the queen and Prince Charles made it clear that this was a matter for Australia, not Britain, to decide.

As British imperial power declined and fell, the structure of government was adjusted step-by-step to reflect the changes in function. Until 1966 there was a *secretary of state for the colonies* heading up a full-fledged department. Then the department was folded into the Department of Commonwealth Affairs, and abolished the following year. In its turn the Department of Commonwealth Affairs was merged with the Foreign Office in 1968. So the evolution from colonial empire to Commonwealth, and then to the declining significance of the Commonwealth was recognized and built into the bureaucratic structure.

Association with Other Nations

Britain had always engaged in alliances with other nations. In Europe these had been part of a strategy to ensure that no nation achieved dominance over the continent. But that had been part of the great power game, with Britain in a leadership role. After World War II, the aim of preventing European hegemony by anyone—particularly the Soviet Union or Germany—remained the same; but now Britain needed alliances not to sustain her position of power but to replace it.

Churchill was not ready to accept this new reality. At war's end he proposed a "three circles" strategy of alliances, with Britain maintaining her global power by being at the focal point of overlapping circles that connected her to the British Empire and Commonwealth, the United States, and Europe. But soon it became clear that only the last two of these mattered in the context of international politics, and that Britain must make the best arrangements she could with the United States on the one hand and Western Europe on the other.

The "Special Relationship." As we saw in chapter 1, the transatlantic connection became central to British foreign policy during and after World War II. Roosevelt and Churchill, Kennedy and Macmillan formed close personal relationships that contributed to the diplomatic bonds between the two countries. Even closer cooperation accompanied the mutual admiration and policy compatibility between Reagan and Thatcher: the United States gave Britain vital logistical support during the Falklands war, Thatcher acceded to Reagan's request to use British bases to bomb Khadaffi's Libya, and the two worked together in opposing Soviet power.

Bush appeared more interested in working with German chancellor Helmut Kohl than with John Major; but it was Britain (which had long been a major stakeholder in Middle Eastern oil and had been instrumental in creating some of the kingdoms and emirates of the area) that fought alongside the United States in the Gulf War.

Of course, no two nations have identical interests on every issue. The British complained of the abrupt termination (as soon as World War II ended) of lend-lease aid from the United States and of the harsh terms attached to the loan that replaced the aid. The Suez fiasco in 1956 ended in humiliation and an open breach between the United States and Britain. Harold Wilson's attempts to act as intermediary between east and west during the Vietnam War was contemptuously dismissed by Lyndon Johnson. Even the Reagan-Thatcher collaboration was marred by Thatcher's refusal to accept the U.S. veto of a west European natural gas pipeline to the Soviet Union, and also by the fact that the United States invaded Grenada, which was still linked to Britain and to the British queen, without Thatcher's prior approval. Then Clinton, who had been personally affronted by the intervention of Conservative party functionaries on behalf of Bush in 1992, disagreed with Major over Bosnia, continued Bush's tilt toward strong ties with Germany, calling the U.S.-German linkage "a truly unique relationship," and irritated the British by intervening in the Northern Ireland issue.

Nonetheless, on one of Major's visits to the United States, Clinton extended an invitation—rarely offered to visiting dignitaries—to spend the night in the White House, and Major was delighted to accept. The Anglo-American relationship might be less than "truly unique," might indeed be less special for the United States than in the past. But it remained a very important component of British policy.

Europe. Britain did not participate in the creation of the Common Market, but joined in 1973, a decision ratified by a national referendum in 1975. Subsequently Thatcher signed the Single European Act in 1987, which prepared the ground for major strides toward economic integration, and in 1990 Britain entered into the exchange rate mechanism (though it was forced to withdraw two years later). Then John Major signed the Maastricht treaty in 1991, which took Britain still further into the European Community.

NATO. The two circles connecting Britain to the United States on one side and Europe on the other merged into one in the form of the North Atlantic Treaty Organization (NATO), a military alliance formed in 1949 to unite the United States and western Europe against the danger of a Soviet attack. Already Britain had handed over great power leadership to the United States; in 1947 Britain had made it clear that it could not provide protection for Greece and Turkey against the possibility of a communist takeover, and the United States assumed the responsibility in the form of the Truman doctrine.

With NATO Britain had, despite Acheson's cutting comment, found a role—that of a participant in the effort to contain Soviet power. Yet it was a role that signified the end of Britain's autonomy as a military power and her dependence on U.S. leadership. So profoundly was this armed alliance embedded in British strategic doctrine that even when the Labour Party's left-wing manifesto of 1983 called for Britain's unilateral renunciation of nuclear weapons and the eventual withdrawal of all U.S. nuclear forces from British soil, it did *not* demand that Britain pull out of NATO.

Thus Britain through its transatlantic and European alliances continued to play an important role in international affairs. But by their nature, these alliances were a recognition that Britain could never again aspire to the great power status of the past.

INCOMPLETE ADJUSTMENTS TO DECLINE

It was one thing for Britain to accept the inevitable, and another to do so consistently and enthusiastically. In fact, the change in Britain's posture came reluctantly, with persistent efforts to play an international role which—if no longer that of a major world power—was still greater than its economic and military resources would seem to justify. Here we consider the controversies that developed over Britain's postimperial military engagements, the building of her nuclear armory, and her troubled involvement with Europe.

Wars to Preserve Residual Imperial Interests

Two military engagements, one an ignominious failure, the other a triumph of arms, resulted from Britain's efforts to preserve remnants of the imperial past.

Suez. The 1956 Suez disaster followed the nationalization of the Suez canal by Egyptian president Gamal Abdel Nasser. An Anglo-French consortium had been running the canal, and prime Minister Anthony Eden saw Nasser's move as threatening Britain's economic links to her former dominions in Asia. Eden then instigated a plan whereby Israel would march on the Suez canal, Britain and France would send forces to stop the fighting—and take back control of the canal.

Unfortunately for Eden, he had not cleared the scheme with President Eisenhower, who was incensed that Britain would act without U.S. approval, creating a crisis during a U.S. election campaign that conceivably could have led to a confrontation between the United States and the Soviet Union. So the United States let the British know that it did not back the action and would not support the British pound against the prospect of a run by currency speculators. The invading forces withdrew, and Britain had been publicly reminded that it could not undertake adventures that ran counter to U.S. interests.

Within a few years, economic pressures had compelled Britain to withdraw most of its remaining military presence east of Suez. The withdrawal was deeply felt by a minority of Conservative leaders, but the impact of the change was largely symbolic, for Britain's interests in the Middle East and in Asia could no longer be served by unilateral military action.

The Falklands. In 1982 Argentina occupied the Falkland Islands, a small British dependency 250 miles off the Argentine coast, which Argentina had long claimed as its own under the name *the Malvinas*. The United States, though not wanting to damage its Latin American relationships, backed a U.N. Security Council demand for Argentina to withdraw. Alexander Haig, the U.S. secretary of state, tried to mediate but failed. Britain sent a naval task force which, though suffering serious losses, took the Falklands back from Argentina.

Afterward there was much criticism of the war from the left in Britain. It was absurd, they said, to have killed so many young men on both sides over an area of no strategic or economic importance to Britain (unless, says Tony Benn, the war was really about access to the oil beneath the ocean near the Falklands). Includ ed among the dead were several hundred on an Argentine troopship, the *General Belgrano*, which, despite British denials, had apparently been steaming away from the war zone at the time it was sunk by a British submarine. (However, in 1994 the Argentine government indicated that the sinking of the Belgrano was a legitimate act of war.) As for the financial cost, it would have been cheaper to have given each of the thousand or so residents of the islands a million pounds to resettle elsewhere.

The critics also insisted that the issue could have been settled by diplomacy at several stages during the crisis; but Thatcher, needing a victory for domestic political purposes, ignored several opportunities for a negotiated settlement. In fact, the crisis should never have blown up in the first place. It could have been resolved by a plan that would have ceded nominal sovereignty to Argentina and given Britain a longterm lease of the islands; however, a succession of British governments had failed to act on the proposal because of a circumstance unusual in British politics—the intimidation of the executive branch by a small but potent group of backbench members of the House of Commons, the so-called Falklands lobby. Finally, the Argentine military had made their move because the Thatcher government, as part of an effort to cut back on defense costs, had withdrawn the sole British navy ship in the South Atlantic, leaving the impression that Britain was no longer interested in protecting the Falklands.

However cogent these criticisms, they made singularly little impression on the British public. Here was a brilliant military victory, reversing a naked act of aggression by a particularly brutal right-wing military dictatorship. For Margaret Thatcher it was a personal triumph; it was generally conceded that any other British political leader of either party would have settled for an outcome short of ultimate success. The victory evoked rapturous enthusiasm among all classes of the population, for they were responding to a deep seated need to reassert national pride after a long period of decline culminating in the Suez fiasco. (In the same way the Gulf War helped erase the United States's sense of humiliation over Vietnam.)

The Falklands also raised Britain's standing in the international community. Other nations had to be impressed by a feat of martial prowess involving the rapid deployment of such a large force over a distance of thousands of miles, as well as by Britain's willingness to stand up against a clear violation of international law.

Yet the ultimate impact on Britain's position in world politics proved to be much less than it appeared in the joyous aftermath of the Falklands affair. This became all too clear in the negotiations over the future of another of Britain's remaining possessions, Hong Kong. Unlike the Falklands, on which sheepherders scratched out a bleak subsistence, Hong Kong was an extraordinarily valuable jewel in the British crown. Britain had forced China to grant a 99-year lease of Hong Kong in 1898. In 1984 Thatcher, after some initially defiant statements, signed an agreement under which Hong Kong would revert to China in 1997. The agreement stipulated that Hong Kong would retain its capitalist system for 50 years after 1997. But clearly this undertaking would be honored only to the extent that China decided that it served its purposes to do so.

Moreover, the Chinese responded with irritation when Hong Kong's last British governor-general, Chris Patten, proposed some modest steps toward greater democratization by increasing the number of elected, as against appointed, members of the legislative council. The Chinese declared themselves unimpressed with Britain's deathbed conversion to democracy after a century of ruling Hong Kong, and announced that they would abolish the council as soon as they took over in 1997.

The Independent Nuclear Deterrent

British scientists had been actively involved in the Manhattan project, which had developed America's atomic bomb. After the war, however, the United States decided that it would not share its nuclear secrets and production facilities with any other nation. The Attlee government therefore decided that Britain should proceed to develop its own nuclear weaponry, and this decision was acted on by the following Conservative government of Winston Churchill.

Subsequently Labour as well as Conservative governments proceeded to develop nuclear and thermonuclear weapons and delivery systems, and this became a source of fierce factional struggle within the Labour Party. The left wing of the party joined the Campaign for Nuclear Disarmament (CND) and other antinuclear groups in protest marches, demonstrations, and sit-ins in the 1950s and again in the 1980s. However, as we have seen, antinuclear politics was bad electoral politics, and eventually leaders of the antinuclear left—Aneurin Bevan in the 1950s, Neil Kinnock in the 1980s—dropped their demand for unilateral nuclear disarmament.

So the nuclear buildup continued until Britain possessed a strike force of 56 Vulcan bombers and 4 Polaris submarines, with the Polaris destined from the mid-1990s to be replaced by the more advanced Trident II, each of which will carry 96 warheads.

Initially the United States had tried to discourage the British from going ahead with their own systems, arguing that the U.S. armory provided a more than ample shield to protect the west, including Britain, from the possibility of a Soviet strike. Britain overruled these objections for two reasons. For one thing, the British, like the French, questioned whether the United States would risk the extermination of its own cities by launching a nuclear strike on the Soviets in the event of a Soviet attack on western Europe. Thus the Soviet Union could only be assured of nuclear retaliation if countries it threatened had their own means of retaliation. In the second place, the British believed that, even though their military and economic position had declined, possession of nuclear weapons would ensure their inclusion in the world power stakes. However, Britain's status as a nuclear power raised a number of awkward questions.

Questions about the Deterrent. First, *did it make strategic sense?* The case for Britain's stockpike was based on the *balance of terror* assumption that any nuclear power would be deterred from attacking another nuclear power by the fear of inevitable catastrophic retaliation on its own cities. This was a credible view in the context of the United States–USSR rivalry. But for a smaller power like Britain, the absence of nuclear weapons might leave it unharmed, whereas its presence would make Britain a likely target in case of a global war.

And the country's vulnerability was painfully obvious. If Britain were to be the victim of a thermonuclear attack its population, crowded together in a small island, would be well-nigh totally destroyed. During the 1950s and 1960s, governments tried to persuade people to become interested in the idea of civil defense. But the suggestions put forward in official pamphlets kept changing abruptly. First there was advice on evacuating children and others from the cities, as if this were to be a reprise of World War II. Then people were told to stay put, tape the windows, get under any kind of shelter, and cover their heads. In time campaigns of this kind were dropped, for their only result was to reinforce people's awareness of Britain's helpless vulnerability should it be attacked in even a limited nuclear war.

Second, *how independent was the independent nuclear deterrent?* By 1960 Britain had decided it could not afford to continue with research on its own *Blue Streak* missile and turned instead to the American *Skybolt*. But in 1962 the United States cancelled production of Skybolt and offered Britain its new Polaris instead—but only in the context of an Atlantic multilateral force. Macmillan negotiated the issue with Kennedy and, as one historian has observed: "Never before had Britain's subservience been so explicit."[2] Kennedy relented and the British were allowed to purchase Polaris missiles which they would mount on their own submarines with their own warheads.

Kennedy, Macmillan, and the Polaris negotiations

SOURCE: Vicky [Victor Weisz], *Evening Standard,* 6 December 1962. Center for the Study of Cartoons and Caricature, University of Kent, Canterbury.

Yet Britain was part of NATO. Could Britain really decide in a crisis to launch missiles that had been supplied by the United States without the specific approval of NATO—and thus without the approval of the United States? The nuclear interdependence of the two countries (or the dependence of Britain on the United States) became even more obvious with the introduction of nuclear-headed cruise missiles—unmanned guided aircraft—into U.S. bases in Britain. And then came the agreement to replace the Polaris with the next generation of submarine-based missiles, the Trident II, provided by the United States on a lease-purchase arrangement, with servicing to be carried out at Kings Bay, Georgia, and most of the warhead design already accomplished by the United States. Moreover, since 1962, all British nuclear tests have been conducted at the Nevada test site in the United States.

But these questions gave way at the end of the 1980s to a new, fundamental question: *why did Britain need a nuclear deterrent against the Soviet threat when, with the collapse of the Soviet empire, that threat had essentially evaporated?* Given the uncertain outlook in Russia and other former Soviet countries there was still a strong argument for maintaining a residual nuclear stockpile in the United States. But the focus was now on negotiations to reduce the level of weaponry, which would lessen the danger of miscalculation by either side and discourage the proliferation of nuclear weapons to other countries. And here were Britain and France refusing to cut their nuclear forces or to allow their weapons to be counted in the western totals for the purpose of east-west negotiations. Moreover, Britain lobbied hard and unsuccessfully against President Clinton's decision for a moratorium on underground nuclear testing. For the United States, the suspension of tests could facilitate nonproliferation negotiations. For the British, it would hamper their efforts to improve the safety and flexibility of the Trident system.

Finally, *could Britain afford it?* Even if Britain's economy improves during the 1990s, it will not provide an adequate base for sizeable conventional forces together with a nuclear armory, especially because the Polaris submarines are scheduled to be replaced with the more expensive Tridents.

Defense Spending Cuts. Indeed, the Defense Department in 1994 announced plans for substantial cuts in defense spending. Ten years earlier Britain was spending 5.3 percent of its gross domestic product on defense. The proportion was down to 3.8 percent in 1992–93, and a further reduction to 2.9 percent by 1996–97 was projected. A contribution to the reduction was to be made by the nuclear weapons program. In 1993 the Under-Secretary of State for Defence had told the House of Lords: "Our plan is for a maximum of about 512 warheads and I am astonished at our . . . moderation."[3] Now that figure was to be further moderated: the number of warheads on each Trident was cut from the original proposal of 128 to 96, for a total of 384. In addition some tactical nuclear weapons were to be eliminated.

But most of the reductions were to come in the area of conventional forces: the army would go down from 120,000 to 114,000, the air force from 70,000 to 57,000, and the navy from 51,000 to 44,000, with consequent cuts in equipment and supplies and in the defense plants and shipyards that produced and maintained them. Efforts would be made to streamline the defense bureaucracy and to reduce unnecessary costs resulting from interservice rivalries (which had not been eliminated when the separate service ministries were integrated into the new defense department in 1967).

Then, continuing the efforts of previous Labour as well as Conservative governments, Britain vigorously sold conventional arms on the worlds's markets. Under the Thatcher government, arms deals with Saudi Arabia may have brought in as much as £20 billion. Iraq, officially on a list of proscribed nations, was still buying weapons-related material from Britain in the late 1980s; as we saw in the last chapter, this led to an official inquiry into charges of a government coverup. And when in 1988 Malaysia signed a deal to buy a billion pounds worth of Tornado jet planes, they secured a protocol promising a foreign aid package of £234 million to build the Pergau dam. The project was of questionable economic soundness and, as the British High Court later found, was financed by an illegal diversion of funds from the overseas development administration budget, for Malaysia is no longer one of the world's poorest nations.

Still, the arms sales would not be enough to prevent the defense budget being cut both in the nuclear and non-nuclear fields. Nonetheless, the four Tridents, with their slightly reduced armory, would still be there, along with a force of nuclear-armed bombers. Nor was it likely that the election of a Labour government would make much difference. Neil Kinnock and his party had changed their minds about unilateral nuclear disarmament, and under Smith and Blair, Labour was not going to be accused of being soft on defense. Even while the party was calling for additional reductions in some areas of defense, Labour was complaining about the layoffs in defense plants and shipyards. As for Trident, Labour argued that four would not be necessary: three would be sufficient—unless it turned out that the cost of cancellation of the fourth boat was more than the cost of construction.

This consensus exists precisely because Britain has fallen from its former great power position and clings to the possession of nuclear missiles as a symbol of international status. Even the dependence on the United States as a supplier of the missiles can be seen as an advantage: it reaffirms the special relationship, for the United States has sold Polaris and Trident to no other country than Britain.

The Reluctant Europeans

From a U.S. perspective, Britain is clearly part of Europe. But the British have been slow to accept a European identity, maintaining a complacent insularity behind the narrow stretch of waters separating it from the Continent. So historically, Britain had aimed at a balance of power in Europe while giving its major attention to the empire/Commonwealth and later to the United States. Consequently, though Britain finally emerged as a full participant in the European Union, it dragged its feet at every stage of the negotiations for European economic and political collaboration, and still remains the most cautious of the EU members about fuller integration.

Thus when France and Germany organized a coal and steel community in 1950, Britain refused to participate. When the Common Market was created in 1957, Britain declined the opportunity to be in at its creation. Nor was the Conservative government's decision criticized by Labour. Hugh Gaitskell, the leader of a party ostensibly dedicated to change, proclaimed that Britain must not turn its back on "a thousand years of history."

The Long Struggle for Entry. In 1962, with Britain's economy in trouble, Prime Minister Harold Macmillan finally applied for admission to the Common Market. But French President Charles de Gaulle, seeing Britain as a surrogate for the enlargement of American influence in Europe, issued a magisterial "Non!" Again, when Labour prime minister Harold Wilson renewed Britain's application in 1967, he was confronted by de Gaulle's "Non!"

At last, when Edward Heath tried again in 1971, de Gaulle had been succeeded by George Pompidou, who said "Oui!" The British Parliament approved the proposal, and in 1973 Britain became a member of the Common Market. Yet this was not the end of resistance to membership within Britain. The parliamentary endorsement was by a narrow margin, for there was intense opposition within both of the major parties. The Conservative right was fearful of a loss of national sovereignty, while the Labour left believed that the cause of socialism would be lost in a capitalist Common Market and in a Europe dominated by conservative Catholic parties.

The left wing of his party represented a particularly difficult problem for Harold Wilson, who had overcome his own early doubts and was not a supporter of Common Market membership. So he finessed the issue by proposing that, if Labour came back to power after the 1974 election, his government would renegotiate the terms of admission and would hold a national referendum on the issue.

Back in office, Wilson did indeed renegotiate the terms, but only on minor technical details. Then he proceeded with the promised referendum. To avoid a destructive internal party battle he suspended the convention of collective cabinet responsibility, and allowed cabinet members opposed to the Common Market to campaign against his own position. Some of them did so and were joined in opposition by a number of right-wing Conservatives. But Wilson and a majority of his cabinet worked with Heath and most of his former cabinet members in a campaign that changed majority sentiment in the country from being against the Common Market to a two-to-one referendum vote for staying in.

This was a brilliant bipartisan accomplishment. Yet Britain's late and hesitant entry carried with it some severe disadvantages. By the time Britain joined, the rules and policies for the Common Market had already been set to serve the purposes of its original members, especially French and German farmers. Consequently British consumers found themselves paying higher food prices, and British taxpayers made a net annual contribution to the Common Market exchequer of over a billion pounds.

Thatcher and Europe. By the time Margaret Thatcher became prime minister, public opinion in Britain had turned hostile to the Common Market. Thatcher spoke for this mood, and at meetings of European leaders she thumped the table and declared: "I want my money back." Her tactics antagonized the other leaders, but she succeeded in changing the formula through which the participant countries paid into and received contributions from the central fund, and Britain's net payment was sharply reduced.

This helped change the public mood back to a more positive attitude to Europe. And the involvement in Europe had steadily grown deeper. In 1950, 11 percent of UK exports went to 12 countries that had joined or would be joining the Common Market. By 1960 the proportion had risen to 15 percent, by 1970 to 29 percent, by 1980 to 43 percent, and by 1988 to a full half of the total. Withdrawal, which the Labour Party manifesto had demanded in 1983, was already out of the question, and the proposal was no longer included in Labour's 1987 manifesto. In 1987 Thatcher signed the Single European Act, providing for the end of tariff and customs barriers by December 31, 1992, as well as movement toward monetary union; and in 1990 Britain tied the pound sterling to the deutschmark by entering the exchange rate mechanism.

Yet, obstinately, the issue continued to be deeply divisive in Britain. Thatcher herself fed the controversy. Although she had signed the Single European Act, her commitment was merely to a Common Market that abolished the barriers to the exchange of goods and services, and not to a European Community. Any suggestion of movement toward a federal Europe was anathema to her. "I think some people are being very superficial," she said in a radio interview, "when they say there is a United States of America, why don't we have a United States of Europe? . . . Europe had a totally different history. It's a history of many different cultures and many different languages. It is not possible to have a United States of Europe."[4]

Certainly she did not intend to have policies forced upon her by Europe that were diametrically opposed to her own positions. Thus in 1989 she declared that Britain would "opt out" of the "social chapter" of the Single European Act, for this aimed at tempering the impact of the single market by providing some underpinning of social programs and workers' rights. She had even stronger reservations about the suggestions for monetary union contained in the Single European Act; and she gave way to the pressure of her chancellor of the exchequer and foreign secretary to enter the ERM despite strong reservations based on her fears that Britain would lose its independence in a Europe dominated by Germany. It was her persistent and vigorous expression of these doubts even after she had given her official approval that led to Geoffrey Howe's resignation from her cabinet and his speech in Parliament, which precipitated her downfall.

Major and Maastricht. By the time John Major came to office, the 12-nation European Community (the United Kingdom, France, Germany, Italy, Belgium, the Netherlands, Luxembourg, Denmark, Greece, Ireland, Spain, and Portugal) was well established, with an extensive structure of policy-making, administrative, legislative, and judicial bodies. These consisted of:

- the *Commission,* headed by 17 commissioners (two each from the five larger countries, one each from the others) with a supporting staff of about 13,000, charged with proposing policies and managing their implementation.
- the *European Council,* made up of the heads of government and foreign ministers of the 12 nations, plus the president and vice-president of the

commission, responsible for setting broad strategies for the European Community.

- the *Council of Ministers,* composed of national representatives, empowered to adopt EC laws, some by qualified or weighted majority voting (i.e., a total of 76 votes was apportioned among the members—Britain receiving 10—and 54 constituted a majority).
- the *European Parliament,* with representatives elected by the voting public in each of the member countries, exercising limited powers of legislative review.
- the *Court of Justice,* charged with interpreting and applying the Treaties and EC laws.

This structure, and the powers of its component units, was the subject of a series of reviews by EC members eager for further moves toward European integration, and in December 1991 the European Council met at Maastricht to consider proposals for the next steps forward.

John Major was ambivalent on the issue. Though he was Margaret Thatcher's chosen successor he declared himself as wanting to be "at the center" of EC decision-making, and he had been instrumental in persuading her to enter the exchange rate mechanism. Yet he was not immune from the traditional British aversion to any loss of sovereignty, and he had to deal with the persistent strong dislike of the EC that came from the right wing of the Conservative party, including Lady Margaret Thatcher herself. Consequently the Maastricht treaty, which he signed in February 1992, and which was submitted to the 12 nations for ratification, included further steps toward cooperation and integration but also some important qualifications.

The strengthening of the bonds between the nations, symbolized by a change in title from European Community to European Union (EU), took a number of forms. There was an increase in the number of topics on which the Council of Ministers could legislate by qualified majority vote rather than by unanimity. The institutions of the treaty itself were supplemented by two coordinating bodies, one relating to foreign and security policy, the other to certain domestic policies including immigration, asylum, combating drug addiction and international fraud, and judicial cooperation. The European Parliament, with its membership increased from 518 to 567, was given the power of veto over legislation in certain fields and over the appointment of the slate of commissioners. The Court of Justice was empowered to impose fines on member states for failing to comply with its decisions or with EU laws. A timetable was set up for further moves toward the establishment of an economic and monetary union (EMU), which was to culminate in the introduction of a single currency and a European Central Bank by 1999.

Qualifying these steps toward integration were some provisions that Major had insisted on as a condition of Britain's agreeing to sign. The word "federal" was expunged from the treaty (though its proponents insisted they intended something much less than the federalism of the United States). The principle of *subsidiarity* was introduced, which the British interpreted as meaning that all matters not specifically mandated by the treaty must be left to the individual countries. Proposals for coordination of foreign and certain domestic policies were seen by the British government as merely advisory, outside the central mandates of the EU treaty. And the most important qualification of all was the right of Britain to "opt out" of the proposed single currency and European Bank. As with the social chapter, Britain insisted on being the one member of the twelve that would have exemption from a key provision of a European treaty.

It was also Britain's view that the EU should be broadened rather than deepened: That is, new members should be admitted, and the task of absorbing them should have priority over further strengthening of the central EU institutions. Indeed, Sweden, Finland, and Austria voted to join in 1994, and, as their economies improved, several eastern European nations would be eager applicants.

Continued Opposition. Offensive though Major's caveats might be to the other European leaders, they fell far short of mollifying his opponents at home, especially those within his own party. For them, a European Community was bad enough; a European Union was intolerable. As they saw it, everything about the Maastricht agreement was obnoxious. The extension of the topics decided by qualified majority votes took away Britain's veto power over laws contrary to its interests. The bureaucracy in Brussels under the European Commission was empowered to interfere in every nook and cranny of British life. And enlargement of the EU membership to 15 would result in more commissioners, a further expansion of the bureaucracy, and an already expensive Parliament increased to 626 members.

Almost every British institution, said the critics, was having to adapt to European requirements. The political parties must divert their resources every five years to elect 87 Members of the European Parliament (each typically covering five to eight Westminster constituencies). The European Parliament, which had begun as an expensive talking shop, was taking on significant legislative powers. Britain's own Parliament at Westminster was having to spend more and more of its time on European affairs, with specialized committees in both Houses wrestling with staggering quantities of technical minutiae. The civil service was becoming Europeanized, with a European secretariat in the cabinet office and European departments or sections in the foreign office, the treasury, and the department of trade and industry. Scotland and Wales had opened their own offices in Brussels, thus bypassing Westminster and Whitehall. Conversely, the EU had set up offices in Edinburgh, Cardiff, and Belfast. Many British local governments, affected by European laws or court decisions, or seeking funds under EU provisions for development of economically deprived areas, appointed EU liaison officers and hired lobbyists to represent them in Brussels. Pressure groups, including trade unions and environmentalists, looked to the EU to overrule their own government and courts.

The skeptics argued, too, that maintaining Britain's barriers against immigration would become much more difficult as frontier controls within the EU were abandoned. The social chapter would be no protection against extensive EU interference in British multinational firms, such as a directive requiring firms employing more than 1,000 workers in Europe to set up works councils, bringing employees into the decision-making and consultation processes.

So Major's narrow victory on Maastricht in Parliament, after his being forced to resort to a vote of confidence, did not end the opposition within his own party. He came under attack when Labour won 62 of the 87 British seats in the European Parliament elections in 1994, leaving the Conservatives with only 18 seats. More fuel for the critics was provided by Major's appointing Neil Kinnock as one of Britain's two European Commissioners in 1994. Kinnock (whose wife had been elected to the European Parliament) promised that he would support the social chapter. Then when the government sought ratification by Parliament of its agreement to increase Britain's financial contribution to the EU, eight of the Conservative Europhobes abstained on the vote, and, as we saw in Chapter 10, were punished by denial of the whip.

In the intensity of their hostility to the EU, the Conservative rebels constituted a small minority in the parliamentary party. Still, a number of their colleagues had strong reservations about Europe. And as suggested by Table 18.1, opinion polls indicated that the British electorate as a whole was far from enthusiastic about closer integration into Europe.

Other polls indicated that only 17 percent of Britons supported the idea of a federal United States of Europe; no more than a third were in favor of a central European bank; less than half believed that, on balance, Britain had benefited from being in the European Union. The "Euroskepticism" reflected in these attitudes was not confined to Britain. The French electorate had approved Maastricht in a referendum by a vote of 51 percent to 49 percent. The Danes had actually voted the treaty down before accepting it in a second referendum. Though Sweden voted to join the EU in a 1994 referendum, 47 percent of the electorate voted no, and Norway actually voted to stay out. So the enthusiastic predictions of a headlong rush to European integration were now being hedged, and the admission of additional member states would further complicate the task of harmonizing the several national interests. There would be no United States of Europe for some decades at least.

Still, on all the issues listed in Table 18.1, the British came close to the bottom

TABLE 18.1 British attitudes toward the EU, 1994

	Positive	**Negative**
Satisfied with how EU being run?	Satisfied: 18%	Dissatisfied: 54%
More integration or looser arrangement?	More integration: 31%	Looser: 61%
Power of European Commission	Too little: 16%	Too much: 58%
Power of European Parliament	Too little: 36%	Too much: 38%

SOURCE: Adapted from MORI, Harris Research Center, EUROBAROMETER, and *The American Enterprise*, September/October 1994, pp. 110–11.

of the list of EU members in their degree of satisfaction with the EU's performance and support for deeper involvement in Europe. This would not mean withdrawal from the EU; it was far too late for that. When pollsters asked in June 1995: "Do you support taking Britain out of the European Union?", the response was 60 percent to 29 percent against withdrawal. And even though 60 percent were opposed to a single European currency, 58 percent said they would not rule it out "forever."[5] The *Chunnel* linking Britain to France would further erode Britain's sense of separateness. Yet among the wide diversity of European cultures Britain persisted in being more "different" than any of the others, and more reluctant to relinquish its past identity as well as its transatlantic links.

That reluctance would again be on display during the review of the European Union's structure and functions scheduled to begin in 1996—just as Britain would be moving toward its next general election. In the course of this review John Major, having survived his leadership reelection test, need not adopt the harshly negative posture urged by the right-wing rebels. And the Euroskeptics did not feature prominently in Major's reconstructed cabinet. On the other hand, Major could not ignore the doubts about Europe held by many in his party. So, while he refused to make any promises on the subject, he did not rule out the possibility of a referendum whenever a single currency became a possibility. And he taunted the Labour Party with the argument that his European policy was much more protective of Britain's sovereignty than theirs.

In response to this, Labour moved to protect its flanks on the issue. They raised the possibility of a British referendum on any changes that might emerge from the 1996 EU review and pose constitutional questions for Britain. And Tony Blair emphasized that, while Britain's role in the world required fuller involvement with Europe, he did not favor federalism, saw "clear limits to integration," and supported a continuation of the British veto over EU voting on immigration and security.

BIPARTISANSHIP IN FOREIGN POLICY

No area of policy has caused more bitter strife in Britain than foreign affairs. In particular, the development of nuclear weapons and the involvement with Europe have aroused intense and lasting hostility. Yet the arenas in which the battles were fought were mostly *inside* rather than *between* the parties. Despite differences, often strongly expressed, by whichever party was in opposition, the party leaders, in and out of government, did not challenge the fundamentals of policy.

This remained true even after Margaret Thatcher came to power. In most other fields she attacked the prevailing consensus. But in foreign policy her differences with previous governments were mostly a matter of style and tone. She raged against the decline in Britain's international standing, and she raised Britain's stature with the Falklands victory. Yet in its broad outlines, her policies reflected continuity rather than fundamental change.

Thus she had accepted the advice of the Foreign Secretary and Foreign Service to bring about the end of white rule in Rhodesia and she had bowed to the inevitable over Hong Kong. Her prized special relationship with the United States was an improved version of the policy of her predecessors. Thatcher's insistence on a new generation of nuclear weapons systems infuriated the Labour left but was fully consistent with the programs of every Labour and Conservative prime minister since 1945. Her distrust of Europe merely echoed the attitudes that had so long delayed Britain's entering the Common Market, and however great her reluctance and her subsequent regrets, it was indeed Thatcher's signature on the Single European Act and Thatcher's decision to enter the exchange rate mechanism.

Thus the Thatcher policies continued along the general lines of British foreign policy since 1945: the shift from three to two circles of influence; the reluctant adjustment to a reduced standing in world politics; the effort to minimize that reduction by playing a larger role than its objective resources justified.

Agreement on these policies extended beyond the two parties. They spoke to the general sentiments of the majority of the public. And they reflected the longterm views of the Foreign Office. The civil service ethos, as we saw in chapter 9, is to carry out the policies of the elected government of the day. But how would the bureaucracy react if the government set out to break the foreign policy consensus? A former head of the diplomatic service put it this way:

> I think that if a government were to decide to take Britain out of Europe, that would be very unsettling and worrying for a large number of members of the Foreign and Commonwealth Office, and I think for home civil servants as well.... I think the withdrawal from NATO, or going wholly unilateralist, would also cause great anxieties in the minds of quite a number of us. But I suppose in foreign affairs there has been a greater tradition of bipartisan policy over the years than on other issues, and it may have been comforting and consoling for us.[6]

In other policy areas Thatcher had railed against the civil service's preference for consensual policies. But even though she distrusted the Foreign Office and brought in her own foreign policy advisors, she did not take Britain out of Europe, or withdraw from NATO, or go unilateralist, or pursue any policy that would be "very unsettling and worrying" for the civil service. The consensus held, and continued to hold under John Major, despite the opposition within his own party. Thus, when Major announced the formation of an Anglo-French rapid reaction force for Bosnia in June 1995, there was criticism from some Conservative backbenchers, but strong support from Tony Blair speaking for the Labour Party.

CONCLUSION

On the fundamentals of foreign policy Britain has achieved a cross-party consensus. But this does not mean that Britain has found the role best suited to its diminished, though not insignificant, place in the world. Thus, while there may be bipartisan agreement that maintaining a nuclear stockpile contributes to Britain's world politics status, building more nuclear delivery systems is not necessarily the best use of the available resources—even when considered solely in the context of defense policy.

Then, too, the consensus on membership in NATO gave Britain a role during the Cold War. But now NATO itself is searching for a new role, and the Bosnian crisis suggests that it will not be easy to define and act on a new set of purposes.

Toward the end of her tenure, Margaret Thatcher made a speech that suggested a valuable new role for Britain. Drawing on her background in science, she presented an urgent warning against the danger of the erosion of the ozone layer, and called for international action to meet the threat. However, her remedies, tied closely to her belief in the competitive market, were less bold than her diagnosis, and subsequently Britain has not taken a strong leadership position on the issue.

Another alternative that has been suggested for Britain would be to cut the military budget still further and become a leader in working with the world's developing nations. However, despite its remarkably generous contribution to Malaysia's Pergau dam, Britain's economic aid spending has been declining. In 1993 it was down to less than 0.3 percent of Britain's gross domestic product—more, proportionately, than the U.S. contribution of 0.14 percent, but well below the Scandinavian countries' 1 percent and the U.N. proposal for a minimum of 0.7% from each developed nation. Given the pressing needs in domestic programs discussed in previous chapters, it seems unlikely that a new consensus will emerge to give a high priority to foreign aid as a key to world economic development.

Finally, it may be questioned whether the determination of successive British governments to link their foreign policy to the United States has always been to Britain's advantage. At times it has imposed on Britain a humiliating dependency, and today there are more and more critics in Britain who argue that clinging to America's coattails contributes to Britain's reluctance to commit itself more fully to its real future, which must lie across the Channel and the North Sea rather than the Atlantic.

SOME QUESTIONS TO THINK ABOUT

Where would you rank Britain among world powers?

How "special" is the "special relationship"? Has the link to the United States been in Britain's best interests?

Should Britain continue to maintain strong military forces? For what purposes?

Should Britain maintain its own nuclear forces? How independent are they?

Should Britain be less cautious about the EU?

How true is it that Britain, having lost an empire, "has not yet found a role"? Does Britain need one? What might it be?

NOTES

1. Harold Macmillan, *At the End of the Day, 1961-1963* (Macmillan, 1973), p. 339.
2. Kenneth O. Morgan, *The People's Peace* (Oxford University Press, 1990), p. 216.
3. Viscount Cranborne, House of Lords, 25 May 1993, *Official Report,* cols. 165-66.
4. Reported in *Manchester Guardian Weekly,* 7 August 1988, p. 6.

5. *The Economist,* 1–7 July 1995, p. 46. Available from MORI/On-Line.
6. Simon Jenkins and Anne Sloman, *With Respect, Ambassador* (BBC Books, 1985), p. 103.

SUGGESTIONS FOR FURTHER READING

On the ending of the British Empire see Brian Lapping, *End of Empire* (St. Martin's Press, 1985), and John Darwin, *The End of the British Empire* (Blackwell, 1991).

For foreign policy in general, see D. Sanders, *Losing an Empire, Finding a Role: British Foreign Policy Since 1945* (Macmillan, 1990), and David Reynolds, *Britannia Overruled* (Longman, 1991); during the Thatcher era, P. Byrd (ed.), *British Foreign Policy Under Thatcher* (Philip Allan, 1988); and post-Thatcher, Christopher Tugenhat and William Wallace, *Options for British Foreign Policy in the 1990s* (Council on Foreign Relations Press, 1988). On defense policy see Michael Dockrill, *British Defence Since 1945* (Blackwell, 1989).

On the Falklands war see Lawrence Freedman, *Britain and the Falklands War* (Blackwell, 1988), Martin Middlebrook, *Task Force* (Penguin, 1987), and Max Hastings and Simon Jenkins, *The Battle for the Falklands* (Pan, 1983). On nuclear policy see Brian Cathcart, *Test of Greatness: Britain's Struggle for the Atom Bomb* (John Murray, 1994).

On the "special relationship," see David Dimbleby and David Reynolds, *An Ocean Apart* (Random House, 1988) and C. J. Bartlett, *"The Special Relationship"* (Longman, 1992).

On Britain and Europe see Stephen George, *Britain and European Integration Since 1945* (Blackwell, 1991) and Stephen George (ed.), *Britain and the European Community* (Oxford University Press, 1992), and Michael Franklin with Marc Wilke, *Britain in the European Community* (Royal Institute of International Affairs, 1991). On the new European institutional structures see N. Nugent, *The Government and Politics of the European Community* (Macmillan, 1992), and Robert O. Keohane and Stanley Hoffman (eds.), *The New European Community* (Westview, 1991).

Two valuable journals are published by the Royal Institute of International Affairs: *International Affairs* and *The World Today.*

19
SUMMING UP
TRANSATLANTIC LESSONS

In our review of British politics and government we have encountered a system different in many ways from our own in the United States. It is not a system that we are likely to adopt; nor will the British consider abandoning their parliamentary institutions in favor of our structure of separated powers. Yet each appears to possess certain advantages over the other, and by looking across the Atlantic in either direction some useful insights might be obtained, and perhaps some specific features might be identified and borrowed.

We consider this possibility in the context first of political and governmental institutions and then of public policies.

INSTITUTIONS

What the British Can Learn from the U.S. System

More Checks and Balances. *Elective dictatorship* as a description of the contemporary British system is clearly an overstatement. Even between elections a variety of constraints exist on the powers of the executive. Nonetheless, power has become concentrated and centralized to an unhealthy degree in the executive branch of government, and within the executive to the prime minister, a small number of cabinet members, and the senior civil service.

A U.S.-style separation of powers would not suit Britain at all; but some additional checks are needed on power at the center.

More Openness. America is far from being a fully open society. McCarthyism and the appalling intrusions of J. Edgar Hoover's FBI into individual liberties are not so far in the past to allow complacency today. The same is true of the various breaches of the constitution by the CIA, and even by the White House during the Iran-Contra affair.

Yet, as any reporter who has worked on both sides of the Atlantic will testify, the U.S. Bill of Rights, Freedom of Information Act, and prevalence of leaks from government offices provide a much greater degree of accessibility to information about government actions than is the case in Britain. There the government's obsession with secrecy has usually been backed by the courts, and if the Thatcher administraton was particularly noted for its rigor in this respect, it was drawing on a long tradition maintained by Labour as well as Conservative governments and by the civil service.

Nothing illustrates the contrast more vividly than the treatment of the defense budgets. In the United States, months of discussion and debate will follow the president's annual proposals for defense spending, and administration officials will be called before Congress to testify on every existing and proposed weapons system. In the United Kingdom, on the other hand, the debate on the annual *Statement on the Defence Estimates* is assigned two days. Moreover, the estimates tend to be cast in very general terms. Thus they revealed to Parliament and the public little or nothing about the Attlee government's plans to build nuclear weapons, or the Churchill government's proceeding to do so, or the modification of Polaris proposed by the Conservatives under Heath and pursued by the Labour governments of Wilson and Callaghan or the Thatcher administration's replacement of Polaris by Trident.

Of course, no nation reveals all of its military secrets, and some of the U.S. administration's data on its weaponry will be classified and presented to Congress under special conditions. Yet the British carry a passion for confidentiality far beyond the real requirements of national security, and reflect an executive branch bipartisan conviction that the public should be denied access to information on perhaps the most crucial of all public issues.

Less Deference. Deference, as we saw in chapter 2, has been declining in Britain. Yet class consciousness, and the influence of a recognizable upper class, remain far stronger than in the United States.

Institutionally this manifests itself in three ways. First, there is the honors system, which has been slightly democratized, but remains primarily a system of status rewards for the higher levels of government, industry, and finance.

Then there is the monarchy. The separation of head of state from head of government is a sound concept lacking in the U.S. system. But inherited monarchies are difficult to reconcile with the principle of democracy, especially in the lavish version maintained by the British.

But if there is still a case to be made for a constitutional monarchy, it is difficult to stretch that case in a democracy to a second chamber made up of an unelected House of Lords.

Reform Proposals. Several proposals gaining ground among opposition parties will be a significant part of future debate, and—unless the Conservatives go on winning—could well be adopted by early next century. Among these are proposals that would bring the British system closer to the U.S. system: creating a bill of rights and a freedom of information act, strengthening the parliamentary select committees, replacing the House of Lords with an elected second chamber, simplifying the monarchy somewhat, and the devolution of much domestic legislation to Scotland, Wales, and local or regional governments.

One other proposal under consideration, proportional representation, would not be drawn from the U.S. model, but if implemented could exercise a more thoroughgoing limitation on the power of the executive than any other reform proposal.

A further source of institutional change that will reduce the authority of the executive branch in Britain will be the European Union. Although there will not be a federal Europe in the foreseeable future, the steps already taken toward closer integration will mean more and more incursions into national sovereignties, even those of a reluctant Britain.

What Americans Can Learn from the British System

The Ability to Make and Implement Decisions. Our system is well-designed to limit power (though more for domestic than for foreign policy); it is poorly equipped, other than in exceptional circumstances, to provide the power necessary to get things done. This is particularly obvious when president and congress are of opposite parties, but the Carter and Clinton experiences are painful illustrations of the tendency of the system toward deadlock even when clear majorities in both Houses are of the President's party.

A Clear Allocation of Responsibility. The diffusion of power in American government, at the state and local as well as the federal level, encourages buck-passing. The blame for failure is too easily shifted to some other part of the system.

It is much easier under the British system to determine who should get the blame for failure or the credit for success.

Relatively Cohesive National Parties. Though intense factional struggles are common to both of the major political parties in Britain, they are still more cohesive, more policy-oriented, and better organized on a national scale than the U.S. parties—especially the Democratic Party. This provides three important advantages. First, despite the tendency to move toward the center as election time approaches, the British parties usually offer clearer alternatives to the electorate than parties in the United States. Second, party discipline in Parliament, though sometimes enforced too stringently, provides a stable base for government. Third, party is the principal mechanism for providing a consistent, organized opposition to government under clearly defined leadership (unlike the United States, where there is usually no generally accepted single leader of the opposition except during a presidential election).

Fewer Access Points for Interest Groups. Organized interests, as Beer and others have observed, play a major role in British politics. But there the focus of their activity is on the executive branch, so their concerns are dealt with in a more systematic, orderly fashion than in the United States where, defeated at one point in the system, they can redouble their efforts at any one of several alternative points of access.

It is true that in Britain there has been an increase of efforts to influence Parliament through paid consultants and other devices; that there is insufficient disclosure of interest group contributions to parties; and that conflicts of interest are not uncommon. Still, there has been no interest group scandal in British politics to compare with the savings and loan disasters in the United States.

Question Time. There are growing criticisms of prime minister's Question Time in the House of Commons. Too often the exchanges have fallen into a tired formula, with the prime minister giving banal answers to questions prepared for his or her backbenchers by the whips, opposition members posing predictable questions designed to embarrass rather than enlighten, and both sides jeering the other in rowdy displays.

Untidy though it is, the process still keeps the government on its toes, making it constantly aware that any of its activities may be the subject of public scrutiny and debate. On the whole it is a more effective system for confronting the leadership than the presidential press conference in the United States, which is called at the president's pleasure rather than on a regular schedule.

It should be noted, however, that this suggested deficiency in the U.S. system is related primarily to the president rather than the executive branch as a whole, for cabinet members, White House staff, and senior bureaucrats are subject to far more intensive cross-examination by Congressional committees than are their counterparts in Britain.

Reform Proposals. The widespread disenchantment with the way the U.S. system is working generated a movement for reform, which received expression in the Republican congress elected in 1994. As a result, committees and staff in the House of Representatives were pruned, Congress was made subject to laws from which it had previously exempted itself, and there was movement toward a presidential line item veto.

Moreover, there is some progress in the direction of more coherent political parties, as southern conservatives turn increasingly to the Republican Party, and as Republicans in Congress, especially the House of Representatives, achieve a much higher level of party unity than in the past.

Even so, both parties remain loose, sprawling coalitions of constituencies even more disparate than those that make up the British parties. Proposals that might bring more consistency between the executive and legislative branches, such as a four-year term for the House of Representatives concurrent with the president's term, are considered only in political science seminars. And there is little immediate prospect of any major reform of a serious defect in the system—the financing of election campaigns.

Thus the current public debate in the United States over the reform of the political system reaches less fundamental issues than is the case in Britain today.

POLICIES

For two decades after World War II, the broad domestic policies of the United Kingdom and the United States moved in divergent directions. The United States was widely seen as the land of competitive, individualist capitalism, opportunity, and incentives. Social welfare programs had expanded considerably under the New Deal; but most of the rhetoric of politicians still favored business over government, private enterprise over government intervention. Britain, on the other hand, was more attached to community values, fair shares for all, the welfare state and the National Health Service, and extensive government intervention in the economy, including nationalization. The standard of living was lower than in the United States, but the slower pace of life and the civility of social relations were cited as compensating virtues.

From the mid-1960s the differences narrowed. In the United States, Lyndon Johnson's *Great Society* programs expanded the welfare state and government's role in a number of areas. In the United Kingdom, maintaining the social services became problematic as economic growth slowed and the once-admired civility eroded.

The convergence of policies became even more marked with the concurrent terms of ideological soulmates, Ronald Reagan and Margaret Thatcher. Reagan attacked the Great Society programs, Thatcher attacked everything that government had done since 1945, and free enterprise and individualism were in the saddle.

In the mid-1990s the differences have widened again. In the United States the Republicans, especially in the House, are intent on pursuing and enlarging the Reagan agenda. In Britain, on the other hand, there is a strong revulsion against further extensions of Thatcherite ideas. Even so, there are powerful resistances in the United States to the abandonment of programs that subsidize large constituencies. And in Britain, Thatcherism has had a profound impact in a number of policy areas, forcing the Labour Party to move away from many of its past positions.

Consequently we encounter both differences and similarities in how the two countries handle their public policy issues, as we see from a brief review of the topics covered in Part IV of this book.

The Economy

Economic performance has clearly been better in the United States than in Britain. The standard of living is higher, productivity is considerably greater, and business is more enterprising and competitive. In the fiscal area, on the other hand, Britain's performance has been more prudent; despite some high deficits in the 1990s, the British are not staggering under the burden of the enormous deficits incurred since the 1980s.

In both countries inflation has been brought under control, in sharp contrast to the experience of the 1970s, let alone that of many other nations today. However, trying to force the rate down to between 2 and 3 percent, if not to 0, could have a dampening effect on the economy and on employment. Indeed, unemployment, especially in Britain, is at higher levels than were considered politically possible in the past. This is one of several factors that have contributed to the growing gap between the top and bottom of the income scales.

In the nineteenth century Disraeli warned of the danger that Britain might become divided into *two nations*, one rich and one poor. But then the poor were a majority and their plight is deeper now that they have become a minority. In both countries the existence of a substantial minority afflicted by a sense of deprivation and hopelessness could become a source of intense social and political tension.

The Welfare State

Although both countries provide a broad array of social programs, Britain's has a longer history and is more extensive. In particular, the United States is still struggling to achieve a health insurance program that will cover most of the population and restrain escalating costs, while the National Health Service, though suffering from budgetary constraints, covers the entire population for less than half the proportion of GNP spent in the United States. Moreover, by measures such as longevity and infant mortality rates the British general health record is comparable with the U.S. record (despite the excessive amounts of sugar and fats in the typical British diet).

On the other hand, Britain has not been more effective than the United States in preventing the rise of homelessness.

Education

The United States and Britain both offer excellent systems of higher education, the United States being particularly strong at the graduate level, while the British are rapidly expanding their first-rate undergraduate programs.

However, there are profound failures of performance in primary and secondary education, for test scores in both countries are below the average for industrialized nations.

Race and Gender

In the United States, despite civil rights laws, court decisions, and the growth of the African American middle class, race remains a deep dilemma. Britain has a much smaller nonwhite population (largely because of holding down the rate of immigration) and its race problem is less acute than in some other European countries. Yet race, a relatively new question for Britain, is severely testing the reputation for tolerance of a highly insular people.

Considerable strides have been made in both countries in the direction of gender equality, though there is still a long distance to go. The United States is yet to come close to Britain's achievement in electing a woman as prime minister.

Civil Liberties

The recent record in this respect is flawed in both countries. On the whole, however, it favors the United States over Britain, where claims of national security—and concern over crime and IRA terrorism—have combined to produce administrative actions, legislation, and court decisions limiting some kinds of individual liberties.

Foreign Policy

Both nations have been strong players in world affairs, but neither maintains the dominant position of the past. Britain, while achieving an impact much greater than its resources would suggest, has been reduced to a generally subordinate role to the United States. For its part, the United States, while the only remaining military superpower, faces some of the same frustrations Britain experienced during its period of decline.

CONCLUSION

Both the British and U.S. systems are functioning, reasonably democratic systems, clearly more so than the many other systems around the world in the throes of deep crises, including Russia, Bosnia, and the autocracies in parts of Africa, Asia, and Latin America.

Both are among the world's rich nations, generating a high standard of living for the majority of their people, and providing a wide range of social services.

However, persistent unemployment, poverty, and racism present threats to the stability of the two societies; and deficiencies in their educational systems and workforce skills may hurt their competitive standing in the global economy.

Moreover, limitations of political will and resources hinder their ability to address the major international problems of the next half century: rapidly increasing population, mostly in already poor countries, the deterioration of the environment, and the proliferation of nuclear weapons.

Improving the capacity to address such problems may require modifications of the institutional structures of the two countries. If this be so, Britain and the United States might do well to study the other's system, recognizing that—despite differences in political culture and constitutional inheritance—each might have some useful lessons for consideration across the Atlantic.

SOME QUESTIONS TO THINK ABOUT

Are there any features of the British system that you would like to see adopted in this country? Are there features of the U.S. system that would be usefully applied to Britain?

How would you rate the two systems with respect to the various policy issues considered in this discussion? If you believe one country has done better than the other on a particular issue, why do you think this has come about?

APPENDIX

GENERAL ELECTION RESULTS, 1945–92

	\multicolumn{5}{c	}{Seats in House of Commons (and Percentage of Popular Vote)}	
	Conservative	Labour	Liberal[a]	Nationalist[b]	Other[c]	Government Majority
1945	213(39.8)	393(48.3)	12(9.1)	0(0.2)	22(2.5)	146
1950	299(43.5)	315(46.1)	9(9.1)	0(0.1)	2(1.2)	5
1951	321(48.0)	295(48.8)	6(2.5)	0(0.1)	3(0.6)	17
1955	345(49.7)	277(46.4)	6(2.7)	0(0.2)	2(0.9)	60
1959	365(49.4)	258(43.8)	6(5.9)	0(0.4)	1(0.6)	100
1964	304(43.4)	317(44.1)	9(11.2)	0(0.5)	0(0.8)	4
1966	253(41.9)	363(47.9)	12(8.5)	0(0.7)	2(0.9)	95
1970	330(46.4)	288(43.0)	6(7.5)	1(1.3)	5(1.8)	30
Feb. 1974	297(37.8)	301(37.1)	14(19.3)	9(2.6)	14(3.2)	−34[d]
Oct. 974	277(35.8)	319(39.2)	13(18.3)	14(3.5)	12(3.2)	3
1979	339(43.9)	269(37.0)	11(13.8)	4(2.0)	12(3.3)	43
1983	397(42.4)	209(27.6)	23(25.4)	4(1.5)	17(3.1)	144
1987	376(42.3)	229(30.8)	22(22.6)	6(1.7)	17(2.6)	102
1992	336(41.9)	271(34.4)	20(17.8)	7(2.3)	17(3.5)	21

[a] Liberal Party 1945–79; Liberal/Social Democrat Alliance 1983–87; Liberal Democrat party 1992–.
[b] Scottish National Party (SNP) and Welsh National Party (Plaid Cymur) combined.
[c] Until 1974 Ulster Unionists affiliated with Conservative Party. Subsequently sat as separate party.
[d] Labour 34 seats short of majority after Feb. 1974 election.

Index

Abortion, 284
Accents, 21. *See also* Dialects
Accountability
   democratic, 40-41, 43
   Major administration and strides toward, 295
Adams, Gerry, 214, 220
Advertising
   campaign, 93
   television, 28
Agee, Philip, 298
Alliance
   election of 1983 and, 64, 84
   formation of, 46, 47, 89, 108
Amalgamated Engineering and Electrical Union (AEEU), 57
Anderson, John, 51
Andrew, Prince, Duke of York, 115
Annual Conference of Conservative Party, 72, 74
Annual Conference of Labour Party, 80
Appellate Committee of the House of Lords, 189
Aristocracy. *See* Upper class
Armstrong, Sir Robert
   as advisor to Thatcher, 161
   background of, 158
   on civil service, 154, 155, 160
Armstrong, Sir William, role in policy making of, 161

Ashdown, Paddy, 89, 177, 241, 252
Association of British Chambers of Commerce, 53
Attlee, Clement
   as compromise party leader, 80, 136
   economic policy of, 226, 227, 229-230
   foreign policy of, 308
   Labour government of 1945-51 under, 42, 81-82, 135-137, 159
   management style of, 161
   nationalization of steel industry and, 69
   social security legislation of, 245
   view of monarchy by, 124
Authority, British vs. American attitudes regarding, 27-28

Backbenchers
   advancement for, 174-175
   explanation of, 171
   Falklands and, 312
   forums for, 180-182
   proposals for legislation by, 179
   use of parliamentary procedures by, 180
Bagehot, Walter, 39-40, 116, 122
Bank of Credit and Commerce International (BCCI), 238
Bank of England, 54
Barings Bank, 238
Barristers, 191, 197

Beaker Folk, 31
Beer, Samuel H., 52
Benn, Anthony Wedgewood
    background of, 83
    on civil service, 159
    leadership contests and, 84
    reform proposals by, 47, 83, 93, 241
    view of monarchy by, 124
Bennett, Alan, 117
Bevan, Aneurin, 213, 227, 231
Beveridge, Sir William, 245
Beveridge Report, 245
Bevin, Ernest, 136, 137
Biden, Joseph, 99
Birmingham Six, 196, 197
Blair, Tony, 21, 59
    education policy of, 265, 266, 268
    election of, 85-86
    as Labour Party leader, 110
    political actions of, 86-87, 240
    social security and, 248
Blunkett, David, 268
Blunt, Sir Anthony, 22
Boothroyd, Betty, 176, 286
British Broadcasting Corporation (BBC)
    background of, 28
    campaign to break monopoly of, 169
    election coverage by, 61
British Empire
    foreign policy and, 308-309
    rise and fall of, 2-3
British Medical Association, 252
British National Health Service, 7
British National Party, 280, 282
British Telecom, 239
Brown, George, 147, 230
Bruton, John, 217
Buckingham Palace, 118-119
Buddhists, 29
Budget deficits, 237
Burger, Warren, 198
Burgess, Guy, 21-22
Burns, James McGregor, 52-53
Burt, Cyril, 262
Bush, George
    budgets of, 42
    campaign in 1992 of, 94, 106
    social background of, 24
Business
    Conservative Party and, 54-55
    overview of, 53-54
Butler, David, 62

Butler, R. A., 70, 74
Butler, Sir Robin
    background of, 158
    letters to editor in *Guardian* newspaper from, 161
    on secrecy issues, 293
Butler Education Act of 1944, 262
Butskellism, 70

Cabinet
    overview of, 128-129
    power of prime minister over, 129-131
Callaghan, James
    defeat of government of, 82
    on education, 263
    error in timing of election by, 132
    leadership style of, 147-148
    media skills of, 98
    resignation as Labour leader by, 83
    Scottish and Welsh Nationalist Parties and, 108, 211
    survival of administration of, 173-174
    view of monarchy by, 124
Cambridge University, 21, 152. *See also* Oxbridge
Campaign for Nuclear Disarmament (CND), 299, 313
Campaigns. *See* Election campaigns
Cannadine, David, 125
Carrington, Lord, 134, 139, 308
Carter, Jimmy, 131
Cash, Bill, 180
Castle, Barbara, 146, 155, 285
Center for Policy Studies, 160
Central Policy Review Staff, 160
Central Policy Review Staff study, 246-247, 254
Chancellor of Duchy of Lancaster, 129
Charles, Prince of Wales
    family problems involving, 115, 116, 119
    political influence of, 122-123
    political leanings of, 124
    taxes paid by, 118
Charles I, confrontation between Parliament and, 35
Charlotte, Queen of England, 117
Charter 88, 47, 301, 304
Chartist movement, 35-36
Childrearing benefits, 245
Church attendance, 29
Church of England
    background of, 28-29
    decline in prominence of, 30

monarch as governor of, 119
role of Parliament in, 30
women priests in, 287
Church of Scotland, 210
Churchill, Winston
on Attlee, 136
bond between Roosevelt and, 8
economic policy of, 226-227
fall of British Empire and, 2
foreign policy of, 133, 134, 309
leadership style of, 144
management style of, 161
media skills of, 133
on policies toward Nazis, 71, 171-172
Churchill, Winston (grandson), 172
Citizen's Charter, 295
Civil liberties
bill of rights and, 303-304, 328
British tradition of, 291, 304, 305
criminal justice system and, 296-297, 302-303
interest groups and, 301
media and, 301-302
threats to, 292-293
in U.S. vs. Britain, 332
Civil servants
career advancement for, 159
code of ethics for, 161
compensation for, 158
educational and class background of, 152-153, 158
as policy or political advisors, 160
political bias of, 158-159
power available to, 156-158
technical expertise of, 153-154
Civil service
constitutional authority and, 160-161
explanation of, 152
subordination and impartiality as issue for, 154-155, 158
Civility, 4
Class system. *See* Social class
Clinton, Bill
budgets of, 42
campaign spending in 1992 by, 94
election of, 87
relationship between Major and, 8, 310
Commission for Racial Equality, 280-282
Commission on Social Justice, 248-249
Common Market, 310, 317, 318
Commonwealth Immigrants Act of 1968, 276-277
Commonwealth of Britain bill, 47
Communist Party, 21-22

Communitarianism, 28
Comparable worth, 286-287
Confederation of British Industries, 53
Congress, U.S.
autonomy of, 169
distribution of professionals in, 167
political advancement for members of, 169-170
resources available to, 167-168
similarities and differences between Parliament and, 164-165, 182
whip system in, 171
Conscience bills, 179-180
Conservative Central Office, 72
Conservative Party
business and financial communities and, 54-55
centralization and, 205-210
educational background of, 21, 167
fundraising by, 94
immigration and, 277-278
leadership succession in, 74-79
locations of power in, 72-74
organization of, 73
overview of conflicts in, 71-72
predominant-party system and, 46
present unpopularity of, 46
profile of, 68-71
prospects for, 109-111
race relations legislation and, 282
relationship with unions, 56-57
transformation in leadership of, 24
voting behavior and, 63-65
women and, 285
Conservativism, 21, 193
Constitution, British
evolution of, 35-36
judicial power and, 38, 40
limitation of government power in, 40-42
pressures for reform of, 44-47
relationship between executive and legislative branches in, 37-38
separation of head of government from head of state in, 39-40
sources for, 36-37
as unwritten constitution, 43-44, 48
virtues of, 42-44
Constitution, U.S.
background of, 36-37, 43
British vs., 42, 43
limitations on power of government in, 40
Conyngham, Lord Simon, 23

Corporatism, 59
Corporatist tendency, 59-60
Court system
　authority of, 38
　lawyers and, 191
　national security issues and, 302
　overview of, 188-189
　property issues and, 300-301
　structure of, 189-191
Crime. *See also* Violence
　increase in, 4, 192, 294
　Major administration and, 194, 295-296
　terrorist, 294
　Thatcher administration and, 194
Criminal Justice Act of 1994, 296
Criminal Justice and Public Order Bill of 1994, 194, 196-197
Criminal justice system
　authority of, 38, 40
　criticisms of, 192-195
　European Court of Justice and, 199
　expeditiousness of, 197-198
　individual liberties and, 296-297
　IRA cases and, 195-197
　reforms in progress in, 198-199
　women's issues and, 288
Cripps, Sir Stafford, 136, 137
Cromwell, Oliver, 35
Crosland, Anthony, 263
Crossman, Richard, 124, 283
　on civil service, 156, 157, 160-161
　parliamentary committees and, 178
　on style of government, 146-147, 161
　on tax issues, 208
Crown Courts, 189-190
Curtice, John, 18, 24-25

Dalton, Hugh, 136
Dalyell, Tom, 211
De Gaulle, Charles, 123, 134
Debates
　election campaign, 96
　in House of Commons, 178-179
　style of political, 8
Delors, Jacques, 61
Democratic accountability, 40-41, 43
Denning, Lord, 193, 196, 198, 298-299
Deregulation, 237-238
Dialects, regional, 6, 17
Diana, Princess of Wales, 115-116, 119, 126
Dicey, A. V., 296-297
Discrimination
　gender, 282-289
　homosexual, 287
　racial, 279-282, 289-290
　religious, 279-280
Disraeli, Benjamin, 55, 72
Divorce laws, 283, 287
Douglas-Home, Sir Alec (Lord Home), 24
　appointment as prime minister, 74
　cabinet government of, 140-141
　foreign policy experience of, 133-134
　media skills of, 98, 102, 133
Dworkin, Ronald, 291, 305

Economic growth
　overview of decline in, 3-4
　U.S. vs. British, 330-331
Economic policies
　Labour Party responses to, 240-241
　of Major administration, 234
　from 1945-79, 226-232
　results of Thatcher-Major, 234-240
　of Thatcher administration, 3, 27-28, 32, 42, 70, 205, 206, 232-233
Eden, Anthony, 311
　foreign policy experience of, 133-134
　prime ministerial government of, 142-143
　resignation of, 74, 120
Education. *See also* Higher education; Public schools; Schools; Secondary education
　elementary, 262
　higher, 269-273
　problems in, 273
　secondary, 261-268
　of upper class, 21, 152-153
　U.S. vs. British, 331
Education Act of 1870, 262
Education Act of 1980, 264
Education Act of 1981, 264
Education Act of 1986, 264
Education Reform Act of 1988, 264
Educational attainment, overview of, 61
Edward VIII, King of England, 117, 119, 124
Eisenhower, Dwight D., 98, 99, 134, 169
Election campaigns
　Americanization of, 98-102
　British vs. U.S., 92-97
　elements of, 102-104
　public interest in, 61
　spending during, 94, 96
Elections
　determinants of, 104-109
　errors in timing of, 132
　local, 204
　power to dissolve Parliament and call new, 132, 173, 181
　prospects for future, 109-111
　results, 1945-92, 333

Elective dictatorship, 326
Elizabeth II, Queen of Great Britain
    criticism of Thatcher policies by, 121-122
    in 1982 Christmas address to Commonwealth, 121, 122
    political leanings of, 124
    on problems of royal family, 115
England
    cultural patterns within, 15, 16
    population of, 15
English language
    as common language, 6-7
    regional dialects of, 6, 17
Entryism, 82
Equal Opportunities Commission, 286
Establishment, 20, 21, 24. *See also* Upper class
Ethnicity. *See also* Immigration
    discrimination and, 280
    overview of, 30-31
Eton, 21, 266, 267, 269
European Community
    British membership in, 31
    cooperation with, 233
European Convention on Human Rights, 302, 303
European Court of Justice, 199
European Union
    background of, 41
    British view of, 320-322
    constitutional significance of treaties with, 37
    power limitations due to participation in, 41
Ewing, K. D., 297, 304
Executive branch. *See also* Cabinet; Civil servants; Prime ministers
    British constitution and, 37-38
    checks on power of, 292, 327
    growing supremacy of, 45
    relations between House of Commons and, 170-174
    secrecy within, 45, 292, 293
    separation of powers and, 39-40

Falklands, 311-312
Family values, 288, 295
Fascist Party, 280
Federalism, 38-39
Ferguson, Sarah. *See* York, Sarah Mountbatten-Windsor, Dutchess of
Feudalism, 27, 35
Filibusters, 180
Financial industry, extent of, 53-54
First Lord of the Treasury, 129. *See also* Prime ministers

Foot, Michael
    as Labour Party leader, 83, 84
    media skills of, 99
Foot, Paul, 231
Ford Motor Company, 173, 181
Foreign policy
    alliances and, 309-310
    bipartisanship and, 322-323
    description of decline in, 308-309, 323
    Europeans and, 316-322
    in Falklands, 311-312
    independent nuclear deterrent and, 313-316
    overview of, 307-308
    prime ministers and, 133-134
    role of prime minister in, 133-134
    U.S. vs. Britain, 332
Foreign trade, 53-54
Foxhunting, 24
Fulton Committee report of 1968, 153

Gaitskell, Hugh, 70, 86, 268, 316-317
Gearty, C. A., 297, 304
General, Municipal and Boilermakers (GMB), 57
George, Lloyd, 213
George IV, King of England, 116
George V, King of England, 117, 118
George VI, King of England, 118
Glorious Revolution of 1688, 35, 291
Gorman, Teresa, 285-286
Government. *See also* Local government
    changes in reputation of, 4-5
    checks on power of, 292, 327
    Conservatives and centralization in, 205-210
    election outcome and performance of, 106
    forces toward centralization in, 202-204
    Labour and centralization in, 204-205
    protests against, 299-300
    reasons for studying, 5-10
    responsibilities of monarch related to, 120-122
Gow, Ian, 216
Great Britain. *See* United Kingdom of Great Britain and Northern Ireland
Griffith, J.A.G., 193, 196, 197, 297, 300, 303-304
Guildford Four, 195-197
Gulf War, 9
Guns, control of, 28

Haig, Alexander, 311
Hailsham, Lord, 23, 74

Hannah, Leslie, 268
Harrow, 21, 266, 267, 269
Hattersley, Roy, 84
Healey, Dennis, 230
    in contest for Labour leader, 83, 84
    on Howe, 77
Heath, Anthony, 18, 24-25
Heath, Edward, 155
    background of, 24
    campaign of 1970 of, 103, 231
    creation of Central Policy Review Staff by, 160
    decision to nationalize Rolls Royce by, 70
    efforts to set wage guidelines during administration, 59
    error in timing of election by, 132
    foreign policy of, 134
    leadership style of, 143-144
    mineworkers strike and, 56
    as party leader, 74-75, 132
    proposal for coalition in 1974, 120
    relationship with Thatcher, 139
Heffer, Eric, 102
Hennessy, Peter, 125
Henry VIII, break with Roman Catholic Church, 35
Heseltine, Michael, 60
    appointment as deputy prime minister, 129, 142
    election of 1992 and, 78
    misconduct in Parliament, 177
    relationship and challenge to Thatcher by, 75, 77, 170
    resignation of, 131
High Court, 189
Higher Civil Service, 152
Higher education
    background of, 269
    Major and, 272-273
    social class and, 21, 152-153
    student composition and, 269-271
    Thatcher and, 271-272
Hindus, 29
Hollis, Sir Roger, 22
Home, Lord. *See* Douglas-Home, Sir Alec (Lord Home)
Home ownership, 255
Homelessness, 258
Homosexuals
    discrimination against, 287
    legislation affecting, 283-284, 286
Honors system, 25
Hosenball, Mark, 298, 299
House of Commons
    backbench forums in, 180
    committees of, 178, 184
    conscience bills in, 179-180
    debates in, 178-179
    duties of monarchy related to, 120
    education and social class of members of, 166, 167
    election of representatives to, 37, 38
    interest group influence on, 168-169
    physical layout of, 171
    political advancement and, 169-170
    power of, 35
    private members' bills in, 179
    proposals for reform of, 184-185
    relations between executive branch and, 170-174
    relations between prime minister and, 132
    representation in, 165-167
    resources of, 167-168
    role of backbenchers in, 174-182
    ten-minute-rule bills in, 179
    use of parliamentary procedures in, 180
    whips and, 171-174, 181-182
House of Lords
    characteristics of, 182-183
    functions of, 183
    honors system and seats in, 25
    partisan makeup of, 183-184
    power of, 35, 38
    proposals for reform of, 185
Housing policy
    homelessness and, 258
    interest rates and, 256
    between 1945-79, 253-254
    privatization and, 254-256
    renter issues and, 257
    tax issues and, 257
Howard, Michael, 194, 196-197, 278
Howe, Geoffrey
    demotion of, 77
    as deputy prime minister, 129
    interest rate actions of, 233
    resignation of, 140, 318
Huguenots, 279
Human Rights Convention, 303
Hume, John, 214
Hurd, Douglas, 76, 134

Immigration
    background of, 31, 275-276
    government view of nonwhite, 30-31
    politics and, 276-278, 289
Immigration Act of 1962, 276
Immigration Act of 1971, 277
Income
    nonwhite, 279

upper class, 21
  of women, 286-287
Individualism
  British vs. American attitudes regarding, 27-28
  communitarianism vs., 28
Ingham, Bernard, 133
Institute of Directors, 53
Interest groups
  civil liberties and, 301
  civil service and, 157
  extent of, 52, 53
  influence on House of Commons, 168-169
  politics and, 52-53, 65, 329
International Monetary Fund, 70
Investments, extent of foreign, 53
IRA Cases, 195-196, 198, 199
Ireland. *See also* Northern Ireland
  historical background of, 15
  reunification of, 218
Irish Republican Army (IRA), 214, 216, 217, 293, 294

James II, 35
Jenkins, Peter, 304-305
Jenkins, Roy, 147, 283
Jews
  discrimination against, 279-280
  population of, 29
Johnson, Lyndon, 134
Joint Framework Document, 217-218
Joseph, Keith, 271
Jowell, Roger, 18, 24-25
Juan Carlos, King of Spain, 126
Judges. *See also* Court system; Criminal justice system
  appointment of, 190-191
  discrimination against women by, 288
  social class and, 192
  types of, 189-190
  women, 286

Kennedy, John F., 98
Kennedy, Paul, 4, 9
Kerner Commission, 280
Keynes, John Maynard, 231
Khrushchev, Nikita, 134
Kilmuir, Lord, 74
Kinnock, Neil, 213
  campaign of, 99, 100, 104, 108
  communication skills of, 170
  derisive treatment of, 177
  educational background of, 268
  National Health Service and, 252

  political views of, 84, 85, 173, 207, 240
  tabloid coverage of, 97, 98, 102
Knighthoods, 25

Labor strikes
  during Thatcher administration, 58
  union power and, 56-57
Labor unions. *See* Trade unions
Labour Party
  background of, 55, 56
  centralizing policies of, 204-205
  constitutional change proposals of, 47
  decline of left in, 84-88
  economic policies of Conservatives and views of, 240-241
  educational background of, 21
  fundraising by, 94
  immigration and, 276-277
  leadership contests in, 83-84
  locations of power in, 80-82
  organization of, 81
  overview of conflicts in, 79-80
  profile of, 68-71
  race relations legislation and, 280-282
  rise of left wing in, 82-83
  social security and, 248-249, 259
  social trends favoring, 105
  trade unions and, 55-56
  view of monarchy by, 124
  voting behavior and, 63-65
  women candidates from, 285
Lane, Lord, 197
Lansbury, George, 80
Lawson, Nigel, 140, 160
Lawyers, 191
Legislative branch, British constitution and, 37-38
Letwin, Shirley Robin, 246, 272
Lewis, Sinclair, 27
Libel laws, 294
Liberal Democrats, 46, 47
  background of, 88-89
  future outlook for, 89
  National Health Service and, 252
  opposition to racism and discrimination, 282
  political views of, 241
  social class and membership in, 63
  women candidates from, 285
Liberal Party. *See also* Liberal Democrats
  background of, 88, 108
  1979 election and, 88
  political positions of, 47
Lilley, Peter, 248
Livingstone, Ken, 206, 207

Local government
  authority granted to, 202
  elections for, 204
  financial issues and, 203-204
  Labour party and, 204, 205
  overview of, 201-202
  reduction in functions of, 202-203
Local Government Act of 1972, 201-202
Local Government Act of 1985, 201
Lord President of the Council, 128-129
Lord Privy Seal, 129

Maastricht treaty, 174, 181, 241, 310, 318-319, 321
MacDonald, Ramsay, 80
Mackay, Lord, 198-199
Maclean, Donald, 21-22
Macmillan, Harold
  campaign of 1959 of, 98, 106
  creation of National Economic Development Council, 59
  firing of members of cabinet by, 131
  foreign policy of, 134, 317
  as housing minister, 253-254
  leadership style of, 144-145
  media skills of, 133
  resignation of, 74, 120
Magistrates' courts, 189
Magna Carta, 35, 36
Major, John
  appointment of women by, 286
  on BBC charter, 28
  cabinet government of, 141-142
  on campaign finances, 94
  civil service cuts by, 154
  communication skills of, 102, 133
  economic policies of, 234, 239-240
  education policy of, 264-267, 272-273
  on firing of members of cabinet, 131
  foreign policy of, 134, 174, 310, 318-321
  on honors system, 25
  law enforcement emphasis of, 194, 295-296
  National Health Service and, 252
  1992 election and, 78-79
  opposition to constitutional change proposals of Labour Party by, 47
  popularity of, 110
  public perceptions of, 247
  relationship between Clinton and, 8
  rise of, 76
  social and educational background of, 24, 272
  union dealings and, 60
Marbury v. Madison, 38, 188
Maudling, Reginald, 74

Maxwell, Robert, 238, 294
McGuire Seven, 195, 197
Media. *See also* Newspapers
  civil liberties and, 301
  national secrecy issues and, 298-299
Meyer, Sir Anthony, 75, 78
Middle class. *See also* Social class
  emulation of upper class by, 25
  profile of, 18, 19
  self-definition of, 19
  voting behavior of, 63, 64
Middlemas, Keith, 59
Miliband, Ralph, 20
Militant Tendency, 82-83, 173
Military Lands Act, 299-300
Miner's strike of 1983-84, 194
Monarchy
  ceremonial duties of, 119-120
  erosion of popularity of, 116-119, 123, 125
  governmental responsibilities and power of, 39-40, 120-122
  influence of, 122-123
  proposals for change of, 123-126, 327-328
  social status of, 20
Monks, John, 86
Morrison, Herbert, 136
Mortgages, 256-257
Morton, Andrew, 115
Mosley, Sir Oswald, 280
Murdoch, Rupert, 54
Muslims, population of, 29

Nadir, Asil, 94
Naruhito, Crown Prince of Japan, 123
National Assistance, as targeted benefit, 245
National Economic Development Council (NEDC), 59, 60
National Executive Committee (N.E.C.)
  explanation of, 80, 81
  expulsion proceedings against Militants by, 84
National Front, 280
National Health Service (NHS), 175
  beds for private patients and, 155
  on Conservative government, 100-101
  creation of, 160, 249-250
  Labour promises for increased spending on, 240
  principles of, 250, 331
  restructuring of, 252-253
  Thatcherism and, 250-252
National Insurance Act of 1911, 249-250
National security
  courts and, 302

journalists and issues of, 298-299
protests and, 299-300
National Union of Conservative and Unionist Associations, 72
Neave, Airey, 216
Nelson, Earl, 23
Newspapers. *See also* Media
   class distinctions and readership of, 19
   coverage of monarchy by, 117
   ownership of, 54
   political coverage by, 61
   role in election campaigns of, 96-98, 102
   support of Conservative Party by, 54, 55, 96
1922 Committee, 180
Nixon, Richard, 98
Nolan committee, 168, 184
North Atlantic Treaty Organization (NATO), 310, 315
Northcote-Trevelyan reforms of 1854, 160-161
Northern Ireland
   historical legacy of, 214
   increase in representation for, 108, 174
   negotiation initiatives in, 217-219
   political parties in, 214-215
   population of districts in, 166
   role of religion in, 30
   sectarian strife in, 213-214
   Thatcher and, 161
   U. S. concern with strife in, 219-220
   violence in, 215-216
Nuclear deterrent, 313-316

Official Secrets Act, 45, 293, 297, 299
Official Unionist Party, 219
Open University, 270-271
Opinion polls, 101, 103
Orders of chivalry, 25
Oxbridge. *See also* Cambridge University; Oxford University
   social class and attendance and, 21, 152, 153, 193
   student composition at, 269-270
   Thatcher and, 271
Oxford University, 21, 152. *See also* Oxbridge

Paisley, Ian, 218-219
Parliament. *See also* House of Commons; House of Lords
   background of, 35
   ceremonial aspects of, 164
   Church of England and, 30
   confrontation between Charles I and, 35
   education and occupation of members of, 166-167
   fixed term for, 184
   overview of, 164-165
   power to dissolve, 132, 173, 181
   prime minister's control of, 131-132
   reform proposals for, 184-185
   right of monarch regarding dissolution of, 121
Parliamentary Conservative Party, 72, 77
Parliamentary Labour Party, 80
Parliamentary sovereignty, 38
Parliamentary system, 5-6
Parsons, Sir Anthony, 159
Party system
   coherence and discipline within, 43
   constraints on power and, 45-47
   function of, 41
   inequalities within, 42-43
   overview of, 51
   third parties and, 46-47
Patronage, 134-135
Patten, Chris, 312
Peel, Sir Robert, 71
Peerages, 25
Perot, Ross, 51, 94
Philby, Kim, 22
Plaid Cymru (Party of Wales), 213
Plant Commission, 63
Police
   function of, 191-192
   problems with, 193-194
   restraints on power of, 195
Police and Criminal Evidence Act of 1984, 194
Policy issues
   civil servants as advisors on, 160
   of Labor Party vs. Conservative Party, 68-69
   similarities of U.S. and British, 7-8
   U.S. vs. British, 330
Political campaigns. *See* Election campaigns
Political parties. *See also specific parties*
   cohesion of national, 328-329
   differences between, 68-69
   extent of identification with, 62-63
   historical background of, 67-68
   listing of various, 62-63
   in Northern Ireland, 214-215
   requirements for contributions to, 54
   in Scotland, 211
   similarities between, 69-71
   social class and identification with, 63-65, 104
   unpopularity of U.S., 67
   in Wales, 213

Politics
    role of religious affiliation in, 30
    women in, 285-287
Poll tax
    background of, 207-209
    Major and, 209, 210
    Thatcher and, 77, 208
Ponting, Clive, 297-298, 302
Poor Law, 244
Poor Law Amendment Act of 1834, 244
Popular culture, overview of, 6
Portillo, Michael, 78, 142, 248
Powell, Enoch, 121, 277
Press Complaints Commission, 296
Prevention of Terrorism Act, 195
Prime ministers. *See also* Executive branch; *specific prime ministers*
    appointments of, 151
    control of Parliament by, 131-132
    election timing and, 132
    foreign policy of, 133-134
    as influence on public opinion, 133
    media coverage of, 148-149
    patronage and, 134-135
    power over cabinet of, 129-130, 148
Primogeniture, 25
Prior, James, 233
Privatization
    housing issues and, 254-255
    in industry, 234-235
Productivity, 238-239
Property rights, 300-301
Proportional representation
    functioning of, 47
    support for, 185, 328
Public schools
    overview of, 266-267
    party politics and, 267-268
    social class and, 21

Quangos, 203
Queen's Bench, 189
Queen's Counsel, 191
Question Time, 43, 175-178, 329

Race
    British distribution by, 278-279
    immigration and, 275-278
Race relations
    immigration and, 278-280, 289
    Labour Party and, 280-282
    present state of, 289-290
    U.S. vs. British, 7-8, 331

Race Relations Act of 1965, 281
Rayner, Sir Derek, 153
Reagan, Ronald
    relationship between Thatcher and, 8, 134
    view of position of United States, 9
Redwood, John
    leadership challenge to Major by, 131
    1992 election and, 78, 79
Reece, Gordon, 99
Rees-Mogg, William, 304
Reisman, David, 27
Religion
    background of, 28-30
    in Britain, 29
    discrimination based on, 279-280
Renter issues, 257
Retirement pensions, 245
Revolutionary Socialist League, 82
Road Traffic Act, 299
Robbins, Lionel, 270
Roedean school, 266
Roman Catholics, 29
Roosevelt, Franklin D., 8
Rose, Richard, 70, 71
Rushdie, Salman, 30, 281-282

Salisbury, Lord, 74
Scarman, Lord, 280, 299
Schools. *See also* Education; Higher education; Public schools; Secondary education
    comprehensive, 262-263
    prayer in, 29
    public, 21, 266-268
    state, 262-266
    for upper class, 21
Scotland
    devolution and independence of, 211-212
    historical background of, 15
    overview of government in, 210-211
    population of districts in, 166
    referendum on devolution of power to, 174
Scottish Nationalist Party, 108, 211
Secondary education. *See also* Education; Schools
    public, 21, 266-268
    state, 262-266
    types of, 261
Secrecy
    changes in issues of, 327
    within executive branch, 45, 292, 293
    government employee breaches and, 297-298
    media and, 301-302
Secretary of state, 129

Sex Discrimination Act of 1986, 286
Sharp, Dame Evelyn, 161, 283
Shaw, George Bernard, 122
Sikhs, 29
Single European Act of 1987, 310, 318
Sinn Fein (Ourselves Alone), 214, 216, 217, 219
Skinner, Dennis, 180
Smith, John, 59, 85-86, 240
Social class
　assessments of system of, 25-27
　decline of, 22-24, 31-32
　election results and, 104
　higher education and, 269, 270
　of judges, 192
　of members of Parliament, 166, 167
　middle class, 18-19, 25
　overview of, 4, 17-18
　persistence of, 24-25
　upper, 20-22, 25, 26
　voting behavior and, 63-65
　working class, 18, 19, 22-23, 104
Social Democratic and Labour Party (Northern Ireland), 214
Social Democratic Party, 46, 108
　election of 1983 and, 84
　formation of, 89
Social security
　background of, 244-245
　Labour Party and, 248-249, 259
　between 1945-1979, 245-246
　Thatcherism and, 246-248
Social Security Act of 1986, 247
Solicitors, 191
Spencer, Herbert, 55
Spycatcher case, 298
Stagflation, 231
State Earnings Related Pension Scheme (SERPS), 246, 247
Steel, David, media skills of, 103
Stevas, St. John, 139
Stevenson, Adlai, 99
Stokes, Donald, 62
Suburbanization, 17
Suez canal, 311

Taxes
　poll, 77, 207-210
　during Thatcher and Major administrations, 236-237
Taylor, Lord, 281
Tebbitt, Norman, 74
Television
　political campaigns and, 98-100, 102
　political coverage by, 62
　political party support and, 54-55
　role in decline of popularity of monarchy, 117, 123
　as source of news, 96, 103
Ten-minute-rule bills, 179
Teviot, Lord, 23
Thatcher, Margaret
　civil service cuts by, 153, 161
　as Conservative Party leader, 73, 161
　economic policy of, 3, 27-28, 32, 42, 70, 205, 206, 232-233, 239-240
　education policy of, 263-264, 267, 271-272
　election in 1987 of, 106, 107
　emphasis on law enforcement, 194
　establishment of parliamentary committees under, 178
　fall from leadership of, 46, 75-77, 131
　foreign policy of, 134, 309-310, 312, 317-318, 322-324
　on French Revolution, 291
　on immigrants, 30
　immigration policy of, 277-278
　media skills of, 98-99, 103
　personal qualities of, 107, 247, 288, 289
　prime ministerial government under, 135, 138-140, 181, 184
　race relations and, 282
　relationship with Heath, 139
　relationship with Reagan, 8, 134
　rise to leadership of, 75, 179
　role of women and, 288-289
　on sanctions against South Africa, 121
　social background of, 24
　social security and, 246-249
　unions and, 57-60
　use of secrecy by, 45, 292-293
　on viewer call-in programs, 96
　Westland affair and, 170
Thatcherism
　economic individualism as element of, 205
　electorate and, 77
　explanation of, 73, 138-139
　housing policy of, 254-258
　law enforcement emphasis of, 194
　National Health Service and, 250-253
　social security and, 246-248
Tisdall, Sarah, 297
Tories, 67
Trade unions
　background of, 55
　decline in power of, 57-59, 233, 234

Trade unions (*continued*)
   Labour Party and, 55-56
   membership in, 58
   relationship between employers and, 59-60
   strikes by, 56-57
   in United States, 55-56
Trades Disputes Act of 1927, 56
Trades Disputes Act of 1965, 301
Trades Union Congress (T.U.C.), 56-57
Traitors, 22
Transport and General Workers Union (TGWU), 57, 86
Trend, Burke, 155
Trotsky, Leon, 82
Truman, Harry, 43

Unemployment
   among nonwhite immigrants, 279
   in industrialized countries, 235
   inflation and, 235-236
   between 1970-1994, 236, 247
Unemployment insurance, 245
Unions. *See* Trade unions
UNISON, 57, 86
United Kingdom of Great Britain and Northern Ireland. *See also* England; Ireland; Northern Ireland; Scotland; Wales
   alliance between United States and, 8-9
   breakdown of civility in, 4
   breakdown in morality in, 295
   cultural diversity within, 15, 17
   districts or constituencies of, 166
   at emergence from World War II, 1-2
   erosion of economic base in, 3-4
   explanation of, 15
   map of, 16
   monarchy as head of, 121-122. *See also* Monarchy
   perceptions of political system in, 4-5
   territories included in, 15
United States
   British investments in, 53
   cabinet in, 130
   Constitution of, 36-37, 40, 42, 43
   court system in, 188
   election campaigns in Britain vs., 92-97
   federal bureaucracy in, 151
   individualism and authority in, 27-28
   as international force, 9-10
   national health insurance in, 249
   nature of party system in, 43
   Parliament vs. Congress of, 164-165, 167
   party system in, 51, 89
   political parties in, 69
   reapportionment issues in, 166
   social class in, 24-25
   unions in, 55-56
   what Britain can learn from, 326-328
   what Britain can teach, 328-330
Universities. *See* Higher education
Upper class. *See also* Social class
   decline in influence of, 23-24
   politics and, 21-22
   profile of, 20-21, 26, 27
Urbanization, 17

Victoria, Queen of England, 117, 152-153
Violence. *See also* Crime
   increase in, 4, 192
   in Northern Ireland, 215-216
   race relations and, 280, 282
   terrorist, 294
Voters
   interests and knowledge of, 61-62
   overview of, 60-61
   party identification among, 62-65, 104
   political involvement of, 62
Voting behavior
   impact of campaigns on, 103-104
   long-term factors in, 104-105
   short-term factors in, 106-109
   social class and, 63-65

Wales
   historical background of, 15
   overview of government in, 212-213
   politics in, 213
   referendum on devolution of power to, 174
Walker, Patrick Gordon, 276
Walker, Peter, 54
Wallace, George, 51
Walters, Sir Alan, 160
Washington, George, 67
Waugh, Evelyn, 269
Webb, Beatrice, 204
Webb, Sidney, 204
Welsh language, 15
Welsh Nationalist Party, 211
Westland affair, 170
Westminster, Duke of, 24
Whigs, 67
Whips
   explanation of, 171
   importance of, 131
   rebellion against, 181-182

Will, George, 124, 126
William IV, King of England, 116-117
William the Conqueror, King of England, 31
Williams, Marcia, 135
Williams, Shirley, 285
Wilson, Harold
   economic policy of, 227-230
   education policy of, 270-271
   election called in 1970 by, 132
   election of 1974 of, 173
   foreign policy of, 134, 309, 317
   on labor strikes, 56
   leadership style of, 146-148, 161, 172
   media skills of, 98, 133
   1964 campaign of, 61
   on Parliamentary questions, 176
   patronage issues and, 135
   union dealings and, 60
   view of monarchy by, 124
   women's rights and, 283
Winchester, 21, 267, 269

Women
   abortion and, 284
   criminal justice system and, 288
   early discrimination against, 283
   family value issues and, 288
   income issues affecting, 286-287
   legislation affecting, 283-284
   social change and, 284-286
   Thatcher and role of, 288-289
   U.S. vs. Britain in strides for, 331
Workfare, 248
Working class. *See also* Social class
   profile of, 18, 19
   shrinking of, 22-23, 104
   voting behavior of, 63, 64
Wright, Peter, 292-293, 298

York, Sarah Mountbatten-Windsor, Duchess of, 115
Young, Hugo, 170
Young, Lord, 54

ABOUT THE AUTHOR

Leonard Freedman, professor of political science at UCLA, grew up in London, England. He graduated from the London School of Economics in 1950, then came to the United States to do graduate work at UCLA, where he earned his doctorate in political science.

He has taught American and British politics at UCLA since 1964, and also served as dean of UCLA's large Extension program for twenty years.

His publications include *Public Housing: The Politics of Poverty* (1969), and *Power and Politics in America* (sixth edition, 1991), as well as a number of articles and anthologies.